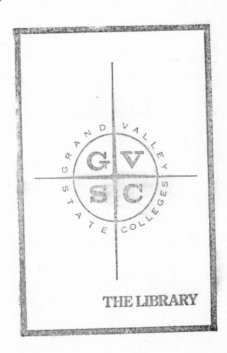

BILLION YEAR SPREE

Billion Year Spree

THE TRUE HISTORY OF SCIENCE FICTION

BRIAN W. ALDISS

Doubleday & Company, Inc., Garden City, New York   1973

ISBN: 0-385-08887-6
LIBRARY OF CONGRESS CATALOG CARD NUMBER 72-92186

To
Jannick Storm
who colonized Denmark

CONTENTS

ACKNOWLEDGEMENTS

My grateful thanks for being able to quote extracts from the novels concerned go to the following individuals and organizations: Edgar Rice Burroughs' *At the Earth's Core* by permission of Edgar Rice Burroughs, Inc., the work Copyright © 1914 by Frank A. Munsey Company; Harry Harrison's *The Stainless Steel Rat* by permission of the author; Frank Herbert's *Dune* by permission of the author; C. S. Lewis' *Out of the Silent Planet* by permission of The Bodley Head, London, and the Macmillan Company of New York; Alun Llewellyn's *The Strange Invaders* by permission of George Bell and Sons, Ltd.; Mervyn Peake's *Gormenghast* by kind permission of Mrs. Maeve Peake; Olaf Stapledon's *Star Maker* by kind permission of Mrs. Agnes Stapledon.

The following chapters have appeared elsewhere in unrevised form: The Origins of the Species, in *Extrapolation* and (in part) in *Works in Progress;* To Barsoom and Beyond, in *Vector;* The Future on a Chipped Plate, in *New Worlds Quarterly.*

Some of the material in the chapter on H. G. Wells was broadcast in the London Weekend Television Company production, *On Reflection: H. G. Wells.*

Rooted as they are in the facts of contemporary life, the phantasies of even a second-rate writer of modern Science Fiction are incomparably richer, bolder and stranger than the Utopian or Millennial imaginings of the past.

Aldous Huxley: *Literature and Science*

Often I sit alone at night, staring with the eyes of my mind into the darkness of unborn time, and wondering in what shape and form the great drama will be finally developed, and where the scene of its next act will be held.

Rider Haggard: the final paragraph of *She*

BILLION YEAR SPREE

Introduction

*Why are the public buildings so high? How come you don't know?
Why, that's because the spirits of the public are so low.*

Or so says W. H. Auden, in a definitive word on town-planners, pinning down a nebulous relationship.

A relationship clearly exists between private fantasy and public events. What that relationship is, I don't exactly know. When you recall that the number of people killed by human agency—through war, genocide, mass extermination, purges, policing operations, ideological extermination, and so on—is estimated as 110 million this century, then I don't want to know what the relationship is.

Science fiction is one of the more secluded parade grounds where private fantasy and public event meet. They call it entertainment, and I have borne that in mind while writing this book.

Science fiction is no more written for scientists than ghost stories are written for ghosts. Most frequently, the scientific dressing clothes fantasy. And fantasies are as meaningful as science. The phantasms of technology now fittingly embody our hopes and anxieties. It is from this angle that I have approached my subject.

Among the lively arts of the last decade, science fiction has played a sizeable but submerged role. Through its formative work

on think-tanks, it has had a dilute effect on government; through
its airing of such issues as overpopulation and pollution before the
general public were aware of them, it has made itself a part of
the general debate of our times; through its popularisation of many
unfamiliar snatches of knowledge and technological developments,
it has served as a form of journalism; through its aspirations as
art, it has added to the literature of the world; through its madness
and free-wheeling ingenuity, it has helped form the new pop
music; through its raising of semi-religious questions, it has become
part of the underworld where drugs, mysticism, God-kicks, and
sometimes even murder meet; and lastly, it has become one of the
most popular forms of entertainment in its own right, a whacky
sort of fiction that grabs and engulfs anything new or old for its
subject matter, turning it into a shining and often insubstantial
wonder.

My objective in writing this first history of the genre is to put
it in perspective. A lot of excitement is going on at present. But
science fiction was exciting from the word "Go"—it's just that nobody until now has been too sure who shouted the word "Go!"

So I have concentrated mainly on the origins of science fiction
in the last century and on its emergence as a genre in this century. Thus the chance is provided for a hunt in splendid rough
territory lying outside the normal estates of literature, where the
game is nothing if not exotic.

No true understanding of science fiction is possible until its
origin and development are understood. In this respect, almost
everyone who has written on science fiction has been (I believe)
in error—for reasons of aggrandisement or ignorance. To speak of
science fiction as beginning with the plays of Aristophanes or some
Mycenaean fragment concerning a flight to the Sun on a goose's
back is to confuse the central function of the genre; to speak of it
as beginning in a pulp magazine in 1926 is equally misleading.

These errors in perspective have led to a curious pecking order
in the sf field, where a few overproductive writers enjoy inflated
reputations at the expense of more interesting figures. I have some
hopes that a clearer grasp of "how it really was" may bring a better
balance, though my intention has not been to debunk. Given
strength, I may write a second volume concentrating on the contemporary scene, investigating my fellow-authors.

The central contention of my book, supported by evidence, is that science fiction was born in the heart and crucible of the English Romantic movement in exile in Switzerland, when the wife of the poet Percy Bysshe Shelley wrote *Frankenstein: or, The Modern Prometheus*. And I seek to show how the elements of that novel are still being explored in fiction, because they are still of seminal interest to our technological society. I seek to show that those elements were combined as they were, when they were, because Shelley's generation was the first to enjoy that enlarged vision of time—to this day still expanding—without which science fiction is perspectiveless, and less itself.

This task is made all the more pleasant because much of the science fiction of last century and this is of perennial fascination. When it concerns itself not only with technological problems but with the affairs of man's inwardness (as does much of the best writing), then it can approach the permanence of myth.

Possibly this book will help further the day when writers who invent whole worlds are as highly valued as those who re-create the rise and fall of a movie magnate or the breaking of two hearts in a bedsitter. The invented universe, the invented time, are often so much closer to us than Hollywood or Kensington. As C. S. Lewis said of one of William Morris' arcadias, "All we need demand is that this invented world should have some intellectual or emotional relevance to the world we live in."

Any definition of science fiction lacks something. I give my definition in Chapter One. Definitions should be like maps: they help you explore the ground; they are not substitutes for exploration. My definition is intended for such guidance. The book as a whole takes cognisance of all the varieties of science fiction, some of which I have already listed.

This is the place to present my credentials and my acknowledgements.

I am a writer; a large part of my work over the last fifteen years is science fiction. I have written novels and short stories and poems. I have edited anthologies, collections, individual novels, and novel series. I co-edit, with Harry Harrison, the well-established *Year's Best*. I have edited, and probably shall again edit, a journal of sf criticism. I have written long critical essays and reviewed hundreds of sf novels over almost two decades.

All of which is well enough. But no history or survey of sf can be attempted with success by anyone who knows sf alone. Beyond the realms of the genre, I was literary editor of a daily newspaper (*The Oxford Mail*) for twelve years; and for that paper and others, for that period and longer, I read and reviewed hundreds of novels and general books. I have also written a travel book, novels, stories, and poems which have nothing to do with sf. Much as I love sf, the greater world beyond it has always meant at least as much. So I shall not lose a sense of proportion too often.

This book has a long history. I began to accumulate notes towards it ten years ago. The title, *Billion Year Spree*, was first mentioned in print in 1964. In that time, I have accumulated many debts of help and friendship.

Such debts include a variety of people. Since science fiction is one of the pivotal factors in my life, it naturally includes many close friends who are also writers; to them go many thanks and much affection. I am grateful to several friends overseas, whose views and conversations have been very persuasive, first among whom I must name Jon Bing, who encouraged me to write a potted history of science fiction for the Norwegian Broadcasting Corporation. And three Swedish friends, Göran Bengtson, expert on Samuel Beckett and Philip K. Dick, Sam Lundwall, and Sven Christer Swahn. Also Jannick Storm, who has done so much for science fiction in Denmark, and to whom this volume is dedicated.

More widely, anyone labouring in these vineyards owes a cultural debt to such friends and critics of the genre in England as Messrs. Kingsley Amis, Robert Conquest, Edmund Crispin, the late C. S. Lewis, Philip Toynbee, and Angus Wilson; and to the publishers who supported science fiction when it was not necessarily a sound financial proposition—Tom Boardman, Jr., Tony Godwin, Herbert Jones (who launched the SF Book Club), Charles Monteith, and Hilary Rubinstein, then a pillar of Gollancz.

As readers of my first chapter will observe, I owe a particular debt to Desmond King-Hele for his contribution to the discussion. Also to Philip Strick, who was to be my collaborator in this project until other commitments overtook him. Also to Philip Harbottle for sterling work at proof stage.

I am also grateful for the patience shown by my English and American publishers, for the kindness of Larry Ashmead—as ever—

and Diane Cleaver at Doubleday, and for aid and encouragement from Faith Evans at Weidenfeld and Nicolson. Also to Margaret Chuter, faithful typist for over fifteen years, who has retyped these chapters more times than she or I care to tell. My wife Margaret knows how absolutely vital her role has been in all this long activity, mapping the possible futures of the past.

> And who feels discord now or sorrow?
> Love is the universe today—
> These are the slaves of dim tomorrow,
> Darkening Life's labyrinthine way.

(Percy Bysshe Shelley)

Heath House   Brian W. Aldiss
Southmoor
June 1972

The Origins of the Species:
MARY SHELLEY

> "The gigantic shadows which futurity casts
> upon the present . . ."
> Percy Bysshe Shelley: *The Defence of Poetry*

"The stars shone at intervals, as the clouds passed over them; the dark pines rose before me, and every here and there a broken tree lay on the ground; it was a scene of wonderful solemnity, and stirred strange thoughts within me." Thus Baron Frankenstein, after an encounter with the creature he has created out of dismembered corpses, while he tries to decide whether or not to build it a mate.

The shattered scenery, the sense of desolation, the baron's dilemma—ghastly but hardly the sort of quandary one gets into in everyday life—are all characteristic of a broad range of science fiction. As for the baron's strange thoughts, science fiction is a veritable forest of them.

That forest, remote and overgrown, is so full of interest, has reached such proportions, that an attempt at formal exploration is necessary. Trails have been blazed, exciting footpaths run here and there; but the present author hopes boldly to drive a new motorway through the heart of the forest. Without marking every tree, we will provide a contour map of the whole science fiction landscape.

To emerge from the undergrowth of our metaphor, this volume investigates the considerable body of writing which has come to be regarded as science fiction, in order to try and illuminate what is obscure, and to increase the enjoyment of what is already enjoyable.

In this first chapter, we attend to three matters. We look at the dream world of the Gothic novel, from which science fiction springs; we identify the author whose work marks her out as the first science fiction writer; and we investigate the brilliant context— literary, scientific, and social—from which she drew life and inspiration.

As a preliminary, we need a definition of science fiction. What is science fiction?

Many definitions have been hammered out. Most of them fail because they have regard to content only, and not to form. The following may sound slightly pretentious for a genre that has its strong fun side, but we can modify it as we go along.

Science fiction is the search for a definition of man and his status in the universe which will stand in our advanced but confused state of knowledge (science), and is characteristically cast in the Gothic or post-Gothic mould.

There's a corollary: the more powers above the ordinary that the protagonist enjoys, the closer the fiction will approach to hardcore science fiction. Conversely, the more ordinary and fallible the protagonist, the further from hard-core.

In many cases, it is impossible to separate science fiction from science fantasy, or either from fantasy, since both genres are part of fantasy.*

One etymological dictionary offers such definitions of fantasy as "mental apprehension," "delusive imagination," and "baseless supposition"—terms which serve equally well to describe certain types of science fiction. H. G. Wells pointed to a similarity between the two genres when he said of his early stories, "Hitherto, except in exploration fantasies, the fantastic element was brought in by magic. Frankenstein, even, uses some jiggery-pokery magic to animate his artificial monster. There was some trouble about the

---

* Nevertheless, one admires the boldness of Miriam Allen de Ford's dictum, "Science fiction deals with improbable possibilities, fantasy with plausible impossibilities" (in her Foreword to *Elsewhere, Elsewhen, Elsehow*).

thing's soul. But by the end of last century it had become difficult
to squeeze even a momentary belief out of magic any longer. It occurred to me that instead of the usual interview with the devil or a
magician, an ingenious use of scientific patter might with advantage be substituted . . . I simply brought the fetish stuff up to date,
and made it as near actual theory as possible."[1]

This is science assimilating fantasy. Fantasy is almost as avid in
assimilating science: in 1705, Daniel Defoe wrote *Consolidator: or,
Transactions from the World in the Moon,* featuring a machine that
would convey a man to the Moon, which was inspired by popular
expositions of Newton's celestial mechanics. In its wider sense, fantasy clearly embraces all science fiction. But fantasy in a narrower
sense, as *opposed* to science fiction, generally implies a fiction lean-
ing more towards myth or the mythopoeic than towards an assumed
realism. (The distinction is clear if we compare Ray Bradbury's
Mars with the painstakingly delineated Mars of Rex Gordon's *No
Man Friday:* Bradbury's Mars stands as an analogy and Gordon's as
a Defoe-like essay in definition.)

You have to understand that the science fiction search for that
"definition of man" is often playful. And what the definition does
not do is determine whether the end product is good, bad, sheer
nonsense, or holy writ (as Heinlein's *Stranger in a Strange Land*
has been taken as holy writ). Definitions, after all, are to assist, not
overpower, thinking.

The definition takes for granted that the most tried and true
way of indicating man's status is to show him confronted by crisis,
whether of his own making (overpopulation), or of science's (new
destructive virus), or of nature's (another Ice Age). And that
there are forms of fiction which may appear to fulfil the definition
but nevertheless are not science fiction—generally because they are
ur-science fiction (existing before the genre was originated), from
Dante's great imaginary worlds of *Inferno, Purgatorio,* and *Paradiso*
onwards—or because they transcend the Gothic format, as do *Moby
Dick,* Thomas Hardy's novels, John Cowper Powys' *A Glastonbury
Romance,* the plays of Samuel Beckett, and so forth.

If all this sounds somewhat all-embracing, nevertheless this
volume errs on the side of exclusiveness. It's more hard-core than
soft.

All the same, I admit to sympathy with the view that many of
the most ancient forms of literature are recognisably kin to science

fiction; that voyages of discovery, mythical adventures, fantastic
beasts, and symbolic happenings are part of the grand tradition in
storytelling which the realistic novel of society has only recently rejected. Thus, The Epic of Gilgamesh, with the world destroyed by
flood, the Hindu mythology, the *Odyssey, Beowulf,* the Bible—and
practically everything down to *Mickey Mouse Weekly*—has been
claimed at one time or another by science fiction fans with colonial
ambitions.

The phrase in my definition about "advanced knowledge" takes
care of that bit of grandiose aspiration. Science fiction is NOW, not
Then.

Nevertheless, Milton's *Paradise Lost,* Book II, with Satan
crossing that "vast vacuity" between his world and ours, looks suspiciously like the pure quill!

Frontiers are by tradition a bit vague. Happily, it is a simple
matter to identify the first true example of the genre.

The term "science fiction" is a recent one. It was coined in the late
1920s, as an improvement on the more ludicrous term "scientifiction," long after the genre itself had come into being. It was then
applied to crudely written stories appearing in various American
magazines, of which *Amazing Stories* (1926 onwards) was the first.
For more respectable forays into the same fields, the label "scientific romance" was used.†

This somewhat parvenu feeling about science fiction has led its
adherents to claim for it, in contradictory fashion, both amazing
newness and incredible antiquity. Potted histories of the genre take
their potted historians back cantering briskly through Greek legends of flying gods like Hermes and satirical voyages to Moon and
stars undertaken by Lucian of Samosata in the second century
A.D. But science fiction can no more be said to have "begun" with
Lucian than space flight "began" in Leonardo da Vinci's notebooks.

On the long struggle upwards from Lucian to the millennial
date of 1926, the historians scoop in Thomas More, Rabelais, Cyrano
de Bergerac, Jonathan Swift, and a whole clutch of eighteenth-cen-

† This volume will use the term "science fiction" (and the abbreviation "sf"), a
widely preferred usage to the hyphenated "science-fiction." Perhaps unease at
the ungrammatical distortion of having a noun do duty as adjective has led to
the fashion for abbreviating the term in a number of ways: SF, sf, sci-fi, sci-fic,
si-fi, si-fic. Only would-be trendies use sci-fi.

tury bishops. One of the more learned anthologists, in a Croatian
science fiction anthology, enlists Dante and Shakespeare to the
ranks,[2] while the first chapter of Genesis has also been claimed,
perhaps with more justification.

Such trawls for illustrious ancestors are understandable, in critics as in families. But they lead to error, the first error being the error of spurious continuity—of perceiving a connection or influence
where none exists; forgetting that writers write with the flux of life
going on about them, scholars rake through their books and pass
over in a couple of pages the thirteen long centuries that lie between Lucian and Ariosto.[3]

The second error to which this ancestor search has led is to in-
terpret science fiction as a series of imaginary voyages to the Moon
and other planets.

The interplanetary flight is certainly a part of science fiction
and, in the nineteen-fifties when space fever was high,‡ seemed a
major part; certainly the development and increasing refinement of
such flight towards scientific reality may be charted, indeed has
been charted, most successfully by Marjorie Hope Nicolson.[4] But
the range of science fiction is far wider than this limitation implies.
It is not necessary to leave this planet Earth to be a science fiction
writer; indeed, it is not even necessary to write about technological
developments; the *effect* of those developments may provide more
imaginative scope.

A Lucian-to-Verne approach to science fiction is mistaken,
leading to misinterpretation of the nature and role of science fiction. A chronological listing of authors who have responded to in-
novatory ideas and discoveries is insufficient for today's more sophisticated needs.

Science fiction, like most branches of art today, is more aware
than ever before of its own nature. The intention of this volume is
not to neglect science fiction's illustrious precursors, who are as essential to it as cathedrals to a study of architecture, but to remove
them from a hitherto perspectiveless gloom.

The greatest successes of science fiction are those which deal
with man in relation to his changing surroundings and abilities:
what might loosely be called *environmental fiction*. With this in

‡ Doubtless, it was in the 1950s that science fiction earned itself the still adhe-
sive label of "space fiction."

mind, I hope to show that the basic impulse of science fiction is as
much evolutionary as technological. While thinking in these terms,
it will be appropriate to regard Lucian and the other pilgrim fathers as near and cherished relations to science fiction writers, as
we regard the great apes as near and cherished relations of man, to
be allowed all due respect for primogeniture.

The evolutionary revolution and the Industrial Revolution occurred
in the same period of time.

The quickening tempo of manufacture becomes most noticeable in Great Britain in the second half of the eighteenth century, at
a time when populations were beginning to increase rapidly. This
traditional incentive to industrial advance was coupled with the
roster of inventions with which we are familiar from school: Har-
greaves' spinning jenny, Cartwright's power loom, Watt's steam engine, and so on.

Industry was not alone in undergoing transformation. The
American Declaration of Independence in 1776 and the French
Declaration of the Rights of Man in 1789 were documents in man's
revision of his attitude to his own kind. It is no coincidence that the
abolition of slavery was a burning issue at this time. Or that Western man now began to alter his attitude towards his God.

It was in this changeable cultural climate that science fiction
first emerges—with a discretely blasphemous nature that it still retains.

Speculations on evolution and natural selection were current
at the end of the eighteenth century. The ancient Greeks had held
enlightened views on these matters, Thales believing that all life
originated in water and Anaximenes holding that life came into being spontaneously from the primaeval slime. But, in Christian Europe, the Bible defeated any such ideas, and a literal interpretation of Genesis still generally held sway.

The debate on whether species were fixed or mutable was a
long one. It gained point and savour in the eighteenth century from
the impact of Pacific exploration. The world of the South Seas—the
first region of the globe to be opened up scientifically—provided
new stimulus to old questions of how our planet, its animals, and
men, had come about.

In the last decade of the century came a remarkable foreshadowing of the theory of evolution, its arguments properly buttressed, and its references up to date. Its author was Darwin—not Charles Darwin of the *Beagle* but his grandfather, Erasmus Darwin.

Erasmus Darwin (1731–1802) was a doctor by profession, and a contemporary of Diderot and the Cyclopaedists, fired by their ideas. He was a witty and forceful talker with an enquiring mind. Many inventions stand to his credit, such as new types of carriages and coal carts, a speaking machine, a mechanical ferry, rotary pumps, and horizontal windmills.

He seems also to have invented—or at least proposed—a rocket motor powered by hydrogen and oxygen. His rough sketch shows the two gases stored in separate compartments and fed into a cylindrical combustion chamber with exit nozzle at one end—a good approximation of the workings of a modern rocket, and formulated considerably before the ideas of the Russian rocket pioneer Tsiolkovsky were put to paper. The best discussion of this most interesting man and his thoughts and inventions is by Desmond King-Hele.[5]

Among all his other capacities, Erasmus Darwin was an able versifier. He gained—and soon lost—fame as a poet. In his long poems he laid out his findings on evolution and influenced the great poets of his day. His is the case of a once-gigantic, now-vanished reputation. Samuel Taylor Coleridge referred to him in 1797 as "the first *literary* character of Europe, and the most original-minded man"; by his grandson's day, he was quite forgotten.

Darwin's mighty work *Zoonomia* was published in two volumes in 1794 and 1796. It explains the system of sexual selection, with emphasis on primaeval promiscuity, the search for food, and the need for protection in living things, and how these factors, interweaving with natural habitats, control the diversity of life in all its changing forms. He also emphasises the great age of the Earth**; evolutionary processes need time as well as space for their stage management.

The philosophical movements of the nineteenth century which were tinged with Darwinism tended towards pessimism; philosophical men like Tennyson were all too aware of "Nature red in tooth and claw." Erasmus, in his heroic couplets, took a more serene view

** In contradiction of the then-accepted view, established by Bishop James Ussher in the seventeenth century, that God performed the act of creation in the year 4004 B.C., probably about breakfast time.

—an eighteenth-century view, one might say: equable, even Parnassian. It is easy to imagine that his century would have withstood the shock of evolutionary theory better than its successor.

> Shout round the globe, how Reproduction strives
> With vanquish'd Death—and Happiness survives;
> How Life increasing peoples every clime,
> And young renascent Nature conquers Time.

The extract is from the last canto of *The Temple of Nature*, posthumously published in 1803. Erasmus concentrated on summing the whole course of evolution so far, from the almost invisible life of the seas to man and man's civilisations. In this poem of four cantos and some two thousand lines, he speaks of the way in which a mammal foetus relives the previous stages of evolution and of the survival of the fittest, as well as prophesying with remarkable accuracy many features of modern life, such as gigantic skyscraper cities, piped water, the age of the automobile, overpopulation, and fleets of nuclear submarines:

> Bid raised in air the ponderous structure stand,
> Or pour obedient rivers through the land;
> With crowds unnumbered crowd the living streets,
> Or people oceans with triumphant fleets.

Thus does Erasmus Darwin qualify as a part-time science fiction writer!

His thrusts at church and state brought opposition and his voice was effectively silenced. Parodies of his verse in George Canning's *Anti-Jacobin* entitled *The Loves of the Triangles* mocked Darwin's ideas, laughing at his bold imaginative strokes. That electricity could ever have widespread practical applications, that mankind could have evolved from lowly life forms, that the hills could be older than the Bible claimed—these were the sorts of madnesses which set readers of the *Anti-Jacobin* tittering, as later generations would scoff at ideas of space travel. Canning recognised the subversive element in Darwin's thought and effectively brought low his reputation as poet.

As for his reputation as scientific innovator—that also was brought into shade; and once the famous grandson appeared luminous on the scene, eclipse was total. Attempts to reinstate this interesting and delightful man are recent.[6]

Despite this long eclipse, Erasmus Darwin's thought was seminal. As we might expect, it particularly affected those poets whose response to nature was closest to his own—the Romantics. Wordsworth owes him something; Shelley's debt is considerable, going far beyond echoes of similar lines. Shelley was a poet of science, a rebel, an atheist, an ardent lover of freedom and the west wind. No wonder he admired Darwin, in whom these qualities were strong.

As we shall see, there is another direction in which Darwin's influence on science fiction is both powerful and direct.

It is worth recalling the names of two novels published in the year that the first volume of Darwin's *Zoonomia* appeared: William Godwin's *Caleb Williams* (regarded as the first psychological pursuit story), and Mrs. Radcliffe's *Mysteries of Udolpho* (regarded as the high point of Gothic).

Although Godwin and Darwin never met, they had connections and sympathies in common, and were pilloried together as atheistical writers, most notably in the *Anti-Jacobin*. Godwin was a novelist and liberal philosopher whose reputation stood high among the poets and writers of his time. He married Mary Wollstonecraft, another contributor to the debate of the age, especially in her *Vindication of the Rights of Women* (1972).

William Hazlitt reported that Coleridge "did not rate Godwin very high [this was caprice or prejudice, real or affected], but he had a great idea of Mrs. Wollstonecraft's powers of conversation." So had the Swiss painter Henry Fuseli, who fell in love with her. After various misfortunes, Mary Wollstonecraft married Godwin and bore him a daughter, Mary.

This Mary grew up to write *Frankenstein;* she is one of the chief subjects of this chapter. Her writings were Gothic in character, *Frankenstein* included. To appreciate *Frankenstein's* full novelty, an understanding of its predecessors of the Gothic school is necessary.

Edmund Burke published his essay on the *Sublime and Beautiful* in 1756. It became an arbiter of taste for many decades, and its influence lingers today. Burke distinguished between beauty, which is founded on pleasure and is placid, and the sublime, which inspires awe and terror and, with pain as its basis, disturbs the emotions. He speaks of "delightful horror, which is the most genuine effect and truest test of the sublime." Note that this is in the middle of the Age of Enlightenment, a comfort perhaps for those who flinch from the amount of horror contained in a forward-looking genre such as science fiction!

Art, as usual, copied art. The Ossianic poems were the first to fulfil Burke's specifications.†† They were counterfeits by an ingenious Scott, James Macpherson, and immediately branded as counterfeit by Horace Walpole, among others; but their enormous Celtic ghosts, giants, cliffs, storms, and buckets of blood thrilled many writers and artists, among them Fuseli, as well as the rest of the literate population of Europe.

The Ossian poems made their appearance from 1760 to 1763. In 1765 *The Castle of Otranto* was published pseudonymously. It was so popular that the author, Horace Walpole, bashfully came forward and admitted his identity in a preface to the second edition.

The Castle of Otranto stands as the earliest Gothic novel. One commentator claims that the whole Gothic revival began with a dream.[7] On a June night in 1764, Walpole had a nightmare in which he saw a gigantic hand clad in armour, gripping the bannister of a great staircase. When he woke, he began writing his novel.[8]

Walpole was a great antiquarian. His most lively monument is not *Otranto* but Strawberry Hill, his residence, which was his own conception, built in Gothic style. He was much influenced by the Prisons of Piranesi[9]—another artist, like Stubbs, in vogue today.

If *Castle of Otranto* owes something to Piranesi, *Vathek* has more of Tiepolo in it. This single and singular novel by the eccentric William Beckford is full of magic and wit. Published in 1786, it nods to both Samuel Johnson's *Rasselas* and the *Arabian Nights*. Beckford's Strawberry Hill was the architecturally daring Fonthill Abbey (too daring—the tower collapsed after some years and the building was demolished).

Beckford wrote *Vathek* in French. Byron called it his Bible. With its Faust-like theme, in which the calif Vathek sells himself to the powers of evil in exchange for the treasures of the pre-Adamite sultans, it had a natural appeal to what might be called the Byronic

†† Perhaps the first painting to meet Burke's definition is George Stubbs' *White Horse Frightened by a Lion* (1770), a masterpiece containing beauty and sublimity. Stubbs was a capable scientist as well as a masterly animal painter.

side of Byron. *Vathek* is a much more enjoyable novel than Walpole's, but both have exerted wide influence—Beckford's not least on Oscar Wilde, a writer with similar predilections, whose *Picture of Dorian Gray* uses a similar theme and bows to Burke's dictum on the sublime.

This was the time of a botanical renaissance, brought about by the classification of plants by the Swede Linnaeus and more especially by the voyages to the South Seas by Sir Joseph Banks and Captain Cook, killed in Hawaii in 1779. Cook carried back to Europe not only fantastic landscapes and images, from the ice world of the Antarctic to the gigantic heads of Easter Island, but a treasury of plants: three thousand species, one thousand of them unknown to botany. The world was alive with news of itself.

These influences show in Erasmus Darwin's poems. In *The Loves of the Plants* (with its Fuseli decoration engraved by William Blake), he makes reference to the Antarctic and tells how

> Slow o'er the printed snows with silent walk
> Huge shaggy forms across the twilight stalk

a couplet which has left its imprint on that very Gothic poem, Coleridge's *Rime of the Ancient Mariner*, when the accursed ship is driven to the Southern Pole:

> And through the drifts the snowy clifts
> Did send a dismal sheen:
> Nor shapes of men nor beasts we ken—
> The ice was all between.

Today, we see oddity in Darwin's method of expressing exact technical detail in heroic couplets and describing the sex life of plants in human terms; we hardly expect Bentham and Hooker to talk like Pope's *Rape of the Lock*. Yet the loss is ours. Before Victorian times, art and science had not come to the division that sf tries to bridge.

By the beginning of the nineteenth century, the Gothic novel—by no means the chief literary form in this brilliantly diverse age—had produced its best-remembered work, including Matthew "Monk" Lewis' *The Monk*, a novel overloaded with licentious monks, romantic robbers, ghosts, and a bleeding nun, as well as episodes of murder, torture, homosexuality, matricide, and incest. Even Lord Byron was shocked. Ann Radcliffe's two most famous novels, *The*

Mysteries of Udolpho and *The Italian,* had appeared, as well as countless "blue books," abridgements or imitations of Gothic novels, selling very cheaply and bearing cheap titles.[10]

These were the sort of fictions made fun of by Jane Austen in *Northanger Abbey.* But fashion was everything; the poet Shelley himself wrote two such novels, *Zastrozzi* and *St. Irvyne,* while still at school.

Thomas Love Peacock (1785–1866) was no Gothic novelist. However, he used the Gothic *mise en scène,* and the very titles of his remarkable novels look back ironically to the fiction of his youth, from *Headlong Hall* (1816) to *Gryll Grange,* published forty-four years later, in 1860. He is of particular interest to science fiction. Not only was he a close friend of Percy Bysshe Shelley and Harriet, Shelley's first wife; his form of discussion novel, in which characters in remote country houses discouragingly discuss the world situation, and anything else that enters their heads, while eating and drinking well, provides a format for later writers of science fiction such as Aldous Huxley.[11]

Mary Wollstonecraft Shelley read Peacock's *Melincourt,* which was published two years before *Frankenstein.* The dangers of a critical method which would explain everything in terms of influence and derivation are well exemplified by this little-read novel. For the central character in *Melincourt* is an orangoutang called Sir Oran Haut-Ton, who does not speak but performs well on flute and French horn. He is a symbol of the natural man, harking back to Rousseau. Is he a literary precursor of Frankenstein's monster? Is he a precursor of Poe's orangoutang in *Murders in the Rue Morgue?* Is he, indeed, with his title and rolling acres, a precursor of Tarzan? We perhaps do better to turn back to Gothic.

Science fiction was born from the Gothic mode, is hardly free of it now. Nor is the distance between the two modes great. The Gothic emphasis was on the distant and the unearthly, while suspense entered literature for the first time—Mrs. Radcliffe was praised by Scott for her expertise in suspense. Nowadays, this quality in her work has worn thin, for more expert practitioners have refined her methods—from Sheridan Le Fanu and Wilkie Collins onward—and what remains to attract in her best work is a dreamy sense of the exotic. Gothic's brooding landscapes, isolated castles, dismal old towns, and mysterious figures can still carry us into an entranced world from which horrid revelations may start.

The revelations may prove a disappointment, as in *The Mysteries of Udolpho*. Then we rouse from our dream to indigestion. We know that some Gothic-Romantic authors relied heavily on dreams for inspiration: Mrs. Radcliffe herself consumed indigestible food in order to induce dreams of terror, just as Fuseli ate raw meat towards the same end, in order to feed his voracious muse. Appropriately, Fuseli's most famous canvas is *The Nightmare*.

The methods of the Gothic writers are those of many science fiction authors, particularly the magazine contributors of the nineteen-thirties, -forties, and -fifties. It would be as absurd to suggest that the latter writers were serious propagandists for the cause of science as that the author of *Romano Castle: or, The Horrors of the Forest* was a serious critic of the evils of the Inquisition—however much both sides may have considered themselves in earnest.

Science fiction writers have brought the principle of horrid revelation to a fine art, while the distant and unearthly are frequently part of the same package. Other planets make ideal settings for brooding landscapes, isolated castles, dismal towns, and mysterious alien figures[12]; often, indeed, the villains may be monks, exploiting a local population under guise of religion.[13] The horrid revelation may be on an imposing scale: that mankind has been abroad in the universe long ago, but was beaten back to his home planet by a powerful adversary[14]; that Earth is merely a sort of Botany Bay or dumping ground for the disposal of the vicious elements of the galaxy[15]; or that mankind is descended from rats which escaped from some interstellar vessel putting in at Earth.[16]

Again, for both Gothic and science fiction writers, distance lent enchantment to the view, as the poet Campbell put it. If something unlikely is going to happen, better to set it somewhere where the reader cannot check the occurrence against his own experience.

So locations in Gothic novels lie in a distant and misty past. Mrs. Radcliffe sets *The Mysteries of Udolpho* in the late sixteenth century; her château commands views of a river, with fine trees (she always particularises about trees and many passages in her novels remind us that this was the age of Gilpin's *Forest Scenery* and Repton's *Landscape Gardening*), and "the majestic Pyrenees, whose summits, veiled in clouds, or exhibiting awful forms . . . were sometimes barren . . . and sometimes frowned with forests of lofty pine." Mrs. Radcliffe is careful with her locations; her imitators were often less precise.

So with science fiction novels. They may locate themselves in distant futures on Earth, or on one of the planets of the solar system, or anywhere in our galaxy, or even in a distant galaxy; or they may occupy a different probability sphere or another time-track entirely (there are at least three brilliant alternate universe novels, Ward Moore's *Bring the Jubilee*,[17] in which the South won the American Civil War; Harry Harrison's *A Transatlantic Tunnel, Hurrah!*, in which George Washington was shot and the American Revolution never happened; and Philip K. Dick's *The Man in the High Castle*, in which the Axis powers won World War II). The Mars celebrated by Edgar Rice Burroughs in his novels is the Mars we know only in name.

The Gothic novel was part of the great Romantic movement. Its vogue passed early in the nineteenth century. But terror, mystery, and that delightful horror which Burke connected with the sublime—all of them have been popular with a great body of readers ever since, and may be discovered, sound of wind and limb, in science fiction to this day. Perhaps this taste set in with the decay of that calm eighteenth-century confidence in hierarchy and rationality expressed by Pope, "whatever is, is right." Shelley was born in 1792, and his is a different outlook with a vengeance!

> While yet a boy I sought for ghosts, and sped
>   Through many a listening chamber, cave and ruin,
>   And starlight wood, with fearful steps pursuing
> Hope of high talk with the departed dead.[18]

The new age had a passion for the inexplicable, as we have in ours; its uncertainties were soon embodied in the pages of the novel written by Shelley's young second wife.

Frankenstein: or, The Modern Prometheus was published in 1818, in the same year as works by Shelley, Peacock, Scott, Hazlitt, Keats, and Byron. The Napoleonic Wars were over; *Savannah* crossed the Atlantic, the first steamship to do so; the early steam locomotives were chuffing along their metal tracks, the iron foundries going full blast; the Lancashire cotton factories were lit by gas, and gas mains were being laid in London. Telford and McAdam were building roads and bridges, Galvani's followers and Humphry Davy were experimenting with electricity. "So much has been done," exclaimed the soul of Frankenstein, "more, far more, will I achieve!" (Chapter 3)

Mary Wollstonecraft Godwin was born in August 1797. Her intellectual and beautiful mother Mary died ten days later, after a severe haemorrhage and an ague, leaving the impractical Godwin to care for the baby and for Fanny, Mary Wollstonecraft's three-year-old child by an earlier liaison. Later, when Shelley took to calling, he and Godwin became very friendly; Godwin eventually drained a fortune from his young friend. Mary eloped with Shelley in 1814. The next year Mary bore Shelley a son, who died. Her eight brief years with Shelley, until his death by drowning in 1822, were the decisive ones in her melancholy life.

In Mary's affairs 1816 marked a vital period. A son, William, was born in January. In May, Shelley, Mary, and Mary's half sister, Claire Clairmont, left England and settled in Switzerland, near Geneva. Here Mary began writing *Frankenstein*, before her nineteenth birthday. Shelley's first wife, Harriet, drowned herself in the Serpentine early in December, and Shelley and Mary were married before the end of the year.

Here is the attractive portrait Trelawny paints of Mary: "The most striking feature in her face was her calm grey eyes; she was rather under the English standard of woman's height, very fair and light-haired, witty, social, and animated in the society of friends, though mournful in solitude."[19] It is hard to resist the idea that this is a portrait of the first writer of science fiction; Mary had imbibed the scientific ideas of Darwin and Shelley; had heard what they had to say about the future; and now set about applying her findings within the loose framework of a Gothic novel.

Frankenstein was completed before Mary was twenty. She lived to write other novels, and died in 1851, the year of the Great Exhibition, aged fifty-three. She is buried in a churchyard in Bournemouth.[20]

Of her three children by Shelley, only one of them, Percy Florence, survived beyond childhood. As Shelley put it in a poem to her,

> We are not happy, sweet! Our state
> Is strange and full of doubt and fear.

To modern readers, Mary's methods of narration in *Frankenstein* may seem clumsy and confusing. Her early readers, to whom the epistolary style of novel as used by Richardson was still familiar, experienced no such difficulty; for them, the flow of documentation from several hands—the letters from Captain Walton to his sister in England, the manuscript by Victor Frankenstein, which contains six chapters of his creature's account of its own life, and finally Walton's narrative again—only added to the general vividness and verisimilitude.

Nor is this narrative arrangement purely arbitrary. Mary may have had Byron and Shelley in mind when conceiving Walton and Frankenstein; her two characters form a strong admiration for each other, and Walton's hazardous voyage is clearly intended to parallel Frankenstein's quest.

The philosophical passages and descriptions of nature would be more welcome in 1818 than they are now. But they are well placed, and the scenic passages in particular are effective, although those set in England, such as the visit to Oxford, seem a little forced, however topographically accurate they may be.

Before growing impatient with the narrative techniques of *Frankenstein*, we should remember that the novelistic tradition behind Mary owed a good deal to Sterne. The idea of the novel as architecture, even the preoccupation with plot, had not yet arrived. In all her novels, Mary Shelley works to produce a quilt of varied colours, of tears, happiness, sensibility, and occasional "strong" scenes.[21] Contrast is what she is after, and in this she succeeds; in *Frankenstein* there is great variety of contrast.

Mary's original impulse was to begin at Chapter Five: "It was on a dreary night of November . . ." Her husband persuaded her to lengthen the tale. After the scene is set, and the tale of Victor Frankenstein's researches told, his composite creation is brought to life. Overcome by horror at what he has accomplished, Victor runs away from it, and a whole summer passes before he meets it again. During that time, his young brother William is murdered; it is for this murder that an innocent woman, Justine, is hanged.

The creature's account of its life since its creation is one of rejection by human society, from its creator onwards. It begins blamelessly like a noble savage—evil is thrust upon it. In this, Mary follows her father's teaching. The monster beseeches Frankenstein to make a female companion; Frankenstein agrees, subject to certain conditions. Before he begins work on the second creature, he moves to the Orkneys. Frankenstein's migratory instincts may seem odd; undoubtedly they reflect the travel-consciousness of this Napoleonic generation—many British were abroad in Europe at the same time as the Shelleys.

When his work is almost finished, the uncertain creator pauses, thinking of the "race of devils" that might be raised up by the union between his two creatures (a curious moment, this, for science fiction, looking back towards Caliban's snarl to Prospero in *The Tempest*—"I had peopled else the isle with Calibans!"—and forward to the monstrous legions of robots which were to be unleashed across the pages of the twentieth-century world!). Victor destroys what he has begun, the monster discovers the breach of contract, utters his direst threat—"I shall be with you on your wedding night!" —and disappears.

The rest is a tale of flight and pursuit, punctuated by death and retribution, with everyone's hand turned against the wretched monster, as much from convention and prejudice as from spite. This section contains much of Godwin's thinking, and of his novel, *Caleb Williams*, which, as its preface announced, was a review of "the modes of domestic and unrecorded despotism by which man becomes the destroyer of man."

In thus combining social criticism with new scientific ideas, while conveying a picture of her own day, Mary Shelley anticipates the methods of H. G. Wells when writing his scientific romances, and of some of the authors who followed him.[22]

For a thousand people familiar with the story of Victor creating his monster from selected cadaver spares and endowing them with new life, only to shrink back in horror from his own creation, not one will have read Mary Shelley's original novel. This suggests something of the power of infiltration of this first great myth of the industrial age.‡‡ (Curiously, the legend of Santa Claus was created at about the same time; it is one of the wholly benign legends of our age.)

‡‡ The cinema has helped enormously to disseminate the myth while destroying its significance. Not long after its original publication, *Frankenstein* was made into a play, performed with great success until the nineteen-thirties. By that time, the cinema had moved in. There were short silent versions, but the monster began his true movie career in 1931, with James Whale's Universal picture *Frankenstein*, in which Boris Karloff played the monster. The dials in the castle laboratory have hardly stopped flickering since. The monster has spawned Sons, Daughters, Ghosts, and Houses; has taken on Brides and created Woman; has perforce shacked up with Dracula and Wolf Man; has enjoyed Evil, Horror, and Revenge, and has even had the Curse; on one occasion, it met Abbott and Costello.

A reading of the novel reveals how precariously it is balanced between the old age and the new. In Chapter Three, Victor Frankenstein goes to university and visits two professors. To the first, a man called Krempe who is professor of natural philosophy, he reveals how his search for knowledge took him to the works of Cornelius Agrippa, Paracelsus, and Albertus Magnus. Krempe scoffs at him. "These fancies, which you have so greedily imbibed, are a thousand years old!" This is a modern objection; antiquity is no longer the highest court to which one can appeal.

Frankenstein attends the second professor, one Waldman, who lectures on chemistry. Waldman condemns the ancient teachers who "promised impossibilities, and performed nothing." He speaks instead of the moderns, who use microscope and crucible, and converts Frankenstein to his way of thinking. Symbolically, Frankenstein turns away from alchemy and the past towards science and the future—and is rewarded with his horrible success.

The hints in the novel as to how the "vital spark" is imparted in the composite body are elusive. In her Introduction to the 1831 edition, however, the author reveals the origins of her story. Like *The Castle of Otranto*, it began with a dream. In the dream, she saw "the hideous phantasm of a man stretched out, and then, on the working of some powerful engine, show signs of life, and stir with an uneasy, half vital motion." It was science fiction itself that stirred.

Greater events were stirring between the publication of the first and second editions of *Frankenstein*. The first volume of Lyell's *Principles of Geology* had just appeared, drastically extending the age of the Earth. Mantell and others were grubbing gigantic fossil bones out of the ground, exhuming genera from the rocks as surely as Frankenstein's creature was patched together from various corpses. Already beginning was that great extension to our imaginative lives which we call the Age of Reptiles—those defunct monsters we have summoned back to vigorous existence.

Other references in the 1831 Introduction are to galvanism and electricity. The Preface to the first edition of 1818 is also instructive. Although Mary had set herself to write a ghost story, her intentions changed; she states expressly in the Preface, "I have not considered myself as merely weaving a series of supernatural terrors." The Preface is an apologia, and Mary Shelley's chief witness for her defence, mentioned in her first sentence, is Erasmus Darwin.

The sources of *Frankenstein* are documented. As Mary Shelley explains, her dream was inspired by late-night conversations with her husband, with Byron, and with Dr. Polidori. Their talk was of vampires and the supernatural; Polidori supplied the company with some suitable reading material[23]; and Byron and Shelley also discussed Darwin, his thought and his experiments.[24]

Mary's dream of a hideous phantasm stirring to life carries a reminder of a nightmare recorded in her journal a year earlier. In March 1815, she had just lost her first baby, born prematurely. On the fifteenth of the month, she wrote: "Dream that my little baby came to life again; that it had only been cold, and that we had rubbed it before the fire, and it had lived." In retrospect, the words have an eerie ring.

The Outwardness of Science and society is balanced, in the novel, by an Inwardness which Mary's dream helped her to accommodate. This particular balance is perhaps one of *Frankenstein's* greatest merits: that its tale of exterior adventure and misfortune is always accompanied by a psychological depth.*

As Mary was commencing her novel, Byron was exiling himself from England forever. He stayed at the Villa Diodati, on the shore of Lake Geneva, where John Milton had once stayed. The Shelley party was near by. "Monk" Lewis also appeared, and read Byron Goethe's *Faust*, translating from the German as he went—thus sowing the seeds of Byron's *Manfred*. As the Shelleys probably introduced Byron to Darwin's ideas about evolution and the future, he introduced them to the *Prometheus Vinctus* of Aeschylus. While at Diodati, Byron wrote his science fictional poem *Darkness*, which is a sort of grim evolutionary vision. It too begins with a dream, or at least a hypnoid fantasy.

> I had a dream which was not all a dream.
> The bright sun was extinguished, and the stars
> Did wander darkling in the eternal space,
> Rayless, and pathless, and the icy earth
> Swung blind and blackening in the moonless air.

* Mary might have said of her drama what Shelley said of *Prometheus Bound*: "The imagery which I have employed will be found, in many instances, to have been drawn from the operations of the human mind, or from those external actions by which they are expressed." (Shelley's Preface to *Prometheus Bound*.)

Something of this grand gloom can be felt in Mary Shelley's novel.

Frankenstein is a unique book. We have noted its form; now to its ingredients.

In many respects it is typical of the Gothic novel, with descriptions of grandiose scenery, with fluttering sensibilities, with talk of charnel houses, mixed with elements of suspense. Yet it was born right in the heart and crucible of a great poetic movement—and still remains some of that vital heat.

Theories of evolution would have been of particular interest to the young atheistic Shelley. If God did not have personal charge of creation, then might not man control it? In Shelley's wife's hands, the scientist takes on the role of creator. The concept of *Frankenstein* rests on the quasi-evolutionary idea that God is remote or absent from creation: man therefore is free to create his own sub-life; this was in accord with Erasmus Darwin's statement that evolution, once it had begun, continued to progress by its own inherent activity and so without divine intervention.

We can see that Erasmus Darwin thus stands as father figure over the first real science fiction novel.[25] The Faustian theme is brought dramatically up to date, with science replacing supernatural machinery. Inside Mary Shelley's novel lie the seeds of all later diseased creation myths, including H. G. Wells' *Island of Dr. Moreau*, and the legions of robots from Čapek's day forward.

The durability of the Frankenstein legend may be accounted for by the fact that it not only foreshadows many of our anxieties about the two-faced triumphs of scientific progress, it is the first novel to be powered by evolution, in that God—however often called upon—is an absentee landlord, and his lodgers scheme to take over the premises.

A parallel situation occurs in Shelley's lyrical drama *Prometheus Unbound*, composed while Mary was writing *Frankenstein*. Jupiter has chained Shelley's Prometheus to an icy rock. Prometheus suffers endless torture, but eventually is made free when Jupiter is dethroned and retires into obscurity.

Before looking at more personal themes in *Frankenstein*, some abstract themes warrant closer examination, in particular the religious one. Again, a precarious balance is preserved between old and new. Against Darwinism, Mary sets the established theology of John Milton's *Paradise Lost*. We know from Mary's journal that

Shelley read *Paradise Lost* aloud to her in 1816, and it is a quotation from that poem which stands on her title page.

The monster likens himself to Adam—but how much less fortunate than Adam, for in this case the creator rushes away from "his odious handywork, horror-stricken." The creature's career roughly parallels Adam's, with the vital exception of the missing Eve: he is first created, and then brought to full intellectual awareness of the world in which he lives—at which stage, "benevolence and generosity were ever present before me" (Chapter 15)—and then undergoes his version of the Fall, "the spirit of revenge enkindled in my heart" (Chapter 16). Now the creature is frequently referred to as "the fiend." In many ways, it becomes less human, more a symbol of inhumanity. "I saw him," says Frankenstein, "descend the mountain with greater speed than the flight of an eagle, and quickly lost him among the undulations of the sea of ice" (Chapter 17).

The fiend increasingly refers to itself in Miltonic terms, saying of itself at last, over Victor's corpse, "the fallen angel becomes a malignant devil."

This change in the nature of the monster enables Mary Shelley to bring out two other aspects of the struggle which are subordinate to the religious theme.

The first is man's confrontation with himself, which the power of creation necessarily entails. The diseased creation myth becomes a Jekyll and Hyde situation, as Frankenstein struggles with his alter ego; their obsessive pursuit of one another makes sense only in these terms.

The second is the disintegration of society which follows man's arrogation of power. We see one perversion of the natural order leading to another. *Frankenstein* is loaded with a sense of corruption, and "the fiend" moves about the world striking where it will, like a disease which, beginning naturally enough in a charnel house, can be isolated and sterilised only on a drifting ice floe.

Here we confront the more personal side of the novel. The struggle between Victor and his fiend is Oedipal in nature. Like André Gide's Oedipus, the fiend seems to himself to have "welled out of the unknown": "Who was I? What was I? Whence did I come?" (Chapter 15), it asks itself. And the mixture of generations may reflect the confusion Mary Shelley felt over her own involved

family situation, surrounded by the half sisters of both her mother's
earlier and father's later liaisons.

Some critics have read into the more macabre scenes of
Frankenstein undertones of vampirism (a favourite with Lord Byron) and incest. "I shall be with you on your wedding night!" cries
the creature to Victor. Sexual tensions move throughout the book.
Incest comes nearest to the surface in the scene where Victor dis-
members that hideous Eve, the female he is building for his macabre Adam. But incest was in fashion at the time, and not only as a
reliable literary titillator: Byron and his dearest Augusta, his half
sister, provided living examples close at hand. If Mary had read De
Sade's novel *Justine,* as seems likely, she would find fathers raping
and ruining their daughters,[26] while in her husband's own verse-
drama, *The Cenci,* the same theme holds court, and old Cenci rants
over his daughter for all the world like one of the divine marquis's
heroes when he cries

> "I do not feel as if I were a man,
> But like a fiend appointed to chastise
> The offences of some unremembered world . . .
> My heart is beating with an expectation
> Of horrid joy." (Act IV)

Algolagnia was certainly not absent from Mary's make-up. She
wrote *Frankenstein* with her baby son William by her side; yet she
makes the monster's first victim a little boy called William, Victor's
younger brother. "I grasped his throat to silence him and in a moment he lay dead at my feet. I gazed at my victim, and my heart
swelled with exhaltation and hellish triumph." Her little William
("Willmouse") died in the summer of 1819.

Mary was a complex person. She certainly had a deep understanding of Shelley, and their mutual passion was strong. One recent
critic, Christopher Small, suggests that in Frankenstein's monster,
Mary was portraying instinctively the two ideas of her husband[27]—
the side that was all sweetness and light, and the charnel side, undoubtedly there if rarely seen.

The Faust theme of the novel, bereft of traditional celestial
vengeance, degenerates into a gritty tale of hatred, pistols fired
from open windows, and exhausting journeys without maps. The
devils and the wrath of heaven have been banished, leaving only a

smouldering fear of nemesis and death's progress through the world, with no promise of afterlife.

If we compare *Frankenstein* with a precursor, *Vathek*, published some thirty years earlier, there too we find a Faustian moral: "Such shall be the chastisement of that blind curiosity, which would transgress those bounds the wisdom of the Creator has prescribed to human knowledge."[†] To us, Frankenstein's transgression is infinitely more worthwhile than the calif's, just as the secret of life is so much more momentous a prize than the treasures of the pre-Adamite sultans. Frankenstein's prime error appears less blind curiosity than blind insensibility to suffering.

But the use of this modernised Faust theme is particularly suited to the first real novel of science fiction: Frankenstein's is *the* modern theme, touching not only science but man's dual nature, whose inherited ape curiosity has brought him both success and misery. His great discovery apart, Frankenstein is a meddler and victim, staggering through a world where heavenly virtues are few (though the fiend *reads* of them). Instead of hope and forgiveness, there remain only the misunderstanding of men and the noxious half life of the monster. Knowledge brings no happiness.

For this critic's taste, the Frankenstein theme is more contemporary and more interesting than interstellar travel tales, since it takes us nearer to the enigma of man and thus of life; just as interstellar travel can yield more interest than such power-fantasy themes as telepathy.

Victor Frankenstein's last words are a feeble hope-against-hope injunction to Walton: "Farewell, Walton! Seek happiness in tranquility, and avoid ambition, even if it be only the apparently innocent one of distinguishing yourself in science and discoveries. Yet why do I say this? I have myself been blasted in these hopes, yet another may succeed." (Chapter 24) Some people never learn.

Frankenstein dies aboard Walton's ship; the ship is becalmed in the regions about the North Pole, stranded amid mist and ice in a manner designedly reminiscent of the *Ancient Mariner*. Walton first sights Frankenstein's monster in a sledge drawn by dogs—"a being which had the shape of a man, but apparently of gigantic stat-

† Later, this judgement would be echoed, although in twentieth-century English, in the closing scenes of several science-horror films: "There are secrets in nature with which man should not meddle!"

ure . . ."—with more than a reminder of the couplet from Darwin already quoted (see page 17). Legend has it that Mary, as a child, hid behind a sofa to listen to Coleridge reading his great poem.

The spirit of scientific enquiry remains subordinate to morbid obsession. Even while the modern Prometheus declares that "life and death appeared to me ideal bounds, which I should first break through, and pour a torrent of light into our dark world" (Chapter 4), he is sinking into a shadowy state beyond reach of other human beings. "Now I was led to examine the cause and progress of this decay, and forced to spend days and nights in vaults and charnel houses. My attention was fixed on every object the most insupportable to the delicacy of human feelings. I saw how the fine form of man was degraded and wasted; I beheld the corruption of death succeed to the blooming cheek of life: I saw how the worm inherited the wonders of the eye and brain." (Chapter 4)

Darwin puts the state of mind succinctly in Canto IV of his *Temple of Nature:*

> There writhing Mania sits on Reason's throne,
> Or Melancholy makes it for her own,
> Sheds o'er the scene a voluntary gloom,
> Requests oblivion, and demands the tomb . . .

Frankenstein solves the riddle of the Sphinx. It brings him torment and death, just as it did Oedipus.

Frankenstein is a triumph of imagination: more than a new story, a new myth. Laboured though parts of it may be, its effect as a science fiction morality is no less powerful today than when it was written, surrounded as we are with so many fiends of our own designing. Yet it is appropriate that its closing words should be ". . . lost in darkness and distance." Science fiction is so often haunted by a sense of corruption. We can never entirely escape the aromas of Frankenstein's "workshop of filthy creation." (Chapter 4)

When we turn to the next great figure in the history of science fiction, we find again an emphasis on incest, darkness, fear, and "the tremendous secrets of the human frame."

Charles Darwin's *Origin of Species* was published in 1859, when its theories gradually won the widest acceptance and its facts had the maximum impact. But those facts and theories were already making their way in the world in Charles Darwin's grandfather's time.

They would grow to influence many aspects of human life. They begin to make themselves felt in *Frankenstein*.

After *Frankenstein*, a pause: not in the larger world of literature but in the infant one of science fiction. The idea of looking to the future was yet to be properly born in anything but a religious sense. Such writings as there were about the future tended to be of a political or satirical nature, such as the anonymous pamphlet *One Thousand Eight Hundred and Twenty-Nine*, published in 1819, which attacked the claims for Catholic emancipation and predicted the restoration of the Stuart kings in 1829.

Mary Shelley wrote other novels, none as successful as *Frankenstein*. Some, like *Valperga* (1823) are pure Gothic. But a word should be said of *The Last Man* (1826), published anonymously, as *Frankenstein* had been.

The Last Man bears on its title page a suitably forbidding motto culled from Milton:

> Let no man seek
> Henceforth to be foretold what shall befall
> Him or his children.

It is the story of Lionel Verney, and set towards the end of the twenty-first century. The king of England has abdicated, bowing to the popular wish, and his son, Adrian, now known as the Earl of Windsor, befriends Verney. Verney's father was a favourite of the king's, but fell from favour, since when Verney has "wandered among the hills of civilised England as uncouth as a savage." He is converted to finer feelings by the friendship with Adrian.

Enter Lord Raymond, a youthful peer of genius and beauty. The date is A.D. 2073, but the Turks are still lording it over the Greeks; Raymond eventually becomes commander of the Greek Army, and besieges Constantinople.

This much, with many complications concerning the various sisters and mothers of the various parties, occupies the first third of the narrative. A modern reader finds his way through it only by recalling that Mary was drawing portraits of people she knew, Shelley being Adrian, Byron Raymond, and Claire Claremont, Perdita, Verney's sister. Several of the infants are also identifiable. None of them has quite as much life and credibility as Frankenstein's creature.

The *roman à clef* involvement is partly abandoned when Constantinople falls to the besiegers. They walk in unopposed, Raymond at their head. The defenders have died of plague: the city is empty.

With the introduction of the plague, the narrative gains pace, dire events and forebodings of worse flock one after the other.

> What are we, the inhabitants of this globe, least among the many that people infinite space? Our minds embrace infinity; the visible mechanism of our being is subject to merest accident. (Volume 2, Chapter 5)

Raymond is killed by falling masonry, Perdita commits suicide by drowning. The plague spreads all over the world, so that "the vast cities of America, the fertile plains of Hindostan, the crowded abodes of the Chinese, are menaced with utter ruin." (Volume 2, Chapter 5)

Back in Windsor, Verney fears for his wife and children, although refugees from plague-stricken spots are allowed to find shelter within the castle walls; the parks are ploughed to provide food for everyone. Adrian is working for the general good in London, where plague has secured a footing. After helping him, Verney returns to Windsor, to find plague in the castle.

> Death, cruel and relentless, had entered these beloved walls. . . . [Later] quiet prevailed in the Castle, whose inhabitants were hushed to repose. I was awake, and during the long hours of dead night, my busy thoughts worked in my brain like ten thousand mill-wheels, rapid, acute, untameable. All slept—all England slept; and from my window, commanding a wide prospect of the star-illumined country, I saw the land stretched out in placid rest. I was awake, alive, while the brother of death possessed my race. (Chapter 7)

Winter halts the deaths. Next summer brings renewed onslaughts, and England is invaded by hordes of Americans and Irish—an invasion force which Adrian quells with peaceful talk.

Adrian and Verney eventually lead the few English who survive from England to France. By then, one of Verney's sons is dead, and his wife dies during a snowstorm.

After various celestial manifestations, and a certain amount of trouble at Versailles, fifty survivors, their numbers still dwindling, move southwards from Dijon. Mary Shelley leaves not a wither unwrung. "Images of destruction, pictures of despair, the procession of the last triumph of death, shall be drawn before thee," she warns her gentle reader.

Adrian and Verney, with two children, Clara and little Evelyn, reach Italy. Typhus claims Evelyn by Lake Como. The three survivors find nobody else alive. The country is desolate. They reach Venice, only to find it ruinous and slowly sinking under the lagoon.

Prompted by Adrian's whim to see Greece again, they set sail down the Adriatic. A storm rises, the boat sinks, they plunge into the water—and eventually Verney flings himself ashore, alone. He is the last man alive.

After indulging in some bitter comparisons between his state and Robinson Crusoe's, he makes for the Eternal City (where Shelley's ashes lay buried). Still he meets with nobody. In Rome, he gluts himself with Rome's treasures, wandering in its art galleries and its libraries, until settling down to write his history.

Our last glimpse of Verney is when he sets out with a dog for company to sail south through the Mediterranean, down the African coast, towards the odorous islands of the far Indian Ocean.

Although Mary Shelley's temperament responded to this gloomy theme, *The Last Man* is no more than Gothic. Its pretence of being set in the future is soon dropped. There are few innovations in her world, apart from steerable balloons. The abdication of the king in favour of a socialistic regime is certainly a novelty (though no more than a pallid reflection of the French Revolution and her father's thinking) but, even there, the introduction of a Lord Protector carries us, not forward, but back to Cromwell's time; while the backward-lookingness is reinforced, not only by the wicked Turks, but by pictures of London which derive strongly from Defoe, who is mentioned in the text. More tellingly, although Mary had an undoubted interest in science,[28] her characters are as powerless against the plague as any citizens facing the Black Death in the fifteenth century. Vaccination was common by the eighteen-twenties, yet Mary makes no extrapolations from it.

Despite these failures to depict anything like a credible future, which of course are more apparent now than they were to Mary Shelley's audience in 1826, there remains the fact that she chose to set her fiction far away in the future, as if feeling that a distance of over two-and-a-half centuries in some way lent additional grandeur to her grand theme. This belief has influenced writers since, though they may not recall—as doubtless Mary did—that passage Shelley wrote, in which, referring to poets as the unacknowledged legislators of the world, he also called them "the heirophants of an unapprehended inspiration; the mirrors of the gigantic shadows which futurity casts upon the present; the words which express what they understand not; the trumpets which sing to battle and feel not what they inspire . . ."[29] In this novel, Mary Shelley frequently becomes a poet in exactly Shelley's sense.

More prosaically, once one has struggled through to Constantinople, the novel presents a tremendously effective suspense element. It is more competent in this than several Gothic novels which have since been reprinted; while, among many passages of tedious moralising and rhapsodising, there are splendid purple patches, not least the scene in which the storm springs up and Adrian is drowned, and the dream in which Raymond's body becomes the pestilence.[30] Here to perfection is Burke's "delightful horror."

The gloom of *The Last Man* is also striking—and often strikingly expressed. Here is Raymond speaking to Lionel.

> You are of this world; I am not. You hold forth your hand; it is even as a part of yourself; and you do not yet divide the feeling of identity from the mortal form that shapes forth Lionel. How then can you understand me? Earth is to me a tomb, the firmament a vault, shrouding mere corruption. Time is no more, for I have stepped within the threshold of eternity; each man I meet appears a corse, which will soon be deserted of its animating spark, on the eve of decay and corruption. (Volume 2, Chapter 2)

Here, the thinking behind *Frankenstein* has grown like a cancer in Mary Shelley's mind, until revulsions that once were applied merely to a freakish monster now infest the whole human race; it is the race, rather than the individual, which is hunted down to exile and extinction. If only Mary had been a great writer instead of merely a good one! What a sombre masterpiece she could have given us!

Overshadowed by her husband's reputation, her writing has been too greatly neglected. Her story "Matilda" was not published until 1959.[31] It was written after the death of "Willmouse," Matilda feels an incestuous love for her father, which is returned. The father disappears, full of guilt. Matilda has a prophetic dream that he may have drowned. She searches for him frantically on the seacoast. "Let him be alive! It is all dark: in my abject misery I demand no more: no hope, no good: only passion and guilt and horror; but alive!"

It is all three Brontë sisters in one! Even more, it presages what would happen three years later, when Mary drove desperately to see if her beloved Shelley had survived the sea.

That drowning echoes back and forth in Mary's life. She seems to have had some genuine prophetic talent.

The sea appears again in another neglected story, "The Transformation," to which no commentator has drawn due attention. It throws singular light on the events of Frankenstein's wedding night.

"The Transformation" appeared first in one of the Keepsakes or Annuals which the early Victorians enjoyed. It was collected together with others of Mary's stories and reprinted with an introduction by Richard Garnett in 1891.

The story is set in Italy. Guido is a dissolute and wealthy young man, betrothed to Juliet until his evil behaviour becomes too much for her.

He has behaved as one possessed. Now he is destitute and wanders along the seashore. He reaches a particularly desolate promontory when a storm breaks. Guido witnesses a ship dashed against a rock and sunk; all aboard are drowned except one man.

He comes ashore. It is not a man but a dwarf, misshapen, a monster—and a magician. Guido and the magician strike a bargain. For three days, they will change bodies. Guido's poverty, exile, and disgrace shall also belong to the dwarf. In exchange, Guido will receive a chest full of money.

Dwarf-as-Guido departs. A week passes and he does not return. Guido-as-dwarf walks to Genoa, to find it full of festivity. Tomorrow, dwarf-as-Guido will marry Juliet!

It is the night before the wedding. Juliet is at her window, whispering Guido's name to the impostor, who stands outside.

The dwarfish shape springs from the shadows and thrusts his dagger towards Guido's throat. They struggle. The present Guido says, "Strike home! Destroy this body—you will still live."

At the words, Guido-as-dwarf falters, and his opponent draws a sword. As the opponent thrusts, Guido-as-dwarf throws himself on the point, at the same time plunging his dagger into the other's side.

When Guido comes to, he is in his own body once more and the dwarf is dead. Juliet tends him lovingly. He has to live remembering that it was the monstrous dwarf who won back Juliet's love, and that the creature she now reviles was himself.

This remarkable treatment of a *doppelgänger* theme lies close to *Frankenstein*. Perhaps both stories express the struggle Mary felt in her own nature between the light and the dark. We can also see that Shelley's death must have seemed to her like her own.

It is all too appropriate that Mary Shelley's work should be neglected. Science fiction has been similarly neglected until recently. As the standing of Mary's reputation is still in the balance, so is science fiction's.

Sufficient at present to point to her solid merits, and the way in which some of her sparklingly dark scenes carry us back to such dramatists as Webster and Tourneur and forward to the Edgar Allan Poe of *The Masque of the Red Death*.

Poe, indeed, is the next considerable writer of science fiction to emerge: another spiritual exile, who can say with Mary's Byronic Raymond, "Earth is to me a tomb!"

NOTES

1. H. G. Wells, Preface to *The Scientific Romances*, 1933.

2. Darko Suvin, *Od Lukijana Do Lunika*, Zagreb, 1965.

3. For instance, Roger Lancelyn Green, *Into Other Worlds*, 1957.

4. Marjorie Hope Nicolson, *Voyages to the Moon*, New York, 1949.

5. *The Essential Writings of Erasmus Darwin*, Chosen and edited with linking commentary by Desmond King-Hele, 1968. References to Darwin in relation to the exploration of the South Seas are contained in Bernard Smith's *European Vision and the South Pacific 1768–1850*, 1960.

6. See Desmond King-Hele's study, *Erasmus Darwin*, 1963.

7. Alethea Hayter, *Opium and the Romantic Imagination*, 1968.

8. Horace Walpole: Letter to the Reverend William Cole, Strawberry Hill, Mar. 9, 1765. Explaining to Cole how he came to write *Castle of Otranto*, he says, "Shall I even confess to you, what was the origin

of this romance! I waked one morning, in the beginning of last June, from a dream, of which, all I could recover was, that I had thought myself in an ancient castle (a very natural dream for a head filled like mine with Gothic story), and that on the uppermost bannister of a great staircase I saw a gigantic hand in armour. In the evening I sat down, and began to write, without knowing in the least what I intended to say or relate . . ."

9. Piranesi engraved his *Carceri* in Rome in 1745, heralding the whole Romantic movement or certainly its gloomier side. For the lighter side, one would have to turn to the etchings of another Italian, the Venetian G. B. Tiepolo, whose *Capricci* appeared at almost the same time as Piranesi's *Carceri*. In these pictures, mysterious figures talk or wait among mysterious ruins; in a later series, the *Scherzi di fantasia*, the beautiful people are surrounded by magic and death, although they are still bathed in Tiepolo's glorious light.

10. For further details, consult, for instance, Margaret Dalziel's *Popular Fiction 100 Years Ago*, 1957.

11. The most interesting point about Peacock is how readable his best novels remain. *Gryll Grange*, published when the author was seventy-five, is an especially delightful satire on progress in Victorian days, with the Reverend Dr. Opimian representing a churlish anti-scientific viewpoint which sounds less strange in our time than it must have done in the 1860s: "The day would fail, if I should attempt to enumerate the evils which science has inflicted on mankind. I almost think it is the ultimate destiny of science to exterminate the human race." (Chap. 19)

12. A fine example is Ursula Le Guin's *The Left Hand of Darkness*, 1969.

13. H. Beam Piper, *Temple Trouble*, 1951.

14. H. B. Fyfe, *Protected Species*, 1951.

15. A. E. van Vogt, *Asylum*, 1942.

16. F. L. Wallace, *Big Ancestor*, 1954.

17. Some while before Ward Moore's novel appeared, a volume was published called *If, or History Rewritten*, edited by J. C. Squire, New York, 1931, which is full of alternative universes dreamed up by scholars and historians. One of the most interesting is Winston Churchill's "If Lee Had Not Won the Battle of Gettysburg." In England, the volume is entitled *If It Had Happened Otherwise*, and was reprinted in 1972.

18. Shelley, *Hymn to Intellectual Beauty*, Stanza 5.

19. Edward John Trelawny, *Recollections of the Last Days of Shelley and Byron*, 1858.

20. The standard biography of Mary Shelley remains R. Glynn Grylls' *Mary Shelley: A Biography*, 1938. It is well documented. More lively is the portrait in Eileen Bigland's *Mary Shelley*, 1959.

21. The point is made with clarity in Miss J. M. S. Tompkins' book

The Popular Novel in England, 1770–1800, 1961. "What their authors aimed at—at least, the best of them—was delicacy and variety of emotional hue. The novel was to be a sort of artificial rainbow, woven of tears and glinting sunshine, but allowing, at times, of more violent contrasts." (Chap. 9)

22. "In its erection of a superstructure of fantasy on a foundation of circumstantial 'scientific' fact . . . it is the first of the Scientific Romances that have culminated in our day in the work of Mr H. G. Wells; in this, as in its suggestion of deeper psychological and sociological implications underlying the story, *Frankenstein* marks an advance on the crude horror of the Radcliffe-Monk Lewis school." R. Glynn Grylls, *op. cit.*

23. It would be interesting to know if Polidori supplied a copy of De Sade's Gothic fantasy *Justine,* published in 1791. There is a Justine in *Frankenstein,* wrongfully imprisoned, and "gazed on and execrated by thousands"—a very De Sade-like situation; though innocent, she perishes on the scaffold. Mario Praz indicates this parallel in *The Romantic Agony;* 1933. Curiously enough, De Sade's Justine perishes by lightning, the force that brings life to Frankenstein's creation in the James Whale film.

24. There is some discussion of this point by M. K. Joseph, in his excellent edition of *Frankenstein,* published in the Oxford English Novels series, 1969.

25. Credit for this observation goes to Desmond King-Hele, in his grand works of Darwinian restoration already cited. He provides plenty of evidence of Darwin's influence on the poets of his time, Shelley in particular.

26. While in *Juliette,* Saint-Fond cries, *"Quelle jouissance! J'étais couvert de malédictions, d'imprécations, je parricidais, j'incestais, j'assassinais, je prostituais, je sodomisais!"*

27. Christopher Small, *Ariel Like a Harpy: Shelley, Mary, and "Frankenstein,"* 1972.

28. Mary contributed lives of "Eminent Literary and Scientific Men of Italy, Spain, and Portugal" and of "Eminent Literary and Scientific Men in France" to *The Cabinet Cyclopaedia* for 1835 and 1838 respectively.

29. Shelley, *The Defence of Poetry,* 1821.

30. This prodromic nightmare is presented in somewhat fustian style but in its intention—to disturb by presenting familiar objects out of context—it is surrealist. Verney has found the beloved Lord Raymond dead in the ruins of plague-stricken Constantinople, and falls asleep:

"I awoke from disturbed dreams. Methought I had been invited to Timon's last feast: I came with keen appetite, the covers were removed, the hot water sent up its satisfying streams, while I fled before the anger of the host, who assumed the form of Raymond; while to my diseased

fancy, the vessels hurled by him after me were surcharged with fetid va-
pour, and my friend's shape, altered by a thousand distortions, expanded
into a gigantic phantom, bearing on its brow the sign of pestilence. The
growing shadow rose and rose, filling, and then seeming to endeavour to
burst beyond the adamantine vault that bent over, sustaining and enclos-
ing the world. The nightmare became torture; with a strong effort I threw
off sleep, and recalled reason to her wonted functions." (*The Last Man*,
Vol. 2, Chap. 3)

Mary Shelley uses the same device just before Victor Frankenstein
wakes to find his "miserable monster" has come to life. There again, the
dream is of someone loved (in this case his fiancée) transformed into a
symbol of horror and disgust:

"I slept indeed, but I was disturbed by the wildest dreams. I thought
I saw Elizabeth, in the bloom of health, walking in the streets of Ingold-
stadt. Delighted and surprised, I embraced her; but as I imprinted the
first kiss on her lips, they became livid with the hue of death; her features
appeared to change, and I thought that I held the corpse of my dead
mother in my arms; a shroud enveloped her form, and I saw the grave-
worms crawling in the folds of the flannel. I started from my sleep with
horror; a cold dew covered my forehead, my teeth chattered, and every
limb became convulsed . . ." (*Frankenstein*, Chap. 5)

For anyone compiling an anthology of evil dreams, Mary Shelley is
essential reading.

31. Edited by Elizabeth Mitchie in *Studies in Philology*, Extra
Series, No. 3.

2

"A Clear-Sighted, Sickly Literature":
EDGAR ALLAN POE

> They who dream by day are cognisant
> of many things which escape those who
> dream by night.
>
> Edgar Allan Poe: *Eleonora*

Mary Shelley had the fortune to live surrounded by literary parents, friends, and acquaintances. Edgar Allan Poe had the misfortune to possess almost no literary friends; perhaps partly as compensation, he created his own literary world: poems, criticisms, reviews, tales, and at least an attempt at a novel.

Poe is a Hamlet of letters; not only isolated, but dandyish, black-clad, and tormented if not actually demented. He still provokes almost as much debate as Hamlet; nearly a century and a quarter after his death, critics have not come to any settled opinion over his merits. That, at least, speaks well for a continuing life in his writings. There are contradictory opinions about the merits of his individual style, the worth of his subject matter, and his status in the world of letters.

These questions are naturally relevant to his position as a science fiction author. A striking early judgement on his writings was passed by the Brothers Goncourt in their journal for 1856:

16 July—After reading Edgar Allan Poe. Something the critics have not noticed: a new literary world, pointing to the literature of the twentieth century. Scientific miracles, fables on the pattern A+B; a clear-sighted, sickly literature. No more poetry, but analytic fantasy. Something monomaniacal. Things playing a more important part than people; love giving way to deductions and other sources of ideas, style, subject, and interest; the basis of the novel transferred from the heart to the head, from the passion to the idea, from the drama to the denouement.[1]

It is a confused remark in some ways. But it points to one thing that Poe's writing has in common with Mary Shelley's, an attempt to balance Inwardness with Outwardness. Poe is the great poet of the Inward; yet he could not resist the scientific miracles, the A+B of which the Goncourts speak. Poe's dark chambers are littered with the gadgets of his age.

Those who enjoy science fiction above all other kinds of writing must enjoy its vitalising bastardy, its immoral interdisciplinary habits, as it feathers its nest with scraps of knowledge seized from the limit of the expanding world. We can only agree with the Aldous Huxley who said, "I have a taste for the lively, the mixed and the incomplete in art, preferring it to the universal and the chemically pure."

Poe's chemical impurities were built into his fibre from birth.

The critic Sam Moskowitz says, "The details of Poe's tortured life would not be believable or acceptable in fiction."[2] Be *that* as it may, it is sometimes difficult to separate the facts from fiction. Poe was born in Boston in 1809 and not 1811, as he later stated. His father was a travelling actor. His mother was Elizabeth Hopkins, an English woman and leading lady in the company of actors. She died in extreme poverty—of the consumption which stalks through nineteenth-century artistic history—when Poe was only two years old; by then, his father had disappeared. Modern child-care experts would no doubt make more of the effect this disaster had upon Elizabeth's infant than have literary critics.

Poe was adopted by a Scottish tobacco merchant, John Allan. Their relationship appears to have been an affectionate one throughout Poe's boyhood, although critics dispute this too. He entered the

University of Virginia, but was sent down for gambling debts. Now began his quarrels with Allan.

His first poems were published in 1827 (*Tamerlane and Other Poems*—forty copies only); by then, he had enlisted in the Army, perhaps prompted by the knowledge that his paternal grandfather had fought in the Civil War.

Always a great embroiderer, Poe made this period of his life out to be full of adventure and travel; in fact, he never left the United States. After demobilisation from the Army, he entered West Point in 1830 and was discharged only a few months later, for disobedience and absenteeism. His movements are often obscure. Although he appears always to have suffered from the difficulties in sustaining personal relationships which characterise children bereaved of their mothers in early years, he began building a reputation with his fiction and acquiring status with an editorial job on the *Southern Literary Messenger*. Much of his excellent literary criticism was written at this time, during the late eighteen-thirties and early forties.

In 1836, Poe married his cousin Virginia, a child of not quite fourteen. Literary theorists, not unnaturally, have smacked their lips over this conjunction; but however terrible his pleasures, Poe's pains seem to have been more terrible. If we are allowed to call as evidence in this relationship Poe's tale *Eleonora*,[3] then Poe and his cousin loved each other deeply, and by no means celibately ("No guile disguised the fervour of love which animated her heart, and she examined with me its inmost recesses"); but of course poor Poe may have found it necessary here, too, to embroider the more banal aspects of life.

However that might be, of his suffering there is no doubt. Virginia wasted before his eyes; she had ruptured a blood vessel while singing and on several occasions fell into a deathlike trance. She died of tuberculosis in 1848. During this game of hide-and-seek with death, Poe took heavily to drink and possibly to opium; he also underwent a lesion on one side of his brain, which rendered him unable to take alcohol without becoming drunk.

It is as well that Poe was the least materialistic of men, for he remained materially poor even when his reputation as poet, critic, and short-story writer was high. During the last year of his life, 1849, he became emotionally involved with three women, and was busy with lecture tours and editing. He died in Baltimore in mysterious circumstances, from brain fever, epilepsy, or a fatal drinking bout. One version of his last days suggests that he was the victim of local press-gang politics—that on his way to a new life in New York, having signed the pledge, he was set upon, drugged, and forced to vote at a number of election booths. Was he a fated victim or an incurable soak? Or perhaps something of both?[4]

More ill luck attended Poe's choice of executor, a literary villain named the Reverend Rufus W. Griswold—indeed a name that would not be believable or acceptable in fiction—who spread many calumnies about Poe, working on the fertile ground of Poe's own inexactitudes.

Poe's reputation is as entangled as his career. His writing was renowned in France, as the extract from the Goncourt journal indicates, at a time when the English-speaking world cared little for its merits. This was in part due to the obsessive attention lavished on his work by Charles Baudelaire. The great poet devoted some sixteen years of his creative life to translating Poe into French. It is difficult to think of a literary parallel to such devotion!

Baudelaire's hero worship had much to do with the absence of moralising in Poe, in an age when morality and literature were becoming increasingly confused. He admired Poe's exploration of mental and moral disease and the terror that was "not of Germany but of the soul."[5] It is on this view of Poe's writings that his best reputation now rests; but English-speaking critics have been reluctant to accept it. They regard Poe either as hopelessly immature[6] or as a stage manager, concerned with little beyond immediate effect—and unfortunately there are a host of tales and poems that support this attitude, which D. H. Lawrence called "the bad taste of sensationalism,"[7] and which Aldous Huxley said contained "those finer shades of vulgarity that ruin Poe."[8]

The most successful tales are those in which some airless room is haunted by the memory of a pale woman, loved yet feared. Then Poe does achieve a haggard grandeur which uniquely mingles immense muffled silences and jangled nerves. The least successful tales—judged as literature—are those in which Poe's predilection for ugly horseplay takes over: the murdered and decomposing Mr. Shuttleworthy popping up out of a crate in *Thou Art the Man;* the homicidal orangoutang, which provides a denouement for *The Murders in the Rue Morgue;* the grotesque mass-drowning in ale in *King Pest;* the setting fire to a party dressed as orangoutangs in

Hop-Frog. This horseplay side of Poe recalls the work of an ill-natured schoolboy.

But his most valid tales—into which category come *The Fall of the House of Usher, Ligeia, Eleonora, The Masque of the Red Death,* and *The Facts in the Case of M. Valdemar,* among others—show a remarkable ability to survive, despite their often overstrained language. Their windowless or curtained chambers provide a valid metaphor for a sunken aspect of the human spirit which had rarely before found such intense utterance. Edgar Allan Poe is the first poet of the Great Indoors; his is an unlikely figure to appear when it did, when the Great Outdoors was being celebrated so heartily by Fenimore Cooper and others. It is this that enables Poe's portrait to be hung in the board room of modernity and science fiction, along with other defunct directors such as Verne and Wells and Mary Shelley.

Nevertheless, Poe had his predecessors in the United States. Charles Brockden Brown (1771–1810), the first professional American writer, dwelt extensively on morbid subjects and died of tuberculosis at the age of thirty-nine. His *Wieland* (1798) is pure Gothic, while *Arthur Mervyn* (1799–1801) is the story of a plague, Brown himself having survived two epidemics of yellow fever. This latter novel is mentioned in Mary Shelley's *The Last Man*.

Nathaniel Hawthorne (1804–64) is a more distinguished literary ancestor, though his most famous novels, such as *The Scarlet Letter* (1850), *The House of the Seven Gables* (1851), and *The Marble Faun* (1860), were all published after Poe's death. Hawthorne was a New Englander greatly preoccupied with the subject of sin, whose writings contain a great deal of allegory and tend, in such short stories as *The Artist of the Beautiful** (1844), towards science fiction.

As a student of morbid psychology, Poe strikingly presents his characters by pictorial descriptions of their surroundings. Most popular representations of Poe's works—the cinema in particular—treat him as a horror-merchant. But Poe's horror is of a special sort. He uses none of the supernatural machinery, the framework of evil gods, manipulated so vigorously by such successors as Machen and

---

* Amid a great display of sensibility, Warland creates an exquisite insect; it may be a steam-driven butterfly. When the girl he admires sees it and asks if he made it, his reply is, "Wherefore ask who created it, so it be beautiful?" Among similar impressive manifestations of the subjunctive, the insect is clobbered by an unfeeling child; but Warland does not mind. He has his Art.

Lovecraft. His are the domestic horrors, the glimpses of little lives riddled with fears of life and sex, with only an occasional occult visitation; any revenants from the grave are likely to be female.

Even hell-fire has died; the terrible frenzies of human desire are banked down under chilling languors and the leukaemias of isolation; the world of Poe is frightening because it is a world of deprivation and of a love that does not dare to breathe its pseudonym. So heavily is the course of love perverted that the inaction (one would hardly speak of action in a typical Poeic tale) generally takes place below ground, to symbolise the depths to which the psyche has foundered.

More than one critic has hailed Poe as "the father of science fiction." According to Professor Bruce Franklin,[9] the first person to do so was an anonymous writer in the *Saturday Review* in 1905, and the notion has rattled about ever since. Although it would seem to be based more on a thorough ignorance of literature than a thorough knowledge of Poe, there is at least some substance in the claim; for Poe holds one of the patents on the short story—and the short story, at least until yesterday, was the ideal form for science fiction.

Among his stories, those most likely to pass muster as science fiction are *The Conversation of Eiros and Charmion* ("Where the approach of a giant comet brings a hideous *novelty* of emotion"), *A Tale of Ragged Mountains, A Descent into the Maelstrom, The Facts in the Case of M. Valdemar, The Narrative of Arthur Gordon Pym of Nantucket, The Unparalleled Adventures of one Hans Pfaall, The Balloon-Hoax, Mellonta Tauta, Mesmeric Revelation, The Colloquy of Monos and Una,* and *The Thousand and Second Tale of Scheherazade.* A handful of tales, and the roll call establishes this: that Poe's best stories are not science fiction, nor his science fiction stories his best.

Certainly Poe was interested in science, in the future of science, and in the effects of science on society. Often he shows remarkable prescience; for instance, in a neglected story, *The Colloquy of Monos and Una,* he perceives certain laws of conservation which were only widely acknowledged in the 1960s. In this potted history of a technologically overwhelmed future, he says, "Meantime, huge smoking cities arose, innumerable. Green leaves shrank before the hot breath of furnaces. The fair face of Nature was deformed as with the ravages of some loathesome disease . . ." He also makes the equation between global pollution and global age-ing: "Prematurely induced by intemperance of knowledge, the old age of the world drew on."

In a letter, he said, "I live continually in a reverie of the fu-ture." But those stories which are most like science fiction are least like stories, more resembling essays or conversations, and often tumbling into the facetious (one of Poe's besetting sins, linked with a habit of giving characters names like von Underduk), as if he found his material intractable.

He may use scientific flavouring, much as Lawrence Durrell does in our day; but this makes him no more a science fiction writer than it does Durrell—in fact, rather less, when we remember the latter's *Nunquam*, with its transvestite Frankenstein motif!

There are excellent stories which are *kin* to science fiction: *MS Found in a Bottle*, featuring a splendid "Flying Dutchman," which has often been turned into a derelict spaceship; *William Watson*, with a *doppelgänger*, which has often been turned into an adroid since Poe's time; but Flying Dutchmen and *doppelgängers* are not in themselves science fiction and were only later smuggled into the sub-genre. Poe wrote stories in which scientific or quasi-scientific theories are present, as mesmerism is in the horrific *Facts in the Case of M. Valdemar*; but that story is, in fact, his most successful science fiction story.

M. Valdemar is the story of a sick man hypnotised; he dies, but his soul cannot leave his decaying body until the hypnotic bond is released. Poe's biological details are good, his manner cool and clinical. He regarded mesmerism as a strange but legitimate new science. But the emotional charge of the story, which is the well-spring of its horrifying success, comes from the fact that Poe is here treading on his favourite unhallowed ground, the territory between life and death.

Cases could also be made out for the curious kind of time-travel in *A Tale of Ragged Mountains* or the mock psychiatry in *The System of Dr. Tarr and Mr. Feather*; and there is Hans Pfaall's balloon journey to the Moon, painstakingly described; and *Arthur Gordon Pym*, to which we shall turn shortly.

But none of these triumph like those Poe mainliners of horror, *The Pit and the Pendulum*, *The Tell-Tale Heart*, *The Masque of the Red Death*, *The Fall of the House of Usher*, and so forth. And, on such a modest science fictional showing, Poe would receive little longer mention in a history of science fiction than his contemporaries and near contemporaries such as Brockden Brown, Hawthorne, and Oliver Wendell Holmes,[10] born the same year as Poe. But there is more to Poe than this.

Beneath Poe's stage machinery, beneath the mock Gothic and his transplanted bits of a never-never Europe, beneath his melodrama, is a retreat from, a sabotaging of the so-called rational world in which he with such difficulty found his way. In his fiction, Poe discards most of the trappings of this world, its politics, its finances, its day-to-day affairs, and most of its people. For he knows of Another World. He cannot tell us where it is: perhaps it is beyond the tomb, perhaps in a lost continent, perhaps through a mirror, perhaps in another state of mind, another time, another dimension. But he knows it is there.

This knowing and being unable to say—it is of the essence of Poe, and lends a necessary ambiguity to what might otherwise seem too obvious. That remarkable prose poem, for instance, *The Masque of the Red Death*—what is it really about? Is the Red Death a plague, like the Black Death? But the opening words of the tale appear to contradict this idea ("The 'Red Death' had long devastated the country. No pestilence had ever been so fatal, or so hideous . . ."). Could "Red Death" be Poe's sardonic way of describing, not death, but life itself?[11] Remembering Poe's ecological interests, we may judge this reading tenable.

Knowing and being unable to say: it is for this reason that Poe's works are scattered with puzzles and cryptograms and cyphers,[12] that baffling clock symbols recur again and again,[13] that strange fragments of foreign tongues are put into the mouths of animals and birds,[14] that he was fond of hoaxes,[15] that he writes stories as articles, using the persona of first-person narrators,[16] that he is full of tricks and curiosities,[17] that his characters have speech impediments,[18] that he could never master anything as long-winded as a novel. All his considerable eloquence points towards a central inarticulacy. He knew of Another World, and could express it only in symbols.

It is in the techniques Poe developed to skirt this central inarticulacy that he has made most impact on other writers. The symbols he uses, the worm-riddled furniture of his sentences, appealed to Mallarmé, Valéry,[19] and the Symbolists[20]; while his pervasive sense of something waiting just out of sight—in the wings, the tomb, or the head—has been reproduced in the writings of science fantasy authors such as Donald Wandrei, Ray Bradbury, Richard Matheson, Robert Bloch, John Ramsay Campbell, and others. And, of course, in Bram Stoker's *Dracula*.

A consideration of Poe's work brings us to a consideration of the whole nature of fiction. We may regard fiction as play, though often play of a serious nature. When children play, they frequently imitate adult situations (mothers and fathers, or doctors), scaling them down so as to come to terms with potentially painful or threatening confrontations. Literature for adults reverses the effect: it produces a play situation in which painful or threatening confrontations are scaled up, helping us to face them via that particular relationship between author and reader which literature—and no other medium—can achieve.

Science fiction is a particular example of scaling, in which one of the axes of the graph is exaggerated, so that threatening situations become particularly precipitous: as if in compensation, the congruence with reality then becomes somewhat less. It is Poe's especial merit—shared with few other writers—that when he is at his best he threatens us with something in which, being ultimately undefined, a part of us must compulsively believe. The resolution of the story leaves that belief intact.

Poe is in considerable measure a Gothic writer[21]; but his nearest literary relations appear to be *Wuthering Heights* and Kafka's *Trial*—the Kafka of what the Goncourts perceptively called "analytical fantasy." It is too easy to say that Poe is obsessed with death; he is an obsessive writer, but the goal of his quest lies just beyond the clutch of death. The narrator in *MS Found in a Bottle* says that he is "hurrying onwards to some exciting knowledge—some never-to-be-imparted secret . . ." and many of Poe's other characters are trapped in the same predicament. This it is which sets them apart from society. Their conscious minds dilate, they become, like Roderick Usher, possessed of extrasensory perceptions. It is the fate of the unsociable in search of the unspeakable to meet with disaster—the knowledge, like Faust's, must be paid for dearly; its "attainment is destruction."

So Poe's heroes in extremis often find themselves in oddly similar situations, bathed in luminous meteorological phenomena (which may be accompanied by Poe's ubiquitous water symbols). The eponymous character in *Metzengerstein* is enveloped in "a glare of preternatural light" as he rides to destruction; the old Norwegian who describes his descent into the maelstrom sees, in the moments of crisis, "the rays of the moon" shining on "a thick mist in which everything there was enveloped"; the traveller to "the Domain of Arnheim" meets with "an effulgence that seems to wreathe the whole surrounding forest in flames"; just before Madeline Usher appears in her shroud and falls upon her brother, he sees "the unnatural light of a faintly luminous and distinctly visible gaseous exhalation which hung about and enshrouded the mansion"; while the wretched Arthur Gordon Pym, drawn towards that "shrouded human figure, very far larger in its proportions than any other dweller among man," is swept along while "out of the milky depths of the ocean a luminous glare arose," to disappear from our ken in a limitless cataract, without sound, which ranges along "the whole extent of the southern horizon." In *The Conversation of Eiros and Charmion* the entire Earth is snuffed out with the same lurid lighting effect: "the whole encumbent mass of ether . . . burst at once into a species of intense flame." That the Undefined should be a blaze of white light is at once a religious and a scientific concept. There are moments when Poe reminds us of another poor visionary, William Blake.

Knowing but being unable to say, Poe is forced to terminate his narrations with these veils of white. Only once does he venture further, in *The Colloquy of Monos and Una,* and then it is to return to his favoured theme of love in or beyond the grave. Yet a new universality is added. This time, the light is "that light which alone might have power to startle—the light of enduring *Love.*" And the climax of the story carries us movingly into all time and space, away from material things!

> The sense of being had at length utterly departed, and there reigned in its stead—instead of all things—dominant and perpetual—the autocrats *Place* and *Time.* For *that* which *was not*—for that which had no form—for that which had no thought —for that which had no sentience—for that which was soulless, yet of which matter formed no portion—for all this nothingness, yet for all this immortality, the grave was still a home, and the corrosive hours, co-mates.

Such quests for the unknown and the infinite are very much in the science fictional vein. Yet the nearer Poe moves towards the actual trappings of science fiction, the less successful are his effects; such stories as *Mellonta Tauta,* which is set in the year 2848 and contains cosmological speculations, and *The Thousand and Second Tale of Scheherazade,* which shows how the Sultan put his wife to death for telling one extra and unbelievable story (which contains nothing but sober nineteenth-century technological achievements) are limp and jocular and without revelation, as are the descriptions of lunar landscape in *Hans Pfaall.* It is as if Poe needed to master a science fictional mode but failed, seeing, despite himself, that there was no solution to his personal problems within the realm of science.

Yet Poe is of the limited company of the world's great short story tellers, and the short story hardly existed as a genre when he wrote, certainly not in America or England. He reached the largest international audience of any of his countrymen last century, proving—to paraphrase his own words—that terror was not of America but of the soul. He was an innovator in both content and form, and in more than one field, for tales such as *Thou Art the Man,* and his stories about Auguste Dupin (*The Murders in the Rue Morgue, The Purloined Letter,* and *The Mystery of Marie Roget*) entitle him to be regarded as an originator of the tale of pure deduction and detection. His best stories—*The Fall of the House of Usher* is his masterpiece—are as alive today as when they were written.

In Poe, so extravagant is his method, success and failure lie close together. His longest work, *The Narrative of Arthur Gordon Pym,* finds room for both failure and success and, in its relationship to science fiction, merits closer inspection.

Pym, first published in 1836, is one of Poe's rare excursions away from the Great Indoors. It begins as a story of sea voyage and shipwreck, of stowaways and mutineers, of villainous cooks and men overboard, in the worst traditions of the sea. Poe also crams in a live burial, a man-eating dog, blood-drinking, cannibalism, an impersonation of a corpse (at which sight, one of the hardened villains of the crew falls back "stone dead"), and a sort of ghost ship manned by a crew of grotesque dead men.

To compensate for all this frantic activity by the author, his hero is as passive as a limbless child in a womb. Only when Pym gets aboard a second ship, the schooner *Jane Guy,* does the narrative gain other than risible interest. As the vessel sails for southern latitudes, the story takes on impetus and moves towards science fiction. There is a reminder of Coleridge's great poem as the *Jane Guy* makes her way among the ice floes of the Antarctic. The captain hopes to find new lands to the south; Poe responds to the theme of the quest, his prose tightens, and we take in our stride polar bears and an increasingly warm climate, for now we are embarked on a marvellous voyage.

The schooner arrives at an island called Tsalal, on which everything is black—soil, vegetation, birds, and human beings, the latter being "the most wicked, hypocritical, vindictive, bloodthirsty, and altogether fiendish race of men upon the face of the globe." These people have black teeth; their fear of anything white extends even to flour and the pages of a book; not unnaturally in these circumstances, they kill all the crew of the schooner—except Pym and a fiendish half-caste, who escape massacre by accident.

Pym and the half-caste find themselves at the bottom of the words of God (another cryptogram), graven deep into the rocks. They manage to climb out of this tangible evidence of the world's damnation and get away from the island in a canoe. It is then that they are swept "with a hideous velocity" over the face of the ocean towards that never-to-be-imparted secret ahead, where there is "a chaos of flitting and indistinct images." That shrouded figure, larger than any man, looms out of the unknown. They rush towards it. The screen goes white.

After its abysmal beginning, *Pym* is marvellous Poe, atmospheric and baffling. It is useless to complain that the end is unsatisfying, or that Poe makes no connections (as Henry James complained); if God speaks only in cryptograms, how should Edgar Allan Poe be more explicit? Pym has reached the end of his quest, and that is that. Destruction is all we may expect—the common and often desired lot of a Poe hero!

Pym is an early model of a Poe hero, the alienated man. Leslie Fiedler[22] calls *Pym* "the archetypal American story, which would be recast in *Moby Dick* and *Huckleberry Finn*." Even allowing that the inner meaning of *Pym*—as Fiedler sees it—rests on a fear of black men, a hatred of women, or a longing for the womb, or all three, and that the whole thing is a parody to boot, it is a remarkably ill-executed, blemished, and melodramatic narrative. If Poe had conceived a science fictional form more clearly, he could have cast the story more effectively; and this applies to most of his few other gestures towards the genre.

Poe preempted a science fictional content, particularly its transcendental content, yet mishandled its form, owing to perverse qualities in his own temperament. Far from being the Father of Science Fiction, this genius bodged it when he confronted its themes directly. Yet he brought off some of its best effects, more or less when looking the other way.

For Poe's is the power to flood a dismal scene with burning light and show us a man on his own confronted by a malignant power he can scarcely understand, let alone master. Zelazny has achieved similar effects. The evil that confronts the Poeian protagonist is not simply external; it is a part of his destiny, if not of himself. This is not an untruthful view of reality—later science fiction authors who change the terms of Poe's equation, making the protagonists gigantic and heroic, and conquering the universe, or making the evil purely external—and so cast in opposition to an innocent mankind—falsify disastrously. Poe may exaggerate; but, in these respects, at least, it is the truth he exaggerates.

The Gothic mode—itself a branch of the Romantic movement—took deeper root and flourished longer in the United States than elsewhere. Its characteristic ingredients—ruined landscapes, haunted characters, the flight from domesticity—might change in the hands of successive practitioners, from Charles Brockden Brown, Fenimore Cooper, and Nathaniel Hawthorne, through Melville, to William Faulkner, John Steinbeck, and Tennessee Williams, but were only recently abandoned.

All these characteristics appear most strikingly in a sub-genre, the Western, the first literary form to find its true strength in another medium: as film. In the cinema, with dusty cow towns taking the place of Renaissance piles and the dated *personae* of monks, aristocrats, and torturers transformed into sheriffs, good guys, and outlaws, the Western has become a vehicle for the endless discussion of the role of the individual and law and order in society; so universal is its appeal that Ranch-House Gothic is one of America's gifts to the rest of the world.

The other remarkable sub-genre is science fiction. As cinema, it cannot rival the Western in popularity (for one thing, the economic factor is against it: science fiction's spectacular special effects cost money to achieve, whereas covered waggons may be hired by the day). On the printed page, science fiction has proliferated enormously. Its special success is to have diversified the Gothic tale of terror in such a way as to encompass those fears generated by change and the technological advances which are the chief agents of change. The Renaissance piles are transformed to subterranean war rooms,[23] fortresses on the Moon,[24] cities under Venusian seas,[25] or an overblown Chicago, eight hundred years in the future[26]; but the Gothic impulse is still at work and, behind it, Burke's dictum about beauty and the sublime, which inspired awe and terror!

It is this prevalence of the Gothic mode which leads to the sort of confusion whereby critics can claim that all or most nineteenth-century authors wrote at least some science fiction. Washington Irving, Melville, Oliver Wendell Holmes, Silas Weir Mitchell, Ambrose Bierce, Mark Twain, Henry James, and all—all are called to serve! Perhaps some of the territorial ambitions which would seek to draw Dante, Shakespeare, and the author of Genesis into the ranks of science fiction writers are at work. We have to recognise that science fiction is merely a sub-genre, however vital, and however often the features that make it attractive are espied elsewhere: for these are features it has imitated and adapted. The converse has not obtained.

Once this distinction is grasped, we have less trouble in perceiving where science fiction begins and ends. In the past, inordinately large claims have been made for the genre—one thinks, laughingly, of Robert A. Heinlein's dictum: "For the survival and health of the human race one crudely written science fiction story containing a single worthwhile new idea is more valuable than a bookcaseful of beautifully written non-science fiction."[27] This is to rate Dick above Dickens, or Priest above Priestley.

But, with modesty and realism intervening, and accepting science fiction as a lively sub-genre of Gothic, we are now able to turn to those earlier writers, the Pilgrim Fathers, whose speculations on an unfolding world about them make them still so attractive, and enjoy their works as cathedrals of an earlier age, whose stones were often appropriated for the hastier buildings of later ages. Although they stand outside the science fiction field, no history of science fiction would make sense without reference to them.

NOTES

1. *Pages from the Goncourt Journal*, edited and translated by Robert Baldick, 1962. The entry is for July 16, 1856.

2. Sam Moskowitz, *Explorers of the Infinite*, Cleveland and New York, N.D.

3. As has at least one critic, David Galloway, editor of *Selected Writings of Edgar Allan Poe*, 1967.

4. A recent life is Edward Wagenknecht's *Edgar Allan Poe: The Man Behind the Legend*, New York, 1963. An illustrious psychoanalytical view is Marie Bonaparte's *Edgar Poe, Étude Psychanalytique*, Paris, 1933, which contains a Foreword by Sigmund Freud.

5. Preface to Poe's *Tales of the Grotesque and Arabesque*, 1840.

6. Cf. T. S. Eliot's remark that Poe possessed "the intellect of a highly gifted young person before puberty" (*From Poe to Valéry*).

7. D. H. Lawrence, "Edgar Allan Poe," *Studies in Classic American Literature*, 1924.

8. Aldous Huxley, "Vulgarity in Literature," *Music at Night*, 1930.

9. H. Bruce Franklin, *Future Perfect: American Science Fiction of the Nineteenth Century*, 1966.

10. Oliver Wendell Holmes (1809–94), most famous for *The Autocrat of the Breakfast-Table*, 1857. He was professor of anatomy at Dartmouth and later Harvard; he wrote three novels with psychiatric themes, of which *Elsie Venner*, 1861, is best known. He also coined the term "anaesthesia."

11. For a discussion of this point, consult Joseph Patrick Roppolo's "Meaning and *The Masque of the Red Death, Tulane Studies in English XIII*," 1963.

12. *The Gold Bug* provides the most eminent example. See also *The Purloined Letter, X-ing the Paragreb*, and *The Narrative of Arthur Gordon Pym*.

13. Particularly interesting in this connection, because of its linking of recurrent clock symbols in many stories with Poe's sexual motivation, and the possibility that the infant Poe observed his parents in the throes of love, is Jean-Paul Weber's article "Edgar Poe or the Theme of the Clock," *La Nouvelle Revue Francaise*, Nos. 68 and 69, 1958.

14. For example, the orangoutang in *Murders in the Rue Morgue*, the birds in *Arthur Gordon Pym*, the raven crying "Nevermore," and the black cat crying murder.

15. He played a part in the Great Moon Hoax of 1836, when a series of articles appeared in the New York *Sun* purporting to describe the lunar world as viewed through Herschel's telescope. There is also *The Balloon-Hoax*, while in *Maelzel's Chess-Player* he unmasks a real-life hoaxer.

16. Examples are *Von Kempelen and His Discovery*, *The Facts in the Case of M. Valdemar*, and *The Premature Burial*.

17. In *The Spectacles*, a man is tricked into virtually marrying his great-great-grandmother. *The Imp of the Perverse* is a man's conscience, which tricks him into confessing a murder.

18. There is a man who is hanged because his powers of utterance are impeded, in *Loss of Breath*, the hiccupping in *Bon-Bon*, and—to name an actual physical obstruction—a length of whalebone down the throat of a corpse in *The Purloined Letter*.

19. Paul Valéry: "Poe is the only impeccable writer. He was never mistaken." In a letter to André Gide, 1891.

20. "That an enthusiasm for Poe should have been shared by the three most influential poets in modern French literature, that this American writer should have become the pivot on which for the past century French literature has turned, this by itself is sufficiently extraordinary. But even this statement of the case does no more than suggest the force of Poe's impact. There is scarcely one French writer from the time of Baudelaire to the present who has not in one way or another paid his respects to Poe. Villiers de l'Isle Adam, Verlaine, and Rimbaud, Huysmans, Claudel, Gide, Edmund Jaloux—these are names at random, but they will serve to indicate the scope of the interest Poe has had for France." Patrick F. Quinn, "The French Response to Poe." Mr. Quinn omits the name of Verne from his list. This essay, together with those mentioned in Notes 11 and 13, are reprinted in *Poe: A Collection of Critical Essays*, edited by Robert Regan (*Twentieth Century Views*), Englewood Cliffs, New Jersey, 1967.

21. Poe specifically mentions "the fancy of Mrs. Radcliffe" in *The Oval Portrait*.

22. Leslie A. Fiedler, *Love and Death in the American Novel*, 1967.

23. As in Eugene Burdick and Harvey Wheeler's *Fail-Safe*, 1962.

24. As in E. C. Tubb's *Window on the Moon*, 1964, and countless other stories.

25. As in Henry Kuttner's *Fury*, first serial publication, New York, 1947. Appeared in "*Astounding Science Fiction*" under the pseudonym Lawrence O'Donnell.

26. As in James Blish and Norman L. Knight's *A Torrent of Faces*, New York, 1967.

27. Robert A. Heinlein, "Science Fiction: Its Nature, Faults and Virtues," *The Science Fiction Novel: Imagination and Social Criticism*, Chicago, 1964.

3

Pilgrim Fathers:
LUCIAN AND ALL THAT

> "If this is the best of all possible
> worlds, what can the rest be like?"
> Voltaire: *Candide*

In this chapter we launch ourselves on the mysterious early seas
of speculative fiction, letting down a bucket now and again. Our
finest catches will be in the eighteenth century, following a quick
inspection of earlier times. Since we shall deal with periods before
the Romantics, we shall find little or nothing that resembles either
Poe's works or *Frankenstein* in feeling, or in what we have called
Inwardness, but much that in content prefigures science fiction.

Poe, as we have seen, had trouble with the *form* of his science
fiction. In most of his forays into the genre, we witness him aban-
doning his usual Gothic-fiction narrative line, employing instead a
sort of straightforward didacticism only thinly disguised as fiction,
or served up as dialogue; examples are *Mellonta Tauta, The Colloquy of Monos and Una,* and *The Conversation of Eiros and
Charmion.* And in this, he shows kinship with his literary ancestors,
the utopianists, the marvellous-voyagers, and the moralists who use
the fantastic to make their point. These older writers do not
seek to involve us in the sufferings of their heroes by tricks of

suspense and character-drawing, as do Ann Radcliffe and her heirs; their intentions lie elsewhere. This holds true even when we look back towards the beginning of the Christian Era to Lucian of Samosata.

The dialogue form of his *Icaro-Menippus* reminds us that Lucian had something of the Socratic spirit. In the *True History*, some of the episodes—particularly the ones in which the adventurers are swallowed, ship and all, by a whale—look forward to Baron Munchausen, as well as back to the tall stories in Homer; while the spirit of Aristophanes' comedies presides fitfully over the whole.

Mention of Socrates and Aristophanes must suffice to recall the truism that much is owed to the Greeks, in science fiction as in science and civilisation generally. Many of the staple themes of science fiction were familiar to the Greeks.

Plato's *Republic*, cast in the form of Socratic conversation, is the first utopia. Aristophanes' comedies sprout utopian ideas and fantastic notions; in his play *The Birds*, war-weary citizens join the fowls of the air in making a Cloudcuckooland between heaven and earth, and the birds become masters of the universe; in the *Lysistrata* we find a theme which has proved still viable in this century, where the women refuse to let their men have sexual intercourse with them until the war is brought to a close; in *The Frogs*, Aristophanes takes his audience on an excursion into another world—to Hell; in *Peace*, performed first for an Athens that had been ten years at war, Trygaeus rides up to heaven on the back of a giant beetle to see Zeus. (Perhaps Lucian was thinking of this flight when his Menippus also ascends.) But such flights of fantasy, permissible in comedy, were forbidden in tragedy; and so it still is today.

In the *True History*, waterspouts and winds carry a Greek ship to the Moon, which proves to be inhabited. The travellers find that the king of the Moon and the king of the Sun are at war over the colonisation of Jupiter. Fantastic monsters are employed in the battles; and the minions of the Sun build a double wall between Sun and Moon, so that the Selenites live in permanent eclipse. They surrender.

One of the clauses of the peace treaty is that both sides shall send a colony to the Morning Star (Venus). The travellers sail their ship to the new colony and then steer for the Zodiac, leaving the Sun to port, until they reach Lycnopolis, a city inhabited by

lamps that speak. They also see Cloudcuckooland, witness a battle of giants, and visit a city built of gold and precious stones. Later,
they come to the Isle of Dreams, where Antiphon invents dreams, of
different kinds:

> Some long, beautiful, and pleasant, others little and ugly; there
> are likewise some golden ones, others poor and mean; some
> winged and of an immense size, others tricked out as it were
> for pomps and ceremonies, for gods and kings; some we met
> with that we had seen at home; these came up to and saluted
> us as their old acquaintance, whilst others putting us first to
> sleep, treated us most magnificently, and promised that they
> would make us kings and noblemen; some carried us into our
> own country, showed us our friends and relations, and brought
> us back again the same day. Thirty days and nights we re-
> mained in this place, being most luxuriously feasted, and fast
> asleep all the time . . .[1]

Thus the first appearance of a Dream Palace, which has made several appearances in the fiction of our day.

Many translators of Lucian, wisely anxious to preserve the
pure Anglo-Saxon world from dirty Mediterranean habits, have
omitted the more titillating passages from his text—for instance his
description of the custom of Lunar inhabitants to wear artificial
private parts, which apparently work quite well. The rich have
them made of ivory, the poor ones of wood. This disgusting information establishes Lucian's claim to be, not only the first writer of
interplanetary fiction, but the first writer to describe prosthetic
limbs and cyborgs.

Lucian's tales now read like pure fantasy, although for centuries they were highly regarded as speculative fiction. A charming example of this change in attitude taking place occurs in a little
Victorian edition of Lucian's two trips to the Moon, published in
Cassell's National Library. This edition contains the following footnote with supplement by later editor, inserted at the point where
Earth is seen hanging in the lunar sky like a Moon: "Modern
astronomers are, I think, agreed that we are to the moon just
the same as the moon is to us. Though Lucian's history may be
false, therefore his philosophy, we see, was true (1780). (The moon
is not habitable, 1887)." The disappointments of progress.

We no longer expect anything but entertainment from Lucian,

and that he provides, though he somewhat spoils his joke by launching on it with the remark that he expects that the reader "will not
only be pleased with the novelty of the plan, and the variety of
lies, which I have told with an air of truth, but with the tacit al-
lusions so frequently made, not, I trust, without some degree of
humour, to our ancient poets, historians, and philosophers, who have
told us some most miraculous and incredible stories . . ."

Under the drift of centuries, interplanetary voyages were forgotten. Spiritual voyages were another matter; the progression of
mankind in his frail coracle of civilisation is itself a spiritual voyage,
which naturally finds its embodiment in tales of difficult journeyings.
But the finest mediaeval minds were in quest for a unity between life
on Earth and the Heavenly Father. In the words of Sir Kenneth
Clarke, "Behind all the fantasy of the Gothic imagination, mediaeval
man could see things very clearly, but he believed that . . . appearances should be considered as nothing more than symbols or tokens
of an ideal order, which was the only true reality."[2]

Perhaps the form of those times closest to science fiction was
the bestiary, derived from Greek sources, in which animals were
endowed with human attributes and enacted moral or satirical
tales, just like aliens in today's science fiction. The history of
Reynard the Fox is the best known of these tales in English-
speaking countries, thanks to a translation printed by Caxton in 1481.
Reynard and Chanticleer the Cock also figure in Chaucer's "Nun's
Priest's Tale" in *The Canterbury Tales*.

Another popular beast was *The Golden Ass* of Apuleius, a
contemporary of Lucian. This is a satire in which a man is turned
into an ass and tells the tale of the follies and vices of his various
owners. The transformation takes place accidentally, through the
carelessness of an enchantress's servant. Such tales, always plentiful,
take us too close to magic and too far from science fiction.

With the dawn of the Renaissance, men developed new ways in
which to think and feel. They rediscovered the classical past and,
among the great tally of its treasures, the writings of its poets, historians, and philosophers, including Lucian.

Lucian's writings in Greek and Latin ran through several
editions in the late fifteenth and sixteenth centuries, and in 1634
were translated into English by Francis Hickes. The translation
was widely read; the influence on later writers, both of the *True*

History and *Icaro-Mennipus,* was considerable. Lucian is said to have inspired Rabelais' *Voyages of Pantagruel,* Cyrano de Bergerac's *Voyage dans la Lune,* and Swift's *Gulliver's Travels,* and no doubt all those eminent authors read their great predecessor avidly, for writers instinctively seek out others of their own persuasion; but there is a great deal of difference between imitation and emulation, and the most original authors often begin on premises laid down by others.° Great authors borrow; little authors steal.

The early seventeenth century was a fantastic age, an age of great voyages and discoveries; of the writing of utopias and death-enriched plays; of a widening universe and the first use of the decimal point; of the sailing of the Pilgrim Fathers; of the discovery of the circulation of the blood and the invention of cribbage; of the founding of colleges and universities, the establishment of colonies and the perfection of the flintlock; and the findings of Galileo, Kepler, and Van Leeuwenhoek. Exploration clearly had an appeal, and the times, rather than literary influence, may be blamed for the increase in fictitious Moon voyages.

Coincidentally, Kepler's *Somnium* (or *Dream*) was published in the same year as Hickes' translation of Lucian, in Frankfurt; Kepler had then been dead four years. Johannes Kepler (1571–1630) was a German mathematician, astrologer, and astronomer who helped lay the foundations of modern astronomy. Kepler's narrative is cast as a dream, and his observer, Duracotus, ascends to the Moon by supernatural means. Once we are on the Moon, however, science takes over, and Duracotus expatiates on that globe as recently revealed by telescope. Cold and heat are more extreme than on Earth; there are dreadful nights a fortnight long, unrelieved by moonlight. As the climate differs from Earth, so does the landscape: mountains are higher, valleys deeper. The ground is perforated by caves and grottoes. Cloud cover and rain prevail over the near side of the lunar globe.

Kepler introduces life to the Moon, but the living things are made to conform to the lunar environment. Although they are not drawn in detail, an impression of variety and grotesquery is given. One sentence gives us a foretaste of Wells' *First Men on the Moon:* "Things born in the ground—they are sparse on the ridges

° Thus, Lucian himself conceived the *True History* as a parody of those Greek historians who magnified every detail into something grander than it began; while Swift's *Gulliver's Travels* began as a minute lampoon of the politics of Queen Anne's reign.

of the mountains—generally begin and end their lives on the same day, with new generations springing up daily."[3]

We acknowledge this as fantasy now. But Kepler conformed to or formed the science of his own day. That claim of scientific accuracy was made on behalf of Jules Verne, two centuries later, as if it were a great novelty.

Kepler had a scientific vision of the Moon; his *Somnium* is straightforwardly astronomical exposition. He established no utopias there. But utopias were still being built. A confusion of wonderful voyages with utopias is of long standing; once a writer has got his travellers to his obscure region on Earth, or to another world, or to the future, he must find something for them to do, and on the whole writers divide fairly sharply between those who have their protagonists lecture and listen to lectures, and those who have them menaced by or menacing local equivalents of flora, fauna, and Homo sapiens.

If this division of interest is still with us, at least the vexing problem of how to reach the Moon has been solved. It has in actuality proved far more costly than any storyteller ever dared guess. Lunar-voyage devices come very inexpensively until we reach the days of Verne and Wells and, even then, the Baltimore Gun Club finances their vehicle, while Cavor has comfortable private means. Before those days, nature, or a balloon, can be relied on to do the trick at a minimum of expense.

Supernatural means of travel were the cheapest of all. Athanasius Kircher, in his *Itinerarium Exstaticum* of 1656, produces an angel who takes the chief protagonist on a Grand Tour of the heavens to complete his education—a pleasant idea that could still be made to work fictionally today.

The next method requiring least human modification was to ascend with the aid of birds. Bishop Francis Godwin's *Man in the Moone: or A Discourse of a Voyage Thither by Domingo Gonsales* appeared in 1638 and remained popular for something like two centuries. Godwin's Gonsales trains some swans until, by degrees, they learn to carry him through the air. The swans or "gansas," twenty-five of them teamed together, save Gonsales from shipwreck. Unfortunately, Gonsales has overlooked the migratory habits of gansas, and his team heads for the Moon, where they hibernate, taking him with them.

Gonsales finds the lunar world a utopia inhabited by giants.

The giants are long-lived and any wounds they receive quickly heal again; even if you get your head cut off, apply a certain herb and it will be joined together once more. But murders are unknown, and all other crimes; while the women are so beautiful that (claims Gonsales) no man ever wants to leave his wife. This peaceful state comes about because the Moon-dwellers detect potential sinners at birth and ship them off to Earth, where most of them are deposited in North America (the first appearance of an idea to enjoy fresh currency in twentieth-century fiction).

Despite these delights, and the beautiful colours on the Moon, Gonsales wants to get back to his family. The Prince Pylonas gives him jewels, and he sets off for Earth with his gansas—landing in China, where he is imprisoned as a magician.

In the same year that this pleasant fiction was published, John Wilkins' *Discovery of a New World* appeared. This is a speculative book concerning the possibilities of travelling to the Moon, with discussions of what life there might be like—what we would call popular science. And, like Godwin's book, it was popular. The times were ripe for it and, with many a reference back to Daedalus, the more *au fait* citizens of the seventeenth and eighteenth centuries began to discuss the possibilities of flight. Although this eagerness to extend man's dimensions of experience has often been mocked, it lies deep in many hearts, and is summed up in John Keats' words, "Ever let the fancy roam, Pleasure never is at home" —though in present context, Milton perhaps puts it better: "Headlong joy is ever on the wing."

From imagining wings that would assist human flight it is a short step to imagining humans with wings. Robert Paltock's *The Life and Adventures of Peter Wilkins* appeared in 1751, and remained popular for many years. After being shipwrecked, Peter Wilkins discovers the country of flying men and women; he marries one of them, Youwarkee, and the loving pair have seven children, some winged, some not.

Also in 1751, *The Life and Astonishing Transactions of John Daniel*, by Ralph Morris, was published, in which human flight is achieved by a veritable "engine," a platform on which two can stand and work the wings by means of levers; John Daniel and his son Jacob take themselves up to the Moon in this machine.

The corniest way of getting to the Moon was the one chosen by Cyrano de Bergerac, in *Voyage dans la Lune*, a comic history first published in 1657, and followed later by *L'Histoire des États et Empires du Soleil.* The two are known together as *L'Autre Monde.*[4]

Bergerac makes himself his own hero, and fastens a quantity of small bottles filled with dew to his body. The Sun sucks him up with the dew, and he lands on the Moon in a couple of paragraphs.

So begins the jolliest of all lunar books, with Cyrano spouting unlikely explanations for amazing phenomena for all the world like a modern sf writer. He does the same in the second book, when he lands on the Sun, glibly explaining why he has no appetite in space, why the Sun's heat does not burn, what causes sleep, how he became invisible, how the inhabitants of the Sun grow from the ground in a sort of spontaneous generation, and so forth.

Cyrano meets Campanella, author of *The City of the Sun,* and together they encounter a woman whose husband has committed a curious crime.

"Since you are a philosopher," replied the woman, addressing Campanella, "I must unburden my heart to you before I go any further.

"To explain the matter that brings me here in a few words, you must know that I am coming to complain of a murder committed against the person of my youngest child. This barbarian, whom I have here, killed it twice over, although he was its father."

We were extremely puzzled by this speech and asked to know what she meant by a child killed twice over.

"You must know that in our country," the woman replied, "there is, among the other Statutes of Love, a law which regulates the number of embraces a husband may give his wife. That is why every evening each doctor goes the rounds of all the houses in his area, where, after examining the husbands and wives, he will prescribe for them, according to their good or bad health, so many conjunctions for the night. Well, my husband had been put down for seven. However, angered by some rather haughty remarks I had addressed to him as we were getting ready to retire, he did not come near me all the time we were in bed. But God, who avenges those who are wronged, permitted this wretch to be titillated in a dream by the recollection of the embraces he was unjustly denying me, so that he let a man go to waste.

"I told you his father had killed him twice over, because by refusing to make him come into existence, he caused him not to be, which was the first murder, but subsequently he caused him never to be able to be, which was the second. A common murderer knows that the man whose days he cuts short *is no more,* but none of them could cause a man *never to have been.* Our magistrates would have dealt with him as he deserved if the cunning wretch had not excused himself by saying that he would have fulfilled his conjugal duty, had he not been afraid (as a result of embracing me in the height of the rage I had put him in) to beget a choleric man."

All writers of fantastic tales feed on their predecessors. Swift took a pinch of wit from Cyrano—about whose book Geoffrey Strachan, its translator, justly says, it "is a poem from an age when poetry, physics, metaphysics, and astronomy could all still exist side by side in one book."

There is no need to detail further flights of fancy to the Moon. In any case, Marjorie Hope Nicolson has already produced a first-rate account, readable and scholarly, of the subject,[5] which is not likely to be bettered; while Philip Grove has defined the genre and provided a list of two hundred and fifteen such voyages published in the eighteenth century alone.[6] These exemptions spare us much that is tedious now or has had time to allow its tediousness to mature.

The great utopias have better claim to our attention, for utopianism or its opposite, dystopianism, is present in every vision of the future —there is little point in inventing a future state unless it provides a contrast with our present one. This is not to claim that the great utopias are science fiction. Their intentions are moral or political. Often they are in dialogue form, as is the great exemplar, Thomas More's *Utopia,* first published in Latin in 1516 and translated into English in 1551—itself indebted to Plato's *Republic.*

> "Now am I like to Plato's city
> Whose fame flieth the world through"

The idea of utopianists, like our town-planners, is to produce something that is orderly and functions well. Citizens have to fit into this pattern as into a town plan. More's Utopia is quite a friendly and sensible place, yet some of its restrictions sound chilly to readers who live in a world of flourishing police states.

When More's Utopians go outdoors, they all wear the same kind of cloak, of one colour. There are a number of cities in Utopia, but all are alike; "whoso knoweth one of them knoweth them all." The citizens must get a licence to travel from one city to another. Furthermore, "dice-play and such other foolish and pernicious games they know not." Farewell, Earth's bliss! Good-bye, Las Vegas! It is of small consolation to learn that they "use two games not much unlike the chess."

More offers higher things. His little world has sane laws and is wisely ruled. The citizens have fine gardens and hospitals. Bondmen perform all the drudgery, mercenaries fight all the wars. Conversation, music, and banquets are welcome, although ale houses and stews are forbidden, as is astrology. Many passages show the human side of More, not least in the question of courtship.

> For a sad and honest matron sheweth the woman, be she maid or widow, naked to the wooer. And likewise a sage and discreet man exhibiteth the wooer naked to the woman . . . The endowments of the body cause the virtues of the mind more to be esteemed and regarded, yea, even in the marriages of wise men.

It is a useful precaution—breakers of wedlock are sternly dealt with in Utopia. For this is a religious land and, although one's own faith may be followed without persecution, only the pious are allowed to teach children and adolescents.

Such sober and worthy plans as More's for a better life on Earth have become remote from us nowadays; our belief in the perfectibility of man and the triumph of altruism over self-interest is less strong than was the case in earlier centuries; a desperate environmentalism has become the new utopianism.

We have seen the noble line of utopias—such as Johann Valentin Andreae's *Christianopolis* (1619), Francis Bacon's *The New Atlantis* (1627), Tommaso Campanella's *Civitas Solis* (1623) (for which Campanella was faced with the Spanish Inquisition), James Harrington's *Commonwealth of Oceana* (1656), and those of the nineteenth century, such as Samuel Butler's *Erewhon* (1872), W. H. Hudson's *A Crystal Age* (1887), and Edward Bellamy's *Looking Backward* (1888)—we have seen this noble line of utopias slide down like sinking liners into such depths of dystopianism as Eugene Zamyatin's *We* (1920) and Orwell's *1984* (1949). Morality, the system whereby man controls himself, has become another weapon in the state armoury, whereby it controls its citizens.

A decline in the general belief in political systems; a profound questioning of the effects of technology; even the retreat from so much as lip service towards established religion; these are some of the factors that render the construction of utopias in the immediate future unlikely. Aldous Huxley's *Island* (1962)—in common with its distinguished predecessors, more a polemic than a novel—may be the last considerable utopia we shall see until the world climate alters; and even on Huxley's well-favoured island, the people sustain themselves with drugs and acknowledge how transient is the *status quo,* threatened with immediate collapse by the end of the book. Had this collapse been threatened by a polluted ocean and broken chains of the life cycle, rather than by invasion by enemy forces, then the message might have seemed more prophetic.

The trouble with utopias is that they are too orderly. They rule out the irrational in man, and the irrational is the great discovery of the last hundred years. They may be fantasy, but they reject fantasy as part of man—and this is a criticism that applies to most of the eighteenth-century literature with which we deal in this chapter. However appealing they may be, there is no room in them for the phenomenon of a Shakespeare—or even a Lovecraft.

And yet, among the distinguished seventeenth-century utopias, there is one which could almost contain Shakespeare and Lovecraft, and even E. E. Smith for that matter. Of course, we have to stretch our terms somewhat wide to think of John Milton's *Paradise Lost* (1667) as a utopia, but of the influence of this great poem there is no doubt. Particularly appealing are its vistas of an unspoilt Earth, while the passages which deal with Hell, and Satan's lonely flight from Hell across the gulfs of space to God's new world, still retain their magnificence. Satan in particular is as puissant as a present-day Apollo when he

> Springs upward like a pyramid of fire,
> Into the wild expanse, and through the shock
> Of fighting elements, on all sides round
> Environ'd, wins his way. (Book 2)

Like his near contemporary, John Donne, Milton infuses his poetry with "the New Philosophy."

From Milton's imagined worlds and exalted poetry, we bring ourselves back to Earth with the aid of Peter Wilkins, the adventurer who married a winged lady and had seven children by her.

For Wilkins' adventures encompass another science fictional device at which we should look; the subterranean journey which discovers human beings living underground. Later—and not much later—this will develop into journeys to the centre of the Earth.

Wilkins' ship gets into trouble near Africa. A strong and remorseless current draws it towards the South Pole and eventually through an archway under an island, into a strange underground world. "I could perceive the boat to fall with incredible violence, as I thought, down a precipice, and suddenly whirled round and round with me, the water roaring on all sides, and dashing against the rock with a most amazing noise." The boat drifts in complete darkness down a subterranean river, delivering Wilkins into an immense cavern, where flying people live.

Here is more than one incident to be found later in Poe. The subterranean descent also carries reminders of a book published ten years before *Peter Wilkins*—Holberg's *Journey to the World Underground*. Holberg's is one of the books, together with Campanella's utopia *The City of the Sun,* which Poe lists as being in Roderick Usher's library—"the books which, for years, had formed no small portion of the mental existence of the invalid."

In turn, Holberg's work owes much to *Gulliver's Travels,* as well as to such earlier subterranean voyages as Athanasius Kircher's *Mundus Subterraneus* of 1665. But Holberg has some curious ideas of his own.

Baron Ludvig Holberg was born in Bergen, Norway, in 1684. He was a great traveller, and his writings, particularly his plays, brought him fame. *Nicolai Klimii Iter Subterraneum* (Holberg wrote it in Latin) was first published in Germany in 1741. It won immediate popularity and was translated and published—and is still being translated and published—into many languages.

Niels Klim is potholing in the mountains near Bergen when he falls down a steep shaft, and keeps falling for some time, for all the world like Alice. He emerges into a wonderland no less remarkable than Alice's, tumbling into the space at the centre of the Earth and becoming one more heavenly body circling about a central Sun.

Klim lands unhurt on the planet Nazar, which proves to be amazingly like Earth as far as the environment is concerned, except that night is almost as light as day. "Nay, the night may be thought more grateful than the day, for nothing can be conceived more bright and splendid than that light which the solid firmament receives from the sun and reflects back upon the planet, insomuch that it looks (if I may be allowed the expression) like one universal moon." Another difference from Earth is that the intelligent species on Nazar is perambulating trees.

This novelty is rather a distraction than otherwise, since, apart from their arboreality, the creatures are there for the same reason as Swift's Lilliputians and Brobdingnagians: to make reasonable man reflect on his own unreasonableness, to make what appears natural seem topsy-turvy. Trees resist serving didactic purposes.

The trees show local differences from land to land, and their paradoxes are paraded for Klim in a series of what might be called mini-utopias: farmers are most highly regarded of all citizens in one land; in another the more honour the state piles on a citizen, the more he acts with humility, since "he was the greatest debtor to the commonwealth"; in another, only the young are allowed to govern, for the older people grow, the more wanton and voluptuous they become; and so on. In one of the most curious countries, the inhabitants never sleep; as a result, they are always in a hurry and confusion, and are obsessed by details—for example, Klim looks into a local bookshop and notices a *Description of the Cathedral* in twenty-four volumes, and *Of the Use of the Herb Slac* in thirteen volumes. But none of these curious situations are developed— Holberg flicks them past our eyes like colour slides—involving Klim in them, for the most part, merely as observer.

Klim does have some adventures. He is banished by bird to the Firmament, which he finds full of monkeys; is wooed by an attractive lady monkey ("I thought it better to be exposed to the vengeance of disappointed love than to disturb the laws of human nature by mixing my blood with a creature not of the human species"); is sent for a galley slave; gets shipwrecked; wins a war; becomes Emperor of the Quamites, Niels the Great; grows overbearing; suffers revolution; escapes; and falls back up the same hole down which he fell twelve years previously!

Klim's journey is now little more than a curiosity. Overshadowing it are the two great books of fake-travel which preceded it, Defoe's *Robinson Crusoe* and Swift's *Gulliver's Travels*. Both books include shipwrecks in remote parts of the globe, both are honourable precursors of the science fiction genre, both are written in the sound style of their age which has guaranteed them wide readership even in ours.

Often when talking of science fiction and the ur-science fiction preceding it, one is like a traveller walking down an unkempt lane, over the other side of the hedge from which lie the cultivated gardens of Literature. But occasionally lane and garden become one, and then the prospect widens out, to the benefit of both wild and sown. So it is in the age of Defoe and Swift, when the enormous advances in pure science of the previous century, the findings of Galileo and Isaac Newton, were still providing speculative fuel.

Swift and Defoe are writers very different in character. Swift belongs to the mandarin tradition of his friend Pope, the great Augustan poet; Defoe is much more of the people. We must resist the temptation here to discuss them and their tremendous variety of writings, Defoe's especially, and concentrate on what we may call the science fictional element in their books.

Daniel Defoe (1659–1731) was the son of a butcher in Cripplegate. His life was filled with cross currents of religion, politics, and economics. He was a Puritan, born on the eve of the Restoration, who lived through the bursting of the South Sea Bubble. All these influences are apparent in his best novel. As for literary influence, this is the place to mention, belatedly, that wonderful journey which was to be found in almost every English home from its first appearance in the sixteen-seventies until the end of the Victorian times: Bunyan's *Pilgrim's Progress*.

After a crowded life, enormously productive as a journalist, Defoe in his sixties took to writing novels, or rather fake memoirs, such as *Moll Flanders* and—a book which Poe surely knew and cherished—*The Journal of the Plague Year*.

The Life and Strange Surprising Adventures of Robinson Crusoe, of York, Mariner was published in 1719. It was an immediate success. Popularity seems to have been a test of merit, for the book has never been out of print since, despite all changes of taste in the past two hundred and fifty years. Crusoe on his lonely island at the mouth of the Orinoco (and he was there for twenty-five years before setting eyes on his man Friday) has as perennial a fascination as Prospero on his island, also marooned in the same quarter of the world.

It is conceivable that if some kind of global ballot were taken to determine the best-known incident in all English literature, then Crusoe's discovery of the solitary footprint in the sand would be voted first, or at least very soon after the apparition of the ghost of Hamlet's father, Oliver Twist's asking for more, and the death of Little Nell! That alien imprint has proved indelible.

The science fictional attractions of *Robinson Crusoe* are obvious: the desert-island theme is eternal, whether transposed to William Golding's island in *Lord of the Flies* or to another planet (as was expertly done by Rex Gordon, paying eponymous tribute to sources, in *No Man Friday*, set on Mars). But beyond this lies a deeper attraction.

In the slow plodding of Crusoe's mind, as he creates in the wilderness of his island a model of the society he has left, and as solitude forces him to come to terms with himself, Defoe builds up a picture of isolation which still stalks our overpopulated times. No imagined planet was ever such a setting for the drama of Man Alone as is *Robinson Crusoe*. Though the emphasis on religion may have little appeal to modern tastes, a patient reading of the text reveals a book that lumbers to real greatness. As one critic has said of Defoe,[7] "He was never brilliant; but he employed dullness almost magically."

Defoe dropped religious orders; Swift took them.

Jonathan Swift (1667–1745) was born in Ireland of English parents. His father died before his birth; he was separated from his mother soon after birth. How far these facts, which find an echo in the life history of Edgar Allan Poe, influenced Swift's sense of separation from humanity, we cannot determine. He was brought to England as a baby, later returning to Ireland to complete his education at Trinity College, Dublin. Thereafter, his hopes, like his lief, vacillated between the two countries. He was ordained in 1694.

Swift became a great pamphleteer, and was deeply involved in the politics of his time. Disappointed in his political ambitions in

England, he returned to Ireland, where he eventually won great popularity as Dean of the Cathedral of St. Patrick. The last few years of his life were tormented by increasing madness, a fate that sometimes overcomes those otherwise most sane.

Swift's was a mysterious life, full of ironies. Romantics and psychiatrists have been attracted to the riddle of Swift's relationships with the two women in his life, his "Stella" and his "Vanessa." His remains lie now in the cathedral in Dublin, beneath the epitaph he composed for himself: *"Ubi saeva indignatio ulterius cor lacerare nequit":* "Where fierce indignation can no longer tear the heart."

Most of his many writings, like his women, appeared under guises, anonymously or pseudonymously. As if in retaliation, the public has always rejected the title of his most famous and living book, *Travels into Several Remote Nations of the World: In Four Parts* (1726), and insists on calling it familiarly *Gulliver's Travels.*

It is fortunate that this masterly work does not count as science fiction, being satirical and/or moral in intention rather than speculative, for, if it did so count, then perfection would have been achieved straightaway, and the genre possibly concluded as soon as it had begun. But the book comes clawing its way out of any category into which critics try to place it.

Swift uses every wile known to Defoe, and more besides—the use of maps, for example—to persuade a reader that he holds yet another plodding volume of travel in his hand. Gulliver seems at first to resemble Crusoe, of York, Mariner—a solid man, a surgeon in this case, using a good plain prose, and as shipwreck-prone as his predecessor. But Gulliver proves to be one of the cleverest heroes a writer ever set up in a work of fiction, at once simple and sly, rash and cowardly, a man who likes to think himself unwaveringly honest and yet who is all too ready to trim his sail to whatever wind prevails. It is a mistake to identify Gulliver with Swift.

But Swift makes it difficult for readers not to identify with Gulliver. He spins so many layers of irony that we are bound to get caught somewhere.

The four voyages lead us ever deeper into Swift's web. We share Gulliver's amusement at the Lilliputians and their petty affairs, so that we are bound to share Gulliver's humiliation at the court of Brobdingnag. In these two first voyages, scale is considered in the worth of human affairs; in the third voyage, to the flying island of Laputa, we see what intellectual endowments are worth;

while, in the last voyage, to the land in which Houyhnhnms and Yahoos are contrasted, we see what our animal nature is worth.

This splendid fourth part has acted like a lodestone on satirists since—on Holberg, as we have seen, and on Wells, Huxley, and Orwell. To the courteous race of horses, the Houyhnhnms, the filthy Yahoos are animals or, at best, peasants and servants. The Yahoos overwhelm Gulliver with disgust. Yet, when his clothes are off, he is almost indistinguishable from them; indeed, once while swimming, he is set on by a lust-mad female Yahoo. The Yahoos are humanity.

It is as if Swift, when drawing his portrait of the Yahoos, had a horror-comical vision of Stone Age hordes, long before theories of evolution had uncovered such an idea to human contemplation. Or he is setting up an image of the Id in contrast to the Super-ego of the Houyhnhnms. One of the book's strengths is its openness to differing readings.

Certainly Swift's mighty satire has gained power and meaning in the last century. It is indestructible, defying time and final exegesis.

Gulliver's Travels has had many interpreters. Thackeray, in mid-Victorian times, spoke for the opposition when (referring in particular to the fourth part) he called it "A monster, gibbering shrieks and gnashing imprecations against mankind—tearing down all shreds of modesty, past all sense of manliness and shame; filthy in word, filthy in thought, furious, raging, obscene." In another category entirely is the Irish bishop—or so Swift claimed in a letter to Pope—who read the book and declared he didn't believe a word of it.

Yet what book can compare with Swift's? It unshakeably has the vote of humanity, selling ten thousand copies in the first three weeks of its long life, and being translated and pirated at once all over Europe. So it has gone on ever since, bowdlerised, truncated, serialised, cartoonised, animated, plagiarised—and read over and over, like a dark obverse of *Pilgrim's Progress*.

The impulse which created this marvellous and mysterious book was complex. Swift intended to amuse a cultivated audience; readers have recognised a strong salting of truth in his view of humanity; and the fantasy of big and little people, of civilised horses, races of immortals, and the quizzing of the dead, all have a perennial appeal. And, one must add, this is some of the rarest wit delivered in some of the finest language.

Many of Swift's best effects are achieved through Gulliver's blind pride, which insists on appealing to something base or petty to bolster what he feels is a worthy claim.

Talking of trade in England ("the dear place of my nativity"), Gulliver tells his master, the Houyhnhnm, how European ships go out to all oceans and bring all sorts of provisions back. "I assured him, that this whole globe of earth must be at least three times gone round, before one of our better female Yahoos could get her breakfast, or a cup to put it in." This is the method of Pope's *Rape of the Lock*. Belinda opens her toilet box:

> Unnumbered Treasures ope at once, and here
> The various offerings of the World appear.

The question is one of reasonable scale.

Again, when "my master" is wondering at the Yahoos' disposition towards dirt and nastiness, compared with a natural love of cleanliness in other animals, "I could have easily vindicated human kind from the imputation of singularity upon the last article, if there had been any *swine* in that country (as unluckily for me there were not), which although it may be a *sweeter* quadruped than a Yahoo, cannot, I humbly conceive, in justice pretend to more cleanliness . . ."

Again, in Laputa, Gulliver's interpreter remarks that he has "observed long life to be the universal desire and wish for mankind. That whoever had one foot in the grave, was sure to hold back the other as strongly as he could."

These brief examples could be infinitely multiplied. They show a kind of *mistaken reasonableness* at work. If we accept *Gulliver* (among all the other things it is) as a great debate on Reason, many of the problems that have confronted commentators in the fourth part will vanish. At the end of his four-decker maze, we meet with Swift's creatures of pure reason, the Houyhnhnms. This is the climax of Gulliver's search, and he is converted to their outlook on life, lock, stock, and barrel—so much so that, when he returns to England, he cannot bear the proximity of his loving wife and children, regarding them as Yahoos.

We must always beware of Gulliver when he admires anything; his name does not begin with "Gull" for nothing. This is part of Swift's "fierce and insolent game," as F. R. Leavis calls it. These horse-shaped children of Reason are cold, uninteresting, and condescending—indifferent alike (as Gulliver becomes) to the lives of their children or the deaths of their spouses. They have limited vocabularies and limited imaginations, which is a fairly strong clue to Swift's real attitude to them. As George Orwell says, they are also racists[8]; yet Orwell, who numbers *Gulliver* among his six indispensable books, makes the mistake of confusing Swift with Gulliver and believing that it is Swift who admires the Houyhnhnms.

What Swift is showing us in the Houyhnhnm culture is a warning: this is what a utopia would be like if governed by pure reason: the nearest thing to death. Horrible though the Yahoos are, they are the oppressed, they have more life and vitality than their oppressors—and they probably have more of Swift's sympathy than is generally allowed.†

In *Gulliver's Travels,* black is never opposed to white: even in despicable Lilliput, wise laws are passed for rewarding virtue; Swift supposes us cultivated enough to be able to compare faulty states of living, and to understand (as we do when reading Aldous Huxley) that the civilised virtues may be represented only covertly in the text, for instance in a pure and urbane prose style. As his subject is Reason, so reason is needed to enjoy his entertainments to the full.

This is why *Gulliver's Travels* works so well over the centuries, why it continues to delight: paralleled by its pure vein of fantasy expressed in terms of naïve realism goes its intellectual paradox, for we have to be better than Yahoos to recognise that they are us, we they. So we are raised to the level of Swift's own ironical vision. Despite the subject matter that Thackeray disliked so much, the effect of this great book is to exalt us.

From the two masterpieces of Augustan prose, *Robinson Crusoe* and *Gulliver's Travels,* we move on over thirty years to glance at two other masterpieces which appeared at the same time—and a glance will have to be sufficient, for neither stand directly in the literary line developing towards science fiction, although, in

---

† Orwell should have got the message, since he appears to feel sympathy as well as distaste for his 1984 Proles—who are literary offspring of the Yahoos.

their concern for the modern human predicament, they contain a great deal that is of interest to science fiction readers.

Voltaire's *Candide* was published in February 1759, to be followed less than two months later by Samuel Johnson's *Rasselas, Prince of Abyssinia.* Johnson was later heard to say that "if they had not been published so closely one after the other that there was no time for imitation, it would have been in vain to deny that the scheme of that which came latest was taken from the other." Coincidentally, Bulwer-Lytton's *The Coming Race* was published just before Butler's *Erewhon* in the following century, when Butler was at pains to deny that the scheme of his book was taken from the other.[9]

Like *Robinson Crusoe* and *Gulliver's Travels, Rasselas* and *Candide* were both immediate successes. Neither have been out of print since. Johnson's book was written in about a week, Voltaire's in three days: facts which should cause the modern denizens of Grub Street to take fresh heart.

Both are cautionary tales against optimism. Voltaire's is much the more sprightly; but any reader susceptible to the cadences of prose will be attracted instantly by the noble melancholy with which Johnson embarks upon his narrative:

> Ye who listen with credulity to the whispers of fancy, and pursue with eagerness the phantoms of hope; who expect that age will perform the promises of youth, and that the deficiencies of the present day will be supplied by the morrow: attend to the history of Rasselas, prince of Abyssinia.

In his attempts to escape from the happy valley in which he lives, Rasselas meets a man "eminent for his knowledge of the mechanic powers," who builds a flying machine. The machine absorbs a lot of work and time, and crashes in the end—not before the designer has made the perceptive remark, "What would be the security of the good, if the bad could at pleasure invade them from the sky?"

Whatever begins well, ends badly; the only consolation is the rueful moral to be drawn from it. In *Candide,* matters begin badly and get worse; the comedy is in the way Candide and his companions, Pangloss and Cunégonde, draw idiotically optimistic conclusions from each fresh disaster. Estrangement between hope and performance is complete; facts exist by the teeming multitude—they are interpreted according to individual temperament.

The nearest the utopian Candide gets to Utopia is in El Dorado, where the streets are paved with gold. There, pleasures are purely material, dinners always excellent. Courts of justice and parliament buildings do not exist; there are no prisons. But the Palace of Sciences has a gallery two thousand feet long, filled with mathematical and scientific instruments. Furthermore, the king's jokes are witty even in translation.

Voltaire, a French philosopher who wrote over ten million words, and produced a voluminous correspondence besides, had indulged his sense of surrealism before writing *Candide,* most notably in the two *contes Zadig, ou La Destinée* and *Micromégas* (1747 and 1752). In the former, Zadig's observation of clues which lead him to deduce that the queen's dog and the king's horse have passed qualify him as a predecessor of Poe's Auguste Dupin.

In *Micromégas,* a gigantic visitor from one of the planets of Sirius and his hardly less gigantic friend from Saturn arrive on Earth and fish a ship out of the Baltic. Holding it in the palm of one hand, the two giants examine it through a microscope and thus observe human beings aboard, with whom they talk. Rabelais was probably an influence here; Swift is also mentioned; but the inversion of having the space journey done *to* Earth rather than *from* it is characteristically Voltairean; so is the conversation. In the end, the two enormous visitors present the creatures of Earth with a volume in which, they promise, the explanation of the universe will be found.

When the secretary of the Academy of Sciences in Paris opens the volume, he finds it contains nothing but blank pages.

A reminder of this incident comes in *Candide,* in a passage of philosophical conversation between Candide and Martin which flows like Marx Brothers' dialogue:

> "While we are on the subject, do you believe that the Earth was originally sea, as is stated in that great book which belongs to the captain?" asks Candide.
>
> "I believe nothing of the sort, any more than I do all the other fancies that have been foisted upon us through the centuries."
>
> "But to what end, think you, was the world formed?"
>
> "To turn our brains."

"Were you not astonished by the story I told you, of the two girls in the country of the Oreillons, who had monkeys for lovers?"

"Not in the least. I see nothing strange in such an infatuation. I have seen so many extraordinary things that now nothing is extraordinary to me."

"Do you think that men always slaughtered one another, as they do nowadays? . . ."

"Do you think that hawks have always devoured pigeons at every opportunity?" (Chapter 21)

Candide was written soon after the Lisbon earthquake, an event which shook civilised Europe as severely as the sinking of the *Titanic* shook Edwardian society. Especially in *Candide* and *Gulliver*, we get a strong impression of the times, and of those weaknesses of the flesh eternally with us—then much complicated by the prevalent scourge of syphilis, to which both authors pay due tribute.

These two remarkable books, together with *Robinson Crusoe* and *Rasselas*, are not quite classifiable as novels by any strict accountancy, in that many of today's science fiction "novels" resemble them. But they are, all four, examples of masculine intellect at work, sketching in character with economy, not concerned with ambivalences of human relationships, interested in telling a tale and, above all, looking outward and drawing conclusions about the world in which the authors find themselves. In this respect, this brilliant eighteenth-century quartet resembles some of today's science fiction—say Thomas Disch's *Camp Concentration* or Robert Sheckley's *Dimension of Miracles*—more closely than the somewhat wishy-washy Moon voyages immediately preceding them.

A more feminine sensibility was to rise and dominate the novel form, exemplified in the next century by the novels of Jane Austen in its early years and Henry James in its late—and by E. M. Forster and Ivy Compton-Burnett and many others in our century. These are the idols that literary critics have, on the whole, preferred; for they provide more scope for rival interpretations; and they have reduced the serious novel to a business of relationships. But, in science fiction, the tradition of looking outwards and measuring man against the world he has made or found, and the tradition linked with it of telling a bold tale (even if it happens to be no more prodigal of incident than Crusoe's long years on his island), have continued, on the whole, uninterrupted. Even the philosophical flavour has been preserved, as in George Stewart's *Earth Abides,* Pohl and Kornbluth's *Wolfbane,* and many other novels.

If it is easy to see how most of the tales and stories in this chapter point towards science fiction, it is equally easy to see how they are *not* science fiction or, at the closest, are ur-science fiction. They remain tall stories mixed with utopian ideas (like Lucian's writings), or extensions of travellers' tall stories (like Godwin's *Man in the Moone*), or parodies of previous stories (like de Bergerac's *L'Autre Monde*), or fake-travels (like *Robinson Crusoe*), or political satires (like *Gulliver's Travels*), or philosophical squibs (like *Candide*), or mixtures of everything (like *Niels Klim*). They are time-locked, unable to visualise change working in their own societies. Their view of man vis-à-vis nature is a modest one—it operates on him, or he on it, randomly. Although they acknowledge fantasy, it is never acknowledged as an internal force, but rather as an outside phenomenon, to be taken seriously or for its own sake—none of the quality of Inwardness, in other words. They operate in the present, without recourse to the wider canvas of past or, more particularly, future.

The greatest of these books would be the greatest of science fiction books if they were science fiction; but they are not, and it is only the growth of the genre since, stimulated by their vigorous example, which makes them seem to resemble it as much as they do.

Walpole's *Castle of Otranto,* already mentioned, was published five years after *Candide.* It inaugurates a new genre, closeted and introspective, in which "atmosphere" usurps the name of action. It lies closer to dreams than to the affairs of the busy world, as Gothic mists curtain the Age of Reason.

When we turn to the nineteenth and twentieth centuries, we find these two streams mingling. Sometimes the external world seems to predominate, sometimes the internal.

Both have their place in science fiction, as in life.

NOTES

1. Translation by Dr. Thomas Franklin.
2. Kenneth Clarke, *Civilisation: A Personal View,* 1969.
3. The translation is Rosen's. The *Somnium* is very short. After it was

written, Kepler added notes, almost one per sentence, which run to many more pages than the *Dream* itself. Kepler's *Somnium: The Dream, or Posthumous Work on Lunar Astronomy*, translated with a commentary by Edward Rosen, Madison, 1967.

4. The best English translation of the two books is *Other Worlds*, translated and with an introduction by Geoffrey Strachan, 1965.

5. Marjorie Hope Nicolson, *Voyages to the Moon*, New York, 1949.

6. Philip B. Grove, *The Imaginary Voyage in Prose Fiction*, 1941.

7. George Sampson, *The Concise Cambridge History of English Literature*, 1941.

8. George Orwell, "Politics vs. Literature," *Collected Essays*, 1961.

9. See the Preface to *Erewhon*, Enlarged Edition, 1901.

4

The Gas-Enlightened Race:
VICTORIAN VISIONS

> Here about the beach I wandered, nourishing
> a youth sublime
> With the fairy tales of science, and the long
> result of Time
>
> Alfred Tennyson: *Locksley Hall*

The wide expanses, the hidden valleys, of the nineteenth century lie like a great continent before any explorer of yesterday's fiction.

A critic gazing at this territory is aware of the falsity of that popular view which regards science fiction as "beginning with H. G. Wells." Wells stands at the end of the century and at the end of the Victorian Age; behind him lie sixty glorious and congested years.

A roll call of all the writers whose works were undoubtedly science fiction, or marginally science fiction, or even far from science fiction and yet of central interest (such as the works of Lewis Carroll) would be a long one. The popular view is correct to this extent, that many of the names on the roll call have been forgotten to all but specialists—deservedly, just as Wells is remembered deservedly.

As we pass through the period, we see how the various themes of a science fictional nature were taken up and used in the debate over and over again, to be drawn together exuberantly in Wells' work.

Piety and materialist optimism were once features of Victorian life about which a good deal was heard; today, as we remake that multicoloured period in our own image, we hear more about scepticism, agonised atheism, and the sort of doubts about a growing mass society as are expressed in de Tocqueville's *Democracy in America*. Most of these grey notes find an echo in the science fiction of the period; from *Frankenstein* on, it has remained most typically a literature of unease.

Typical too is that other *Frankenstein* theme, the duality of man, expressed markedly in Victorian times by a duality of society —the Rich and the Poor, dramatically labelled by Disraeli "the two nations."

The eighteen-thirties, as literary historians have remarked, were a time of decline for the novel in general, as well as for the Romantic movement.[1] After the death of Sir Walter Scott in 1832, fiction was in recession, to come bouncing back in the forties with a power that rendered the novel the dominant form in imaginative literature for the rest of the century. Among the remarkable new novels of the eighteen-forties, were Thackeray's *Vanity Fair*, several of Dickens' novels—including *Martin Chuzzlewit* and *Dombey and Son*— Disraeli's *Coningsby* and *Sybil*, novels by all three of the Brontë sisters—*Wuthering Heights, Jane Eyre*, and *Tenant of Wildfell Hall* —as well as novels by Mrs. Gaskell, Harrison Ainsworth, Melville, Borrow, Charles Kingsley, and Trollope.

Most of these names were new to the reading public. A few novelists, by reason of age or stamina, bridged the ebb tide of the thirties. Among them were Shelley's friend, Thomas Love Peacock, and Bulwer-Lytton.

The life cycle of the Bulwer-Lytton is almost as complicated as an insect metamorphosis; and his name underwent as many changes. He ended as Edward George Earle Lytton Bulwer, First Baron Lytton, having begun life as a fairly simple Bulwer and somewhere along the line narrowly missing becoming Lord South Erpingham. He finished life as one of the dullest pillars of Victorian society, having begun as a young Regency sprig who imparted ideas of dandyism to Disraeli.

Two years after the fashionable publisher Henry Colburn had

published Mary Shelley's *The Last Man* in three volumes, Lytton's dandy novel, *Pelham*, appeared from the same house in the same format. Later, Lytton turned successively to novels about crime and criminals (such as *Eugene Aram*), historical novels (such as *The Last Days of Pompeii*), the occult (such as *Zanoni*), and novels of peaceful everyday life in the manner of Trollope (such as *My Novel*); he also wrote plays.

"What will Bulwer become? The first author of the age? I do not doubt it. He is a magnificent writer,"[2] wrote Mary Shelley. But our interest in him must here be confined to *The Coming Race* (1871), a novel about supermen.

The Coming Race is the story of a human being who enters a coal mine, stumbles down a ravine, and discovers a human-like race living peaceably under the Earth's crust in well-lit caverns. This race has air boats, automata, mechanical wings, formidable weapons, and grand buildings. And scenery that seems to owe much to John Martin[3]:

> My host stepped out into the balcony; I followed him. We were on the uppermost story of one of the angular pyramids; the view beyond was of a wild and solemn beauty impossible to describe—the vast ranges of precipitous rock which formed the distant background, the intermediate valleys of mystic many-coloured herbage, the flash of waters, many of them like streams of roseate flame, the serene lustre diffused over all by myriads of lamps, combined to form a whole which no words of mine can convey adequate description: so splendid was it, yet so sombre; so lovely, yet so awful. (Chapter 5)

Burke's sublime with a vengeance!

The race that lives in these caverns is called the Vril-ya, after a beneficent and all-purpose force, *vril*, with which they control their world. Vril is a "unity in natural energetic agencies."* But the Vril-ya are far from warlike—hunting dangerous animals (a few antediluvian monsters still survive) is left to children, because hunting requires ruthlessness and "the younger a child the more ruthlessly he will destroy." Lytton spoke as a family man.

Most of the novel is taken up by pedestrian descriptions of how the subterranean world differs from ours, in the manner of all utopias. There is a slight humorous element, since one of the alien

---

* Which later lent its name to Bovril, a fortifying beef beverage.

women falls in love with our hero—and these women are larger and altogether more formidable than human women, taking the initiative in courtship. Our anonymous hero admits that Zee "rather awed me as an angel than moved me as a woman."

He admires the subterranean world but finds it dull, and eventually escapes back to his own world, carried in the arms of the woman who loves him. The somewhat philosophical narrative ends on a subdued note of menace:

> The more I think of a people calmly developing, in regions excluded from our sight and deemed uninhabitable by our sages, powers surpassing our most disciplined modes of force, and virtues to which our life, social and political, becomes antagonistic in proportion as our civilisation advances—the more deeply I pray that ages may yet elapse before there emerge into sunlight our inevitable destroyers.

Here is a submerged nation, perhaps an echo of Disraeli's.[4]

The Coming Race was descended from tribes living on the Earth's surface. Records suggest that their retreat underground took place "thousands of years before the time of Noah." But that does not accord with current theories in geological circles, "inasmuch as it places the existence of a human race upon earth at dates long anterior to that assigned to the terrestrial formation adapted to the introduction of mammalia." In this way and in others, Lytton shows a somewhat confused interest in evolutionary theory.

The year after the publication of his novel, a much bigger gun was turned towards the same target.

Samuel Butler (1835–1902) is one of those brilliant writers who never lives up to his brilliance. The two books for which he is now best remembered are his posthumous novel *The Way of All Flesh* and his satirical utopia, *Erewhon* (1872), in which Butler's wit combines with his interest in science (and particularly in Darwinism, with whose adherents Butler skirmished through many books and many years) into a somewhat Swiftian whole. The result is a much more living book than *The Coming Race*, though Butler recognised their similarity. Nor need plagiarism be suspected; when it is time to think about a subject, a lot of people will be thinking about it.

Whereas the use of *vril* and all its forces has made Lytton's people strong and impressive, the Erewhonians are strong and impressive because they have banned the use of machines.

Butler deploys his arguments with something of Swift's skill, though without the same liveliness.

> There is no security against the ultimate development of mechanical consciousness, in the fact of machines possessing little consciousness now. A mollusc has not much consciousness. Reflect upon the extraordinary advance which machines have made in the last few hundred years, and note how slowly the animal and vegetable kingdoms are advancing. The more highly organised machines are creatures not so much of yesterday, as of the last five minutes, so to speak, in comparison with past time. Assume for the sake of argument that conscious beings have existed for some twenty million years: see what strides machines have made in the last thousand! May not the world last twenty million years longer? If so, what will they not in the end become? Is it not safer to nip the mischief in the bud and to forbid them further progress? (Chapter 23)

Such reasoning would not have been possible a generation before Butler. And there are other pleasant reversals of what we regard as normal, the best known being the way in which Erewhonians are treated as criminal when they are sick, and sick when they are criminal. Higgs, Butler's protagonist, sees these methods working at first hand, for his host, Mr. Nosnibor, is a respected embezzler.

> I do not suppose that even my host, on having swindled a confiding widow out of the whole of her property, was put to more actual suffering than a man will readily undergo at hands of an English doctor.

Erewhon has a love affair—the standard one. Higgs falls in love with a girl called Arowhena and, despite all obstacles, eventually manages to escape with her by balloon.

Witty though *Erewhon* is, like its successors it remains little more than a debate on current themes, the nature of society, etc. We see an immense difference if we contrast it with the books H. G. Wells was writing twenty-five years later, where we catch vivid glimpses of a Butlerian society in which machines have reached supremacy, from *The Time Machine* onwards.

Samuel Butler speaks of machines reproducing themselves,[5]

and of men becoming their slaves: "Consider also the colliers and pitmen and coal merchants and coal trains, and the men who drive them, and the ships that carry coals—what an army of servants do the machines thus employ! Are there not probably more men engaged in tending machinery than in tending men?" (Chapter 24)

H. G. Wells *shows* us, for instance in *When the Sleeper Wakes*, what happens when men are slaves to technology. Wells is involved, Butler merely a commentator.

The difference between the two methods lies not only in the changes that took place between the publication of *Erewhon* and Wells' novels, but in radical differences of temperament: Butler cautious and—when all is said—ever looking back; Wells the new man, eager—when all is said—for the next thrilling chapter in human history, whatever it might bring. Yet the contrasts between the two men are not so great. Butler's is a keen sardonic eye. Both he and Wells would have concurred with Tennyson's great line: "Better fifty years of Europe than a cycle of Cathay."

Speaking as one who had experienced more than fifty years of Europe, the old novelist Peacock presented a thoroughgoing scepticism to modern improvements of any kind in his last novel, *Gryll Grange* (1861). There he invoked an ancient spirit, to return from the dead with the wish that

> . . . with profoundest admiration thrilled,
> He may with willing mind assume his place
> In your steam-nursed, steam-borne, steam-killed,
> And gas-enlightened race. (Chapter 28)

Butler and Lytton seized eagerly and early on the theory of evolution. Both of them employ it in their fiction as essentially an aesthetic object (the phrase is Butler's). This is the way in which most scientific theories, whether invented for the occasion or not, are employed in science fiction.

The Coming Race and *Erewhon* rank among the nineteenth century's utopian novels. Like the seventeenth century, the nineteenth yields many utopias, most of them occasioned by fresh aspects of existence revealed by increasing industrialisation. We can do no more than nod towards such utopian philosophers as John Ruskin—whose stature is still growing—Carlyle, Thoreau, Emerson, and, to some extent, William Morris. But a word should be said about *Looking Backward*, because its theories are somewhat more than aesthetic object; they are its very existence.

That existence, it must be said, is a pale one now. What was never literature cannot become literature. But, when it was published in 1888, the book was a tremendous living force.

Its author is Edward Bellamy (1850–98). Bellamy was born and died in Chicopee Falls, Massachusetts, but his novel is set in a Boston of the future. The protagonist, Julian West, suffers from insomnia and passes his nights in a subterranean chamber, where a mesmerist occasionally puts him to sleep. This is presumably a late echo from the world of Poe and M. Valdemar. But when West awakes he is no corpse; the year is 2000, and he fell asleep in 1887.

What follows is a socialist utopia, in which nineteenth-century Boston is unfavourably compared with a Boston of the future. "The glorious new Boston with its domes and pinnacles, its gardens and fountains, and its universal reign of comfort . . ." Industrial organisations have evolved into something larger, resulting in a sort of state socialism where every man is worthy of his hire. In consequence money is abolished. So how does a man pay his way abroad? "An American credit card is just as good in Europe as American gold used to be."

There are other deft touches which prove the shrewdness of Bellamy as a thinker. But his optimism got in his way; marriages are not made only for love, any more than machinery provides us with nothing but pleasure. Nor do we occupy our leisure time peacefully and profitably, listening to sermons or whatever. The human animal, operating within a non-human scheme of affairs, always defies the rationalists. Possibly it is this realisation which has spawned so many dystopias in our century. Dusty though Bellamy's book has become, there is still a touching faith and hope in it we can envy.

Looking Backward was taken up by followers of Henry George, the revolutionary economist, and by socialist groups then struggling for coherence inside the United States. The influence of the book spread to Europe, and provoked attack and counter-attack. Its effect was not only on the literary.

The same can be said of two other socialist-inclined utopias of the period, one British, one Austrian, both published in 1890, two years after Bellamy's fable. William Morris, influenced by Ruskin, depicted a mediaeval-type future in *News from Nowhere,* in which the people have destroyed the machines, handicrafts are the thing, and longevity is practised without the aid of geriatic wards. Morris was a man of many parts, who sought to establish utopia in a practical way by maintaining mediaeval standards of craftsmanship against the shoddy standards of his own day; he was also an artist and designer—many of us still enjoy William Morris designs on our wallpapers and fabrics. Later in his life, he wrote of strange realms that bear a resemblance to mediaeval worlds, which many find remote and haunting ("No mountains in literature are as far away as distant mountains in Morris," said C. S. Lewis of him[6]); these will be discussed later.

A German, Theodor Hertzka, described a practicable utopia in *Freeland: A Social Anticipation* (as the English translation of 1891 is called). The utopia of Freeland, established in Africa, is a modified capitalist state which makes full use of modern inventions, plus a few of its own. Many societies sprang up, trying to put Hertzka's propositions into effect—one even set sail for Africa, but the experiment was not a success.

Such books played a part in the debate of their period, and perhaps helped to soften its rabid capitalism, if by nothing more than an infusion of hope.

Evolution was used opportunistically by Lytton in *The Coming Race.* It was more central to Samuel Butler's work. He devoted four volumes to discussion of it.[7] We shall see how large a part it played in Wells' writing; but there is a writer greater than any of them in whom the evolutionary revelation works throughout most of his literary life.

In 1873, a novel was published which contains a situation not unfamiliar to readers of thrillers, although this was no thriller. A man has fallen part way down a cliff, and is clinging there, the sea below him, with slender chances of rescue.

> By one of those familiar conjunctions of things wherewith the inanimate world baits the mind of man when he pauses in moments of suspense, opposite Knight's eyes was an imbedded fossil, standing forth in low relief from the rock. It was a creature with eyes. The eyes, dead and turned to stone, were even now regarding him. It was one of the early crustaceans

called Trilobites. Separated by millions of years in their lives,
Knight and this underling seemed to have met in their place
of death. It was the single instance within reach of his vision
of anything that had ever been alive and had had a body to
save, as he himself had now.

The creature represented but a low type of animal existence, for never in their vernal years had the plains indicated by
those numerous slatey layers been traversed by an intelligence
worthy of the name. Zoophytes, mollusca, shell-fish, were the
highest developments of those ancient dates. The immense
lapses of time each formation represented had known nothing
of the dignity of man. They were grand times, but they were
mean times too, and mean were their relics. He was to be with
the small in his death. (Chapter 22)

The passage continues with a lecture on life before man—poetic
and striking as well as learned, but out of key with the rather trivial
love-story-with-ironies in which it is embedded.

The author is Thomas Hardy, the novel, *A Pair of Blue
Eyes*. It is one of the weakest of the Wessex novels,† although Tennyson much admired it and Proust declared it to be "of all books
the one which he would himself most gladly have written."[8] Yet it
provides early evidence of Hardy's tremulous awareness of the in-
significance of individual human lives when set against the encom-
passing mysteries of space and time, which he would develop
more fully in other novels and in poems, and in his mighty verse-
drama, *The Dynasts*.

A recent and perceptive guide to Hardy's thought emphasises
the effect Darwin's writings had on him.[9] Hardy's is the loneliness of the long-distance eye; his is perhaps the first zoom lens in
literature, and from the picture of ancient Egdon Heath, where
"the distant rims of the world and of the firmament seemed to be a
division in time no less than a division in matter," in *The Return of
the Native* (1878), through such novels as *The Woodlanders*
(1887) and *Tess of the d'Urbervilles* (1891), to the exalted poetry
of *The Dynasts*[10]—less a historical play than a long meditation on
the evolution of consciousness—Hardy presents a unique panorama

---

† Wessex is, in Hardy's hands, an example of a dream world, although its
boundaries lie very near the boundaries of reality. Hardy himself referred to
Wessex's "horizons and landscapes of a partly real, partly dream-country."
(Preface to *Far from the Madding Crowd*)

of man in relationship to his environment, where time and chance are as influential as the seasons.

Consider this extract from *Two on a Tower* (1882). It is a monologue by Swithin St. Cleeve, the astronomer hero, punctuated by Lady Constantine's comments, as they stand at the top of his tower and gaze at the night sky:

> "You would hardly think, at first, that horrid monsters lie up there waiting to be discovered by any moderately penetrating mind—monsters to which those of the oceans bear no sort of comparison."
>
> "What monsters may they be?"
>
> "Impersonal monsters, namely, Immensities. Until a person has thought out the stars and their inter-spaces, he has hardly learnt that there are things far more terrible than monsters of shape, namely, monsters of magnitude without known shape. Such monsters are the voids and waste spaces of the sky. . . . Those are deep wells for the human mind to let itself down into, leave alone the human body! . . . So am I not right in saying that those minds who exert their imaginative powers to bury themselves in the depths of that universe merely strain their faculties to gain a new horror?"
>
> Standing, as she stood, in the presence of the stellar universe, under the very eyes of the constellations, Lady Constantine apprehended something of the earnest youth's argument.
>
> "And to add a new weirdness to what the sky possesses in its size and formlessness, there is involved the quality of decay. For all the wonder of these everlasting stars, eternal spheres, and what not, they are not everlasting, they are not eternal; they burn out like candles . . ." (Chapter 4)

In *The Dynasts* (1904), Hardy presents his final grand development of those evolutionary speculations present in the passage already quoted from *A Pair of Blue Eyes*, concerning the growth of consciousness and intelligence.

The scene in *The Dynasts* moves from Earth to the Overworld —where the final stage of evolution will occur when the Immanent Will that rules us all (with "eternal artistries in Circumstance") eventually achieves consciousness and fashions a better universe, more in accordance with human thoughts and wishes. No bolder speculation than this comes our way until Olaf Stapledon's works in the nineteen-thirties.

Hardy's work‡ is shot through with perceptions newly formulated for his generation, and alive with observations honed on his peculiar temperament by the scientific findings and developments of his time; yet it would be absurd to regard Hardy as a science fiction writer.

Firstly, Hardy does not introduce his changes in the natural or the old order for the sake of novelty or sensationalism, though he is not averse to sensationalism in other respects; the changes he records go to buttress deep feelings and movements in the novels and remain subordinate to the lives of his characters (who in any case live in surroundings where most changes appear transitory). Secondly, and more subtly, there is a question of *tone*. The tone of science fiction is characteristically rapid and light, and this is far from Hardy's voice—Swift, for instance, is several degrees nearer to it. Thirdly, there is the matter of genius. Genius does what it must; talent does what it can. Hardy, for all his faults, is a genius; while science fiction—as yet at any rate—has only attracted writers of talent, with one or two possible exceptions. Those with greater or lesser attributes work elsewhere.

The example of Thomas Hardy—and, even more, of a writer who greatly admired him, John Cowper Powys[11]—should confirm us in our opinion that it is not enough for a writer's *oeuvre* to contain what might be called science fictional speculation for us to claim him as a science fiction writer. Sf is as much a matter of form as content.

We detect a fairly early split between science fiction, or the novels that will have most influence on emerging science fiction, and other novels which also concern reactions between character and environment or characters and change. In other words, the way to modern science fiction (such as, say, Philip Dick's) lies through Udolpho and Mary Shelley's territory via Sheridan Le Fanu's *Uncle Silas* and Wilkie Collins' *The Moonstone*, rather than

‡ The most immediate shaping force on the range of verse in *The Dynasts*, on its different metres, its various spirit voices, and, to an extent, its subject matter, is Hardy's favourite poet, Percy Bysshe Shelley, and particularly his *Prometheus Unbound*. This poem, as we noted, bears certain filial duties to Erasmus Darwin's poetry.

through (say, again) the Brontës, *Great Expectations,* and Hardy.
Tone here is a more reliable guide than subject matter.

For reasons connected both with space and the haste of critics, this
book concentrates on Anglo-Saxon contributions to the field; in
many respects, it celebrates an extraordinary cultural interchange
between Britain and North America. But, with Jules Verne looming
ahead like Poe's monstrous figure in the ice fields, we should remind
ourselves that science fiction was never a national prerogative.

The French could probably claim a figure as considerable as
Erasmus Darwin in the writer best known to the English-speaking
world for *Monsieur Nicolas,* Restif de la Bretonne (1734–1806).
One of De la Bretonne's biographers salutes him as "a prophet
who foreshadowed the atom, the sputnik, flying men and air squad-
rons, interplanetary missiles, bacteriology, atomic energy, Com-
munism, etc."[12] Most of this claim rests on De la Bretonne's
work *La Découverte Australe, par un Homme-Volant* (four volumes, Paris, 1781).

Of this work, which may have been suggested by Peter Wilkins,
a distinguished French scholar has written that it "not only described a heavier-than-air flying machine which was a combination
of helicopter and parachute, and foretold the creation of airborne
fleets whose bombs would leave 'in the immense space of future
time a trail of infamy, fear and horror,' but looked forward beyond
that period of war to the creation of a communist society in which
property should be abolished." This last vision was no vague
utopian daydream: in *La Découverte Australe* and other works,
Restif elaborated detailed practical plans for the institution of
collective farms, a five-hour day, a five-and-a-half-day week, com-
munal refectories, organised leisure activities, and changes in the
penal system, all designed to achieve "a general reform of manners
and through that reform the happiness of mankind." Finally, not
content with describing the present and prophesying the future, he
looked back to the very springs of life, sketched out a theory of
microbes a hundred years before Pasteur, described a system of
creative evolution which foreshadowed Bergson, and asserted his
belief in "a divine electro-magnetico-intellectual fluid," which in
our times Teilhard de Chardin was to call the "noosphere."[13]

From Restif de la Bretonne, a sedulous scholar may trace a
thread to surrealism and Dadaism and the pop art movements

that feed on them. For De la Bretonne's work fired that strange character Gérard de Nerval, an eccentric, a bohemian, a tormented man later to be extolled by Proust, a suicide.

Nerval's best-known work is *Aurelia* (1854), with an opening often praised. "Our dreams are a second life. I have never been able to penetrate without a shudder those ivory or horned gates which separate us from the invisible world . . ."[14] In its disorganised way, *Aurelia* presents many striking images, not least when it bursts into a kind of evolutionary fantasy:

> . . . I imagined myself transported to a dark planet where the first germs of creation were struggling. From the bosom of the still soft clay gigantic palm trees towered high, poisonous spurge and acanthus writhed around cactus plants: the arid shapes of rocks stuck out like skeletons from this rough sketch of creation, and hideous reptiles snaked, stretched, and coiled in the inextricable network of wild vegetation. Only the pale light of the stars lit the bluing perspectives of this strange horizon; yet, as the work of creation proceeded, a brighter star began to draw from it the germs of its own future brilliance.

Nerval is a romantic figure. He makes no attempt to impose his visions on the exterior world; his interior landscapes are presented as just that; and such "action" as there is is interior.

Another romantic of slightly later date whose work, like Nerval's, seems to presage another age, is Villiers de l'Isle-Adam. He is generally regarded as the first symbolist. He lived and breathed in the exotic world peopled by the spectral presences of Byron, Hoffmann, Baudelaire, Hugo, and Poe.

Despite these illustrious shades, De l'Isle-Adam had his own original viewpoint, embodied in his famous play *Axel* (1890), with its well-known line, "*Vivre? Les serviteurs feront cela pour nous*," and writings which more closely approach science fiction, as they approach surrealism.

Notable among these are the *Contes Cruels* and *L'Ève Future*. In the latter, published in 1887, De l'Isle-Adam tells of an inventor who creates a beautiful automaton, whom he christens Hadaly. Hadaly closely resembles a real woman; she can sing and carry on conversations, being powered by electricity and carrying a stack of gramophone records inside her metal breast.

This splendid creature looks back to the beautiful but mechanical Olympia in E. T. A. Hoffmann's *The Sandman,* who dances and sings to clockwork perfection. Olympia was given an extension of life in Offenbach's opera *The Tales of Hoffmann.*[15]

De l'Isle-Adam's *Cruel Tales* (first published in book form in 1883) have a Poe-like strangeness and Poe's dislike of materialism, together with a wider spectrum of interest than Poe could command.

The *Cruel Tales* are less cruel than unusual. They concern a duke suffering from a rare kind of leprosy, a duel which one of the seconds persists in regarding as a stage performance, a beautiful woman isolated from her lovers by deafness, a new machine for guaranteeing a play's success, the use of the night sky for advertising, and so on. In this latter story, *Celestial Publicity,* as in many others, De l'Isle-Adam turns his sense of humour against the mercenary traits of the *bourgeoisie:*

> A moment's reflection is enough to allow one to imagine the consequences of this ingenious invention. Would not the Great Bear herself have cause for astonishment if, between her sublime paws, there suddenly appeared this disquieting question: "Are corsets necessary?"[16]

In his sonnet to De l'Isle-Adam, Aldous Huxley concludes with the words:

> you bade the soul drink deep
> Of infinite things, saying, "The rest is naught."

Jules Verne (1828–1905) was born ten years earlier than De l'Isle-Adam. On him, as on the younger man, the writings of Poe in Baudelaire's translation had a stimulating effect; one of Verne's earliest stories, *Cinq Semaines en Balloon* (*Five Weeks in a Balloon*), published in 1863, bears a clear relationship to Poe's *The Balloon-Hoax* of 1844.

Poe's use of scientific detail must have attracted Verne; he would have liked, too, the way in which the Poeian protagonist stands outside society, as do Verne's great heroes. But where Poe is the doomed poet of the Inward, Verne is the supreme celebrant of the Outward; the subterranean chamber gives way to the sea, the elements. Yet, even towards the end of Verne's career, he still fishes in Poe's wake. In 1897, he published *Le Sphinx des Glaces* (known in English as *The Sphinx of the Ice Fields* or *An Antarctic Adventure*), a sequel to *The Narrative of Arthur George Pym*, which Verne believed to be incomplete.

Verne's career began in the theatre. He wrote plays, light opera, and sketches, and met Dumas *fils*, collaborating with him on several occasions.

Voyage au Centre de la Terre (*Journey to the Centre of the Earth*) (1864) was an early success; from then onwards, Verne wrote prolifically and enjoyed immense fame in a line "which I have invented myself," as he put it. That line was science fiction. Even if Verne did not invent it, he was the first to succeed in it commercially, which is perhaps as great a thing. And he was the first and last to be blessed by the Pope for so doing.

Verne was born at Nantes, and so was familiar from birth with ocean-going ships and the traffic of ports. As a boy, he tried to run away to sea, was caught and beaten; but his father seems to have been an understanding man, who later subsidised Verne's early writing. Although a misogynist, Verne had the sense to marry well and raise a large family. He went into local government, became a pillar of society, and enjoyed sailing his own yacht on that sea which comes breaking in as a symbol of freedom in so many of his books.

On the surface, Verne remained as good a Catholic as De l'Isle-Adam was a bad one. On one of his cruises in the Mediterranean, he was received by the Pope, who praised him as a moral and didactic writer.[17] He died full of years and honours at Amiens, where his remains are interred under a grandiose tomb which depicts him rising again in full marble.

One of Verne's critics, Marcel Moré,[18] has argued that behind Verne's industrious and bourgeois façade lay a more anguished personality, the key to which is the way the novels concern only masculine relationships and where women, the few there are, are mere cyphers. In the words of a British biographer, Verne "never sullied his pages by descending to scenes of lust."[19]

Michel Butor, a novelist and critic to be respected, has another view of Verne, seeing him as "a cryptologist of the universe," composing imaginative variations on the themes of the four elements, earth, air, fire, and water, with electricity as a pure form of fire.[20] His characters forever oppose the unruliness of the world with logic; the poles are sacred places because they form still points in a turning world.

Such theories illuminate some aspects of the novels. More centrally, it needs to be said that *Les Voyages Extraordinaires* (the collective title of Verne's novels) span the last four decades of the last century, and cover the globe, moving from one place to another in which struggles for liberty were being waged. He wrote in the great imperialist age; like Wells, he is not on the side of the imperialists. Unlike later sf writers such as Robert Heinlein and Poul Anderson, Verne is quietly against conquest. His typical hero is a rebel or outcast from society, the most notable example being Captain Nemo, the nationless figure at the centre of *Twenty Thousand Leagues Under the Sea* (1870).

More amazing than the lack of women is the lack of religious feeling; throughout that great turbulent landscape of the novels, there is scarcely a priest or a church to be had and, in extremities, the protagonists utter only a conventional cry to Providence.

In the early novels, detailing tremendous voyages to the centre of the Earth, to the bottom of the sea, to the Moon, or off on a comet, Verne celebrates man's progress. Everything works like mad. Both machines and machine-builders exist apart from society as a whole. But society comes creeping up. The tone of the novels changes, the atmosphere darkens with time. The later novels clog with satanic cities instead of super-subs, with Stahlstadt, Blackland, Milliard City. Even the brave scientists show signs of deterioration, eccentricity, blindness. The heroic age of the engine is done. Things fall apart, the centre will not hold.

Verne's great land of the future, America—setting of twenty-three of his sixty-four novels—develops increasingly negative aspects. Dollar diplomacy enters, expansionism takes over, the machine-mentality triumphs. Robur, benevolent hero of 1886's *Robur le Conquérant* (generally translated as *Clipper of the Clouds*) returns in a 1904 sequel as a destroyer (*Maître du Monde—Master of the World*). Men and societies are going down into eclipse, driving and driven by their dark angels, the machines.[21] Sam Smiles has moved over to make room for Nietzsche.

The poverty of English translations of Verne has not diminished his popularity, merely his chance of better critical appraisal. His tone is flat, his characters are thin, and he pauses all too frequently for lectures; his is a non-sensual world. These are his negative features, and very damaging they are, even if his books are regarded as fit merely for boys.

His positive features include a fascination with scientific possibilities, a passion for geography on the hoof, his undying affection for liberty and the underdog, an awareness of the political realities of his own time which parallels H. G. Wells', and his relish for a good story. These qualities have rightly carried his books to treasured and meagre bookshelves round the world. Of course, his negative qualities have been found most available to imitation by his successors.

There is little point in discussing *Les Voyages Extraordinaires* individually.[22] A characteristic passage from an early novel must serve instead.

This is from *Hector Servadac*, sometimes known as *Off on a Comet*. A comet has grazed the Earth, carrying a portion of North Africa, the Mediterranean, and the Rock of Gibraltar off into space. Along with this chunk of world go Captain Hector Servadac and his orderly, Ben Zoof. At first, they are unable to account for the strange phenomena which surround them, but the truth of their exceptional situation gradually becomes clear to them. They meet other survivors of various nationalities in their travels, as they are whirled further from the Sun and the temperature becomes chillier.

> Telescopes in hand, the explorers scanned the surrounding view. Just as they had expected, on the north, east, and west lay the Gallian Sea, smooth and motionless as a sheet of glass, the cold having, as it were, congealed the atmosphere so that there was not a breath of wind. Towards the south there seemed no limit to the land, and the volcano formed the apex of a triangle, of which the base was beyond the reach of vision. Viewed even from this height, from which distance would do much to soften the general asperity, the surface nevertheless seemed to be bristling with its myriads of hexagonal lamellas, and to present difficulties which, to an ordinary pedestrian, would be insurmountable.
>
> "Oh, for some wings, or else a balloon!", cried Servadac, as he gazed around him. And then, looking down at the rock upon which they were standing, he added, "We seem to have been transplanted to a soil strange enough in its chemical character to bewilder the savants at a museum."

"And do you observe, Captain," asked the count, "how the convexity of our little world curtails our view? See, how circumscribed the horizon is!"

Servadac replied that he had noticed the same circumstance from the top of the cliffs of Gourbi Island.

"Yes," said the count. "It becomes more and more obvious that ours is a very tiny world, and that Gourbi Island is the sole productive spot upon its surface. We have had a short summer, and who knows whether we are not entering upon a winter that may last for years, perhaps for centuries?"

"But we must not mind, Count," said Servadac, smiling. "We have agreed, you know, that, come what may, we are to be philosophers."

"True, my friend," rejoined the count, "we must be philosophers and something more; we must be grateful to the good Protector who has thus far befriended us, and we must trust His mercy to the end . . ."

Before the evening of this day closed in, a most important change was effected in the condition of the Gallian Sea by the intervention of human agency. Notwithstanding the increasing cold, the sea, unruffled as it was by a breath of wind, still retained its liquid state. It is an established fact that water, under this condition of absolute stillness, will remain uncongealed at a temperature several degrees below zero, while experiment, at the same time, shows that a very slight shock will often be sufficient to convert it into solid ice.

. . . Servadac . . . assembled his little colony upon a projecting rock at the extremity of the promontory, and having called Nina and Pablo out to him in front, he said:

"Now, Nina, do you think you could throw something into the sea?"

"I think I could," the child replied, "but I am sure that Pablo would throw it a great deal further than I can."

"Never mind, you shall try first."

Putting a fragment of ice into Nina's hand, he addressed himself to Pablo:

"Look out, Pablo; you shall see what miracles Nina can accomplish! Throw, Nina, throw as hard as you can."

Nina balanced the piece of ice two or three times in her hand, then threw it forward with all her strength.

A sudden thrill seemed to vibrate across the motionless waters to the distant horizon, and the Gallian Sea had become a solid sheet of ice![23]

Absurd perhaps, but colourful and dramatic. Burke's sublime gets its first chromium-plating. A myth-making trait in Verne's writings has allowed them to survive—dated though their details may be—when more serious work has died. The cinema has mined him extensively, following Walt Disney's successful Cinemascope production of *Twenty Thousand Leagues Under the Sea* in 1954, with James Mason playing Captain Nemo. The novel was first filmed as early as 1905. Verne clearly has a long publishing life still before him.

Verne's huge success is coincidental with the establishment of railway bookstalls with their proliferating cheap editions, of popular lending libraries, and of various education acts.[24] Sensationalism, often coupled with a vague air of uplift, was much in demand, and sermons on science were becoming as respectable as sermons on morality.

Verne, who preached a sermon of work and militant liberty, seems fusty now; but a good translation of his best novels might effect a revaluation of his vast *oeuvre*.

Before leaving France, mention must also be made of the draughtsman, engraver, and writer, Albert Robida, one of the first men to grasp how the technologies of the nineteenth century might be turned to total warfare. Robida's visions began to appear in a periodical, *La Caricature*, in 1883; they were published in Paris in book form in 1887 as *La Guerre au Vingtième Siècle* (*The Twentieth Century War*), and provide an extraordinary panorama of new weapons of the future, illustrated in Robida's delightful and spectacular style. Also in the 1880s, Robida produced a second novel, *La Vie Electrique*. Both novels are set in the 1950s. I. F. Clarke has said of Robida that his is "the first major vision of technological warfare ever presented." But Robida's outlook is essentially lighthearted, his illustrations almost gay, and many of his incidents comic—for instance, food kitchens on a mammoth scale supply the needs of his future city, the nutrients being pumped through enormous iron pipes; but a pipe bursts and floods Robida's hero's home with soup.

Despite this blithe approach, Robida made many remarkable forecasts. It was a game that all could play. At the turn of the century, in particular, looking forward became a hobby. Although would-be inventors or cartoonists could easily dream up a personal flying-machine with pack and propellor strapped on the back and flapping wings above, they could scarcely imagine what wide-scale effects such an innovation would have on society. Instead, they contented themselves with picturing the appliance simplifying courtship or complicating a game of tennis.[25]

From the ascent of the first hot-air balloon, despatched by the brothers Montgolfier in 1783, onwards, it was a pleasant exercise of the imagination to visualise aerial warfare. Those first paper novelties were soon recognised as omens of something less pleasant —yet the tone is generally half facetious, for men were still not trained to regard the future with great seriousness.** Before long, balloons were used in reality for military ends. The first air raid in history took place in 1849, when the Austrians used pilotless montgolfieres to bomb Venice. Gas balloons were extensively employed during the siege of Paris, 1870–71.

During this period, a more earnest note enters speculation on future warfare, coinciding with the growing imperialisms of the European powers. Critics owe a debt to the researches of I. F. Clarke for his exhumation of the literature of this subject and period,[26] and for his resurrection of the otherwise forgotten pamphlet *The Battle of Dorking*, published in 1871, when the balance of power in Europe had been so remarkably altered by the German invasion of France.

The Battle of Dorking, published anonymously, was by Colonel George Tomkyns Chesney, and his story is purely didactic in intent: to warn England of Germany's rearmament and of her own unpreparedness.

His narrator is a volunteer who fought in the engagements he is

** In this respect, one of the earliest balloon paintings remains the most striking. Towards the end of his long life, Francesco Guardi, the contemporary of those other Venetian masters, G. B. Tiepolo and Canaletto, painted the *Ascent of the Montgolfier Balloon, 1784*. There it sails over the Giudecca, while the Venetians watch it under their colonnades; dressed in their finery, they huddle and gawp at the new thing as helplessly as any bunch of peasants. Through Guardi's fingertips, we watch the old order confronted by the ascendance of the new.

describing to his grandchildren. He tells of an invasion of England in the near future, in which modern Prussian forces sweep away a native army still attempting to fight as it did at Waterloo. It is beaten and broken. Fortitude is not enough. At Guildford, the First Army Corps is falling back; everywhere, British troops have to retreat in disorder; Woolwich, the country's only arsenal, is captured by the enemy. London falls, the country surrenders and is stripped of its colonies.

Darwinism gave new point to the knowledge that only the fittest army will survive; it also produced the perspectives into which a tale of the future could be painted. But a more immediate inspiration for *Dorking* was those new breechloaders rolling out of Krupp's.

Chesney tells his story with vigour and sure military knowledge. Even his polemics come in the same forthright prose, without waste of words.

> Truly the nation was ripe for a fall; but when I reflect how a little firmness and self-denial, or political courage and foresight, might have averted the disaster, I feel that the judgment must have really been deserved. A nation too selfish to defend its liberty, could not have been fit to retain it. To you, my grandchildren, who are now going to seek a new home in a more prosperous land, let not this bitter lesson be lost upon you in the country of your adoption.

Chesney's story was immediately effective. Fear and interest were aroused on all sides. Gladstone spoke out against the pernicious pamphlet; "Unfortunately these things go abroad, and they make us ridiculous in the eyes of the whole world."

Go abroad they did. For Chesney had hit upon a formula and a nerve centre. The device of future war, sudden invasion, beggarly unpreparedness, inevitable defeat, and national disgrace was open to all. Parodies, counter-arguments, translations, imitations, appeared at home and in European countries; while in the United States, Canada, Australia, and New Zealand, more editions of Chesney's story were rapidly printed. A new fashion in Dreadful Warnings had begun.

As I. F. Clarke puts it, "Between 1871 and 1914 it was unusual to find a single year without some tale of future warfare appearing in some European country." France, the mood of *la revanche*

upon it, was the first country to produce a revised version of
Chesney, with *La Bataille de Berlin en 1875*—a story of comfort
rather than discomfort.

Such was the prestige of Chesney's story that, almost thirty
years later, in 1900, another colonel, also anonymously, published
The New Battle of Dorking—clearly confident that the reference
would be widely understood. The last edition of Chesney's story
was a German translation—published by the Nazi regime in 1940,
as England lay awaiting possible invasion.

Last century's tales of future wars which never took place
make dusty reading now. Sufficient to note that the tradition was a
flourishing one, and that H. G. Wells' *The War of the Worlds*
belongs to that tradition. Wells wrote many books about war, and
was not alone in that. He may be contrasted with William le Queux,
who specialised in war scares. A new Le Queux was the by-product
of every European crisis. Franco-Russian amity in 1893 produced
Le Queux' *The Great War in England in 1897*, published in a
journal that year. It was widely popular, was issued in book form,
and inspired many imitations, including several by Le Queux
himself. We find him still going strong just before the outbreak of
war in 1914.[27]

Scientific rationalism and a general authoritarianism in society had
set up diluted realism as the most proper channel for the novel in
the sixties; but, just as respectability sought to smother its opposite,
so a rich vein of fantasy flowed beneath the sort of realistic social
novel with which Trollope was most successful.[28]

> The whole great wicked artificial civilised fabric,
> All its unfinished houses, lots for sale, and railway outworks

as Clough called it, might be laid bare in the novels of Dickens,
Charles Reade, and Mrs. Gaskell, but the best fantasy did not
entail an entire abandonment of reason and responsibility. The
reforming novelist Charles Kingsley turned to *The Water Babies*
(1863); Meredith's *The Shaving of Shagpat* (1855) is a mixture of
Arabian Nights and Gothic. George MacDonald entered the lists
with his symbolic fairy tale *At the Back of the North Wind* (1871),
while uncanny fantasy was secure in the hands of Sheridan Le Fanu,
an Irish poet and journalist whose writings include *The House by
the Churchyard* (1863) and *Through a Glass Darkly* (1872), which

contains much-anthologised short stories, such as "Green Tea" and "Carmilla."

Le Fanu's sinister masterpiece, *Uncle Silas,* was published in 1864 and is still justly enjoyed today. Also at high table with Le Fanu sits Wilkie Collins, the friend of Dickens; he published *The Moonstone* in 1868, when half awash with laudanum—a powerful early tale of detection with fantastic elements, sinister Orientals, double lives, crime committed under the influence of drugs, and a strong undercurrent of superstition, which was not without its impact upon Dickens' last and unfinished novel, *The Mystery of Edwin Drood* (1870).

It is in the next decade, the eighteen-eighties, that a storyteller of a different kind emerges, with a dark and powerful fantasy containing several layers of meaning. This is Robert Louis Stevenson, whose *Dr. Jekyll and Mr. Hyde* was published in 1886.

Framed in a narrative contributed by three different hands, it relates, as every schoolboy worth his salt must still know, how an Edinburgh doctor discovers a concoction which releases his baser nature. Unhappily, the drug is habit-forming. The baser nature, Mr. Hyde, takes over, commits murder, and is finally hunted down. Like several other works we have noted, *Dr. Jekyll* began as a dream, which RLS wrote down when he awoke.

> Late one accursed night, I compounded the elements, watched them boil and smoke together in the glass, and when the ebullition had subsided, with a strong glow of courage, drank off the potion.
>
> The most racking pains succeeded: a grinding in the bones, deadly nausea, and a horror of the spirit that cannot be exceeded at the hour of birth or death. Then these agonies began swiftly to subside, and I came to myself as if out of a great sickness. There was something strange in my sensations, something incredibly new . . . I knew myself, at the first breath of this new life, to be more wicked, tenfold more wicked, sold a slave to my original evil.

Even in a volume like this one, dedicated to strange stories, *Dr. Jekyll* remains a very strange story. Stevenson was conscious of its allegory; but what exactly is the allegory? Is it concerning the duality of man's nature, with "angel and fiend" (in Jekyll's words) in one flesh? Is it about the struggle between rationality and instinct? Or is what Jekyll calls "the brute that slept within me," playing its "apelike tricks," a mythical reinterpretation of the Descent of Man? Whichever of these readings Stevenson favoured (and there is no reason why they should not all have been in his mind), there is little doubt that the *doppelgänger* relationship between Jekyll and Hyde parallels the one between Frankenstein and *his* bundle of retribution, the monster.[29]

We see Stevenson now through time's diminishing glass, but he achieved great fame in his day, partly for his personal history of illness and retreat to the South Seas. H. G. Wells was later to admit to his influence, for Jekyll is one of the line of meddling savants from Frankenstein to Wells' Moreau and Griffin and so on to yesterday's "mad scientist."

Before *Dr. Jekyll*, Stevenson had written other fantasies, *The New Arabian Nights*, and a real heart-knocker, *Thrawn Janet*, among them. *Thrawn Janet* is about a black man who takes over —and occasionally takes off—a dead woman's body; so that we may regard it as a sort of Ur-Jekyll. But Stevenson's main influence was as a teller of splendid romantic tales, such as *Treasure Island* and *Kidnapped* and we shall come across several novelists of the nineties in a later chapter who emulate something of his swash-buckle, if not his vein of dark fantasy.

Lewis Carroll's kind of fantasy stands apart, not only from Stevenson's, which it predates, but from everyone else's.

For the sf buff, 1871 is a vintage year. It saw the publication not only of *The Battle of Dorking* and Lytton's *The Coming Race* but of an adult fantasy masquerading as a child's book, *Through the Looking Glass*.

> . . . And certainly the glass was beginning to melt away, just like a bright silvery mist.
>
> In another moment, Alice was through the glass, and had jumped lightly down into the looking-glass room. The very first thing she did was to look whether there was a fire in the fireplace, and she was quite pleased to find that there was a real one, blazing away as brightly as the one she had left behind. . . . Then she began looking about, and noticed that

what could be seen from the old room was quite common and uninteresting, but that all the rest was as different as possible.

Through the Looking Glass is inseparable from its predecessor, *Alice in Wonderland* (1865). These two unique Victorian dreams, though nominally addressed to children, contain profound veins of symbolism, imagination, satire, and metaphysical terror, as well as a reinterpretation of the Victorian submerged-nation theme noted in Disraeli, Kingsley, and Lytton. (The first Alice book was originally called *Alice's Adventures Underground.*) Adults discern these veins below a delightful surface play of upended logic.

"Take some more tea," the March Hare said to Alice, very earnestly.

"I've had nothing yet," replied Alice in an offended tone, "so I can't take more."

"You mean you can't take *less*," said the Hatter: "it's very easy to take *more* than nothing." (*Alice in Wonderland,* Chapter 7)

The eternal Alice and her adventures do not form part of science fiction. Equally, her ventures into other dimensions and her experience of situations where the commonplace is weirdly distorted ("Now, here, you see, it takes all the running you can do, to keep in the same place. If you want to get somewhere else, you must run at least twice as fast as that," says the Red Queen) relate to the surreal aspect of science fiction. Carroll's various amazing animals, often mythological, often grotesquely dressed, stand between the worlds of Beatrix Potter and the universe of Gray Lensman.

Carroll's logical inversions have had a marked effect on the field, though his adroit mixture of fantasy, seriousness, and wit is less easily imitated; it has occasionally surfaced in the writings of Eric Frank Russell, Ray Bradbury, and Robert Sheckley, among others.

Carroll's method has also been assimilated. "Gulliver is a commonplace little man and Alice a commonplace little girl," says C. S. Lewis in his essay on science fiction.[30] "To tell how odd things struck odd people is to have an oddity too much." This rule has generally been observed, though Carroll's tales have never been surpassed.

Beside the major figure of Carroll we may set a minor one, another scholar with an interest in mathematics, Edwin A. Abbott. Abbott was a Shakespearean scholar and theologian, now best remembered for that slender sport *Flatland*, first published in 1884 and still surviving by reason of its wit and originality.

Flatland—subtitled *A Romance of Many Dimensions* (and published as by A. Square)—describes a world where the inhabitants live in two dimensions; they are of various shapes, triangles, squares, circles, pentagons, and so on, but can see each other only as straight lines because they have only length and breadth. It is a terrible place in many other ways; law and order are major preoccupations in Flatland, and women, being sharp-pointed, are penalised.

This slender work is hardly science fiction, conforming to our original definition in content but not form, which is of the straight expository kind, aided by blackboard diagrams. But it has always attracted sf readers, not least because its lucid account of dimensions reminds us that we may be relatively as imperceptive of the reality of our universe as were the inhabitants of Flatland. Perhaps for this reason, the book was a favourite of C. S. Lewis.

This survey demonstrates that science fiction and many of its themes were flourishing towards the end of last century—even if they had not always converged in the same target area. The diversity of the nineteenth century—its achievements and disappointments under which we still labour—guarantees that.

One theme remains to be treated, a theme which has achieved greatest popularity in our century: the theme of Nature Coming Back into Its Own. Its relationship to evolutionary thought is clear. If mankind does not prove fit enough to rule the world he arrogantly claims as his, then nature will return and overwhelm him. It has its connections with the guilty fear of the Disraelian "two nations" theme, that the suppressed and oppressed will rise up again.

It was given memorable expression in 1884 by a naturalist and journalist already suffering from a terminal case of consumption. Richard Jefferies' *After London* begins with a survey, somewhat Hardyesque in tone, of what happens to the land "after London ended." Jefferies hated London and the age in which he lived; he shows little of the ambiguous feelings characteristic of greater Victorians, shares none of Hardy's or Tennyson's cautious welcome of change and "the thoughts that shake mankind." He sat defeated in Brighton, phthisically writing off change, thought, and the metropolis.

Jefferies could not visualise a catastrophe devastating enough to demolish a capital city (our generation has more sophistication in such matters), so he dispenses with all explanations. This lends his text an agreeably sinister and Kafkaesque taking-the-unaccountable-for-granted air.

The triumph of nature is described in grand style:

> Footpaths were concealed by the second year, but roads could be traced, though as green as the sward, and were still the best for walking, because the tangled wheat and weeds, and, in the meadows, the long grass, caught the feet of those who tried to pass through. Year by year the original crops of wheat, barley, oats, and beans asserted their presence by shooting up, but in gradually diminished force, as nettles and coarser plants, such as the wild parsnips, spread out into the fields from the ditches and choked them.
>
> Aquatic grasses from the fields and water-carriers extended in the meadows, and, with the rushes, helped to destroy or take the place of the former sweet herbage. Meanwhile, the brambles, which grew very fast, had pushed forward their prickly runners farther and farther from the hedges till they now had reached ten or fifteen yards. The briars had followed, and the hedges had widened to three or four times their breadth first, the fields being equally contracted. Starting from all sides at once, these brambles and briars in the course of about twenty years met in the centre of the largest fields.
>
> Hawthorn bushes sprang up among them, and, protected by the briars and thorns from grazing animals, the suckers of elm-trees rose and flourished. Sapling ashes, oaks, sycamores, and horse-chestnuts lifted their heads. Of old time the cattle would have eaten off the seed leaves with the grass so soon as they were out of the ground, but now most of the acorns that were dropped by birds, and the keys that were wafted by the wind, twirled as they floated, took root, and grew into trees. By this time the brambles and briars had choked up and blocked the former roads, which were as impassable as the fields. (Chapter 1)

Unfortunately, interest dies when Jefferies introduces characters into his feral landscape; his people enjoy considerably less animation than his plants. Perceptive naturalist though he was, Jefferies' gifts as a novelist are small, and—as many later writers bear witness—imagination is of little use unless teamed with the other necessary talents of a writer.

While Jefferies was writing his strange book and dying of tuberculosis, another tubercular young man was living and working in the sooty, hammer-and-tongs London Jefferies was destroying. This young man, Herbert George Wells, was attending Professor Thomas Huxley's lectures in biology and zoology. Time was approaching when he would prove himself to have in superabundance the necessary talents of a writer—and a towering and ferocious imagination besides.

NOTES

1. George Saintsbury, in *The English Novel*, speaks of a "half-ebb" in the novel.

2. Mary Shelley, *Journal*, Jan. 11, 1831.

3. John Martin (1789–1854), painter of awful spectacles, was the Cecil B. de Mille of the Romantic movement. His grand gloomy canvasses and engravings had tremendous influence on other artists (Turner imitated him in such paintings as *The Destruction of Sodom*) and writers. The little Brontës slept with Martin's engravings hanging over their beds. In France, his vogue was such that an adjective "Martinien" (an early example of Franglais) was coined for mighty extravaganzas. Martin's canvas *The Last Man*, of which more than one version exists, was based on the poet Thomas Campbell's poem of the same name: "I saw a vision in my sleep . . ." Another imitator was Francis Danby, whose *Opening of the Sixth Seal* was bought by Beckford in 1828; but Beckford was friendly with many artists, and had Martin sketch Fonthill for him.

Martin, like Erasmus Darwin, was a forward-looking man; he proposed grandiose schemes for the modernisation of London, including farsighted plans for sewage disposal. It may be wondered how such men as Martin and Erasmus Darwin were so easily forgotten by their fellow-countrymen; the answer lies in a conservative streak in the English, which sets itself against innovation.

4. Or perhaps not. Disraeli's *Sybil: or The Two Nations* was published in 1845. Later novels had taken up the "two nations" theme. The

propagandist novelist Charles Kingsley deals with the rural poor in *Yeast* (1848–a good year for such a topic). In *Yeast,* the labourers are portrayed as hopelessly degenerate beings; young Lancelot wonders if they are "even animals of the same species." Recent works such as Steven Marcus' *The Other Victorians* have shown how the exploitation of the "nation" in the darkness was not only financial but sexual. This grave moral division lay at the basis of Victorian hypocrisy. Lytton was well aware of the Victorian underworld, and the concluding passage of *The Coming Race* may contain an echo of it.

Later, this great Victorian theme of the submerged nation, the hidden life awaiting the hour of its revenge, expressed so often in novels (Dickens' among others) and paintings, finds science fictional embodiment in Wells' *Time Machine,* with its subterranean Morlocks.

5. What Frankenstein's monster hoped for, sf writers later accomplished. The funniest application of the idea of machines reproducing themselves is to be found in John Sladek's *The Reproductive System,* 1968 (U.S. title *Mechasm*), that most Butlerian of novels. The inventors explain the system to a general who has been called in:

> During the week they explained, the boxes had devoured over a ton of scrap metal, as well as a dozen oscilloscopes with attached signal generators, thirty-odd test sets, desk calculators both mechanical and electronic, a pair of scissors, an uncountable number of bottle caps, paper clips, coffee spoons and staples (for the lab and office staff liked feeding their new pet), dozens of surplus walky-talky storage batteries and a small gasoline-driven generator.
>
> The cells had multiplied—better than doubled their original number—and had grown to various sizes, ranging from shoeboxes and attaché cases to steamer trunk proportions. They now reproduce constantly but slowly, in various fashions. One steamer trunk emitted, every five or ten minutes, a pair of tiny boxes the size of 3×5 card files. Another box, of extraordinary length, seemed to be slowly sawing itself in half.
>
> General Grawk remained unimpressed. "What does it do for an encore?" he growled. (Chap. 4)

6. C. S. Lewis, "William Morris," *Selected Literary Essays,* edited by Walter Hooper, Cambridge, 1969.

7. *Life and Habit,* 1877, *Evolution, Old and New,* 1879, *Unconscious Memory,* 1880; *Luck or Cunning?,* 1886.

8. Remark by Proust recorded in Harold Nicolson's diary for June 21, 1933, and quoted by J. I. M. Stewart in his *Thomas Hardy: A Critical Biography,* 1971. One may speculate pleasureably that the entire germ of *A la Recherche du Temps Perdu* might be contained in a

sentence of Hardy's closely following the passage quoted: "Time closed up like a fan before him."

9. F. R. Southerington, *Hardy's Vision of Man.* "Perhaps the most powerful influence of all, however, was that of Darwin . . ." (Chap. 14) Darwin's somewhat valetudinarian life and his enormous patience in unravelling gigantic riddles as well as the habits of earthworms are in tune with Hardy's whole tenor of being; Darwin, in Hardy's phrase, "was a man who used to notice such things." In Florence Emily Hardy's *Life of Thomas Hardy,* an entry records Hardy's presence at Darwin's funeral, adding, "As a young man he had been among the earliest acclaimers of *The Origin of Species.*" (Chap. 12)

10. Perhaps the best-known passage in this long and difficult work— it occurs near the beginning—is a stage direction.

> The nether sky opens, and Europe is disclosed as a prone and emaciated figure, the Alps shaping like a backbone, and the branching mountain-chains like ribs, the peninsular plateau of Spain forming a head. Broad and lengthy lowlands stretch from the north of France across Russia like a grey-green garment hemmed by the Ural mountains and the glistening Arctic Ocean.
>
> The point of view then sinks downwards through space, and draws near to the surface of the perturbed countries, where the peoples, distressed by events which they did not cause, are seen writhing, crawling, heaving, and vibrating in their various cities and nationalities.

The methods of D. W. Griffiths, Eisenstein, and De Mille are here presaged.

11. John Cowper Powys' best-known novel is *A Glastonbury Romance,* 1932. Among his other novels is *Up and Out,* 1957, in which a hydrogen bomb blows a big chunk of the Earth into space; four people survive on it, a husband and wife created by vivisection called Org and Asm, and an ordinary man and woman. The chunk of matter meets Time, which is a slug, and kills it; it also encounters Eternity ("pitifully unimpressive"), Aldebaran, the devil, and God.

12. Marc Chadourne, *Restif de la Bretonne ou le Siècle Prophétique,* Paris, 1958.

13. Robert Baldick, in the Introduction to his translation of *Monsieur Nicolas: or The Human Heart Laid Bare,* 1966.

14. Gérard de Nerval, *Selected Writings,* translated by Geoffrey Wagner, 1958.

15. For derivations of automata before De l'Isle-Adam and Hoffmann, see the curious inter-disciplinary book by John Cohen, *Human Robots in Myth and Science,* 1966.

16. Villiers de l'Isle-Adam, *Cruel Tales*, translated by Robert Baldick, 1963.

17. Even *The Times* called his "wonderful books . . . terribly thrilling and absolutely harmless." It is quoted as doing so in a cheap edition (one shilling) of *Around the Moon*, issued by the authorised publishers, Sampson Low, Marston, Searle, and Rivington, 1876.

18. Marcel Moré, *Le Trés Curieux Jules Verne*, Paris, 1960.

19. I. O. Evans, *Jules Verne, Master of Science Fiction*, 1956.

20. Michel Butor, *Répertoire*, Paris, 1953.

21. The best and most thorough examination of this grand theme is contained in Jean Chesneaux, *The Political and Social Ideas of Jules Verne*, translated by Thomas Wikeley, 1972.

22. An exception to this sweeping remark may be made for *Les Cinq Cents Millions de la Begum*, 1879, known more briefly in English as *The Begum's Fortune*. This is Verne's only utopia, and it enters that category but narrowly.

The fortune of the title is divided between Sarrasin, a French authority on hygiene, and Schultz, a German professor of chemistry. The two men use the money to build rival towns in Oregon. Frankville is established as a model city, Stahlstadt is a small police state. Verne was clearly feeling a touch of *revanchisme* when he wrote, although the Franco-Prussian War had been over for several years. Stahlstadt tries to destroy Frankville, but Schultz happily blows himself up.

Some commentators see this story as a prophecy of German militarism to come. The utopian aspects concern the use or misuse of modern machinery and capabilities. But the unlikeliness of the events and the somewhat ludicrously diagrammatic plot makes it unlikely that readers will take the social reformer as seriously as the patriot.

23. *Hector Servadac*, in *Novels by Jules Verne*, selected and edited by H. C. Harwood (Chap. 22). This is the authorised translation also used—although there "abridged and modernised"—in the Ace Books edition, retitled *Off on a Comet*, 1957.

24. The dates in England: W. H. Smith secured the rights to sell books and newspapers on railway stalls in 1848. "Railway libraries," "Yellow Backs," and other numerous series, featuring novelists such as Lytton, were published to stock the stalls. The Education Act was passed in 1870. Circulating libraries had been operative in various forms since the eighteenth century; Mudie's, the most well known, was opened in London in 1842. The official tax on paper was abolished in 1861.

25. Illustrations of a set of French postcards dating from about 1900 and depicting such advances as dictaphones, underwater hunting, automated learning, and mechanised beauty parlours (if indeed these are advances) are to be found in the last chapter of *The Nineteenth Cen-*

tury: The Contradictions of Progress, edited by Asa Briggs, 1970. Some examples of Robida's work are also included.

26. I. F. Clarke's preliminary skirmish with the subject is contained in *The Tale of the Future: From the Beginning to the Present Day,* 1961, which is a check list. His brilliant full-scale operation is *Voices Prophesying War 1763–1984,* 1966.

27. The Bodleian Library lists 142 titles by Le Queux (1864–1927). He seems to have been afflicted by a lust for war, and was as right wing in his opinions as were most of the writers of future war stories—Wells being a notable exception to this rule. Among Le Queux' titles are *German Atrocities,* published in 1914, and presumably intended to whip up war lust. In 1915, he published a science fiction title, *The Mystery of the Green Ray.*

28. As one literary critic puts it, when speaking of the eighteen-sixties, "*Lorna Doone* and *Harry Richmond* are isolated outcroppings of romance in a decade when realism was entrenching itself in the English novel. It must also be observed, however, that the same decade witnessed a remarkable output of fantasy. Indeed, not until then is fantasy (when not used merely as a device for satire) identifiable as a distinct mode in English fiction." Lionel Stevenson, *The English Novel: A Panorama,* 1960.

29. There is an interesting discussion of the meaning of *Dr. Jekyll and Mr. Hyde* in Chap. 4 of *Into the Unknown* by Robert M. Philmus (Berkeley and Los Angeles, 1970), which considers various interpretations. It also touches on Stevenson's reference to "Mr. Darwin's theory" in 1874. Philmus adds a great deal to our appreciation of Stevenson's story by his perceptive look at the other characters involved in Dr. Jekyll's downfall, showing how, for instance, Utterson, acting as detective, embodies an approach to the mystery of human nature which is antithetical to Jekyll's, thus underlining the point that more than one approach to inner truth is possible.

30. "On Science Fiction" is collected in C. S. Lewis, *Of Other Worlds: Essays and Stories,* edited by Walter Hooper, 1966.

5

The Man Who Could Work Miracles:
H. G. WELLS

> The battle hurtles on the plains,
> Earth feels new scythes upon her.
> Elizabeth Barrett Browning: *The Cry of the Human*

There have been many books written about Herbert George Wells, but only one really good one, and that he wrote himself: *Experiment in Autobiography.*[1]

Here is the passage, from Chapter 6, in which Wells describes the London he knew, and the housing constructed early in the nineteenth century:

> Private enterprise spewed a vast quantity of extremely unsuitable building all over the London area, and for four or five generations made an uncomfortable incurable stress of the daily lives of hundreds of thousands of people.
>
> It is only now, after a century, that the weathered and decaying lava of this mercenary eruption is being slowly replaced —by new feats of private enterprise almost as greedy and unforeseeing. To most Londoners of my generation, these rows of jerry-built unalterable houses seemed to be as much in the nature of things as rain in September and it is only in retrospect

that I see the complete irrational scrambling planlessness of which all of us who had to live in London were the victims. The multiplying multitude poured into these moulds with no chance of escape. It is only because the thing was spread over a hundred years and not concentrated into a few weeks that history fails to realise what sustained disaster, how much massacre, degeneration and disablement of lives, was due to the housing of London in the nineteenth century.

How much of Wells, his negative and positive sides, reveals itself in this passage! His hatred of muddle, his hope for something beyond the profit motive, his sense of melodrama, his irascibility, his dramatic feeling for the organic flow of history—all are here, as well as whispers of that didacticism which rose up and choked off his great creative ability.

The passage tells us much about Wells' background. Life for him was a battle for health and success. Whereas most writers in the England of his time lived in large comfortable country houses, Wells was a poor man's son and made his way without any assets other than his genius.

He was born in his parents' little china shop in the High Street of Bromley, Kent, in 1866.

Wells' mother had been in service when she met and married H.G.'s father, then working as a gardener. The shop was their first hopeful matrimonial venture together; it failed by degrees, year after year. Wells wrote with love and some exasperation of his mother, "Almost as unquestioning as her belief in Our Father was her belief in drapers." After some elementary schooling, his first job was in a draper's shop in Windsor. He was no good at it, and they told him he was not refined enough to be a draper. He got the sack.

This was the man of whom the fastidious Henry James was later to cry—in the nearest the Master ever got to a fan letter—"Bravo, bravo, my dear Wells!" in response to two of Wells' books, admitting "They have left me prostrate with admiration!"[2]

Wells became a teacher, educating himself as he went along, and so moved into journalism and authorship. His first books appeared in 1895, when he was almost thirty. Around him, a raw new London was emerging, consciously becoming the Heart of Empire—an expanding capital trapped in the contracting houses Wells described with such hatred. The central figures of many of his early

novels are chirpy Cockney "little men" with whom he was entirely
familiar—their accents came to him through the flimsy bedroom par-
titions of his various digs. Wells exhibits them for inspection rather
than admiration.[3]

In this submerged metropolitan world, taking lessons from
Thomas Huxley, thinking great thoughts and struggling with great
illnesses, Wells lived and survived. In 1895, he got one hundred
pounds from W. E. Henley for his short novel *The Time Machine*. Its
sceptical view of the present, and its pessimistic view of the future
of mankind—and of life on Earth—challenged most of the cosy ideas
of progress and the new imperialism then current.

Except for a collection of essays, *The Time Machine* was the
first of Wells' one hundred and twenty odd books, and it is very
nearly his most perfect. It was an immediate success.[4]

Here is part of the famous passage in which the time-traveller
stands alone at the end of the world and looks about him:

> "The darkness grew apace; a cold wind began to blow in
> freshening gusts from the east, and the showering white flakes
> in the air increased in number. From the edge of the sea came
> a ripple and a whisper. Beyond these lifeless sounds, the world
> was silent. Silent? It would be hard to convey the stillness of
> it. All the sounds of man, the bleating of sheep, the cries of
> birds, the hum of insects, the stir that makes the background of
> our lives—all that was over. As the darkness thickened, the ed-
> dying flakes grew more abundant, dancing before my eyes;
> and the cold of the air more intense. At last, one by one,
> swiftly, one after the other, the white peaks of the distant hills
> vanished into blackness. The breeze rose to a moaning wind. I
> saw the black central shadow of the eclipse sweeping towards
> me. In another moment the pale stars alone were visible. All
> else was rayless obscurity. The sky was absolutely black.
>
> "A horror of this great darkness came on me . . . I felt
> giddy and incapable of facing the return journey . . ."

As Bernard Bergonzi has stressed in his excellent study of
Wells' science fiction,[5] *The Time Machine* is very much a *fin de
siècle* book. One glimpses in it some of the despairs of Hardy's vision; while the Eloi, those pale, decadent, artistic people that the
time-traveller discovers, derive a flavour of the aesthete from the
eighteen-seventies, and are echoed in those pale lost lilies of peo-

ple who haunt Beardsley's and Walter Crane's drawings and Ernest Dowson's poems.

The Eloi live aboveground, in idyllic surroundings. Below ground live the dark and predatory Morlocks, appearing at night to snatch the helpless Eloi. The innocence and laughter of the Eloi are only an appearance; below the surface lies corruption. The theme is a familiar Victorian one; it had vivid meaning for urban generations striving to install efficient modern sewers under their towns. One finds it, for instance, in Oscar Wilde's *The Picture of Dorian Gray*, published in 1891, where the sinner stays young and fair; only his portrait, locked away from prying eyes, ages and grows dissipated and obscene.

But the Eloi and Morlocks have historically deeper roots. They are a vivid science fictional dramatisation of Disraeli's two nations. Wells tells us as much in a later book, *The Soul of a Bishop*:

> "There's an incurable misunderstanding between the modern employer and the modern employed," the chief labour spokesman said, speaking in a broad accent that completely hid from him and the bishop and every one the fact that he was by far the best-read man of the party. "Disraeli called them the Two Nations, but that was long ago. Now it's a case of two species. Machinery has made them into different species. . . . We'll get a little more education and then we'll do without you. We're pressing for all we can get, and when we've got that we'll take breath and press for more. We're the Morlocks. Coming up."

This "submerged-nation" theme, coupled always with the idea of retribution, is essentially a British obsession, occurring in writers as diverse as Lewis Carroll, S. Fowler Wright, and John Wyndham. The essential American obsession, as we shall see, is with the Alien —also coupled with the idea of retribution.

Wells in his thirties was prodigious. Most of his best books were published before his fortieth birthday: *The Island of Dr. Moreau, The Invisible Man, The War of the Worlds, When the Sleeper Wakes* (later revised as *The Sleeper Awakes*), *Tales of Space and Time, The Food of the Gods*, and the two novels before which the Master was prostrate, *A Modern Utopia* and *Kipps*, as well as such non-sf works as *Love and Mr. Lewisham* and *Anticipations*.

Still to come after that first decade of writing were many good things, among them *Mr. Polly, The New Machiavelli, The War in the Air, Ann Veronica,* and a number of lesser and later books which would have looked well in the lists of a lesser writer: *Tono-Bungay, The World Set Free, The Shape of Things to Come, All Aboard for Ararat,* and *Men Like Gods* (about which more will be said in Chapter 7), as well as his excursions into popular education, such as *The Outline of History, The Health, Wealth and Happiness of Mankind,* and *The Rights of Man.* Wells is also remembered for a number of remarkable short stories; indeed, he was one of the forgers of this genre of England, following the example of De l'Isle-Adam, De Maupassant, and others in France. Among his stories are some that won immense popularity in their time, such as "The Country of the Blind," "The Door in the Wall," "The Truth About Pyecraft," "The New Accelerator," "The Crystal Egg," and "The Man Who Could Work Miracles." Most of them belong to Wells' early creative phase.

In many of these stories, Wells proved himself the great originator of science fictional ideas. They were new with him, and have been reworked endlessly since. He seems to have been the first fiction writer to use the perspectives of evolution to look backwards as well as forwards. His *The Grisly Folk* (1896) is a tale of humankind struggling against the Neanderthals as the glaciers retreated. "Great Paladins arose in that forgotten world, men who stood forth and smote the grey man-beast face to face and slew him."

Tales of prehistory have always remained a sort of sub-genre of science fantasy. Wells also wrote *A Story of the Stone Age* (1897), and Jack London dealt with the confrontation of human with prehuman, but it is not until William Golding's *The Inheritors* that this theme yields anything like a masterpiece. Wells' mind is the first to venture so far into past as well as future.

Among science fiction writers past and present, Wells, with Stapledon, is one indisputable giant. His debt to Hawthorne, Poe, and Swift, which he acknowledged, is apparent; he mentions also the novels of Holmes and Stevenson[6] in this context. It is true that Wells lacks the Inwardness we perceive in Mary Shelley; but he has an abundance of imagination as well as inventiveness—the two are by no means identical. Wells has his weaknesses, among which his inability to create any psychological depth of characterisation must be conceded. But it seems to this critic that the virtues which lift Wells above his successors (and above Verne) are threefold.

Firstly, he inherited something of the enquiring spirit of Swift—and science is, when all's said, a matter of enquiry; and from this spring the other two virtues, Wells' ability to see clearly his own world in which he lived (for without such an ability it is impossible to visualise any other world very clearly), and his lifelong avoidance of drawing lead characters with which readers will uncritically identify and thus be lulled to accept whatever is offered.

To see how these virtues work in practice, we may examine two of the early novels, *The War of the Worlds* and *The Island of Dr. Moreau.*

The War of the Worlds was published in serial form in 1897 and in book form a year later. It describes what happens when Martian invaders land on Earth. The story is told by an English observer, who sees the invaders move in on London against all the Army can do to hold them off. London is evacuated before the invaders die, killed by common microbes.

Even this brief outline shows that *The War of the Worlds* is part of the literary lineage which includes Chesney's *The Battle of Dorking.* But Wells makes a twofold progression. This time the invader is from another planet. This time, the invader is effortlessly more powerful than the invaded.

These two steps forward are not merely a development of wandering fancy; they form a development of the moral imagination. For Wells is saying, in effect, to his fellow English, "Look, this is how it feels to be a primitive tribe, and to have a Western nation arriving to civilise you with Maxim guns!"

This element of *fable* or oblique social criticism in Wells' early work is marked, from the novels to such short stories as "Country of the Blind" and "The Door in the Wall." Yet it remains always subservient to the strong flow of his invention; only when invention flagged did moralising obtrude and the tone become shrill.

In *The Invisible Man,* one is not intended to identify with Griffin in his strange plight. The moral beneath the fable is that scientific knowledge should be shared and not used for selfish gain (as Moreau uses his knowledge for personal satisfaction and so is damned just like Dr. Jekyll); but this moral is so profoundly part of the fabric of the story that many reviewers and readers missed the point, and complained that Griffin was "unsympathetic." Similar obtuseness confronts a science fiction writer today. His audience is accustomed to powerful heroes with whom they can unthinkingly identify. A mass audience expects to be pandered to. Wells never pandered.

Of course, Wells provides plenty of sensationalism in *War of the Worlds*. There is the carefully detailed destruction of the London of his day, followed by the horrible appearance of the Martians. Cunningly, Wells refrains from describing his invaders—we have seen them only in their machines—until over halfway through the book. They are then as ghastly as you please.

After a description of their external appearance comes an account of their internal anatomy when dissected. Wells' manner is cool and detached. From description, he turns to a discussion of the way in which the Martian physiology functions ("Their organisms did not sleep, any more than the heart of man sleeps") in matter-of-fact detail, going on to consider Martian evolution. The telling stroke, when it comes, lifts the whole remarkable passage to a higher level. "To me it is quite credible that the Martians may be descended from beings not unlike ourselves, by a gradual development of brains and hands . . . at the expense of the rest of the body." It is this linking of the Martians with humanity, rather than separating them from it, which shows Wells' superior creative powers. At the same time, he prepares us for the surprise and the logic of his final denouement.

C. S. Lewis was later to attack Wells for peopling our minds with modern hobgoblins. But it was Wells' successors in the pulp magazines, the horror merchants with no intent but to lower the reader's body temperature as fast as possible, who managed that. Wells' non-humans, his Martians, Morlocks, Selenites, and Beast-People, are creatures not of horror but terror; they spring from a sophisticated acknowledgement that they are all part of us, of our flesh. It was the later horror merchants who made their creatures alien from us, and so externalised evil. Wells' position is (*malgré lui*) the orthodox Christian one, that evil is within us. His non-humans are not without Grace but fallen from Grace.

In *War of the Worlds* we can distinguish Wells using three principles to produce this masterly piece of science fiction. Firstly, he begins by drawing a recognisable picture of his own times, "the present day." While we acknowledge the truth of this picture, we are being trained to accept the veracity of what follows. Secondly, he uses the newer scientific principles of his times, evolutionary theory and the contagious and infectious theories of micro-organ-

isms, as a hinge for the story.[7] Thirdly, he allows a criticism of his
society, and possibly of mankind in general, to emerge from his
narrative.

To these three principles must be added Wells' ability to write
effectively. There are few openings in science fiction more promising, more chilling, than that first page of *War of the Worlds,* including as it does the passage, "Across the gulf of space, minds that are
to our minds as ours are to those of the beasts that perish, intellects
vast and cool and unsympathetic, regarded this earth with envious
eyes, and slowly and surely drew their plans against us." How
beautifully underplayed is that adjective "unsympathetic"!

Yet Wells' early readers were puzzled over the question of his
originality. How original was he? This question of originality is
bandied about with regard to today's writers, all of whom stand in
Wells' portly shadow. Wells himself has an amused word to say on
the subject in his autobiography.

> In the course of two or three years I was welcomed as a
> second Dickens, a second Bulwer Lytton and a second Jules
> Verne. But also I was a second Barrie, though J.M.B. was
> hardly more than my contemporary, and, when I turned to
> short stories, I became a second Rudyard Kipling. I certainly,
> on occasion, imitated both these excellent masters. Later on I
> figured also as a second Diderot, a second Carlyle and a sec-
> ond Rousseau[8] . . . These second-hand tickets were very con-
> venient as admission tickets. It was however unwise to sit
> down in the vacant chairs, because if one did so, one rarely got
> up again.[9]

The War of the Worlds enjoyed an immediately favourable reception from readers and critics. Yet many of its aspects were ignored or misunderstood. It was felt in some quarters that the novel
was not very *nice.* The reviewer in the *Daily News* declared that
some episodes were so brutal that "they cause insufferable distress
to the feelings." *The Island of Dr. Moreau* had had the same effect
two years earlier.

Despite its merits, *The War of the Worlds* contains at least two
aspects of Wells' writing which tell against it increasingly as time
goes by. They turn out to be aspects of the same thing, Wells as a
delineator of "the little man." I mean his penchant for humour, par-

ticularly Cockney humour, and the general scrubbiness of his characters.

An old man is rescuing his orchids as the Martian invasion force draws near. " 'I was explainin' these is vallyble,' " he says. Wells' London is populated by shop assistants, cabmen, artillerymen, and gardeners. There is a curate, too, but he, like most of the clergy in Wells' works (and in his disciple, Orwell's), is used as a comic butt and talks nonsense. " 'How can God's ministers be killed?' " he asks. There are no characters in *The War of the Worlds,* only mouths.

In Wells' best book, this fault does not obtrude.

The Island of Dr. Moreau, published in 1896, contains for all practical purposes only three human beings: Moreau, the scientist ahead of his time; Montgomery, his assistant, a drunken doctor in disgrace; and Prendick, the common man, the narrator. Prendick has none of Bert Smallways' or Mr. Polly's or Kipps' cocky chirpiness, while the Beast-People hardly crack a joke between them. If the characters are in part cliché, this is in part because they serve symbolic roles, and there is a symbolic quality about the whole that gives it a flavour of Poe or the French writers.

Moreau begins in a businesslike way, in the manner of *Gulliver's Travels,* with a sea voyage and a shipwreck. Prendick survives the wreck and arrives at an unnamed island, owned by Moreau. A mystery surrounds the place, there are strange shrouded creatures, cries in the night. If this is Prospero's island, it is peopled by Calibans. In the way Prendick's mind leaps to terrible nameless conclusions, we come to that nervous playing on unvoiced things which is the essence of science fiction.

Incident flows smoothly on incident, each preparing us for the next: Prendick's unwelcome arrival; the mystery of the "natives"; Prendick's suspicion that Moreau experiments on human beings to bestialise them, and then the revelation that Moreau is in fact creating something like humanity from animals by the extreme application of vivisection techniques; then we meet the grotesque population of the island, the fruits of Moreau's surgery, the Hyena-Swine, the Leopard Man, the Satyr, the Wolf Bear, the Swine Woman, the faithful Dog Man. Then we have the death of the Leopard Man; the escape of the female puma on which Moreau is operating; the death of Moreau himself in the ensuing hunt through the forest; Prendick's shaky assumption of control; Montgomery's drunken carousal with

the Beast-Men, in which he is killed; the destruction of the strong-
hold; and the whole awful decline, as Prendick is left alone with
the Beast-People while they slowly forget what language they have
learned, and lapse back into feral savagery.

Nobody has quite decided what *Moreau* is, apart from being a
splendid and terrifying story. But it is clear that Wells has something more in mind, something larger, than a thrilling adventure.*

In the main, Wells' first critics and reviewers expressed
shocked horror at the whole thing, and would look no further; in
short, he was condemned rather than praised for his artistry—a reception which was to have its due effect on Wells' future writings.
Yet it is not difficult to see what he intended.

For some time, we are kept in suspense with Prendick about
the nature of the island's population. Is it animal or human? This is
not merely a plot device; as with the scientific hinge on which *War
of the Worlds* turns, Moreau's experiment links with the entire
philosophical scheme of the novel. And even after we learn the
true meaning of the Beast-People, Wells carefully maintains a poign-
ant balance between animal and human in them. At their most
human, they reveal the animal; at their most animal, the human.

The point may be observed at the moment when Prendick,
now in the role of hunter, catches up the Leopard Man in the forest:

> "I heard the twigs snap and the boughs swish aside before
> the heavy tread of the Horse-Rhinoceros upon my right. Then
> suddenly, through a polygon of green, in the half darkness un-
> der the luxuriant growth, I saw the creature we were hunting.
> I halted. He was crouched together into the smallest possible
> compass, his luminous green eyes turned over his shoulder re-
> garding me.
>
> "It may seem a strange contradiction in me—I cannot ex-
> plain the fact—but now, seeing the creature there in a per-
> fectly animal attitude, with the light gleaming in its eyes, and
> its imperfectly human face distorted in terror, I realised again
> the fact of its humanity. In another moment others of its pur-
> suers would see it, and it would be overpowered and captured,
> to experience once more the horrible tortures of the enclosure.

---

* Just as one of this novel's descendants, Golding's *Lord of the Flies,* is more
than a thrilling adventure.

Abruptly I slipped out my revolver, aimed between his terror-struck eyes and fired."

It is clear that *Moreau*, at least in one sense, speaks against transplant surgery, the consequences of which are revealed in the ghastly Law which the Beasts chant (a Law which some critics have seen as a parody of the Law of the Jungle in Kipling's *Jungle Books*, though the dry, sublimated humour of Swift is also present):

"Not to suck up Drink: that is the Law. Are we not Men?
Not to eat Fish or Flesh: that is the Law. Are we not Men? etc.
His is the Hand that Wounds. His is the Hand that Heals."

We are put in mind—not accidentally—of liturgical chant. "For His Mercy Is on Them That Fear Him: Throughout All Generations." We recall that Wells labelled the novel "an exercise in youthful blasphemy." Moreau is intended to stand for God. Moreau is a nineteenth-century God—Mary Shelley's protagonist in his maturity—Frankenstein Unbound.

Furthermore, Moreau's science is only vaguely touched on; the whole business of brain surgery, on which the novel hinges, has none of Wells' usual clarity. We can infer that he wanted to leave this area sketchy, so that we no more know what goes on in Moreau's laboratory than in God's. This vagueness, by increasing our horror and uncertainty, is a strength rather than otherwise.

When God is dead, the island population reverts to savagery, though he hovers invisible above the island. Prendick tells the Beasts: "For a time you will not see him. He is there—pointing upward—where he can watch you. You cannot see him. But he can see you."

Blame for the wretched state of the Beasts is set firmly on Moreau. "Before they had been beasts, their instincts fitly adapted to their surroundings, and happy as living things may be. Now they stumbled in the shackles of humanity, lived in a fear that never died, fretted by a law they could not understand."

At this moment, Wells is trying to create a synthesis between evolutionary and religious theory. Not to put too fine a gloss on it, he does not think highly of the Creator. Nor does he of the created. Moreau says it for Wells, declaring that he can "see into their very souls, and see there nothing but the souls of beasts, beasts that perish—anger, and the lusts to live and gratify themselves." There is that Biblical phrase which echoes in the opening of *War of the Worlds:* "beasts that perish." As for the two real humans, Prendick and Montgomery, they also are poor things. Prendick is certainly not there for us to identify with, any more than the Invisible Man is. His shallowness, his lack of understanding for Montgomery, his lack of sympathy for the Beasts, is perhaps a mark against the book—the darkness of any painting can be enhanced by a highlight here and there. Or perhaps it is just that Prendick is a commonplace little man, as Gulliver was a commonplace little man and Alice a commonplace little girl.

Moreau stands in an honourable line of books in which man is characterised as an animal. *Gulliver's Travels* is one of the best-known examples of the genre, and the one to which Wells paid homage, but such stories stretch back to the Middle Ages and beyond. Wells, however, revived the old tradition, gaining additional power because he and his audience were aware of evolutionary theory. They are the first generation to understand that it was no mere fancy as hitherto to regard man as animal; it was the simple betraying truth, and formalised religion began to decay more rapidly from that time onwards.

Prendick eventually returns to "civilisation," rescued from the island by a boat with dead men in it. His fears pursue him back to England. "I could not persuade myself that the men and women I met were not also another, still passably human, Beast People, animals half-wrought into the image of human souls; and that they would presently begin to revert, to show first this bestial mark and then that." The Leopard Man, *c'est moi.*

This is the final triumph of *Moreau;* that we are transplanted from the little island, only seven or eight square miles in extent—say about the size of Holy Island—to the great world outside, only to find it but a larger version of Moreau's territory. The stubborn beast flesh, the beast mentality, is everywhere manifest.

The ending has a sombre strength.† As with the climax of *War of the Worlds,* it comes not just as a surprise but as a logical culmination. Wells has subtly prepared us for it, so that it is revelation rather than punch line, for instance in his Hardyesque remark that

† Not least, one would imagine, for George Orwell, who may have found in the passage last quoted inspiration for what was later to become *Animal Farm.*

"A blind fate, a vast pitiless mechanism, seemed to cut out and shape the fabric of existence."

In this early novel, Wells amply fulfilled his conscious intentions. The exercise in youthful blasphemy worked. It is apparent that he also exorcised something that obsessed him during that period. Although *Moreau* is the darkest of his novels, it is not strikingly different in attitude from its companions. We find a horror of animality, an almost prurient curiosity about flesh, and the cultural shock of evolution stamped across all Wells' early science fiction. As the Beast-People are our brethren, so the Martians could be us at another stage of our development; while the Morlocks, that submerged nation in *The Time Machine* whose *vril* is flesh of Eloi—they are descended from us, our flesh could grow into such nocturnal things. "I grieved to think how brief the dream of human intellect has been," says the time-traveller.

The cannibalism practised by the Morlocks is paralleled by the flesh-eating of the Beast-People. Although the Invisible Man divests himself of flesh, he does not lose a vicious competitive streak. The Selenites of *The First Men on the Moon* are one long nightmare of distorted flesh; like the Morlocks, they live underground. They are forced into arbitrary shapes by social usage almost as cruelly as if they came under Moreau's scalpel. In *The Food of the Gods,* flesh runs amok—like *Moreau,* this novel, too, is in part an allegory of man's upwards struggle.

With a frankness remarkable for its time, Wells has told us much about his early sexual frustrations. He was a sensuous man and, with success and wealth, found the world of women open to him. It may be that this gradually assuaged his old obsessions; though he never achieved peace of mind, his later books do not recapture that darkly beautiful quality of imagination, or that instinctive-seeming unity of construction, which lives in his early novels, and in his science fiction particularly.

The rest of Wells' career must be looked at briefly, bearing in mind the question of why the hundred books that followed do not share the brilliance of the early handful.

As soon as Wells' public became accustomed to one Wells, up would pop another. There was *A Modern Utopia,* the last of the

great utopias and the first to realise that from now on, with improved communications, no island or continent was big enough to
hold a perfect state—it must be the whole world or nothing. Later,
he developed the idea of a World State. This was H.G. flexing his
Fabian and political muscles. *Tono-Bungay,* a social novel full of
autobiographical background material, and *Ann Veronica,* which
roused a great storm because the heroine practised free love, saw
publication in 1909. There were two gorgeous and sensible books
for children before the Great War broke out, *Floor Games* and *Little Wars.*

In 1914, just before the outbreak of hostilities, *The World Set
Free* was published. It contains some of the most amazing of Wells'
predictions, in particular of atomic warfare, but also—more accurately and horribly—of trench warfare. His speculations on tank
warfare had already appeared in a short story, "The Land Iron-
clads." We have seen how Wells' warfare books were written very
much in the *Battle of Dorking* tradition—yet he was remarkably
more successful in predicting what actually happened than his rivals, perhaps because he was no reactionary (as were most of the
rivals), and therefore tended less to view the future in terms of the
past; and also because he actually hated war (though with the ambivalent feelings many people experience) unlike such men as Le
Queux, who pretty clearly longed for it.

The World Set Free is full of shrewd preachments, exciting
home truths writ large, and radical diagnoses of human ills, all of
which made the book (novel it hardly is) exciting and immediate
at the time.

Here's Karenin in the future, when London is being cleared up
after extensive bombing. He is looking back and talking about a
1914 which bears resemblance to the 1970s.

> "It was an unwholesome world," reflected Karenin. "I seem
> to remember everybody about my childhood as if they were
> ill. They were ill. They were sick with confusion. Everybody
> was anxious about money and everybody was doing uncthe-
> nial things. They ate a queer mixture of foods, either too much
> or too little, and at odd hours. One sees how ill they were by
> their advertisements . . . Everybody must have been taking
> pills. . . . The pill-carrying age followed the weapon-carry-
> ing age . . ." (Chapter 5, 4)

The World Set Free is successful in every way but the ways in which the early Wells books were successful. It is full of lively ingredients; it has no organic life. Wells the One-Man Think-Tank has burst into view. His books are no longer novels but gospels.

After World War I, this more solemn Wells developed further into the Wells who produced solid and effective works of scientific popularisation and started the vogue for one-volume encyclopaedias. Wells was on the way to becoming the most popular sage of his day.‡ And he was still producing novels every year.

During the thirties, Wells the Novelist faded out before Wells the World Figure. He was a famous man, busily planning a better world, chatting with Lenin, arguing with George Bernard Shaw, flying to the White House to talk to Roosevelt, or to the Kremlin to talk to Stalin. Remembering the muddle of the London of his youth, he hated muddle, and saw a World State as the tidiest possible way of governing mankind for its own happiness.

Unlike Verne, he was never in danger of being blessed by the Pope.

Wells proved himself one of the few men capable of spanning the great gulf between the mid-Victorian period when he was born and our modern age. He had grasped the principle of change. He was a visionary and not a legislator, yet he worked for the League of Nations during World War I and, during the Second, helped draw up a Declaration of the Rights of Man which paved the way for the Universal Declaration of Human Rights adopted by the UN after Wells' death. He died in 1946, having witnessed the dropping of an atomic bomb he had predicted many years earlier.

To the Establishment, the idea of change is always anathema.** It never took Wells to its lordly bosom, just as it has never taken

‡ An edition of *The World Set Free* published by Collins in the twenties heralds Wells, on the cover, as "The most widely read author in the world."
** Wells' shrewd and uncomplaining view of this curious matter should be given, if only in a footnote. He speaks of "the supreme importance of individualities, in other words of 'character' in the fiction of the nineteenth century and early twentieth century. Throughout that period character-interest did its best to take the place of adjustment—interest in fiction. . . . It was a consequence of the prevalent sense of social stability. . . . Throughout the broad smooth flow of nineteenth-century life in Great Britain, the art of fiction floated on this same assumption of social fixity. The Novel in English was produced in an atmosphere of security for the entertainment of secure people who liked to feel established and safe for good. Its standards were established

science fiction, possibly for the same reason. It disliked him for the things he did best, and thought him a cad. So did the literati, perhaps with more reason, for Wells' ill-timed attack on his old friend Henry James in *Boon* (1915) was a poor thing, and most orthodox writers sided with James.

The literati still do not accept Wells to the sacred canon. In a volume such as Cyril Connolly's *The Modern Movement* (1965), which claims to list books "with the spark of rebellion," there is room for Norman Douglas and Ivy Compton-Burnett but none for Wells, except in an aside. However, some real writers, like Vladimir Nabokov, appreciate his true worth as innovator and creative spirit.

The current received idea of Wells seems to be that he began modestly and well as an artist (*The Time Machine* and all that) and then threw it all up for journalism and propaganda purposes.[10] There is a grain of truth in the charge. Many of his books were hastily written or scamped; he says himself, "It scarcely needs criticism to bring home to me that much of my work has been slovenly, haggard and irritated, most of it hurried and inadequately revised, and some of it as white and pasty in texture as a starch-fed nun."[11] What humility and honesty! Lesser writers today would not dare admit anything of the sort.

For all that, the facts do not entirely bear out either the received idea or Wells' own declaration (what writers say of themselves always should be greeted with scepticism). Wells began as a teacher and continued as one. He had a strong didactic example from his teacher, Thomas Huxley, one of the great controversialists of the century. For a while, in those earlier novels, Wells followed the doctrine of art for art's sake (then in favour with those writers and artists who were, like Wells, against the "done thing"); in that period, he took care to incorporate his central point into the imaginative whole. When he did so, when his point was so well integrated as not to be obvious, his audience misunderstood him or failed to get the point, as was the case with *Moreau, Invisible Man,* and *War of the Worlds.*

---

within that apparently permanent frame and the criticism of it began to be irritated and perplexed when, through a new instability, the splintering frame began to get in the picture.

"I suppose for a time I was the outstanding instance among writers of fiction in English of the frame getting into the picture." (Experiment in Autobiography, Chapter 7, 5)

Wells hated muddle and misunderstanding. He took to making the message clearer and clearer. His characters became mouthpieces, the fiction became lost in didacticism. The amplifiers were turned up. Wells gained volume and lost quality, but he was always a man with an amplifier, not content to whisper in corners. Indeed, the controversial nature of science fictional themes is such that only careful control—the control Wells found and lost—deflects the fantasy from the sermon.

Moreover, despite his fecundity and his joy in producing a different-coloured rabbit from his hat with each performance, Wells was consistent in his career. As early as 1912, he turned down an invitation to join the Academic Committee of the Royal Society of Literature. However much we may regret it, he wanted to deal with life, not aesthetics. Perhaps he failed to recognise that he was a creator, not an administrator. He could exhort but not execute. Eventually, the exhortations took over from the imagination.

Much of Wells' work has been filmed. *The Time Machine* was not filmed until 1960, in an indifferent version produced by George Pal for the MGM Studios. *The Island of Dr. Moreau* was filmed as *Island of Lost Souls* in 1932. Paramount made it with Charles Laughton as the doctor. Considerable liberties were taken with the story.

In the following year, Universal filmed *The Invisible Man* directed by James Whale, who made the original *Frankenstein*. Both Universal and Whale were full of expertise in the matter of horror, and the tricks of invisibility—for instance, the long grass crushed under unseen footsteps—were remarkable for their time. Claude Rains, unseen for most of the film, played Griffin. Universal made a sequel in 1940, with Joe May directing and Sir Cedric Hardwicke in the eponymous role. This was *The Invisible Man Returns*. The same year saw a saucy comic variation on the theme, *The Invisible Woman*, with the delightful Virginia Bruce revealing generous amounts of leg as she unexpectedly becomes visible again.

Paramount made *War of the Worlds* in 1953, with George Pal producing. The story was updated and the location shifted from England to California. The machines are altered radically, and the comic curate becomes one of the film's (incinerated) heroes. It is generally agreed that this is a successful sf film, criteria being low in the genre.

The British *First Men on the Moon*, made in 1964 and directed by Nathan Juran, was a poor thing, despite special effects by Ray Harryhausen and jovial performances from Lionel Jefferies and Edward Judd as Cavor and Bedford. There was an early version in 1919—the first of Wells' books to be filmed.

In 1936, two Wells films appeared, *The Man Who Could Work Miracles*, and *Things to Come* under Wells' supervision. Alexander Korda was in charge of production, William Cameron Menzies directed. A particularly fine musical score was provided by Arthur Bliss. The design of the film was stunning, while Raymond Massey and Ralph Richardson and the other actors did not allow themselves to be entirely dwarfed by the impressive sets, or a story that moved many years into the future. However shaky some of *Things to Come*'s ideas have proved (the reign of technocracy, for example), the film remains grand and striking, one of the classics of the cinema, and certainly Wells' best memorial there.

Many of his non-sf novels have also been filmed, among them *Love and Mr. Lewisham, Kipps* (a memorable performance from Michael Redgrave), *Ann Veronica,* and *The History of Mr. Polly. Kipps* also turned up as a musical entitled *Half a Sixpence* with Tommy Steele.

In October 1938, CBS broadcast an adaptation of *War of the Worlds.* This was an early venture in the career of young Mr. Orson Welles. So effective was the broadcast that a wave of hysteria swept the United States. Although consistently dismissed as nonsense, science fiction has always been effective on the "unknown fear" level, as was demonstrated on this occasion.

Wells did not change the world as he would have liked to do. He did alter the way millions of people looked at it. He was the first of his age to convey clearly that our globe is one, the people on it one—and the people beyond this globe, if they exist. He helped us understand that present history is but a passing moment, linked to distant past and distant future. It was Wells who said, "Human history becomes more and more a race between education and catastrophe." As the human race struggles and sinks beneath its own weight of numbers, we see how his words remain contemporary.

Perhaps a writer who views human history as a race between

anything and catastrophe is doomed to write hastily and carelessly, as Wells often did. Yet Wells was loved by men and women far beyond his personal acquaintance, far beyond the normal readership a novelist gathers if he merely has staying power. He was witty and honest, he spoke for his generation—and for more than one generation. George Orwell conveyed something of what a symbol H. G. Wells became:

> Back in the 1900s it was a wonderful thing to discover H. G. Wells. There you were, in a world of pedants, clergymen, and golfers, with your future employers exhorting you to "get on or get out," your parents systematically warping your sex life, and your dull-witted schoolmasters sniggering over their Latin tags; and here was this wonderful man who could tell you all about the inhabitants of the planets and the bottom of the sea, and who *knew* that the future was not going to be what respectable people imagined.[12]

Orwell was speaking of the beginning of the century. Thirty years later, as this writer can vouch, the same state of affairs held true. Wells was still at it, stirring everyone up. He saw that the one constant thing was change, and the dynamic for change that he found in the world about him was echoed in his own being; this accounts for his turning from one role to another, and from one woman to another.

He spread his energies widely. To regret that he did so is hardly profitable, for it was in his nature to do so.

Much of his activity has been dissipated. His novels remain. The science fiction is read more than ever.

Wells was born in the year dynamite was invented; he lived to witness the birth of the nuclear age. Inaccurately, Orwell characterised Charles Dickens' novels as "rotten architecture but wonderful gargoyles"; it is Wells' gargoyles, his Martians, the Selenites, the Morlocks, the Beast-People we most relish today, when Kipps and Polly grow faint. We may no longer accept Wells' faith in the improving potentialities of education, but we long ago conceded his point that we show "first this bestial mark and then that."

It is undeniable that if we compare Wells' novels with Dickens' most Wells-like novel, *Great Expectations* (assuming *Great Expectations* to be about Pip's escape from a menial life at the forge into the wider world of London!), then we are confronted with Wells' shortcomings as a novelist. But such a comparison would be unfair to almost any writer. Within his own wide domain, Wells was *sui generis*. Within the domain of scientific romance, he managed three unique achievements. He elevated the freak event —a visit to the Moon, an invasion from another planet—into an artistic whole. In consequence, he greatly extended the scope and power of such imaginings. And he brought to the genre a popularity and a distinctness from other genres which it has never lost since, despite the blunders of many following in his wake.

Wells is the Prospero of all the brave new worlds of the mind, and the Shakespeare of science fiction.

NOTES

1. H. G. Wells, *Experiment in Autobiography*, 2 Vols., 1934.

2. James to Wells, letter dated Rye, Nov. 19, 1905. The two books to which James refers are *A Modern Utopia* and *Kipps*. The letter, brimming with rare enthusiasm, is quoted in a biography by Vincent Broome, *H. G. Wells*, 1952.

3. A fair example is Bert Smallways, hero of *The War in the Air*. "Bert Smallways was a vulgar little creature, the sort of pert, limited soul that the old civilization of the early twentieth century produced by the million in every country of the world. He had lived all his life in narrow streets, and between mean houses he could not look over, and in a narrow circle of ideas from which there was no escape. He thought the whole duty of man was to be smarter than his fellows, get his hands, as he put it, "on the dibs," and have a good time. He was, in fact, the sort of man who had made England and America what they were." (Chap. 3)

4. For a thoroughgoing account of the reception of Wells' books as they were published, see Ingvald Raknem, *H. G. Wells and His Critics*, Oslo, 1962.

5. Bernard Bergonzi, *The Early H. G. Wells: A Study of the Scientific Romances*, Manchester, 1961.

6. *Experiment in Autobiography*, Chap. 6.

7. Mention should be made also of the good psychological timing of *War of the Worlds*. The new journalism was bringing word of the solar system to Wells' public, while Mars in particular was in the general

consciousness. It had been in close opposition in 1877, 1879, and 1881, and Percival Lowell's first book on Mars, containing speculations about the "canals" and possibilities of life there, had been published in 1895.

8. Wells does not mention himself as a second Camille Flammarion. The parallels between the great French astronomer's novel *La Fin du Monde* (published in 1893 and translated into eleven European languages) and Wells' *The Star* are striking. There is a discussion of this derivation and others in Raknem, *op. cit.*, Chap. 22.

9. *Experiment in Autobiography*, Chap. 8.

10. This assumption lies behind the otherwise sympathetic biography by Lovat Dickson, *H. G. Wells: His Turbulent Life and Times*, 1969.

11. *Experiment in Autobiography*, Chap. 1.

12. George Orwell, "Wells, Hitler, and the World State," *Critical Essays*, 1946.

6

The Flight from Urban Culture:
WELLS'S COEVALS

> Of all things human which are strange and wild
> This is perchance the wildest and most strange,
> And showeth man most utterly beguiled,
> To those who haunt that sunless City's range;
> That he bemoans himself for aye, repeating
> How time is deadly swift, how life is fleeting,
> How naught is constant on the earth but change.
>
> James Thomson: *The City of Dreadful Night*

As the nineteenth century drew to its close, the inhabitants of the congested cities of Europe and America found themselves increasingly in need of distraction. Not only religion but fiction also became the opium of the people. Sf is the hard stuff of fiction.

In Wells' heyday, there was a literary revolution taking place of fully as much importance as the paperback revolution of the nineteen-fifties. Wells and his contemporaries were fortunate; they enjoyed expanding markets where new journals and periodicals were springing up every week, catering to a new reading public. Disraeli's submerged nation was coming up for air.

This was the age when many of the great newspapers were founded, and with them the fortunes of their proprietors. In London, this was the day of Newnes, Pearson, and Northcliffe. Among his other good and profitable works, George Newnes started the first modern magazine, the *Strand,* in 1890.

The new literate and semi-literate public devoured newsprint. The number of novels published in England in 1870, the year of Dickens' death, was 381; by the turn of the century, it had swollen to over two thousand. This tremendous increase is traditionally ascribed to the Education Act of 1870. In fact, a similar, though proportionately smaller, increase in novels published may be noticed at the end of the eighteenth century*; while in the eighteen-fifties, Railway Library and Yellow Back novels were exploiting a poor and less cultivated reading public.

In the United States, the dime novel flourished. Among its proliferating numbers was a series still cherished by hard-case sf fans, the futuristic adventures of "Frank Reade, Jr.," written by one Luis P. Senarens, an industrious hack who turned out some forty million words in thirty years. Senarens, who used many pen names, certainly started one enduring sf tradition—of sending first drafts out uncorrected to the printer. Following "Frank Reade, Jr.'s," success came the "Tom Swift" series, many written pseudonymously by H. R. Garis. The arrival of the pulps gradually forced the dime novel out of existence, as the slicks later forced out the pulps, and paperbacks the slicks.

The great spate, the torrent of modern publishing, was in motion. New publishers, new magazines, new writers! It is hardly surprising that many authors regarded their potential audience as merely one to be exploited. It is evident, then as now, that the authors most eager to write for the quick buck are the ones most easily exploited by publishers.

A diversity of publications meant a diversity of themes, and a slow stepping up of the luridness of the content, as well as the emergence of a type of modern power fantasy which has less to do with the conditions of life than the fairy story, traditionally a cautionary form. We call such fantasy "escapism." It relates to daydreaming and is found in its purest form in areas which border closely on science fiction. Its appearance has bedevilled the history, the criticism, and the writing of science fiction ever since.

In this chapter, we are concerned with some of the fantasy and science fiction writers who were active between the 1890s and the 1920s. The main characteristic of their work lies in its embodiment of a wish to escape from claustrophobic urban culture.

At the same time, the escape is often shown to be the proverbial one, from frying pan into fire. It's nice to get away for a quiet weekend in the Amazonian jungle—where the ferocious

---

* The *Monthly Review* for 1796 notices twice as many novels as in 1795. By 1800, novels were so numerous and so bad that some magazines (e.g. *Scots* and the *Gentleman's Magazine*) ceased to notice them at all.

Stone Age tribes will capture you! Such seems to be the moral of Conan Doyle's *Lost World,* typical of its time.

The other characteristic tale of the period is the one that deals with war—often the real war that came about in 1914, but sometimes a war against nations in the Far East. War, too, is an escape from personal responsibilities and problems.

Such escapes represent a way of dealing with man's anxieties about his ability to cope with day-to-day existence. Some of the authors we are going to talk about, from Rider Haggard onwards, express a common anxiety about death. Fantasy painlessly lets us acknowledge our deepest fears, of inadequacy or death or whatever it may be; science fantasy lets us acknowledge more recent cultural fears, as androids often symbolise a fear of depersonalisation.

Even a "teller of tales" such as Robert Louis Stevenson produced a disturbing allegory of modern consciousness in *Dr. Jekyll and Mr. Hyde.* Between 1890 and 1920, we find a sort of neutral time zone, where tale-telling has no particularly focussed infrastructure of significant new myth, except in the earlier works of Wells; that is to come. On the Western shores of the Atlantic, the British appear to be forgetting their obsession with submerged nations—again, except for Wells. While on the Eastern shores, the Americans have not yet become obsessed with the vanished Red Indian, who will later return to haunt their science fiction.

Even of such a neutral period, one appreciates the force of what Susan Sontag has said of sf as a life-normalising agent. It is true that her statement was made with reference to the sf film; yet it seems to me one of the most effective—in its deliberately refraining from claiming too much or too little—explanations ever made of the function of science fiction:

> Ours is indeed an age of extremity. For we live under continual threat of two equally fearful, but seemingly opposed, destinies: unremitting banality and inconceivable terror. It is fantasy, served out in large rations by the popular arts, which allows most people to cope with these twin spectres. For one job that fantasy can do is to lift us out of the unbearably humdrum and to distract us from terrors—real or anticipated—by an escape into exotic, dangerous situations which have last-minute happy endings. But another of the things that fantasy

can do is to normalise what is psychologically unbearable, thereby inuring us to it. In one case, fantasy beautifies the world. In the other, it neutralises it.

The fantasy in science fiction films does both jobs. The films reflect world-wide anxieties, and they serve to allay them. They inculcate a strange apathy concerning the processes of radiation, contamination, and destruction which I for one find haunting and depressing. The naive level of the films neatly tempers the sense of otherness, of alien-ness, with the grossly familiar. In particular, the dialogue of most science fiction films, which is of a monumental but often touching banality, makes them wonderfully, unintentionally funny . . . Yet the films also contain something that is painful and in deadly earnest.[1]

Deadly earnestness, between 1890 and 1920, was not greatly in favour. The heroes are strong and serious and good. But by and large the crises in which they are involved concern only their own immediate circle and not the great globe itself; their job is to save themselves and not the world. And this they frequently do with more than a swash of their gleaming buckles. Action is the thing. RLS is more of an influence than LSD.

Dr. Jekyll and Mr. Hyde, that strange tale which has gained power since the dark star of psychoanalysis rose over the horizon, is something of a sport in Stevenson's output. Stevenson's main influence was as a romancer. The impact of his *Treasure Island* (in book form in 1883) and *Kidnapped* (1886) is reflected in the novels of his contemporaries—in Henry Rider Haggard's *King Solomon's Mines* and its successors; in Anthony Hope's *Prisoner of Zenda* and its sequel, *Rupert of Hentzau;* and in the once popular novels of Stanley Weyman, such as *Under the Red Robe.* Also of the nineties are Conan Doyle's early historical novels such as *The White Company,* and Doyle's greatest creation, the unlikely but mesmeric Sherlock Holmes, issuing from his fog-swathed lodgings in Baker Street.

On a different level, William Morris published *The Wood Beyond the World* in 1895 and *The Well at the World's End* in the following year. These are fantasies of an imaginary Middle Ages, the Middle Ages with none of the grossness of that period and all of the anaemic grace of the paintings of Morris' friend, Burne-

Jones. *The Wood Beyond the World* belongs to the tushery school
("She said, in a peevish voice: 'Tush, Squire, the day is too far
spent for soft and courtly speeches; what was good there is naught
so good here.'" Chapter 14), and has recently been hailed as "the
first great fantasy novel ever written."[2]

Also in mid-decade, Rudyard Kipling published his two *Jungle
Books*. These, and Kipling's vision of India in his short stories and
(later) *Kim*, and the other colourful tales and genres, all contain
elements which were soon to be incorporated into science fiction.
Exotic territories ruled over by exotic women, remote countries
contested by doubles, quests for kingdoms, pretty uniforms, mad
adventures, hard riding, talking animals—not to mention a sackful
of latter-day tushery—all could be accommodated within the happy
hunting grounds of later science fantasy.

One of this group of romantic writers was to have an influence on
science fantasy at least as strong as Wells'. As we have seen, Wells'
was an analytical fiction, not the sort of thing craved by broad
public taste. To satisfy that, brave and good heroes, stirring exploits and pageantry, and an escape from the prodromic troubles
of the present (Wells' hunting grounds) were needed—and it was
these ingredients that Rider Haggard (1856–1925) supplied in
abundance, staging them far from the overcrowded cities of London
and New York.

Paradoxically, Haggard himself never wrote science fiction,
unless one counts the posthumously published *Allan and the Ice-
Gods* (1927), Haggard's version of the Ice Age. As a young man,
he went to South Africa as secretary to Sir Redvers Bulwer, the
governor of Natal; there he came to know the country which
provides the background for the best of his long string of romantic
novels.

The first of these novels was written as the splendidly unlikely
outcome of a shilling bet with his brother that he could write a
better book than Stevenson's *Treasure Island*. It was published in
1885—*King Solomon's Mines*—an immediate and striking success.
Like Kipling, and unlike his imitators of later date, Haggard knew
whereof he spoke, and the best of his novels, like *She* and *Allan
Quatermain*, still have vigour, even if the mood of our times has
turned against them.

Haggard had a vivid and curious imagination. The horrific scene in *She* (1887) in which the immortal Ayesha bathes herself in life-giving flame and then dies when it fails her—dies and dwindles to a ghastly thing—echoed through science fiction for many years (see, for instance, the last chapter of John Russell Fearn's *The Golden Amazon*, 1944): "She, who but two minutes gone had gazed upon us—the loveliest, noblest, most splendid woman the world has ever seen—she lay still before us, near the mass of her own dark hair, no larger than a big ape, and hideous—ah, too hideous for words!" The corpse is referred to as "the little hideous monkey frame."

Richard Kyle, in a critical essay, has this to say of this famous passage: "Pale Ayesha . . . died after two thousand years of life, turned into a large and ancient ape—even as Haggard's generation saw divine, God-created Man dying with the birth of evolution, after two thousand years of Christianity, leaving behind only a large and ancient ape."[3] Kyle presents a convincing argument for deriving some of the substance of Burroughs' early Mars books from *She* and *Cleopatra*.[4] From Haggard on, crumbling women, priestesses, or empresses—all symbols of women as Untouchable and Unmakeable—fill the pages of many a scientific "romance."

Haggard is remembered. Edwin Lester Arnold is forgotten. But that is not entirely true; in the sf field, nobody is ever totally forgotten, not even Otis Adelbert Kline.

It is true to say that the fame of Edwin Lester Arnold (1857–1935) was eclipsed by the fame of his father, the Sir Edwin Arnold whose much reprinted *Light of Asia* brought Buddhism into many an antimacassared Anglican home. The son wrote two novels on the theme of reincarnation, *Phra the Phoenician* (1891) and *Lepidus the Centurion* (1901), in both of which souls journey across the centuries. Mysticism, like crumbling women, is something close to sf's adolescing heart, and we shall meet it again. Roger Lancelyn Green calls *Lepidus* "a far finer book,"[5] but *Phra* has its merits, and the story of the Phoenician trader who survives to chat with Good Queen Bess is told in appropriate language:

> So I was a prisoner of the Romans, and they bound me, and left me lying for ten hours under the side of one of their stranded ships, down by the melancholy afternoon sea, still playing with its dead men, and rolling and jostling together in its long green fingers the raven-haired Etrurian and the pale, white-faced Celt. (Chapter 1)

Which stands comparison with similar imagery in Tourneur's Jacobean plays.

Phra was reprinted in *Famous Fantastic Mysteries* for September 1945, and nobody seemed to find it incongruous.

Reincarnation also awaited Arnold's third novel (after which he gave up): *Lieut. Gulliver Jones: His Vacation,* published in 1905, and destined to lie fallow until Richard Lupoff discovered it in 1963 and persuaded Donald Wollheim of Ace Books to publish it, in its first American edition, as *Gulliver of Mars.*

It is a delightful book. Jones gets to Mars by wish and magic carpet, and finds there a gentle race, not quite male or female, which lives in the ruins of a long-decayed civilisation, not unlike the Eloi in *The Time Machine.* They, too, are threatened by a submerged nation. Their Morlocks are the dreaded Thither-folk, who descend every so often to extract goods and lovely slave girls from the decadent culture. The beautiful princess whom Jones is going to marry is carried off by the nasty ape-like Ar-hap. Jones, in true fairy tale fashion, sets off to rescue her.

Even today—but why the "even," for in the dream worlds of sf nothing changes?—passages of Arnold's book come over with amazing force. Here's what he sees when he is cast upon an alien shore:

> All the opposite cliffs, rising sheer from the water, were in light, their cold blue and white surfaces rising far up into the black starfields overhead. Looking at them intently from this vantage-point I saw without at first understanding that along them horizontally, tier above tier, were rows of objects, like— like—why, good Heavens, they were like men and women in all sorts of strange postures and positions! Rubbing my eyes and looking again I perceived with a start and a strange creepy feeling down my back that they *were* men and women!—hundreds of them, thousands, all in rows as cormorants stand upon sea-side cliffs, myriads and myriads now I looked about, in every conceivable pose and attitude but never a sound, never a movement amongst the vast concourse.
>
> Then I turned back to the cliffs behind me. Yes! they were there too, dimmer by reason of the shadows, but there for certain, from the snowfields far above down, down—good Heavens! to the very level where I stood. There was one of

them not ten yards away half in and half out of the ice wall, and setting my teeth I walked over and examined him. And there was another further in behind as I peered into the clear blue depth, another behind that one, another behind him— just like cherries in a jelly.

It was startling and almost incredible, yet so many wonderful things had happened of late that wonders were losing their sharpness, and I was soon examining them almost as coolly as though it were only some trivial geological "section," some new kind of petrified sea-urchins which had caught my attention and not a whole nation in ice, a huge amphitheatre of fossilised humanity which stared down on me. (Chapter 14)

A whole nation in ice! Arnold's picture is reminiscent of an Yves Tanguy or a Max Ernst canvas. Lupoff argues convincingly that this novel was the formative influence on Burroughs' Mars.[6] Is this derivation correct, or is Kyle's, through *She*? Perhaps the answer is that neither are incorrect. All fantasy ideas are amazingly alike; no man is an island—and that applies with especial force to writers.

At this juncture, it is as well to remind ourselves that the real Mars was, at the end of the last century, a striking and mysterious object for speculation, just as quasars are in our time—though Mars was certainly much more accessible than quasars, with respect both to proximity and popular comprehension. When the Red Planet was in opposition in 1877, 1879, and 1881, the Italian astronomer G. V. Schiaparelli made studies and charts of its surface. Schiaparelli noted straight lines running across the surface, which he labelled *"canali"*—a word generally meaning "channels." Translated into English as "canals," it started a whole new train of thought . . .

The canals were confirmed by French astronomers in 1885 and, a few years later, the American Percival Lowell built his famous observatory at Flagstaff, Arizona, in order to study Mars and its mysterious features. Lowell, too, saw the canals, and firmly believed that Mars was the abode of life. His two books, *Mars* (1895) and *Mars and Its Canals* (1906), aroused considerable interest. Lowell perhaps raised a red gleam in the eyes of Wells and Arnold; Percy Greg's *Across the Zodiac*, however, predates Lowell's books.

Across the Zodiac was published in 1880. It is possibly the first interplanetary journey to be made by spaceship. Like Verne, Percy

Greg produces painstaking facts and figures for his remarkable craft. It even carries a rudimentary hydroponic system to recycle air, and boasts walls of metal three feet thick. The space travellers find an advanced civilization on Mars, with polygamy and atheism being the established thing, and apathy well set in. The plot involves an underground subversive movement in which the narrator, by marrying a Martian woman, Eveena, becomes entangled. Eveena is killed, and the hero comes back to Earth, brokenhearted.

Greg's ship was powered by a mysterious force called "apergy." The same driving force is used on the interplanetary trips featured in *A Journey in Other Worlds* (1894) by John Jacob Astor. In order to escape the monotony of the utopian Earth of the year A.D. 2000, a venturesome party visits Jupiter and Saturn. The former is equipped with the giant reptiles of prehistory, whereas the latter contains spirits, and the travellers enjoy some Biblical experiences. Perhaps Astor was undecided between the rival attractions of *The Descent of Man* and the Old Testament.

Under the pen name George Griffith, G. C. G. Jones wrote a number of inventive and popular science fiction novels on warlike themes. *The Angel of the Revolution* appeared in 1893, with a sequel, *Olga Romanoff*, in the following year. This features a colossal power struggle, in which a British-German alliance is saved from defeat by a French-Russian alliance through the intervention of the Americans. However, a successor of the last Czar stages a comeback, and is about to take over the world when a passing comet burns almost everyone to a cinder. Other novels by Griffith include *The Great Pirate Syndicate* (1899) and—in a much more peaceful vein—*A Honeymoon in Space* (1900), in which the newlyweds sing "Home Sweet Home" and "Old Folks at Home" to the angels who live on Venus.

"Grant Allen and I were in the tradition of Godwin and Shelley," said Wells.[7] Grant Allen was a Darwinian. Like Wells, he used the future to mirror the evils of the present, and his *The British Barbarians* (1895) presents a scientist from a distant future working as an anthropologist among a savage tribe in an English suburb, as he investigates the current shibboleths on class, sex, property, and creed. Grant Allen's best-known novel is *The Woman Who Did*, also published in 1895, about a woman who bears and cares for an illegitimate child—a daring theme at the time, which may have moved Wells towards the writing of *Ann Veronica*.

The name of Frank Stockton grows faint, but still rings pleas-
antly, mainly because of one clever and teasing short story, "The
Lady or the Tiger." His novel *The Great Stone of Sardis* was published in 1897. It is based on the remarkable premise that there was
once a comet consisting of a huge diamond. It was captured by the
Sun, whereupon the surface of the diamond burnt to ashes and became soil; the main body of the diamond became the Earth. Twentieth-century men bore down beneath the crust and find the great
diamond still intact. Stockton's work, as one encyclopaedia puts it,
"was very unequal in interest."

Also in 1897, a thousand-page novel was published in Germany: *Auf Zwei Planeten* (*On Two Planets*), by Kurd Lasswitz. It
became very popular and was translated into several European
languages, although its translation into English had to wait until
1971. As in *The War of the Worlds*, appearing serially in the same
year, Martians land on Earth—at the North Pole. They capture two
Earthmen and take them back to Mars. Lasswitz' Martians are
much more humane than the Wellsian variety. Prettier, too. La,
daughter of the engineer Fru, has large eyes, which change colour,
and hair of "a reddish shimmering blonde like that of a tea-rose."
When she first appears, she is having trouble with Earth gravity.

> Leaning against the railing, she moved with difficulty as
> if she were bent under a heavy burden. She winced with pain
> when her foot touched the next lower step with a desperate
> thump. Then with as much pain and difficulty she passed
> through the corridor, leaning always with her hands on the
> railing. Now she touched the door, which seemed to roll itself
> open without a noise.[8]

Mass slaughter does not appeal to the Martians—although they
don't draw the line at wiping out the British Navy. After several
forays they establish a world state, with Martians and Earthmen
working together. Of this book, the Austrian critic Franz Rottensteiner says appositely, "The writing is plausible, with the role of
individual people not being ridiculously exaggerated as in many
later works of science fiction"[9]—thereby putting his finger on the
weakness of much current sf.

M. P. Sheil was an Irishman who also exploited the obsession
with war. *The Yellow Danger* was published in 1898, after being
serialised. It tells, as the title so subtly hints, of a menace out of

Asia, which wipes out half the world before being wiped out itself by the inscrutable British, who thus become rulers of the world. Sheil still has a faithful band of followers. He was scarcely the worst writer in the field—the competition for that honour being too fierce—but his prose is prize-winningly grotesque.

As a brimming maiden, out-worn by her virginity, yields half-fainting to the dear sick stress of her desire—with just such faintings, wanton fires, does the soul, over-taxed by the continence of living, yield voluntary to the grave, and adulterously make of Death its paramour.

This is a sentence, not from *The Yellow Danger,* but from one of M. P. Sheil's short stories, entitled, appropriately enough, "The S.S." If ever there was a fascist, Sheil was he. He was as violently anti-Semitic as he was anti-Asian. If ever there was a dangerous vision, in the full sense of that sometimes misapplied term, it is contained in "The S.S." The eponymous Society of Sparta is murdering thousands of people all over the world, in order to make the race eugenically pure, taking what the author terms "very moderate pains" to obliterate those with any disease or disability whom medical science has spared. "Less death, more disease"; that is the motto. This farrago is wrapped up in purple prose and in a nonsense cypher which strives to outdo Poe, and is not readily accessible to sense.

Small surprise that Sheil's most readable novel, *The Purple Cloud* (1901), adapts Mary Shelley's theme of the Last Man. Sheil's last man bears the throat-clearingly significant name of Adam. He sets out from the North Pole in a world full of corpses embalmed by the gas which killed them off, rejoicing in his solitude and setting fire to cities now and then, Calcutta, Peking, San Francisco. . . . For a writer as strange as Sheil there was perhaps no recourse open but to science fiction!

The last figure in our nineties gallery is an astronomer, Garrett P. Serviss. His *Edison's Conquest of Mars* was serialised in *The New York Evening Journal* in 1898, and only reached book form in 1947. In it, the inventor, Thomas Alva Edison, with other scientists, builds a fleet of spaceships and sets forth to *strafe* the Martians for daring to invade Earth, as related by H. G. Wells.

Over in France, Wells' old rival for the young imagination,

Jules Verne, was still writing—although, like the century itself, he was now past his best.

And when the century changed, it affected very little but calendars. The twentieth century was, for well over half its length, to prove but the nineteenth in extension, sharing magnified versions of its problems and triumphs. And its science fiction.

One immediate effect of World War I on fiction was to kill dead the future-war story—though resurrection came with the thirties. Men like William le Queux were put out to grass, although in 1906 he is still going strong with *The Invasion of 1910*, later highly successful in book form.

The Germans invade again. Aided by maps and proclamations, Le Queux relates the progress of the war until the all-conquering German armies take London. The Kaiser sends a telegram to his commander in chief: "Your heroic march, your gallant struggle to reach London, your victorious attack and your capture of the capital of the British Empire, is one of the greatest feats of arms in all history."

It would be wrong to suggest that Le Queux just petered out when the war he had so often dreamed of came about (and proved so much less fun than it had done in imagination). He went on writing,[10] and among his daunting output are such titles as *Tracked by Wireless* and *The Voice from the Void*.

Many stories such as Le Queux' can be seen to play upon the jingoism, fears, and prejudices of the peoples involved. Better and more lasting examples of the obsession with war are H. G. Wells' *The War in the Air* (1908), in which Bert Smallways, "a vulgar little creature," becomes involved with a mighty German fleet of airships which destroys New York; Wells' prophetic *The World Set Free* (early 1914); Conan Doyle's short story, "Danger" (published in the *Strand Magazine* just one month before hostilities broke out in Europe), which predicted submarine warfare, with merchant ships being sunk until food supplies give out and Britain sues for peace; and H. H. Munro's *When William Came*, published late in 1913, a few months before William (the Kaiser) actually started to march. Slightly earlier than these novels is a remarkable novel pitched in a different key, Erskine Childers' *The Riddle of the Sands*, published in 1903.

The Riddle of the Sands, as its subtitle says, is "A Record of

Secret Service." There are superb passages in it, and a great feel for
the pleasures of sailing and the open air, as well as a well-founded
German invasion plot which is gradually unravelled. Childers reads
like the precursor of Buchan, which he was; his book became a
minor classic, still being reprinted in the thirties. It was reprinted in
England in hard-cover in 1972.

When William Came is a pungent tale of German occupation
of Britain, as much domestic as military in tone. H. H. Munro is
better known by his pseudonym, "Saki," under which he wrote
many spiky and clever short stories in the Edwardian era—stories
which enjoyed a long vogue. By 1913, though only forty-three, his
literary career was in the main behind him. He enlisted in the Army
when war came, and was shot in the trenches on the Western Front
in 1916. His apotropaic vision had not preserved him from evil,
and it remains a debatable question whether talking about or preparing for such a dire event as war averts it or merely hastens its
fulfilment.[11]

Future wars apart, one receives the generalised impression that the
period was a welter of variously coloured plagues, invisible airships,
mysterious civilisations under volcanoes, poisonous clouds of gas,
new versions of the Flood, bouts of immortality, and Mars splitting
in two; while only slightly nearer to reality are the warnings about
New York being destroyed, socialism taking over, women ruling
the world, radium power bringing the millennium, and a transatlantic tunnel being built.

Some of the authors of the period still have a faithful, if ageing,
band of followers. Konrad Lorentz has shown how young ducklings
become imprinted by their mother's image at a certain tender age
(when even a false mother would do the trick), after which they
can accept no substitutes for her, and the same effect is observable
in many species, not excluding our own; tastes in the arts may be
formed in this way. It is hard to understand otherwise the furore
that greeted the early works of Merritt, Lovecraft, and Otis Adelbert Kline. Nevertheless, these and other authors had their audiences, often to be numbered in millions, and they do repay a closer
look.

A few of the better authors who wrote some science fiction
made their reputations in other fields.

Among them is numbered Rudyard Kipling, with such stories

as *With the Night Mail* (1905), a glimpse of the world of the year 2000, in which flying has become so important that the A.B.C. (Aerial Board of Control) rules the world. A sequel, *As Easy as A.B.C.* (1912), continues the same theme, showing how it develops, with the A.B.C. ruthlessly trying to maintain law and order. In general terms, Kipling's fancy was not incorrect: international scheduled flying has changed the world, just as scheduled railway services changed it in the 1830s and 1840s.

G. K. Chesterton, that master of paradox, wrote a number of fantasies, among which the best-known and most enjoyable is *The Man Who Was Thursday* (1908), a story of a group of anarchists who have been interpenetrated entirely by detectives until no anarchists are left. The narrative itself is free-flowing and ingenious.

> Syme was increasingly conscious that his new adventure had somehow a quality of cold sanity worse than the wild adventures of the past. Last night, for instance, the tall tenements had seemed to him like a tower in a dream. As he now went up the weary and perpetual steps, he was daunted and bewildered by their almost infinite series. But it was not the hot horror of a dream or of anything that might be exaggeration or delusion. Their infinity was more like the empty infinity of arithmetic, something unthinkable, yet necessary to thought. Or it was like the stunning statements of astronomy about the distance of the fixed stars. He was ascending the house of reason, a thing more hideous than unreason itself. (Chapter 9)

Not science fiction, perhaps, yet nearer to science and rationality than the science fantasy which is the hallmark of the period. Chesterton's *The Napoleon of Notting Hill* (1904), a novel of revolution, his clever short stories, "The Club of Queer Trades" (1905), and the better-known Father Brown stories, beginning with "The Innocence of Father Brown" (1911) are all related by their ingenuity and exuberance to science fiction, particularly science fiction in its Carrollian aspect.

Conan Doyle's science fiction belongs to this period: *The Lost World* was serialised in 1912, while *The Poison Belt* appeared the year after. There are other, later, novels which pass for science fiction (*The Land of Mist, The Maracot Deep*), but it is the earlier two which are remembered with pleasure. There are also some short stories, of which the most reprinted is "When the World

Screamed," in which the thrusting Professor George Challenger penetrates the Earth's crust to pierce living matter below.

The Poison Belt is a tepid performance, much under Wells' influence. Challenger and Co. spend a night sipping oxygen while the Earth ploughs through toxic interstellar gas. Next morning, the whole world is dead, and the surviving party tours a picturesquely deserted London that we shall meet again in *The Day of the Triffids* and elsewhere. But it turns out that the gas induced not death but catalepsy; people revive, and everything returns to normal. After the 1914–18 war, such meek reversions to the prosaic would no longer be possible.

Like Doyle's more famous creation, Sherlock Holmes, Professor Challenger is an unlikely and inhuman figure; but he does allow for a certain crispness in the dialogue.

Challenger is the first to diagnose what is about to happen. Gathering his friends about him in his house, he explains the threat poised by the gas in lofty terms:

> "You will conceive a bunch of grapes," said he, "which are covered by some infinitesimal but noxious bacillus. The gardener passes it through a disinfecting medium. It may be that he desires his grapes to be cleaner. It may be that he needs space to breed some fresh bacillus less noxious than the last. He dips it in the poison and they are gone. Our Gardener is, in my opinion, about to dip the solar system; and the human bacillus, the little mortal vibrio which twisted and wriggled upon the outer rind of the earth, will in an instant be sterilized out of existence."
>
> Again there was silence. It was broken by the high trill of the telephone-bell.
>
> "There is one of our bacilli squeaking for help," said he, with a grim smile. (Chapter 2)

The Lost World is one of the great adventure stories, to rank with the best of Rider Haggard's—to which it is probably indebted. Professor Challenger and his cronies find a mighty volcano in the Amazon basin, in the crater of which, isolated from the outside world, a fragment of prehistoric world has survived, Stone Age tribes, ape men, dinosaurs, and all. Doyle happened on the perfect setting for adventure.

Filmed more than once—most recently with Michael Rennie

negligently dropping half-smoked cigarettes into the jungle and exclaiming "There goes a Brontosaurus now" as a Stegosaurus lumbers by—*The Lost World* tells an exciting and imaginative story that no schoolboy in his right mind can resist. The atmosphere of the lost world is vividly conveyed, and its creatures gustily described, as we move towards the final battle when Challenger and Lord John Roxton lead "a host of the stone age" into victorious battle against the ape men. In the end, they escape from what Doyle by this time calls "a dreamland of glamour and romance," and return safely to London and Roxton's chambers in the Albany. Our feeling is very much that we have enjoyed the literary equivalent of a good hard game of Rugger before tea.

The last author we need name whose reputation was made beyond the science fantasy field is the redoubtable Jack London (1876–1916). There is something engaging in the story of this self-made man of letters, "at fifteen a man among men,"[12] to quote his own words. He lived hard, gulping down Washington Irving's *The Alhambra* and Ouida's novels while working on ranches, selling newspapers, becoming an oyster pirate, going seal-hunting in the Pacific, joining in the rush for gold in the Klondike and other characteristically American occupations of the period.

London was only forty when he died, his fifty-odd books all appearing during the last seventeen years of his life. Such books as *The Call of the Wild, White Fang, The People of the Abyss* (which is informed by London's strong socialist sympathies), and *The Sea Wolf,* many times filmed, were tremendously popular, and won him world-wide reputation. They contain something of London's own rough kindness, something of his imaginative and empathic response to life, and a lot of his vitality.

His place in the history of science fiction is secured by three books, among which the most eminent in reputation is a dystopian tale of future dictatorship, *The Iron Heel* (1907). Alas for reputation, *The Iron Heel* is hard to take today. Its honest sympathies with the poor and the oppressed are never in doubt, but they come clothed in clichés, with alternate spates of denunciation and sentimentality. "This delicate, aristocratic-featured gentleman was a dummy director and a tool of corporations that secretly robbed widows and orphans" (from Chapter 5), combines both modes.

London has no real vision of a future; his future is just the present and past, only more so.

Though time has not improved *The Iron Heel*, it still retains sporadic life, notably towards the end, where London's heroine, Avis, witnesses the revolt of the proletariat in Chicago. In a manner that brings to mind Dickens' revulsion for the mob in *Barnaby Rudge* and *A Tale of Two Cities*, Avis, loyal supporter of the popular struggle, suddenly sees the horde with fresh insight:

> The inner doors of the entrance were locked and bolted. We could not escape. The next moment the front of the column went by. It was not a column, but a mob, an awful river that filled the street, the people of the abyss mad with drink and wrong, up at last and roaring for the blood of their masters. I had seen the people of the abyss before, gone through its ghettos, and thought I knew it; but I found that I was now looking at it for the first time. Dumb apathy had vanished. It was now dynamic—a fascinating spectacle of dread. It surged past my vision in concrete waves of wrath, snarling and growing carniverous, drunk with whisky from pillaged warehouses, drunk with hatred, drunk with lust for blood—men, women, and children, in rags and tatters, dim, ferocious intelligences with all the godlike blotted from their features and all the fiendlike stamped in, apes, and tigers, anaemic consumptives and great hairy beasts of burden, wan faces from which vampire society had sucked the juice of life, bloated forms swollen with physical grossness and corruption, withered hags and death's heads bearded like patriarchs, festering youth and festering age, faces of fiends, crooked, twisted, misshapen monsters blasted with the ravages of disease and all the horrors of chronic malnutrition—the refuse and the scum of life, a raging, screaming, screeching, demoniacal horde. (Chapter 23)

London certainly knew how to pile on the agony. In *The Star Rover* (1915), the hero goes berserk and slays some two hundred seals. "Indeed, quite bereft was I of all judgment as I slew and continued to slay." (Chapter 19)

The Star Rover is an uneven book; its hero is Darrell Standing, whose soul can flip from one existence to another, reliving his past lives. He works his way back through one period of time to another, remembering such gods as Ishtar and Mitra, until he becomes a prehistoric man.

> I was Ushu, the Archer, and Igar was my woman and mate. We laughed under the sun in the morning, when our manchild and woman-child, yellowed like honey-bees, sprawled and rolled in the mustard, and at night she lay close in my arms and loved me and urged me, because of my skill at the seasoning of woods and the flaking of arrowheads, that I should stay close by the camp and let the other men bring me the meat from the perils of hunting. (Chapter 21)

Ouida was evidently a lasting influence.

This story is told within the framework of Standing's confinement to a strait jacket in a death cell in San Quentin, where a sadistic warden tortures him. He escapes from the torture by skipping back in time.

London himself had skipped back in time before this. His *Before Adam*, published in book form in 1906, is a story of the Stone Age. Again racial memory comes into it. A city child dreams he is Big-Tooth, growing up with the Cave People, braving the terrors of the past world. Anthropologists may find fault with many of the facts of London's reconstruction, but the book has a sort of wild lyric truth, and some of his guesses about prehistory still appear sound—for instance that inventions might come about through the necessities of old age; the use of gourds to store water is credited to old Marrow-Bone, who kept a store of water in his cave to save him visiting the stream; gourds had previously been mere playthings.

Big-Tooth himself had racial memory dreams.

> For Big-Tooth also had an other-self, and when he slept that other-self dreamed back into the past, back to the winged reptiles and the clash and the onset of dragons, and beyond that to the scurrying, rodent-like life of the tiny mammals, and far remoter still, to the shore-slime of the primaeval sea. I cannot, I dare not, say more. It is all too vague and complicated and awful. I can only hint of those vast and terrific vistas through which I have peered hazily at the progression of life, not upward from the ape to man, but upward from the worm. (Chapter 9)

Other writers before London had ventured into the neolithic world. H. G. Wells' forays have been mentioned. And there was Stanley Waterloo's *The Story of Ab* (1897), a romance of the uniting of paleolithic and neolithic cultures.

London was accused of plagiarism by Waterloo; but, from this time onwards, the sheer bulk of publication and the contemporaneousness of writers makes the question of plagiarism almost irrelevant (though in a field naturally dependant upon surprise and sensationalism, it remains an interesting question). At any time, there are common moods, currents of thought, even catchwords—"atavism" being one catchword that runs through the science fiction of this period and later—which give society a mysterious unity. The prospect of nuclear doom which transfixes the nineteen-fifties, the fascination with drugs in the late sixties and seventies: such general preoccupations are naturally reflected in the fiction of the period.

One general feeling which London's *Before Adam* reflects is the wish to escape from urban civilisation. Nowadays, drugs are a defeatist symbol of the same longing. At the beginning of the present century, that longing more healthily found refuge in the still untamed regions of Earth. Hence the success of Kipling's *Jungle Tales* and *Kim*, followed by the African tales of Edgar Wallace in *Sanders of the River*, and Edgar Rice Burroughs' Tarzan novels, also set in Africa. Hence, also, the success of Conan Doyle's *The Lost World*, which manages to get in a Stone Age civilisation as well as a remote region of Earth.

So we come to two writing prodigies of the period, one British, one American—Edgar Wallace and Edgar Rice Burroughs. Burroughs belongs far more centrally to the history of science fiction, and lords it over our next chapter. But Wallace has an honoured place, for his name, with Merian C. Cooper's, adorns the credits of the greatest monster-science-fiction movie of them all, *King Kong*. He was working on the script in Hollywood when death overtook him —a fittingly bizarre place in which to end his amazing career.

Wallace was born in the same year as Burroughs, 1875, the illegitimate son of an actress. He ran away to sea as a youth, soldiered in the Boer War, and worked as a reporter before beginning to write stories and plays. He had an immediate success with *Sanders of the River*.

He became tremendously prolific in middle age, writing one hundred and sixty-seven novels in fourteen years. The *Sanders of the River* stories, set in the Congo, were wildly popular, and based on firsthand knowledge of Africa. They ran from 1909 until well into the nineteen-twenties. Wallace also wrote some science fiction, such as *The Day of Uniting* (1926), a Wellsian tale about the threat of a large comet which, in its close approach to Earth, causes humanity to unite as never before. In 1929, he published *Planetoid 127*, about the discovery of a planet "on the far side of the sun"—the traditional location of the hypothetical planet Vulcan.

His main output was devoted to crime, his favourite locale the London underworld and the race track, which Wallace knew much better than Vulcan. His biographer relates how he stood for Parliament at the height of his success, and did not endear himself to his constituency by admitting in a public speech that one reason why he wanted to get into the House of Commons was that "a writer of crook stories ought never to stop seeking new material."[13]

During the most prolific period of his life, there was a joke current about the appearance of "the noonday Wallace." In England, in the late twenties, he became the second best seller after the Bible. He was made a chairman of British Lion Films, sometimes directing his own scripts from his own novels. A Rolls would wait outside the Carlton, London's most expensive hotel, in case he wished to go somewhere. He liked to live well, was magnificently generous, and enjoyed his success to the full.

It is estimated that Wallace's sales have probably topped twenty million, while some one hundred and ninety films have been made, silent and talkie, from his books and plays, in the United Kingdom, the United States, Germany (an especially faithful market) and elsewhere.[14] His biographer was guilty of no exaggeration when she called him a phenomenon. A phenomenon is a very different thing from a writer; but Wallace had his merits.

Among Edgar Wallace's successors is Ian Fleming, with his redoubtable hero, James Bond. Both these authors set their protagonists in the contemporary world, or a version of it, however fantastic the goings-on therein. Wallace's coeval, Burroughs, opted for the wide-open spaces, the remote. Burroughs utilises ruthlessly a wish to escape from city living which was only casually pressed to serve by RLS, Haggard, Doyle, and their ilk. When he arrives at his formula, the unique prescription of present-day sf is almost fulfilled.

NOTES

1. *Against Interpretation*, by Susan Sontag. The essay in which the quoted passage occurs, "The Imagination of Disaster," is included in *Science Fiction: The Future*, edited by Dick Allen, New York, 1971.

2. See cover of Ballantine's "Adult Fantasy" Edition, New York, 1969. C. S. Lewis' essay on Morris is worth reading.

3. Richard Kyle, "Out of Time's Abyss: The Martian Stories of Edgar Rice Burroughs, A Speculation," *Riverside Quarterly*, Vol. 4, No. 2.

4. *Ibid.*

5. Roger Lancelyn Green, *Tellers of Tales*, Chap. 14, 1965.

6. Lupoff's argument is presented in the Introduction to *Gulliver of Mars*, New York, Ace, N.D., and more fully in his *Edgar Rice Burroughs: Master of Adventure*, New York, Chap. 3, 1965. In the latter volume Lupoff argues that Burroughs derived Barsoom from *Gulliver of Mars* and the character of John Carter from *Phra*. Since neither Phra nor Carter has much in the way of character beyond muscle, this argument must remain open.

7. H. G. Wells, *Experiment in Autobiography*, Chap. 8.

8. Kurd Lasswitz, *Auf Zwei Planeten* (*On Two Planets*), a novel, translated by Hans H. Rudnick, Carbondale and Edwardsville, 1971. This brief extract gives some sample of its quality. An Afterword is provided by Mark Hillegas, who points to the continuing validity of Lasswitz' ideas, and speaks of their influence on German astronomical thought, and on the scientists and technicians at Peenemünde, the German base from which those proto-spaceships, the V-1's and V-2's, were launched at England in the closing stages of World War II.

9. Franz Rottensteiner, *"Kurd Lasswitz: A German Pioneer of Science Fiction,"* reprinted in *SF: The Other Side of Realism*, edited by Thomas D. Clareson, Bowling Green, Ohio, 1971.

10. "William Le Queux (who was born in 1864 and died in 1927) must have been one of the most prolific writers of all time. Edgar Wallace was hardly in the same class. I have sixty books of his on my shelves (with the imprints of fifteen different publishers) and I doubt

whether I have one book in four of his total output. All, he claimed, were written in his own hand: he never dictated or used a typewriter." Hugh Greene, *The Rivals of Sherlock Holmes*, 1970.

11. Such fears have been expressed over every armament escalation, such as the installation of ballistic-missile and missile defence systems. They occurred, too, to Erskine Childers. A note by M. A. Childers in a late edition of *The Riddle of the Sands* reads as follows: "Erskine Childers advocated preparedness for war as being the best preventive for war. During the years that followed, he fundamentally altered his opinion. His profound study of military history, of politics, and, later, of the causes of the Great War convinced him that preparedness induced war. It was not only that to the vast numbers of people, engaged in fostered war services and armament industries, war meant the exercise of their professions and trades and the advancements of their interests; preparedness also led to international armament rivalries, and bred in the minds of the nations concerned fears, antagonisms, and ambitions, that were destructive to peace." Admirably put!

12. "Jack London By Himself," used as Autobiographical Introduction to the 1963 edition of *The Star Rover*, New York, The Macmillan Company.

13. *Edgar Wallace: The Biography of a Phenomenon*, by Margaret Lane, 1938. Wallace is one of the few best-selling writers, or writers outside the world of established letters, whose life has been written in such literate terms.

14. Information kindly supplied and verified by Edgar Wallace's daughter, Mrs. Penny Halcrow.

7

To Barsoom and Beyond:

ERB AND THE WEIRDIES

> I glanced up to find the great orb still motionless
> in the centre of the heavens. And such a sun! I had
> scarcely noticed it before. Fully three times the size
> of the sun I had known throughout my life, and ap-
> parently so near that the sight of it carried the con-
> viction that one might almost reach up and touch it.
> "My God, Perry, where are we?" I exclaimed.
> "This thing is beginning to get on my nerves."
>
> Edgar Rice Burroughs: *At the Earth's Core*

Let's compare two novels published in book form in 1923. Both
qualify as science fiction. One was written by H. G. Wells, one by
Edgar Rice Burroughs.

In *Men Like Gods,* one of Wells' little men, a Mr. Barnstaple,
drives in his car into the fourth dimension, and there finds a utopia
of beautiful and powerful (and frequently nude) people. With
him is a diverse group of his contemporaries who do their best to
wreck the utopia. Barnstaple defeats them with utopian aid, and
eventually returns through the dimensional barrier, back to the
real world.

Pellucidar, after a brief prologue intended to establish the "reality" of what follows, is the story of a world at the hollow centre of

the Earth, the Inner World, where one David Innes searches for his lady love. He is reunited with her after many strange adventures, travelling through savage country populated by monsters and primitive creatures.

Described like this, the two novels sound not dissimilar. Both are fantasies, both use people as symbols, both have their excitements. Yet their differences are many.

The fourth dimension is perhaps as unlikely as a hollow earth, and Barnstaple's adventures no more probable than Innes'. However, Wells' fantasy device, the fourth dimension, serves merely to lead us to his utopia; the utopia is so much the thing, that the feasibility of the device which gets us there does not much matter, provided it is dealt with briefly and interestingly. On the other hand, Burroughs' Inner World is the whole story, and the narrative is largely taken up with the stones and arrows loosed there, and the fangs and claws bred there.

Burroughs' characters are exotic and bear strange and beautiful names, of which perhaps the best is Pellucidar itself. Barnstaple is allowed his handle "Mr." throughout, while the characters he is involved with are based on real politicians of the day, such as Balfour and Winston Churchill.

The action in *Men Like Gods* is leisurely, so that there is plenty of time for discussion, which mainly consists of contrasting our world unfavourably with utopia and airing Wells' ideas about world government. In *Pellucidar*, events move fast; one threat succeeds another, one scrape succeeds another; conversation is practically limited to threats, or to explanations of what has happened or is about to happen.

When Barnstaple returns in his battered old car to our world, it is a recognisable dull world of hotels with waitresses serving tea, the *Daily Express, The Times*, chat about Poland, the Chinese, and sport. Our world in *Pellucidar* is represented by a telegram from Algiers, the finding of a mysterious telegraphic instrument buried in the Sahara, a call to action!

In short, Wells' is a serious tale, enlivened by a little humour, whose main aim is to discuss entertainingly the ways in which mankind might improve himself and his lot. Whereas Burroughs' story is pure fantasy adventure which we do not for one minute take seriously.

The publishing history of the two novels is also interestingly in contrast. Wells' novel was published in hard-cover in 1923 and only achieved paperback publication forty-seven years later.[1] Burroughs' novel was serialised in *All-Story Cavalier Weekly* in 1915, to appear in hard-cover in 1923, since when it has made many paperback appearances.

Which of the two is the "better" book? If the question has any meaning, my answer would be that *Pellucidar* is the better. If one's choice of company lies between a fatigued schoolmaster and an inspired anecdotalist, one's better bet is the anecdotalist.

Burroughs, in this novel, writes about as well as he can write, which is not well but very serviceably, while his fertile imagination pours out lavishly the details of his preposterous world. Wells appears constipated beside him. Wells' novel is laborious, and, whatever it was in 1923, it takes an effort to read now, whereas Burroughs still slips down easily. With Burroughs you have (moderate) fun; Wells here gives off what Kingsley Amis categorises as "a soporific whiff of left-wing crankiness."[2]

So why does one obstinately respect Wells the more? It must be because, whatever else his failings, he is trying to grapple with what he sees as the real world, whereas Burroughs—however expertly, and he can be a mesmerist—is dishing out daydreams.

Linked with this is another important distinction between the sort of fiction the two men are writing. Wells does not expect anyone to identify with his stuffy little central character; Barnstaple is just an ordinary fellow, not held up particularly for approval or ridicule. The characters who surround him are mildly satirised, though not grotesque. And all this may account for the reason why Wells was never a popular author as popular authors go. Whereas all Burroughs' main characters can claim the old title "hero"—not only in the novels dealing with Pellucidar but in all the other Burroughs series, Tarzan's jungles, Napier's Venus, Carter's Mars. Burroughs wants us to identify, to sink into his dream countries and exclude the outside one. Barsoom is a million miles from Wessex.

Wells is teaching us to think. Burroughs and his lesser imitators are teaching us not to think.

Of course, Burroughs is teaching us to wonder. The sense of wonder is in essence a religious state, blanketing out criticism. Wells was always a critic, even in his most romantic and wondrous tales.

And there, I believe, the two poles of modern fantasy stand defined. At one pole stand Wells and his honourable predecessors such as Swift; at the other, Burroughs and his imitators, such as Otis Adelbert Kline, and the weirdies, horror merchants, and the Never-Never-Landers, such as H. P. Lovecraft, and so all the way to Tolkien. Mary Shelley stands somewhere at the equator of this metaphor.

At the thinking pole are great figures, although it is painfully easy to write badly; at the dreaming pole are no great figures—though there are monstrous figures—and it is terribly difficult to write well.

Although reading is for pleasure, one should try to be pleased by whatever can reward with the highest pleasure. A swimming pool is a poor place in which to swim when there is a great ocean near by.

Burroughs, in his proliferating series and titles, is one of the most commercially successful authors of this century, certainly the most commercially successful science fantasy author. His sales still grow. His influence has been immense, and often deadening.

It was Edgar Wallace's boast that he always kept his stories clean—by which he meant sex-free—however much blood was shed. Edgar Rice Burroughs could say the same.

The creator of Tarzan was born in the same year as the creator of King Kong, in 1875, in Chicago. As a young man, he enlisted in the U. S. Cavalry, and saw something of a West that was still wild, meeting men who had fought Sioux and Apache. Later, he was discharged, tried gold-prospecting, and then ran through a series of miserable jobs, including railroad cop and candy salesman. He was into his thirties, married and with a family to support, before he tried his hand at writing. His success was immediate.

Burroughs published some seventy books, fifty-nine of them during his lifetime. His world sales have probably topped one hundred million. His Tarzan character alone has appeared in countless films, comic strips, and comic books, and been imitated by other hands in countless variations.[3]

Eight years after writing his first story, Burroughs was able to purchase rolling acres and a press baron's palace near Los Angeles. This site is now the township known as Tarzana—the word made flesh, or at least bricks and mortar. When in his sixties, in World War II, Burroughs was appointed war correspondent and spent some while in Hawaii. When he died he left behind readers all over the world and a staunch body of fans known, proudly and collectively, as ERBdom, from the initials of their hero's name.

His first published story was a six-part serial, which ran in one of the grand old pulps, the *All-Story*, in 1912. This was *Under the Moons of Mars*, now better known under its later book title, *A Princess of Mars*. With this first effort, Burroughs brought the novel with an interplanetary setting into science fiction to stay.

Burroughs launched out on a series of interconnected novels set on the Red Planet, which was known to its inhabitants as Barsoom. *A Princess of Mars* was published in book form in 1917, soon to be followed by two sequels, *The Gods of Mars* (1918), and *The Warlord of Mars* (1919). As one of his more literate admirers puts it, "To the schoolboy in his early teens, Burroughs can open magic casements with the best . . . Those who read him at the right age owe a great debt of gratitude to Edgar Rice Burroughs" (Roger Lancelyn Green, *Into Other Worlds*).

Wafted by mystical and Blavatskian means across the gulfs of space, John Carter finds himself on Mars. In no time, he gets himself opposed to a great fifteen-foot-high Martian, green, four-armed, and sharp-tusked. Action and blood follow thick and fast in all Burroughs' books. A hasty ingenuity is his.

Yet the world of Barsoom, its history and geography, is painted in with a generous brush. Barsoom is dying, its seas drying, of the old civilisations little is left but ruin and deserted cities; its tribes, which vary in skin colour, are deadly enemies. In the first book Carter falls in love with the princess, Deja Thoris, a beautiful red woman. All Martian women are oviparous, although this does not stop them mating with Earthmen.

Here is a colourful passage where a company of green Martians and their animals, together with Carter and Deja Thoris, move across one of the dried-out sea beds:

> We made a most imposing and awe-inspiring spectacle as we strung out across the yellow landscape; the two hundred and fifty ornate and brightly coloured chariots, preceded by an advance guard of some two hundred mounted warriors and chieftains riding five abreast and one hundred yards apart, and followed by a like number in the same formation, with a score or more of flankers on either side; the fifty extra mastodons, or

heavy draft animals, known as zitidars, and the five or six hundred extra thoats of the warriors running loose within the hollow square formed by the surrounding warriors. The gleaming metals and jewels of the men and women, duplicated in the trappings of the zitidars and thoats, and interspersed with the flashing colours of magnificent silks and furs and feathers, lent a barbaric splendour to the caravan which would have turned an East Indian potentate green with envy.

The enormous broad tyres of the chariots and the padded feet of the animals brought forth no sound from the moss-covered sea bottom; and so we moved in utter silence, like some huge phantasmagoria, except when the stillness was broken by the guttural growling of a goaded zitidar, or the squealing of fighting thoats. The green Martians converse but little, and then usually in monosyllables, low and like the faint rumbling of distant thunder (from the chapter "Sola Tells Me Her Story").

This passage also shows Burroughs' carelessness—to speak of turning potentates green gives the game away, for this is clearly what he is doing, by transposing an Eastern sumptuousness to Mars. Nevertheless, the first three novels make an enormous paella of colour, mystery, and excitement for a hungry adolescent stomach.

Unfortunately, Burroughs could never resist ruining a good thing. The success of his trilogy of Martian novels led him to continue with more sequels, until we find him still spinning them out into the 1940s, with *Synthetic Men of Mars* and so forth. But Burroughs claimed never to write for anything but money.[4]

Tarzan of the Apes was Burroughs' second story. It was published in 1912, also in *All-Story*. It reflects to perfection the wish to escape from urban civilisation, where there are lousy jobs like railroad cop going.

Mystery surrounded John Carter's birth. Tarzan's origins provide a perfect invitation to daydreamers; in Burroughs' immortal words, "the son of an English lord and an English lady nursed at the breast of Kala, the great ape." Rousseau's Noble Savage has been ennobled. Tarzan is not only the great killer of the jungle; he is also Lord Greystoke, heir to a fortune in England, and the plot of his first Tarzan novel juggles effectively between these incongruities.

Is Tarzan science fiction? His ability to talk "apish" makes him a borderline case. But there is no doubt that he is a magnificently successful embodiment of fantasy; if the blood of Mowgli, child of the wolves, runs in his literary veins, then he in turn has fathered many fictional progeny, and must surely be accounted at least one of the godfathers watching over Tolkien's legions in Middle Earth.

ERB's reincarnation of noble savagery (bad ideas never die) came swinging through the trees onto cinema screens very early in his career. The first Tarzan movie was produced in 1917, since when ape man movies have proved more permanent on the screen than custard pies. At one time, Tarzan was played by Buster Crabbe, who then went on to the title role in Universal's Flash Gordon serials, inspired by Alex Raymond's elegant science fantasy strip. One of the most popular Tarzans was Johnny Weissmuller in the thirties. There was also a newspaper comic strip based on Burroughs' novels and scrupulously drawn by Hal Foster; this strip was later taken over by Burne Hogarth and other artists.

At first, Burroughs seemed genuinely interested in working out the complex, if fictional, problems which would confront a man with such a conflicting inheritance as Tarzan's. In *The Return of Tarzan*, these problems are already being laid aside in favour of a rather trite exposure of the decadence of civilisation compared with the ethical codes of the jungle. Already, duelling Frenchmen, beautiful Russian countesses, unsavoury Europeans, brutish black men, survivors of Atlantis, and lost treasure cities ruled over by lovely priestesses, are creeping in, until Africa bears about as much relationship to reality as does Barsoom.

Burroughs could resist anything but success.

Tarzan of the Apes was followed in time by some two dozen sequels, straggling on throughout ERB's career—and after! Tarzan also makes a guest appearance in a third series he was hatching at the same time as the first two, the Pellucidar series, which commenced with *At the Earth's Core*, first published as a serial in 1914.

The *donnée* of this series is that the Earth is hollow. Its inner lining supports a whole world of savage tribes and amazing creatures. This is Pellucidar. Pellucidar is lit by a miniature Sun burning in the centre of the hollow; the Sun has a small satellite revolving round it in a twenty-four-hour orbit. Inner Space indeed!

To enquire whether Burroughs derived this idea from Niels

Klim is idle, though the similarity of concepts is striking. The truth is, that when one is hard up for secret worlds, one can find them under the Earth, in a puddle, in an atom, up in the attic, down in the cellar, or in the left eyeball: and all of these vantage points have been explored by hard-pressed fantasists. Furthermore, we need no longer enquire whether extrapolations of Mars or Venus derive from such astronomers as Lowell or Arrhenius; for the generations of writers now close ranks and begin to derive their ideas from one another. This is known as a continuing debate.

David Innes, Burroughs' new hero, arrives in Pellucidar via a giant mechanical mole, boring down through the Earth's crust. There he undergoes a number of remarkable adventures which parallel fairly closely the crises, hairbreadth escapes, and cliff-hangers of Carter and Tarzan. Only the cliffs are different. Burroughs is in fine form in at least the first two novels in this series, *At the Earth's Core* (book form 1922) and *Pellucidar*, and something of his excitement and interest in creating a new world comes over.

Here is a passage from the first of the two novels, which shows, even in slight abridgement, the dextrous way Burroughs had of moving along from one exotic focus of interest to another, with a smoothness that perhaps no other fantasy writer has managed. David Innes and his friend Perry are taken to an arena to watch the punishment of two slaves—one a man, one a woman—to be held in an arena, and watched over by the ruling race, the Mahars:

> For the first time, I beheld their queen. She differed from the others in no feature that was appreciable to my earthly eyes, in fact all Mahars look alike to me; but when she crossed the arena after the balance of her female subjects had found their bowlders, she was preceded by a score of huge Sagoths, the largest I ever had seen, and on either side of her waddled a huge thipdar, while behind came another score of Sagoth guardsmen . . .
>
> And then the music started—music without sound! The Mahars cannot hear, so the drums and fifes and horns of earthly bands are unknown among them. The "band" consisted of a score or more Mahars. It filed out in the centre of the arena where the creatures upon the rocks might see it, and there it performed for fifteen or twenty minutes.
>
> Their technique consisted in waving their tails and moving

their heads in a regular succession of measured movements resulting in a cadence which evidently pleased the eye of the Mahar as the cadence of our own instrumental music pleases our ears. Sometimes the band took measured steps in unison to one side or the other, or backward and again forward—it all seemed very silly and meaningless to me, but at the end of the first piece the Mahars upon the rocks showed the first indications of enthusiasm that I had seen displayed by the dominant race of Pellucidar. They beat their great wings up and down, and smote their rocky perches with their mighty tails until the ground shook . . .

When the band had exhausted its repertory it took wing and settled upon rocks above and behind the queen. Then the business of the day was on. A man and woman were pushed into the arena by a couple of Sagoth guardsmen. I leaned far forwards in my seat to scrutinise the female—hoping against hope that she might prove to be another than Dian the Beautiful. Her back was toward me for a while, and the sight of the great mass of raven hair piled high upon her head filled me with alarm.

Presently a door in one side of the arena wall was opened to admit a huge, shaggy, bull-like creature.

"A Bos," whispered Perry excitedly. "His kind roamed the outer crust with the cave bear and the mammoth ages and ages ago. We have been carried back a million years, David, to the childhood of a planet—is it not wondrous?"

But I saw only the raven hair of a half-naked girl, and my heart stood still in dumb misery at the sight of her, nor had I any eyes for the wonders of natural history. (Chapter 6)

Again, Burroughs never knew when enough was enough. Six Pellucidar novels were published in his lifetime, and a seventh, *Savage Pellucidar* (1963), was cobbled together after his death. One of the six is *Tarzan at the Earth's Core* (1930).

In 1932, *Argosy* began to serialise the first novel in Burroughs' fourth major series. This time the setting is Venus. Carson Napier is a typical Burroughs hero, even down to some oddities surrounding his birth, for he was the son of a British army officer and an American girl from Virginia, born in India and brought up under the tutelage of an old Hindu mystic who taught Carson many odd things, "among them telepathy"!

Also conforming to precedent, Burroughs frames his narrative in introductory matter which mentions real names and places, to ease one into the incredible happenings which are to follow. The framework in *Pirates of Venus* mentions David Innes and Pellucidar, for the author seems to have had a vague idea of linking his entire *oeuvre* together, rather in the way that Anthony Trollope provided links within his Barchester novels.

This new Barsoomian Barchester, although generously supplied with strange topography, people, and adventures, never has quite the zip of the Martian series. But then, Venus has never been the best planet for the imagination. Its shrouded surface has damped the creative urge. Drawing out a very slender thread of reasoning, the Swedish astronomer Arrhenius proclaimed in 1917, "Everything on Venus is dripping wet"—and the depressing thought has stuck.[5] The writerly imagination has been clouded.

Burroughs' Venus possesses a year-long axial rotation, so that it always turns the same face to the sun, and regions of ice surround the hot equatorial region. Mile-high trees grow in the tropics.

Three more Venus novels followed the first, in true Burroughs fashion, and a fourth was started but not completed. World War II got in the way. Burroughs died in bed one day in 1950, while reading a comic book—a man of seventy-four still dreaming up wild refuges for his somewhat gory imagination.

Besides the novels mentioned, he wrote many others, some of them also in series. *The Moon Maid* (serialised in 1923) launched a series which depicts an inner world on the Moon. No wonder that Burroughs founded his own publishing house, still flourishing in Tarzana, California, to cope with his massive output!

Many readers consider Burroughs' best novel to be *The Land That Time Forgot* (first published in book form in 1924). It consists of three novelettes, each purportedly written by a different person; they are, *The Land That Time Forgot, The People That Time Forgot,* and *Out of Time's Abyss.* The beginning of the story contains echoes of both Poe and Conan Doyle, where a submarine is drawn towards an uncharted magnetic island, sighting icebergs as it goes. On one of the island's rare beaches, a dead man is sighted, reminding one of the crew of a prehistoric man. They find the subterranean channel of an inland river flowing into the sea;

the submarine navigates the channel, thus entering the world of Caprona, or Caspak as it is known to its inhabitants.

And what inhabitants! The mystery of this lost world is solved, typically enough, by a story told to Bradley while he is imprisoned in a foul pit in the Blue Place of Seven Skulls. Evolution is not a unitary process involving all phyla on Caspak; it is an individual process. The tribes through which the sailors have passed from south to north are each representatives of an upwards evolutionary process; all individuals pass through this evolutionary process, in their own bodies recapitulating a whole cycle from tadpole to fish or reptile, and so to the ape, and from then—if they are lucky—to Man. The women lay their multitudinous eggs into warm pools.

This evolutionary fantasy is nicely worked out, and the stages well visualised, although the novel is blemished by its cast of disagreeable Germans and stage Cockneys ("'Wot s'y we pot the bloomin' bird, sir?'").

Wherever they are set, all Burroughs' novels are vaguely similar, heroes and incidents being often transposable, as crocodile fights were transposed from one Tarzan film to the next. Since the people are almost characterless, beyond bearing exotic names, they experience nothing of the difficulties of personality with which we all wrestle in real life. ERB specialised in unreal life, and his novels offer to a remarkable degree every possible facility for identifying with the hero and daydreaming through his triumphs. No harm in such facility, perhaps; but self-exploration is as important as self-indulgence, and there is always the possibility of becoming permanently drugged by such brightly coloured pipe dreams.[6]

So what, finally, are we to make of ERB, that supreme example of the dichotomy of taste, between critics who see no virtue in him, and fans who see no fault?

A peculiar feature of Burroughs' output is the frequency with which mystery surrounds birth. The lead figures in the major series all have oddities attending their infancy, except for David Innes. This is most extreme in the hero of the best series, John Carter of Mars, who could almost pass for Ayesha after a sex-change. Carter recalls no childhood, has always been adult, and remains at about the age of thirty. Other instances of children, like Tarzan, lost to or estranged from parents are many—a comic example is the eponymous cave girl in a lesser series which begins with *The Cave Girl*

(1925); she is revealed to be the daughter of a vanished count and countess. The women of Mars, like the women of Caspak, are oviparous; in other terms, children are born away from or rejected by their mothers, rather as Tarzan is fostered by an inhuman creature. More widely, in psychoanalytical terms, to live on the Moon or another planet is to accept loss of contact with humanity.

Was there confusion as well as an attempt to glamorise his own origins in ERB's statement, "I was born in Peking at the time that my father was military adviser to the Empress of China, and lived there, in the Forbidden City, until I was ten years old." (*Edgar Rice Burroughs, Fiction Writer*)

Sexual dimorphism is common in Burroughs' world, as the hideous males of Opar in the Tarzan series differ markedly from the beautiful females. (Though in *Tarzan and the Ant Men* [1924], it is the females, the Alalis, who are hideous because they have achieved sexual dominance.) The males generally have a tough life, though rarely quite as hazardous as in *The Land That Time Forgot*, until they finally win the hand—and little more than the hand—of some attractive girl.

Despite a considerable amount of nudity in ERB's novels, no sexual intercourse is mentioned or even implied; we might be in a prepubertal world. This is bowing to more than the literary conventions of the times. Thuvia, maid of Mars, spends fifteen years as a "plaything and a slave" of the egregious White Martians, and runs around naked to boot, yet survives to flaunt her virginity in the very title of the novel!

Yet the *danger* of sex is always there. One industrious critic, Richard D. Mullen, has calculated the omnipresence of the threat of rape in Burroughs' world, and found female virtue in danger no less than an obsessive seventy-six times in the novels written between 1911 and 1915! The menaces include a marvellously miscegenously-inclined throng of apes, usurers, black sultans, Negroes, green, white, and yellow Martians, cavemen, hairy men, monster men, orangoutangs, and Japanese head-hunters.[7] In every case, chastity is successfully preserved.

In Carl Jung's *Memories, Dreams, Reflections,* he recounts the vivid psychosis of one of his female patients, who believed that she had lived on the Moon. She told Jung a tale about life there. It appears that the Moon people were threatened with extinction. A vampire lived in the high mountains of the Moon. The vampire kidnapped and killed women and children, who in consequence had taken to living underground. The patient resolves to kill the vampire but, when she and it came face to face, the vampire revealed himself as a man of unearthly beauty.[8]

Jung makes a comment which could stand on the title page of this book: "Thereafter I regarded the sufferings of the mentally ill in a different light. For I had gained insight into the richness and importance of their inner experience." Without imputing mental illness to Burroughs, I believe that Jung provides a key to fantasy writing in general, and to the echoing of themes. He does illuminate something compulsive and repetitive in Burroughs' output.

For this reason, it is foolish to protest that the Burroughs books depart from facts—that an oviparous woman is a contradiction in terms, that Mars has no breathable atmosphere, that a child raised by apes would be incapable of learning human language when older, that Venus rotates and is intolerably hot, that a sun inside Earth would turn it into a nuclear bonfire, and so on. Burroughs is not interested in the facts of the external world. As one critic has observed, by so doing he throws away many advantages—for instance, by not preserving the distinction that Lowell clearly made between old Martian sea beds and barren plateaus, and thus forfeiting a clearer realisation of his Barsoom[9]; but Burroughs was reporting from his own internal Pellucidar. Burroughs' Mars is like Ray Bradbury's later Mars; it reports on areas which cannot be scrutinised through any telescope.

A failure to make a simple distinction between two sorts of vision, the Wellsian and the Burroughsian, or the analytic and the fantastic, bedevils all criticism, especially sf criticism—as well it might, for the distinction is particularly hard to draw in science fiction. Lowell's Mars—in its time the latest factual study science could produce—is now itself as much a fantasy world as Barsoom!

One further general point before leaving Burroughs. ERB's stories are much like Westerns, and the Chicago in which he was born still retained elements of a frontier town. The vanishing redskin was not far away in space or time. Burroughs often wrote about him, directly or indirectly; his writings are a welter of racial fantasy —even Tar-Zan means White Skin in the language of the apes. Any critic whose piercing vision has found in Poe's work obsessional fears of coloured people will achieve as much in Burroughs' work with one eye tied behind his back.

Burroughs fits very neatly into Leslie Fiedler's synthesis of the myths which give a special character to art and life in America. Fiedler's synthesis culminates in *The Return of the Vanishing American*. The one passage in that volume which deigns to mention Burroughs is so apropos to the hordes of odd-coloured and -shaped creatures which were about to descend on twentieth-century man via science fiction that it must be quoted.

Fiedler, putting his case against the American male, shows how the image of a white girl tied naked to a stake while redskins dance howling round her appeals to both our xenophobia and a sense of horror. Often such images were used as crude magazine illustrations.

> And, indeed, this primordial image has continued to haunt pulp fiction ever since (often adorning the covers of magazines devoted to it); for it panders to that basic White male desire at once to relish and deplore, vicariously share and publicly condemn, the rape of White female innocence. To be sure, as the generations go by, the colour of her violators has changed, though that of the violated woman has remained the same: from the Red of the Indians with whom it all began, to the Yellow of such malign Chinese as Dr. Fu Manchu, the Black of those Africans who stalk so lubriciously through the pages of Edgar Rice Burroughs's Tarzan books, or the Purple or Green Martians who represent the crudest fantasy level of science fiction.[10]

This theory does not hold water—or rather, holds more water than Fiedler thinks, for Sax Rohmer, the creator of Dr. Fu Manchu, was an Englishman; and we have seen that the two most likely sources of Burroughs' Mars lie in *Gulliver of Mars* and *She*, both written by Englishmen. Americans are not alone in obsessional fears about sex and colour. Indeed such fears are also observed in deepest Africa. Suffice it to say that Pocahontas and Ayesha really started something. With those mother-figures, the guilts of their respective doomed continents merge. Burroughs let the spectral Red/Black/Yellow/Green men into sf, and they have been on the warpath ever since—all the way to the stars!

Burroughs marks a retreat to the primitive. Other writers took other paths in their flight from urban culture and rational thought. The prime attraction of George Allan England's *Darkness and Dawn,* first published in 1912, was that it presented a picture of a great city—New York—in ruins. Two modern Rip Van Winkles, Barbara and Allan, wake on the forty-eighth storey of a skyscraper to find that they have slept for some fifteen hundred years and that civilisation has crumbled away all about them.

England (1877–1936) wrote several other serials for the pulps of this period, among them *The Empire of the Air* and *The Golden Blight,* as well as two sequels to *Darkness and Dawn.* Like Wells, and unlike most of his fellow writers, he was a socialist, with a small if not a large S. His characters are conventional, his prose slightly pretentious. He has not worn as well as Burroughs, although he was once regarded as Burroughs' rival.

As much might be said about Otis Adelbert Kline, though his imitation of Burroughs seems fairly open. Kline's *Planet of Peril* was published in serial form in 1929 and set on Venus. An inevitable sequel followed. Later, Kline moved in on Mars with *The Swordsmen of Mars,* and in on Tarzan with *Tam, Son of the Tiger,* and *Jan of the Jungle*—made indiscriminately into a Universal film serial, just as Tarzan had been. And so on.

Others of the great obscure include Austin Hall and Homer Eon Flint, authors of *The Blind Spot* (1921) polished off adequately by Damon Knight in a chapter entitled "Chuckleheads" in his *In Search of Wonder;* and Ralph Milne Farley, an ex-senator from Wisconsin, whose *The Radio Man* of 1924 was followed up (or down) by *The Radio Beasts, The Radio Planet,* and *The Radio Minds of Mars.* There are also Ray Cummings, best remembered for *The Girl in the Golden Atom*—Gulliver down the microscope—Charles B. Stilson, Victor Rousseau, and J. U. Gisey, author of the attractively titled *Palos of the Dog Star Pack,* which ran as a serial and of course spawned sequels.

Croft, the hero of *Palos,* travels to that distant star by astral projection, the means by which John Carter reached Mars, or the anonymous traveller in the 1741 *A New Journey to the World in the Moon* reached the lunar world. Mysticism in one form or another never dies, and sf has its due freight.[11] It may be regarded either as another form of retreat from the materialist problems of urban culture, or as a convenient plot device to remove a hero far and fast from an everyday situation to a bizarre one; but these alternatives do not necessarily conflict.

One way of escape lay through the macabre, to the shadowy worlds where the rational could be set aside by the supernatural. Whatever we care to say about Burroughs' worlds, he does present us with a great frieze of prancing and capering beings, full of pulp life, engaged in hearty struggle with their contemporaries and their environment. On Hodgson, Merritt, Lovecraft, and their ilk, the shadow of the grave lies as heavy as it did across Poe; these practitioners stand nearer to what we have termed "the dreaming pole" than does ERB.

William Hope Hodgson, born in Essex in 1877, served in the British Merchant Navy. He was a courageous and active man, killed in the trenches in 1918, in the war that killed Saki and millions of others. Hodgson's total output is modest, and he never wrote a really perfect book; yet he produced two novels which have embedded in them visions as colossal and impressive as any mentioned in this volume. They are the basis for a reputation that has grown slowly since Hodgson's death. Of course, he is not in DNB, and no standard reference book mentions his name.

The House on the Borderland (1908) is a strange house indeed, a massive stone affair in which the narrator lives with his old sister. The house is built over a pit, from which swine-things (another submerged nation?) emerge and go through the traditional uncanny, nocturnal, and nauseous antics of all swine-things.

So far, so undistinguished. But the centre of the story is something different. The pit is in some vague fashion connected with the universe. The narrator stands transfixed at his window while time accelerates outside. The Sun begins to whirl across the heavens until it is an arc of fire, a Sun stream.

> From the sky, I glanced down to the gardens. They were just a blur of a palish, dirty green. I had a feeling that they stood higher than in the old days; a feeling that they were nearer my window, as though they had risen, bodily. Yet they were still a long way below me; for the rock, over the mouth of the pit, on which this house stands, arches up to a great height.
>
> It was later, that I noticed a change in the constant colour of the gardens. The pale, dirty green was growing ever paler and paler, towards white. At last, after a great space, they became greyish-white, and stayed thus for a very long time. Fi-

nally, however, the greyness began to fade, even as had the green, into a dead white. And this remained, constant and unchanged. And by this I knew that, at last, snow lay upon all the Northern world.

And so, by millions of years, time winged onward through eternity, to the end—the end, of which, in the old earth days, I had thought remotely, and in hazily speculative fashion. And now, it was approaching in a manner of which none had ever dreamed.

I recollect that, about this time, I began to have a lively though morbid curiosity, as to what would happen when the end came—but I seemed strangely without imaginings.

All this while, the steady process of decay was continuing. The few remaining pieces of glass, had long ago vanished; and, every now and then, a soft thud, and a little cloud of rising dust, would tell of some fragment of fallen mortar or stone.

I looked up again, to the fiery sheet that quaked in the heavens above me and far down into the Southern sky. As I looked, the impression was borne in upon me, that it had lost some of its first brilliancy—that it was duller, deeper hued.

I glanced down, once more, to the blurred white of the world-scape. Sometimes, my look returned to the burning sheet of dulling flame, that was, and yet hid, the sun. At times, I glanced behind me, into the growing dusk of the great, silent room, with its aeon-carpet of sleeping dust . . .

So I watched through the fleeting ages, lost in soul-wearing thoughts and wonderings, and possessed with a new weariness . . .

It might have been a million years later, that I perceived, beyond possibility of doubt, that the fiery sheet that lit the world, was indeed darkening.

Another vast space went by, and the whole enormous flame had sunk to a deep, copper colour. Gradually, it darkened, from copper to copper-red, and from this, at times, to a deep, heavy, purplish tint, with, in it, a strange loom of blood.

Although the light was decreasing, I could perceive no diminishment in the apparent speed of the sun. It still spread itself in that dazzling veil of speed.

The world, so much of it as I could see, had assumed a

dreadful shade of gloom, as though, in very deed, the last day of the worlds approached.

As the house crumbles, the Sun begins at last to grow dull. Finally, it hangs in the sky, stationary, like a bronze shield. The air falls as snow round the shell of house. The Central Suns approach. Earth itself is a forgotten thing.

What did this overpowering spectacle of the Remote mean to Hodgson?

His mystical vision, which comes through clear and unforcedly, carries an echo of the mystical initiation of Harmachis, in the fourth chapter of Haggard's *Cleopatra* ("Behold the world that thou has left," said the Voice, "behold and tremble"); but Hodgson's scope and verve are his own. The whole vision, a mingling of astronomy and psychic experience, extends through several chapters—a bravura piece of writing, full of wonder, excelling in its scope anything written up to that date, and bursting far beyond the tawdry horror story in which it is set.

The Night Land (1912) flares into similar magnificence and dies into unreadability. Here Hodgson makes the strategic error of embedding his main story, which is set far into the future, within a preposterous seventeenth-century framework, and of writing in mock-antique. It is a very long book, and a reader may be forgiven if he never gets to the end even of the abridged edition, issued in 1921; yet within its length appears a morbid drama of great and powerful splendour, the drama of the Last Redoubt.

This drama is set far in the future, where the remainder of humanity wait under siege. The old world has been laid waste by "Monsters and Ab-human creatures," which have been permitted, through the agency of long-past human science, to pass "the barrier of Life." The Last Redoubt is a pyramid, seven miles high, set on a desolate plain.

The Redoubt is powered by electricity drawn from the Earth. Fantastic creatures gather on the plain from the Night Lands, awaiting the exhaustion of this power. Greatest among these creatures are the Watchers. The Watchers are enormous, immobile, silent, and have been so throughout unknown thousands of years, awaiting the end that must come.

> Before me ran the Road Where The Silent Ones Walk; and I searched it, as many a time in my earlier youth had I,

with the spy-glass; for my heart was always stirred mightily
by the sight of those Silent Ones.

And, presently, alone in all the miles of that night-grey
road, I saw one in the field of my glass—a quiet, cloaked figure,
moving along, shrouded, and looking neither to right nor left.
And thus was it with these beings ever. It was told about
in the Redoubt that they would harm no human, if but the human did keep a fair distance from them; but that it were wise
never to come close upon one. And this I can well believe.

And so, searching the road with my gaze, I passed beyond
this Silent One, and past the place where the road, sweeping
vastly to the South-East, was lit a space, strangely, by the light
from the Silver-fire Holes. And thus at last to where it swayed
to the South of the Dark Palace, and thence Southward still, until it passed round to the Westward, beyond the mountain
bulk of the Watching Thing in the South—the hugest monster
in all the visible Night Lands. My spy-glass showed it to me
with clearness—a living hill of watchfulness, known to us as
The Watcher Of The South. It brooded there, squat and tremendous, hunched over the pale radiance of the Glowing
Dome.

Much, I know, has been writ concerning this Odd, Vast
Watcher; for it had grown out of the blackness of the South
Unknown Lands a million years gone; and the steady growing nearness of it had been noted and set out at length by the
men they called Monstruwacans; so that it was possible to
search in our libraries, and learn of the very coming of this
Beast in the olden-time.

This compelling situation has a brooding quality which reminds
us of the tale Jung's woman patient told him about the monster—
in her case a vampire—tyrannising everyone on the Moon. The situation in *The Night Land* is never resolved, as perhaps some
trauma in Hodgson's personal life was never resolved. We are left
with the image of those monstrous things, implacably sitting out
the span of humanity, and infinity.

What can one say of the great A. Merritt? It is a name that still
stirs the dusty pulses of old-time fans, who recite the names of his
fantasies like a litany. Merritt is really not a science fiction writer,

but his dreamy, suffocating tales were reprinted in science fiction magazines and well received.

Abraham Merritt (1884–1943)[12] went much further along the fantasy trail than Burroughs. At least one may look into the night sky and observe Mars and Venus, and have something to speculate upon; Merritt fled to never-never lands without benefit of Morris. His heroes are forever stepping through strange jewels, galloping through great doorways in mountains, discovering stairways leading down into extinct volcanoes, or arriving at temples full of unhallowed mysteries in some lost oasis. He is right up the dreaming pole.

Merritt's best-known titles, *The Moon Pool* (and its inevitable sequel, *The Conquest of the Moon Pool*), *The Ship of Ishtar, Seven Footprints to Satan, Dwellers in the Mirage,* and *Burn, Witch, Burn!,* all appeared in the flourishing pulps from 1918 to 1932. Two of them were filmed. Merritt's overheated style exactly matched his plots, which were up to here in serpents, feathers, fur, great black stallions, freaks, naked women, evil priests, golden pigmies, talismen, monsters, lovely priestesses, sinister forces, and undefined longings. Merritt believed in fairies.

> I heard a sweet, low-pitched voice at the other side of the tower trilling the bird-like syllables of the Little People—
> And then—I saw Evalie.
> Have you ever watched a willow bough swaying in spring above some clear sylvan pool, or a slender birch dancing with the wind in a secret woodland and covert, or the flitting green shadows in a deep forest glade which are dryads half-tempted to reveal themselves? I thought of them as she came towards us.
>
> > She was a dark girl and a tall girl. Her eyes were brown under long black lashes, the clear brown of the mountain brook in autumn; her hair was black, the jetty hair that in a certain light has a sheen of darkest blue . . . [etc., etc.] . . . Her skin was clear amber. Like polished fine amber it shone under the loose, yet clinging, garment that clothed her, knee-long, silvery, cobweb fine and transparent. Around her hips was the white loin-cloth of the Little People. Unlike them, her feet were sandalled.
> > But it was the grace of her that made the breath catch

in your throat as you looked at her, the long flowing line from ankle to shoulder, delicate and mobile as the curve of water flowing over some smooth breast of rock, a liquid grace of line that changed with every movement.

It was that—and the life that burned in her like the green flame of the virgin forest when the kisses of spring are being changed for the warmer caresses of Summer . . . [etc.] . . .

I could not tell how old she was—hers was the pagan beauty which knows no age . . .

The small soldiers ringed her, their spears ready.

(*Dwellers in the Mirage*, Chapter 8)

As the critic Moskowitz perceives, Merritt was "escaping from the brutalities and injustices of the world." His world ends not with a bang but a simper.

Merritt's later stories turned progressively to the darker side of the occult, which was just about where H. P. Lovecraft began.

So we come to that kind, lonely, and influential man, Howard Phillips Lovecraft, born 1890, departed this life 1937. With him, the flight to the irrational has become complete. Darkness rules at the dreaming pole. His literary ancestry includes Poe and the remarkable Lord Dunsany (1878–1957), who wrote many delicate fantasies of never-never lands while soldiering in the Coldstream Guards in the Boer War and the Royal Inniskilling Fusiliers in World War I, and living at other times a sporting outdoor life. Lovecraft, on the other hand, is a prisoner of the library and the cold damp hand. Horror, the abnegation of personality, seems to be his only permanent interest. Although horror can make a good literary seasoning if sparingly used, like salt it makes an indigestible banquet. The conclusion of Lovecraft's first story to be published, *Dagon* (1919), shows how he means to go on:

The end is near. I hear a noise at the door, as of some immense slippery body lumbering against it. It shall not find me. God, *that hand!* The window! The window!

The macabre, the eldritch, is Lovecraft's province. He developed a demoniac cult of hideous entities, the spawn of evil, which were seeking to take over Earth—Cthulhu, Yuggoth, Yog-Sothoth, Nyarlathotep, the Magnum Innominandum, and other titles which recall anagrams of breakfast cereal names. He had a fondness for the device used by Hodgson to conclude the main manuscript of *The House of the Borderland,* the first-person narrator who continues desperately scribbling his journal until the very moment that he goes insane or that his head is bitten off by the menace. (Indeed, the conclusion of *The House of the Borderland* manuscript is perhaps the model of *Dagon* a few years later: "There is something fumbling at the door-handle. O God, help me now! Jesus— The door is opening—slowly. Somethi—")

Here, even Merritt's world of titillation and adventure has faded and gone. The only culture possible in Lovecraft's universe is a fevered search for old books of black magic. Attempt anything else, and the monstrosities start tramping dankly up from the foundations.

Ghastly writer though Lovecraft is, predictable though the horrors are, somewhere buried in his writing is a core of power that remains disconcerting when all the adjectives have fallen away like leaves. Colin Wilson indicates this quality when he says that Lovecraft's writing holds interest as a psychological case history, even if it fails as literature. "Here was a man who made no attempt whatever to come to terms with life. He hated modern civilization, particularly in its confident belief in progress and science. Greater artists have had the same feeling, from Dostoevsky to Kafka and Eliot . . . Possibly future generations will feel that Lovecraft is 'symbolically' true."[13]

This is arguable. Lovecraft's hatred of science and progress is part of a hatred of life. And the mistrust of science, its ends and means, finds more rational expression in later science fiction authors such as Ray Bradbury, who has acknowledged his debt to Lovecraft. Indeed, Lovecraft's influence on the field has often been through later authors—not always fortunately—for talented, intelligent, and sensitive writers such as August Derleth (whose memoirs in *Walden West* are much to be cherished) and Robert Bloch (perhaps best known for his novel *Psycho*) may have been deflected from their true course by Lovecraft's too easy vein of grave-haunting. Perhaps as much is true of the unreadable Clark Ashton Smith. (Ah, but how I loved his *City of Singing Flame* as a lad!)

One or two of Lovecraft's stories rank as science fiction, for instance *Herbert West—Reanimator,* an exercise on a Frankenstein theme. West's lifework is the reanimation of the dead. The First

World War provides him with plenty of corpses. Lovecraft is about his old business of chilling the blood, however ludicrously:

> For that very fresh body, at last writhing into full and ter-
> rifying consciousness with eyes dilated at the memory of its
> last scene on earth, threw out its frantic hands in a life and
> death struggle with the air; and suddenly collapsing into a
> second and final dissolution from which there could be no re-
> turn, screamed out the cry that will ring eternally in my aching
> brain:
> "Help! Keep off, you cursed little tow-headed fiend—keep
> that damned needle away from me!"
>   (From *Dagon and Other Macabre Tales*)

One may find Lovecraft funny, and his most dramatic effects overloaded. But he had and still has staunch supporters. August Derleth and Donald Wandrei founded a publishing imprint, Arkham House, in 1939, simply to publish the treasured works of HPL in a form more permanent than magazines; and those early publications are now valuable, scarce, and much sought after. Truly, friends are better than critics.

NOTES

1. North Hollywood, California, Leisure Books Inc., 1970.

2. Kingsley Amis, *New Maps of Hell*, Chap. 1, 1961.

3. By way of comparison, to show how the pace has hotted up since Wallace's and Burroughs' day, the James Bond novels of Ian Fleming had sold seventy million copies by 1967. Films of the Bond novels are highly profitable. Box-office takings on *Diamonds Are Forever*, 1972, totalled $24,568,915, in its *first twelve days* of release in some 1,000 cinemas round the world. Figures given in Roger Eglin and Iain Murray, The Gilt-Edged Bond. *Business Observer*, Sunday, Jan. 16, 1972.

4. "I was not writing because of any urge to write nor for any particular love of writing. I was writing because I had a wife and two babies . . . I loathed poverty . . ." Autobiographical article in *Open Road* magazine, Sept. 1949, quoted in Chap. 12 of Richard Lupoff's sympathetic biography of Burroughs.

5. For an investigation of imaginative treatments of Venus through the years, see my *Farewell, Fantastic Venus! A History of the Planet Venus in Fact and Fiction*, 1968.

6. And worse than drugged. "The Story of Kirk" in Robert Lindner's *The Fifty Minute Hour, and Other True Psychoanalytic Tales*, New York, 1954, relates the case of a young man, Kirk, who identified with an interplanetary hero much like John Carter, whose adventures spread over a long series of fantasies; though the evidence presented by Lindner suggests the series might be, not Burroughs', but the Lensman series by E. E. Smith (see Chap. 9). By coincidence, the hero has the same name as Kirk's (an assumed name). Soon, Kirk is away with his fictional namesake, "far off on another planet, courting beautiful princesses, governing provinces, warring with strange enemies." The identification becomes part of a self-sustaining psychosis, which Lindner ameliorates only with great difficulty. (This "Story of Kirk" is included in *Best Fantasy Stories*, 1962, edited by the present writer.) I am indebted to Dr. Leon Stover for evidence that "Kirk" is, in fact, the pseudonym for the politician who later wrote science fiction himself under another pseudonym—Cordwainer Smith.

7. For the full list, consult Richard D. Mullen, the Elder, "Edgar Rice Burroughs and the Fate Worse Than Death," in *Riverside Quarterly*, Vol. 4, No. 3.

8. The dream is related in "Psychiatric Activities," *Memories, Dreams, Reflections*, Chap. 4, 1963.

9. Richard D. Mullen, "The Undisciplined Imagination: Edgar Rice Burroughs and Lowellian Mars," *SF: The Other Side of Realism*, 1971.

10. Leslie A. Fiedler, *The Return of the Vanishing American*. The chapter on "The Basic Myths, III: Two Mothers of Us All." To be guided entirely by Fiedler's theories would probably cause one to see the alienations surrounding the births of ERB's characters as explicable in terms of the latter's rejection of his European (or European cultural) ancestry. "What a lovely American dream—to be born as a fatherless Indian boy from a husbandless Indian mother, to have no father at all, except for the Forest itself: all fear of miscegenation washed away in the same cleaning metaphor that washes away our European ancestry," says Fiedler.

11. For a discussion of mysticism in one sf magazine of the thirties see Leland Sapiro's "The Mystic Renaissance: A Survey of F. Orlin Tremaine's *Astounding Stories*," *Riverside Quarterly*, Vol. 2, Nos. 2–4.

12. Once one has read Damon Knight's description of Merritt's appearance, one never forgets it: "Merritt was chinless, bald and shaped like a shmoo." *In Search of Wonder*, Chap. 2, 1967.

13. Colin Wilson, *The Strength to Dream*, Chap. 1, 1962. Since publishing this book, Wilson has increasingly fallen under the spell of Lovecraft, whom he likens to W. B. Yeats and Peter Kurten, the Düsseldorf murderer. He has written two novels which utilise the Lovecraftian cult of Cthulhu.

8

In the Name of the Zeitgeist:

MAINLY THE THIRTIES

> Those find, who most delight to roam
> 'Mid castles of remotest Spain,
> That there's, thank Heaven, no place like Home;
> So they set out upon their travels again.
> > Aldous Huxley: *Ninth Philosopher's Song*
>
> For thirty hours he had been struggling
> across the surface of the Moon. Hours of toil
> in a world of utter silence, of pitchy black
> shadows and harshly glaring light, of treach-
> erous pitfalls and mountainous barriers. His
> heart thudded audibly; sweat streaked his face
> and body; his muscles groaned against the
> torture of prolonged, superhuman effort.
> > Yet behind the spherical glassite helmet of
> his space suit, the boyish face of Jerry
> Blaine bore an expression of triumph that no
> weariness could mar. His blue eyes twinkled
> joyously.
> > Lloyd Arthur Eshbach: *Dust*

Like C. S. Lewis, I have never accepted that enjoyment of Shakespeare's plays precludes pleasure in the comics, or that those who
visit Barsoom should not feel at home in Hardy's Wessex. There are
more things for more occasions than Lit. Crit. will ever allow.

All the same, the authors who assemble in this chapter present a real challenge to catholic appreciation. Between the humanitarian concerns of a Čapek and the gadget-mindedness of a Gernsback stretch light-years of traditional cold shoulders.

We have seen a division occur in science fiction—a division not present in *Frankenstein*—between the analytical fiction that Wells wrote and the adventure or fantasy fiction that Burroughs wrote; or between the thinking and dreaming poles, as we have termed them.

This division later became institutionalised by the establishment of magazines that specialised in science fiction. The great flourishing age of the magazine gave way to an age of specialisation, just as some dinosaurs specialised in grotesque armour in their later period. General magazines became a thing of the past, as category fiction crept in. The contrasted epochs are marked by the publication of the *Strand* in 1890 and *Amazing Stories* in 1926.

After this later date, and for many succeeding years, we find that the analytical type of science fiction is published outside the magazines, while the magazines are inundated by many kinds of fantasy, often imitating Burroughs and often—less attractively—anti-Burroughsian. This latter is a third type of science fiction, most conveniently labelled Gernsbackian. Neither culture nor dreams warm it; it exists as propaganda for the wares of the inventor.

Monoculture brings its dangers, whether in literature or agriculture. It became impossible for writing with any serious intent to appear in the specialised magazines. Although there are a few minor exceptions, the authors of the thirties one thinks of with respect, who actually contributed anything new, had probably never even heard of science fiction.

It is as difficult to imagine Franz Kafka, Aldous Huxley, Karel Čapek, *et al.*, submitting their works for serialisation in *Amazing Stories* or *Weird Tales*, as it is to think of E. E. Smith, creator of the Gray Lensman, as a moulder of Western thought. The gulf between two similar sorts of reading matter has become complete.*

This chapter is a survey of the writers who wrote for their fellows rather than for the magazines. As such, it includes some great names, among them the most brilliantly imaginative writer science

---

* But sf is a literature of surprises. In fact, *Amazing Stories* for August 1927 published *The Tissue-Culture King*, a story by Aldous Huxley's elder brother, Julian Huxley!

fiction has known. And it concludes bathetically by inspecting the first "scientifiction" magazines.

Those who saw one of the few performances that Sadler's Wells Opera gave of *The Makropoulos Case* in 1971 were privileged—and more privileged than they knew at the time. By the end of that year, the gorgeous Marie Collier, who sang the lead role, was dead. Ironically, Miss Collier played Emilia Marty, the beautiful young woman who is several hundred years old when the curtain goes up. Emilia Marty drank an elixir of longevity in 1565. We meet her in 1907, the year in which the opera is set, when she is torn between a desire to recover the secret of the elixir (buried in the complicated Makropoulos estate), thus prolonging a meaningless life, and a desire to yield to the death she has eluded so long. Her existence, once so bright and warm, has come to depend on a formula. Eventually, this brilliant and terrifying figure collapses; all that is left is a little fragile and broken burden in her lover's arms.

The musical score is by Janáček, based on a play (translated as *The Makropoulos Secret* in 1927) by the Czech dramatist Karel Čapek. As the curtain rises on the first act, we are taken into a dusty office filled with wooden desks and files. In these cobwebby pigeonholes, valuable documents are lost for years, or forgotten secrets suddenly materialise. This is Prague in the fusty days of the Austro-Hungarian Empire, the Prague of secrets and conspiracies. It may have reminded the Sadler's Wells audience of similar gloomy rooms to be found in the strange unfinished novels appearing in the very year that Čapek's play was translated into English.[1] I mean the novels of Franz Kafka.

Kafka's unique formulations were pieced together only after his death. It was Čapek's reputation which spread first, although he was Kafka's junior by seven years.

Čapek was a great humanist—and a humorist as well, two characteristics he shared with that other internationally popular Czech writer Jaroslav Hašek, author of *The Good Soldier Schweik* —born the same year as Kafka. Čapek's humour was gentler than the anarchistic wit of Hašek, and has worn less well. But there is still force in his best-known work, the play *R.U.R.*, first performed in the capital of the new Czechoslovakia in 1921, and shortly thereafter all round Europe and in the United States.

R.U.R. stands for Rossum's Universal Robots. It is a satire on capitalist methods and, more deeply, an embodiment of Čapek's fears that increasing automation and regimentation would dehumanise mankind. Old Rossum has invented a formula whereby artificial people can be made in a factory. His robots are simplified versions of human beings; they have no soul and do nothing but work (the word "robot," which is Čapek's coinage, comes from a Slav root meaning "work"). In the end, the robots take over and wipe out humanity. They cannot breed, but two aberrant robots, a male and a female, are left to start all over again.

Nowadays, the word robot is reserved for creatures of metal; Čapek's robots are what we would term "androids." His theme is a logical development of the Frankenstein theme. Victor's solitary product has become the staple of a conveyor belt.

R.U.R. was written in collaboration with Karel's elder brother, Josef, a painter of some renown whose reputation was made in the Cubist school. The brothers collaborated on *The Insect Play*, another success of the early twenties, again concerned with the theme of regimentation.

Karel Čapek was art director of the National Theatre of Prague. He later established his own theatre (staging Shelley's *The Cenci* among other plays) and was editor of an eminent cultural periodical. He travelled a great deal, and wrote many travel and gardening books; he was also a close friend of Thomas Masaryk, the first Czech president, writing the latter's life story in the thirties.

His versatility was tremendous, as his fondness for themes bordering on science fictional was constant. *Tovarna na Absolutno* is a novel, published in 1922 and translated into English a few years later as *The Absolute at Large*. This is a Wellsian discussion of the relativity of human values, with a company setting itself up to manufacture and sell—not robots this time, but atom-powered machines, locomotives, cars, ships, guns. As in *R.U.R.*, war breaks out and all is destroyed. Čapek would have agreed with Erskine Childers' conclusion that "preparedness induced war." His novel *Krakatit* (1924, and translated as *An Atomic Phantasy*) relates how atomic energy is discovered and, through human dishonesty, causes widespread destruction.

In 1936, Čapek published *Valka s Mloky*, translated as *War with the Newts*, a rambling and intermittently amusing novel which repeats the author's old theme with variations. The Newts are child-

sized, a docile race of creatures who live in the sea and are enslaved by man for profit. Like the robots, they eventually revolt,
undermine the continents, and so bring about the downfall of man.

In the real world, Hitler's robots were undermining the Continent. Masaryk's republic was well prepared for war; but France
and Britain were not, and the United States was isolationist in attitude. Czechoslovakia was persuaded to give in to Hitler's threats,
and the Wehrmacht rolled into the Sudetenland in 1938. The dis-
memberment of the Czech state commenced. Čapek, a great and
liberal man, died on Christmas Day in 1938, a mere atom in the
general darkness engulfing Europe. As for the elder brother, Josef,
he was sent to German concentration camps, and died in Belsen in
1945.

Franz Kafka (1883–1924) was Austrian, born in Prague, son of a
forceful Jewish businessman. Unlike Čapek, he wrote in German,
not Czech. By dying young, he avoided the horrors that awaited so
many of his compatriots. But his novels seem to look, not only
backwards to the sordid and dusty files of the Dual Monarchy,
where precious documents could be lost forever, but forward to
the *Nacht und Nebel*† of Nazi Germany, in which individuals and
families could be lost forever.

The world Kafka created in his two major novels, *The Trial*
and *The Castle,* is as coherent and as original as the world of Swift
or of Lewis Carroll, and so formidable that it has become the target
of a whole library full of interpretations. It is not simply that
both major novels deal with a puzzle which is never resolved, or
that Kafka's manner of relating the puzzle is oblique, but that, on
the surface, the furniture of his novels is an ordinary world with
which we are all familiar: yet we are adrift in it.

As one of his commentators, Erich Heller, puts it, the Kafka
universe is "like the reader's own; a castle that is a castle and 'sym-
bolises' merely what all castles symbolise: power and authority; a
telephone exchange that produces more muddle than connections;
a bureaucracy drowning in a deluge of forms and files; an obscure

† *"Nacht und Nebel Erlass*—'Night and Fog Decree.' This grotesque order . . .
was issued by Hitler himself on December 7, 1941. Its purpose, as the weird
title indicates, was to seize persons 'endangering German security' who were
not to be immediately executed and make them vanish without a trace into
the night and fog of the unknown in Germany." William L. Shirer: *The Rise
and Fall of the Third Reich*, Bk. 5, "The New Order."

hierarchy of officialdom making it impossible ever to find the man authorised to deal with a particular case; officials who work overtime and yet get nowhere; numberless interviews which are never to the point; inns where the peasants meet, and barmaids who serve the officials. In fact, it is an excruciatingly familiar world, but reproduced by a creative intelligence which is endowed with the knowledge that it is a world damned for ever."[2]

One need not agree with that final phrase (for Kafka's is too humdrum for the drama of damnation, and more concerned with corruption) to accept the truth of the rest. Alice was a commonplace little girl. Kafka's is a commonplace little world; yet the spell of terror—an oddly comic terror—lies over it.

Kafka does not seem to be writing allegory, although many commentators would not agree with that, nor does he fit into the symbolist camp. He goes about his own business—and so thoroughly and so convincingly that an ordinary reader might be scared off by the litanies of scholarly praise which have risen like incense on all sides, from W. H. Auden's "Had one to name the author who comes nearest to bearing the same kind of relation to our age as Dante, Shakespeare, and Goethe bore to theirs, Kafka is the first one would think of," onwards.

Against the higher criticism one arms oneself with the recollection of Kafka's friend, Max Brod, saying that Kafka's friends burst into laughter as he read passages of *The Trial* aloud to them. Kafka's atmosphere of foreboding is shot through with humour (a very peculiar humour), while his diaries[3] reveal a constipated, father-dominated, but slyly amusing man. Dickens, the Dickens of the Circumlocution Office, stands prominent in Kafka's literary ancestry.

Little of Kafka's work was published in his lifetime, although he had gained a reputation in Czechoslovakia and Germany by the time of his death. His executor, Max Brod, had instructions to burn his literary remains, but fortunately disobeyed orders. So his three posthumous novels appeared, *Der Prozess* (*The Trial*, 1925); *Das Schloss* (*The Castle*, 1926); and *Amerika* (1927, translated under the same title). These were all unfinished works, set into order by Max Brod.

The Trial is the story of Joseph K., perplexingly arrested on a charge which is never specified and eventually executed on the sentence of a judge he has never seen, despite his efforts to clear himself.

The Castle is the story of K., who claims to be a land surveyor and arrives in a village dominated by a castle, in which K. seeks work; but the forces in the castle are impressively passive, and never accept him, so that the situation remains unresolved.

These are Kafka's two long works, which come near to a spirit of science fiction. Manifestly, they are not sf, although it would need only the revelation (but Kafka's is, of course, not a literature of revelation) that the judge is K.'s *doppelgänger*, or that the Castle has been taken over by aliens, to reduce both novels to traditional science fiction. And yet the baffling atmosphere, the paranoid complexities, the alien motives of others, make the novels a sort of *haute* sf. The towering stature of Kafka's writing, particularly since World War II, relates it to several kinds of writing by the influence it has had. Yet its oneirocritical faculties are so powerful, that one has only to contrast it with more orthodox kinds of science fiction—say, Wells' *Mr. Britling Sees It Through* or Burroughs' *Jungle Tales of Tarzan*, both written when Kafka was writing *The Trial*—to see how Kafka had a terrifyingly different kind of imagination, which has haunted a whole generation. Like Poe, he has the three "I"'s—Inwardness, Imagination, and Invention.

Because one of his strengths is to weave a web of suspicion, propitiation, and innuendo, Kafka's potent effect is not easily conveyed by extracts, but here is a quotation from early in *The Castle*, when K. is exploring the village and passing the school.

> The children were just coming out with their teacher. They thronged round him, all gazing up at him and chattering without a break so rapidly that K. could not follow what they said. The teacher, a small young man with narrow shoulders and a very upright carriage which yet did not make him ridiculous, had already fixed K. with his eyes from the distance, naturally enough, for apart from the school-children there was not another human being in sight. Being the stranger, K. made the first advance, especially as the other was an authoritative-looking little man, and said: "Good morning, sir." As if by one accord the children fell silent, perhaps the master liked to have a sudden stillness as a preparation for his words. "You are looking at the Castle?" he asked more gently than K. had expected,

but with the inflexion that denoted disapproval of K.'s occupation. "Yes," said K. "I am a stranger here, I came to the village only last night." "You don't like the Castle?" returned the teacher quickly. "What?" countered K., a little taken aback, and repeated the question in a modified form. "Do I like the Castle? Why do you assume that I don't like it?" "Strangers never do," said the teacher. To avoid saying the wrong thing K. changed the subject and asked: "I suppose you know the Count?" "No," said the teacher turning away. But K. would not be put off and asked again: "What, you don't know the Count?" "Why should I?" replied the teacher in a low tone, and added aloud in French: "Please remember that there are innocent children present." K. took this as a justification for asking: "Might I come to pay you a visit one day, sir? I am to be staying here for some time and already feel a little lonely. I don't fit in with the peasants nor, I imagine, with the Castle." "There is no difference between the peasantry and the Castle," said the teacher. "Maybe," said K., "that doesn't alter my position. Can I pay you a visit one day?" "I live in Swan Street at the butcher's." That was assuredly more of a statement than an invitation, but K. said: "Right, I'll come."

The encounter has the lucidity and the enigmatic quality of an actual encounter between two people. Kafka offers plenty of data, little interpretation. In this respect, he contrasts markedly with another Central European Jew whose work was set amid the obfuscations of Franz Josef's Dual Monarchy: Sigmund Freud.[4]

More directly science fictional are some of Kafka's short stories, of which the best known is "Metamorphosis" (*"Die Verwandlung,"* first published in 1916), about the man who wakes up one morning and finds himself transformed into a gigantic insect. The family are a little stuffy about it at first, but rapidly adapt themselves to the change. This story looks forward to Ionesco's *The Rhinoceros* and the Theatre of the Absurd. "In the Penal Colony," with its horrendous torture machine, also approaches science fiction. "The Giant Mole," which concerns exactly what the title claims, is a sort of humorous fantasy; J. G. Ballard produced a pastiche of it, "The Drowned Giant," which is a Kafka story in its own right.

Working in Prague today is another very interesting and individual science fiction writer, Josef Nesvadba, many of whose stories have been translated in the West[5] and in the USSR. Although a Nesvadba story is unmistakeably by Nesvadba, he is heir to the somewhat grim and labyrinthine humour of Kafka and, to a lesser extent, Čapek.

The reluctance of the Anglo-Saxon world to translate from or become conversant with other languages than English means that many writers famous in their own countries are unknown in the parts of the world which chiefly concern us. To give an instance, while Kafka was writing *The Castle*, Mihaly Babits was publishing his fantasy *The Nightmare* in Hungary (1916). This short novel is about a case of split personality and clearly owes much to philosophical thought and new scientific findings.[6]

Another Hungarian writer, the popular Frigyes Karinthy, added two further books to the four of *Gulliver's Travels*, one of which (*Faremido*, 1917) features an automated robot culture, and the other (*Capillaria*, 1921) a country ruled by women. The latter book was accompanied by an introductory letter to H. G. Wells on its first appearance.[7]

The culture on Faremido is far more advanced than the rough-and-ready world Čapek later dreamed up. The "*solasis*" robots are all metal. "Not even the tiniest fragment of their body consisted of that certain matter which, according to our conception, was the only possible carrier and condition of life, and which was called, in common parlance, organic matter." Karinthy's latter-day Gulliver describes the brains of these strange beings, and goes on to explain how they come into being:

> A glance at the face of the *solasi* convinced me that it was manufacturing this same product which it needed—eyes. Now it became evident how these amazing creatures or mechanisms came into being: they themselves manufactured their equals from metals and minerals, and they themselves activated the finished *solasi* through the sources of energy (electric accumulators, steam, gases, etc.) placed within their bodies. (Chapter 4)

The *solasis* live a calm and pleasant life. Thought, inward thought, is an infection; organic life on Earth is no more than a disease. In true Swiftian fashion, Karinthy's Gulliver is converted to his hosts' point of view, and begs to be turned to metal. He is given an injection, after which he saw "heat, thermal energy flowing around me in a multicoloured, wavering stream, lapping over my body," and other remarkable things besides. But his body and mind are too immature for the shot to have its desired effect, and Gulliver returns sadly to Earth.

A few years later, an English writer turned his attention to a world where automation had set in and extra-uterine babies were the fashion. This was Aldous Huxley, whose *Brave New World* was published in 1932. In part, it was a reply to H. G. Wells' utopian ideas,[8] and superseded the overpraised *The Machine Stops* (1909), by E. M. Forster, which was described by its author as "a reaction to one of the earlier heavens of H. G. Wells."

Forster's story is all very back-to-the-wombish. There is an underground world in which everyone lives in separate rooms and is completely tended by the Machine. In the end, most people die, the machine breaks down, including the central character with his body of white pap, but a few lucky ones are left to tramp about in "the mist and the ferns." Humanity has learnt its lessons. So much for English middle-class dreams of a quiet garden suburb! *Brave New World* has a lot more punch, and no easy solutions or moralising.

Brave New World is arguably the Western world's most famous science fiction novel.

Years later, and in a changed world, Huxley's novel remains of great interest. This is partly because its central debate on how far people should be induced to surrender their individuality for the benefit of a smooth-running state remains ever topical, and partly because a good deal of wit eases us through this utopia— unlike most other utopias.

Aldous Huxley (1894–1963) opens his novel briskly and without compromise—in the future, in the year 632 A.F. (After Ford). This is something none of his predecessors had done; even Wells liked to begin his novels cautiously, in the present day. Huxley is also wholehearted about his future civilisation. Instead of introducing one major change, for instance, the extra-uterine production of babies, or the cloning methods of obtaining identical people ("Bokanovsky's Process" it is in the book), or the disappearance of Christianity, and so on, Huxley draws an altered society where several such major changes interact.

On the first page, we are swept into the London Hatchery, to a dazzling and polemical tour of this atrocious but well-reasoned future. Unlike poor E. M. Forster, Huxley shows us a world that indeed does have its insidious attractions. We can believe in it.

The weakness of the book (apart from an occasional descent into facetiousness) lies in the character of the Savage, whom Huxley introduces to symbolise the world of the spirit which the Ford-founded utopia has banished. The Savage is never credible; in all Huxley's novels, there is generally a wise old figure who spouts at length, like Propter in *After Many a Summer* or Rontini in *Time Must Have a Stop*, who comes on strong about Vermeer, Pergolesi, Pascal, the Spirit, and kindred topics of enlightenment. The Savage is a wise young man who quotes Shakespeare too much and never ceases to be a twenties stereotype of untrammelled youth drawn by a man who had known D. H. Lawrence personally.

One takes this in one's stride, assisted in doing so by the light jazzy arrangement of the blocks of prose. The book bubbles with invention and aphorism, as the smug society, with its ever-available girls and the slugs of *soma* when needed, parades its monstrous virtues. The saxophones wail, the feelies go full blast ("There's a love scene on a bearskin rug; they say it's marvellous. Every hair of the bear reproduced"), everyone talks, everyone copulates, Ford's in his Flivver, all's right with the world.

"All men are physico-chemically equal."

"When the individual feels, the community reels."

"Was and will make me ill. I take a gramme and only am."

Art has gone by the board. It would rock the boat too much. "That's the price we have to pay for stability. You've got to choose between happiness and what people used to call high art." Scientific progress too has had to go. Knowledge and truth are dangerous. "What's the point of truth or beauty or knowledge when the anthrax bombs are popping all round you?" God also has been abolished for the general good. "Anybody can be virtuous now. Christianity without tears—that's what *soma* is."

The Controller sums it up. "Industrial civilisation is only possible when there's no self-denial. Self-indulgence up to the very limits imposed by hygiene and economics. Otherwise the wheels stop turning." The philosophy of conspicuous consumption.

The moulded personalities of Huxley's new world may owe something to Wells' Selenites in their inspiration, but on the whole the novel has a pleasing originality still evident today, long after all the "shocking" aspects which helped or retarded sales in the thirties have evaporated.

Huxley was a noted essayist as well as novelist, covering not merely a wide range of subjects, but covering them—and often dramatically juxtaposing them—in a single essay. He wrote other novels which qualify as his own special kind of science fiction.

After Many a Summer (1939), the wittiest of his novels, includes a view of Los Angeles which was later expanded on by Evelyn Waugh in *The Loved One*, a beautiful pastiche of an eighteenth-century diary, and Huxley's acerbic comment on evolution.

The wretched English poet Jeremy Pordage goes out to California to catalogue a millionaire's book collection. The lusts of the flesh are all about him (Huxley was always keen on *them*); even the tame baboons in the grounds rut for human delight, and when the dumb blonde calls dreadful Dr. Obispo an "ape-man," both she and he are aware of the flattery involved.

Stoyte, the millionaire, dreads death. When Pordage discovers that the lecherous Fifth Earl's two-centuries-old journal discloses the secret of immortality, Stoyte takes the whole party to England. There, beneath the Fifth Earl's house, in a stinking cellar, they find the old boy still alive—two hundred years old, and apelike in appearance and habit. The foetal anthropoid has been able to come to maturity! What a long way this cruel joke is from Čapek's handling of the immortality theme!

Ape and Essence (1949) shows man again surrendering to the ape in him. This novel, cast as a screenplay with a foreword relating its ironic provenance, uses a post-World War III society in which God and Devil have reversed roles to point to the twin evils of Progress and Nationalism. Radiation has upset mankind's genetic structure, so that "romance has been swallowed up by the oestrus" and mating is a seasonal mass orgy (which Huxley views with his usual lip-licking disgust).

Admittedly, *Ape and Essence* does not make pleasant reading, partly because of an occasional shrillness of tone. But the coolness

of its initial reception was undeserved. Huxley has to a large
extent overcome his old difficulty of the omniscient Propter-figure
who lectures on art and morality by introducing two such figures,
both slightly comic. One is the Narrator of the scenario, whose in-
cursions are always brief and pointed. The other is the Arch-
Vicar, a comic-sinister figure who can munch pig's trotters while
he lectures (as Huxley-cleverly as ever!).

Even Poole, the central character, who begins from the usual
ineffectual-intellectual Huxleyan position—though quoting Shelley to
good effect—retrieves himself vigorously by opting for the well-
padded No's of sex!

Another reason for the book's initial cool reception is one which
applies to many works falling within the science fiction category.
Huxley's prophetic vein runs a good deal deeper and stronger than
that of his critics. They may think he is indulging in exaggeration
or fancy. In fact, he is diagnosing a condition which will only be
generally recognised after his death. Here is the Arch-Vicar, swig-
ging from his bottle and chatting familiarly of the Devil:

> From the very beginning of the Industrial Revolution He
> foresaw that men would be made so overwhelmingly bump-
> tious by the miracles of their own technology that they would
> soon lose all sense of reality. And that's precisely what
> happened. These wretched slaves of wheels and ledgers began
> to congratulate themselves on being the Conquerors of Nature.
> Conquerors of Nature, indeed! In actual fact, of course, they
> had merely upset the equilibrium of Nature and were about
> to suffer the consequences. Just consider what they were up to
> during the century and a half before the Thing. Fouling the
> rivers, killing off the wild animals, destroying the forests, wash-
> ing the topsoil into the sea, burning up an ocean of petroleum,
> squandering the minerals it has taken the whole of geological
> time to deposit. An orgy of criminal imbecility. And they
> called it Progress. Progress! (II)

Huxley here is as perceptive, as prophetic, as previous, and as
impressive, as ever H. G. Wells was.

It is still difficult to arrive at conclusions about that difficult
and diffuse novel *Island* (1962), except to say that it may not be a
shapely novel, or a light entertainment, but it is a fine piece of
polemic. *Island* is Huxley's last novel, filled with all the matters

that preoccupied him, and standing most of the precepts of *Brave New World*, written thirty years earlier, on their head.

For instance, drugs are now valued as gateways to new perception, and free love is advocated as opening the personality; even the children's rhymes of the previous book are here made delightful, an easy way of learning. And the precarious little state of Pala, an island somewhere near Indonesia, is indeed a utopia, full of happiness.

Unfortunately, it is full of slop too. The old Huxleyan disgust and irony have been put away. Here his people talk their big ideas in baby talk. Chapter 6 begins:

> "Golly!" the little nurse exploded, when the door was safely closed behind them.
>
> "I entirely agree with you," said Will.
>
> The Voltairean light twinkled for a moment on Mr. Bahu's evangelical face. "Golly!", he repeated.

An earlier Aldous Huxley could never have written the sort of dialogue which fills *Island*. Was he trying to show us that the inhabitants of this utopia are not priggish just because they are perfect, or had he by this date gone soft? I prefer to believe the case as Philip Toynbee stated it at the time *Island* was published:

> This book, then, is an act of genuine virtue and love. Mr. Huxley has renounced his natural material because he no longer believes that mere disgust is enough to change us. He has deliberately stepped into an area where he is automatically turned into a stutterer and crude fumbler with words. He has done this, I believe, because he is far more concerned with helping the world forward than with writing a praiseworthy book. And it seems to me that it is our duty to look beyond the evident failure . . . to hear what it is that he means us to hear. If we do this I think we shall find a great deal of wisdom, and indeed help, in these awkward pages.[9]

Aldous Huxley was the grandson of the great T. H. Huxley, the supporter of Darwin who became Wells' instructor late in life. He achieved at least three reputations, as a cynic, as a mystical philosopher, and, after his death, as a sort of godfather of the hippies. He was erudite, saintly, and a man of marvellous gifts, which showed through more in his life, possibly, than in his books.[10]

That enquiring spirit of Huxley's never allowed him to rest on any one plateau of achievement. He could without much distortion be made to stand as one shining and eccentric example of the way the twentieth-century world has gone. For this scion of a noted English family, this son of Eton and Balliol, likened to Noel Coward during the period of his post-war success, moved ever outwards, rejecting accepted religion and much else, until he worked his way through Hindu faiths to a philosophical position of detachment and concern.

Speaking of him during this later period, Isaiah Berlin, in a memorial volume dedicated to Huxley, says:

> He would—at least in public—speak of nothing but the need for the reintegration of what both science and life had divided too sharply: the restoration of human contact with non-human nature, the need for antidotes to the lopsided development of human beings in the direction of observation, criticism, theory, and away from the harmonious development of the senses, of the "vegetative soul," of that which man has in common with animals and plants.[11]

It was in 1954 that Huxley published his *Doors of Perception*, an account of his experiences with mescalin. How much it and its successor, *Heaven and Hell*, have contributed to the widespread use of drugs cannot be assessed; but Huxley's delighted account of his experiences made at least one reader hasten round to his local chemist next day (but mescalin was not in the Pharmacopoeia).

When Huxley's first wife died, he married an American woman in 1956, settling in California. He makes a noble father-figure for the hippie cult. His library, with a lifetime's collection of books and manuscripts, was destroyed during a canyon fire, but he did not grieve. He and his wife took LSD and enjoyed many happy psychedelic days together, in search of enrichment rather than escape. In this atmosphere, *Island* was written, and the knowledge should help us to understand that novel better.

Huxley was by no means cut off from the world—eighteen months before his death in 1963, he maintained a fairly heavy schedule of lecturing and seminars, in California and farther afield. When he died, he went forth on a tide of *moksha*-medicine, talked into the beyond by his wife whispering to him of love.[12]

What Huxley has left behind is a sizeable body of work which —at present at least—is undervalued. His writing is formidable in its variety and in its unceasing quest for the nature and enrichment of the free individual. His life is formidable for the way it embodies a whole remarkable movement of our times, from the strictness of a Victorian English upbringing, through immense popularity, to the luminous Californian freedom of gurudom.

Huxley died on 22 November 1963, the day that President J. F. Kennedy was assassinated. Almost within twenty-four hours, Professor C. S. Lewis was dead. He died in Headington, Oxford.

Like Huxley, Lewis also was a seeker of truth; he found its illuminations within the Christian belief. Like Huxley, he called forth affection and respect from all who met him, even those opposed to his views. Again like Huxley, he was drawn to science fiction as a medium of expression.

With the possible exception of Huxley, C. S. Lewis was the most formidable and respected champion of science fiction the modern genre has known.

Clive Staples Lewis (born 1898) spent most of his working life at either Oxford or Cambridge. He served in the infantry in the First World War, and was wounded in 1918. He was elected Fellow and Tutor in English Literature at Magdalen College, Oxford, in 1925, a position he held until 1954. It was during his Oxford period that he wrote the trilogy which has earned him an enviable place in science fiction history, *Out of the Silent Planet* (1938), *Perelandra* (1943), and *That Hideous Strength* (1945).

No journey from Earth to another planet was ever of more consequence than the one which took Devine and Weston to Lewis' world of Malacandra (Mars). For their voyage broke the ages of quarantine which have kept Thulcandra, the Silent Planet (Earth), from the converse of the planets and of the solar system —known as the Field of Arbol to the *eldila*, the angel-like beings who tend it. Great questions are now open again as a result of the voyage.

In the first volume of the trilogy, Ransom is kidnapped and taken to Mars by Devine and Weston. The latter two are caricatures of the materialist point of view, and of the progressive scientist.

Ransom is at first terrified by the whole idea of Malacandra

and its inhabitants. "His mind, like so many minds of his generation, was richly furnished with bogies. He had read his H. G. Wells
and others." But Malacandra's inhabitants are entirely amiable, as
he finds on his first encounter with a *hross*, a seal-like being. Later,
Ransom meets the tall *sorns*, the froglike *pfifltriggi*, and the great
Oyarsa, the *eldil* who rules Malacandra.

Since he is a philologist, Ransom learns to speak the language
of Oyarsa with some ease. Weston and Devine have only a toe-
hold in the language, which leads to one of the most comic and
telling scenes in the book. Weston addresses Oyarsa in the sort
of terms that H. G. Wells or Olaf Stapledon might use, and Ransom
interprets for him. Only the terms come out a little strangely in
translation:

> "Life [says Weston] is greater than any system of moral-
> ity; her claims are absolute. It is not by tribal taboos and
> copy book maxims that she has pursued her relentless march
> from the amoeba to man and from man to civilization."

> "He says," began Ransom, "that living creatures are stronger
> than the question whether an act is bent or good—no, that
> cannot be right—he says that it is better to be alive and bent
> than to be dead—no—he says, he says—I cannot say what he
> says, Oyarsa, in your language. But he goes on to say that the
> only good thing is that there should be very many creatures
> alive. He says there were many other animals before the first
> men and the later ones were better than the earlier ones; but
> he says the animals were not born because of what is said to
> the young about bent and good action by their elders. And he
> says these animals did not feel any pity."

> "She—" began Weston.

> "I'm sorry," interrupted Ransom, "but I've forgotten who
> She is."

> "Life, of course," snapped Weston. "She has ruthlessly
> broken down all obstacles and liquidated all failures and today
> in her highest form—civilized man—and in me as his repre-
> sentative, she presses forward to that interplanetary leap which
> will, perhaps, place her forever beyond the reach of death."

> "He says," resumed Ransom, "that these animals learned
> to do many difficult things, except those who could not; and
> those ones died and the other animals did not pity them. And

he says the best animal now is the kind of man who makes the big huts and carries the heavy weights and does all the other things I told you about; and he is one of these and he says that if the others all knew what he was doing they would be pleased. He says that if he could kill you all and bring our people to live in Malacandra, then they might be able to go on living here after something had gone wrong with our world. And then if something went wrong with Malacandra they might go and kill all the *hnau* in another world. And then another—and so they would never die out." (Chapter 20)[13]

Oyarsa decides to return the humans to Earth, though Ransom may stay on Malacandra if he so desires. His answer, "If I cannot live in Thulcandra, it is better for me not to live at all," might be a reproof to John Carter of Mars. So he returns unharmed, completing one of the most delightful space voyages in the literature.

The whole trilogy is informed by the powerful religious nature of Lewis' mind. He takes great pleasure in invention, like any good storyteller, but sometimes a wish to be improving gains the upper hand. Both the invention and the preachment are stronger in the second volume, although Lewis categorically denied that he wrote primarily for a didactic purpose.[14]

Perelandra is Venus, on which watery planet the scene is set. The description of the planet, its floating and flexible rafts of islands contrasted with the Fixed Land, set in the midst of a summery and non-salt ocean, is delightful.

Ransom is transported from Thulcandra by Oyarsa's powers. On one of the floating islands he meets the Green Lady. She is at present separated from her king, who is elsewhere. Perelandra is as yet a sinless world, and the Green Lady its Eve (though we are warned that history never repeats itself exactly). The Serpent arrives in the form of Ransom's old enemy, Weston, who is taken over bodily by the Bent One, the devil himself. "Weston" tries to tempt the Green Lady to stay on the Fixed Land, which Maleldil has forbidden her to do.

The temptation goes on for many days, with Ransom speaking up, not always effectively, for good. Eventually, it comes down to a physical battle between him and "Weston," and the Bent One is vanquished. Ransom then has some adventures in a subterranean world before rejoining the Green Lady and her king for a grand finale at which the *eldils* are also present. Perelandra has been preserved from evil.

Lewis manages to convey both the horror of the thing that is no longer Weston, together with the misery of all things concerned with it, and, contrastingly, the beauty and happiness of things Venerian, or Perelandrian; he also displays with considerable skill the force and truth behind Christian myth—i.e., the importance of individual life, however puny-seeming. What he cannot do is to make non-Christians believe in his overall design, though it is undeniable that he can sometimes make them squirm with embarrassment, as in the psalm-singing ending.[15]

It is a mark of much original work that it shows traces of its ancestry, as Shakespeare's dramas exhibit their debts to Holinshed's chronicles and old Tudor plays. The first two Lewis novels reveal fairly clearly one line of their descent.

Out of the Silent Planet was in some measure inspired by a favourite novel of Lewis', *A Voyage to Arcturus,* by David Lindsay. Lindsay roars along like a late member of *Sturm Und Drang,* although his extravagant story was published in 1920. It relates how one Krag persuades Nightspore and Maskull to travel in a spaceship to Tormance, a planet where weird metaphysical adventures confront them. Read as allegory, these adventures defy interpretation; so they have to be accepted as vision.

Perelandra is much more allegory than vision. But it derives power from that great allegory *Paradise Lost,* a poem with which Lewis was thoroughly familiar. How far this is from saying that *Perelandra* is similar to *Paradise Lost* (although it does have its similarities) we can see when we recall that a very different novel, Mary Shelley's *Frankenstein*—as dark and atheistic as Lewis' Venus is religious and well lit—also owes much to Milton. The more one considers it, the greater is every English fantasy writer's debt to Milton; and that includes Lindsay.[16]

So we turn to the third book of Lewis' trilogy.

The forces of "Progress" which will ruin the world have become much more powerful in *That Hideous Strength.* Devine is now Lord Feverstone, backing a National Institute for Coordinated Experiments. N.I.C.E.'s programme is vague and grandiose, including a massive programme of vivisection and the reeducation of man, together with prenatal education. N.I.C.E. begins to take

over Edgestow, using a mixture of circumlocution and secret
police. Victory would be theirs, had they not already broken
Earth's quarantine, which permits good *eldils* to enter from outside and help man to frustrate them.

The somewhat ragged forces opposing N.I.C.E. include Ransom, now a man of some power. Happily, Edgestow is the site of
ancient Logres. Merlin is resurrected and he and Ransom, operating
as the Pendragon, rout N.I.C.E. utterly by using Earth-magic.

This is a curious novel which seeks to operate on several different levels, from realistic through to symbolic. H. G. Wells appears
as Jules, the figurehead of the Institute, and is shot. The Institute
for Coordinated Experiments is full of Kafkaesque obfuscation,
making it difficult for us to believe that it could represent a major
threat to anything but progress. Moreover, its grasp on science is
too nebulous for the sort of villainy Lewis seeks to portray. Devine
has visited Mars, and one of his objectives through N.I.C.E. would
surely have been to duplicate Weston's space flight and to attempt
to control the forces there, forces of whose presence he is dimly
aware.

On the other side, it is hard to believe in the Christians,
trailing clouds of Arthurian romance with them and subscribing
to both a high moral creed and a love of a bucolic little England.

The total effect is rather as if C. P. Snow and Charles Williams
took turns to rewrite Rex Warner's *The Aerodrome*: remarkable
rather than successful.

What remains vital about *That Hideous Strength,* and the
trilogy of which it is part, is that it tries to answer the Wellsian
position in vaguely Wellsian terms. It is not dystopian; it is against
the idea of utopia. As such, it represents a genuine minority viewpoint.

In a short book on C. S. Lewis,[17] Roger Lancelyn Green, his
noted disciple, quotes a letter from Lewis in which the latter says:

> What immediately spurred me to write was Olaf Staple-
> don's "Last and First Men" and an essay in J. H. B. Haldane's
> *Possible Worlds,* both of which seemed to take the idea of
> such [space] travel seriously and to have the desperately
> immoral outlook which I try to pillory in Weston. I like the
> whole interplanetary ideas as a *mythology* and simply wished to
> conquer for my own [Christian] point of view what has always

hitherto been used by the opposite side. I think Wells' *First Men on the Moon* the best of the sort I have read . . .

Nevertheless, Lewis' attitude to Wells was ambivalent[18]; Wells awoke Lewis' imagination and his moral dislike at one and the same time. So with Stapledon: "I admire his invention [though not his philosophy] so much that I feel no shame to borrow," says Lewis in his preface to *That Hideous Strength*.

An interesting footnote to *That Hideous Strength* is that it shows other influence besides the Wells-Stapledon axis, the influence of two of Lewis' close friends at that time in Oxford, J. R. R. Tolkien and Charles Williams. The latter is present in the Logres material, the former in rather cryptic references to Numinor and the True West, with a tantalising word in the Preface about "the MSS. of my friend, Professor J. R. R. Tolkien."

Tolkien's *Lord of the Rings*, when it finally began its monstrous appearance, proved every bit as anti-Wellsian as Lewis' trilogy, and every bit as fantastic. By the way it was clutched to the chests and bosoms of sf readers, one can see that their true interest is not in the writer's viewpoint, but in his imagination. Lewis or Wells, Stapledon or Tolkien, Burroughs or Heinlein—in one sense, all are equal in the eyes of the reader; what they have in common is greater than what they have against each other; the medium is the message.

Wells, escaping from the horrors of a lower-class Victorian environment, saw the hope that science offered of a better world. Those who argued against him, like Lewis and Forster, saw only the eternal human condition, which science could not improve when regarded from a religious viewpoint. Wells also saw the human condition, and loathed it—hence his strong vein of pessimism —but he believed it was malleable, not eternally the same. Alas, he may be right, if there is truth in the predictions about future biological control of living organisms!! Wells both hopes and fears. Since his day, his fears have been accepted, his hopes rejected— or, where challenged, as by Huxley, Forster, and Lewis, challenged largely in Wells' terms.[19]

We turn now to the greatest of Wells' followers, who said of Wells' influence, "A man does not record his debt to the air he breathes." This is Lewis' bête noire, W. Olaf Stapledon.

Stapledon was born in 1886, in the Wirral, Cheshire, England.

Much of his childhood was spent in Egypt. He received a good education, and was a rather unlikely product of Balliol. He served in an ambulance unit in World War I. He lectured in philosophy at Liverpool University and wrote several works of philosophy. All his novels may be classified as speculative fiction, even his slender last book, *A Man Divided*, which has autobiographical elements. It was published in 1950, the year Stapledon died. None of the standard works of literary reference see fit to mention his name, but this shameful state of affairs may improve.

The atmosphere Stapledon generates is chill but intoxicating. Reading his books is like standing on the top of a high mountain. One can see a lot of planet and much of the sprawling uncertain works of man, but little actual human activity; from such an altitude, all sense of the individual is lost.

The best of Stapledon is contained in two long works of fiction and two shorter novels. His most famous work is the first he published: *Last and First Men: A Story of the Near and Far Future*. It appeared in 1930.

Last and First Men is evolutionary fantasy on a gigantic scale. It begins at Stapledon's Now, 1930, to move steadily further and further into the future, two thousand million years hence, until the last species of man, the Sixteenth Men, settle on Neptune, and there resign themselves to extinction as the Sun begins to disintegrate.

The author himself regarded—or said he regarded—his chronicle as expendable; for the next generation, it would "certainly raise a smile." Well, there is no doubt that Stapledon's version of events from 1930 to the present is ludicrous. It is worth close attention if one wishes to savour how wrong prediction can be, in both fact and spirit. Almost anything Stapledon says about Germany and America is incorrect. Only when one climbs through the leaden opening chapters of the book does one start to soar on the wings of inspiration—"myth," Stapledon called it. Politics then gives way to an inquiry into life processes.

One thing is never at fault: the invention. The Second Men, for instance, are bothered by Martian invasions; although the idea may have been derived from Wells, the Martians are cloudlike beings and derive only from Stapledon.

Moreover, the invention is sustained, nourished by imagination, and the successive panoramas of life which Stapledon unrolls

are always varied and striking. They are variations on the theme of
mankind as a creature like any other, fatally victim of its surroundings, so that whatever is godlike in the creature is brought to
nothing by blind happenstance. Like Hardy, Stapledon was influenced by Schopenhauer's philosophy of being, as well as Speng-
ler's philosophy of the cyclic nature of history; his view is at once
more prideful and more pessimistic than Hardy's.

Here is one of his final visions, which science fiction readers
evidently find profoundly moving—though it is the kind of passage
that Lewis found profoundly irritating:

> But in the fullness of time there would come a far more
> serious crisis. The sun would continue to cool, and at last
> man would no longer be able to live by means of solar radia-
> tion. It would become necessary to annihilate matter to supply
> the deficiency. The other planets might be used for this pur-
> pose, and possibly the sun itself. Or, given the sustenance for
> so long a voyage, man might boldly project his planet into the
> neighbourhood of some young star. Thenceforth, perhaps, he
> might operate upon a far grander scale. He might explore and
> colonise all suitable worlds in every corner of the galaxy, and
> organise himself as a vast community of minded worlds. Even
> (so we dreamed) he might achieve intercourse with other
> galaxies. It did not seem impossible that man himself was the
> germ of the world-soul, which, we still hope, is destined to
> awake for a while before the universal decline, and to crown
> the eternal cosmos with its due of knowledge and admira-
> tion, fleeting yet eternal. We dared to think that in some far
> distant epoch the human spirit, clad in all wisdom, power, and
> delight, might look back upon our primitive age with a certain
> respect; no doubt with pity also and amusement, but none the
> less with admiration for the spirit in us, still only half awake,
> and struggling against great disabilities. (Chapter 16)

Such a chilly vision is best conveyed as fiction or music; as
architecture or government, it would be intolerable. Note how the
eschatology of this passage takes us a long way beyond the passage
we quoted from William Hope Hodgson's *The House on the
Borderland*. We may suspect that Stapledon's alienation was at
least as severe as Hodgson's; but Stapledon's powerful intellect
has shaped his mental condition into a metaphysic.

In 1932, Stapledon published *Last Men in London*, a pendant to the earlier book. His greatest work appeared in 1937, when the shadow of another war was stretching over Europe. In his Preface, Stapledon makes an apology for writing something so far removed from the sounds of battle, and says of those in the thick of the struggle that they "nobly forgo something of that detachment, that power of cold assessment, which is, after all, among the most valuable human capacities"—a very suspect claim; there is no denying that he set great store by a detachment he probably could not help but feel. His was among those "intellects vast and cool and unsympathetic" to which Wells made reference in another context.

The Star Maker begins, in some respects, where *Last and First Men* left off. An unnamed human being, the disembodied "I" of the book, falls into a kind of trance, a "hawk-flight of the imagination," while sitting amid the heather on a hill close to his home. The "I"'s essence is drawn away from Earth, into the solar system and then beyond, farther and farther, and faster.

This is a new—and so far unsurpassed—version of the spiritual voyage. A fresh generation has brought fresh knowledge; Einstein's perceptions, and the popularisations of Eddington and James Jeans, add calibre to Stapledon's new model of the universe:

> After a while I noticed that the sun and all the stars in his neighbourhood were ruddy. Those at the opposite pole of the heaven were of an icy blue. The explanation of this strange phenomenon flashed upon me. I was still travelling, and travelling so fast that light itself was not wholly indifferent to my passage. The overtaking undulations took long to catch me. They therefore affected me as slower pulsations than they normally were, and I saw them therefore as red. Those that met me on my headlong flight were congested and shortened, and were seen as blue.
>
> Very soon the heavens presented an extraordinary appearance, for all the stars directly behind me were now deep red, while those directly ahead were violet. Rubies lay behind me, amethysts ahead of me. Surrounding the ruby constellations there spread an area of topaz stars, and round the amethyst constellations an area of sapphires. Beside my course, on every side, the colours faded into the normal white of the sky's familiar diamonds. Since I was travelling almost in the

plane of the galaxy, the hoop of the Milky Way, white on either hand, was violet ahead of me, red behind. Presently the stars immediately before and behind grew dim, then vanished, leaving two starless holes in heaven, each hole surrounded by a zone of coloured stars. Evidently I was still gathering speed. Light from the forward and the hinder stars now reached me in forms beyond the range of my human vision.

As my speed increased, the two starless patches, before and behind, each with its coloured fringe, continued to encroach upon the intervening zone of normal stars which lay abreast of me on every side. Amongst these I now detected movement. Through the effect of my own passage the nearer stars appeared to drift across the background of stars at greater distance, the whole visible sky was streaked with flying stars. Then everything vanished. Presumably my speed was so great in relation to the stars that light from none of them could take normal effect on me. (Chapter 2)

The traveller moves ever on in quest for planets that might support humanlike life, and eventually arrives on Other Earth. A full description of its societies is given before the traveller passes on; there is some mild satire of terrestrial behaviour, as well as occasional comments which foreshadow the writings of more intelligent modern sf writers including C. S. Lewis and James Blish. "Shortly before I left Other Earth a geologist discovered a fossil diagram of a very complicated radio set," suggests the extraordinary reality-reversions of Philip K. Dick.

Travelling faster than light, the traveller meets other mental cosmic adventurers. They explore endless worlds, endless modes of life, in which Stapledon's ingenuity in creating varied species of men as demonstrated in *Last and First Men* is completely eclipsed. Here, under all sorts of alien conditions, he shows us many "strange mankinds," as he calls them—among them centaurs, which are fairly common in the universe (recalling Van Vogt's comment in his novelette *The Storm* that the centaur family is "almost universal"), human echinoderms, and intelligent ships, as well as symbiotic races, multiple minds, composite beings, mobile plant men, and other teeming variants of the life force. Utopias, interstellar-ship travel, war between planets, galactic empires, terrible crises in galactic history, telepathic sub-galaxies going down in madness . . . until a galactic utopia becomes a possibility. In all this, the history of *Last and First Men* appears as a couple of paragraphs, lost among greater things. Stapledon is truly frightening at times.

He keeps turning the volume up. We move to para-galactic scale. Stars also have mentalities, and the minded worlds establish contact with them. As the galaxy begins to rot, there is perfect symbiosis between stars and worlds. Meanwhile the "I" observes "the great snowstorm of many million galaxies." A full telepathic exploration of the cosmos is now possible, yet the "I" still remains a mystery to itself.

Again the scale increases. The "I" is now part of the cosmic mind, listening to muttered thoughts of nebulae as it goes in quest of the Star Maker itself. This Supreme Creator is eventually found, star-like and remote. It repulses the raptures of the cosmic mind— for the created may love the creator but not vice versa, since that would merely be self-love of a kind.

This encounter brings a sort of dream to the cosmic mind. In the most fantastic part of the book, the cosmic mind visits earlier versions of the cosmos with which the young Star Maker experimented. These are toy versions of the universe. They cannot and should not be detailed here, for their place is exactly where Stapledon sets them. Suffice it to say that one of these "toy" cosmoses consists of three linked universes which resemble a Christian vision of the world. In the first of these universes, two spirits, one "good" and one "evil," dice or play for possession of souls of creatures. According to whether they are won or lost, the souls plunge into the second or third linked universes, which are eternal heavens or hells, and there experience either eternal torment or eternal bliss of comprehension!

The range of cosmoses is continued, up the scale, as the Star Maker's own skill and perception are improved by his models—he perpetually and tragically outgrows his creatures. Later creations show greater economy of effort than ours, but suffering is always widespread. The creations pour on successively, until the cosmic mind is fatigued; then it comes to the ultimate cosmos.

Beyond that, the cosmic mind wakes from its "dream" and understands that it has encountered the consciousness of the Star Maker, which comprehends all lives in one timeless vision. Such contemplation is its greatest goal.

The "I" now returns to Earth, is back in the present, may take refuge in littleness. The man may go home to his wife. Yet private happiness remains mocked by public calamity. The world is faced with another crisis. All we can do is fight for a little lucidity before ultimate darkness falls.

Time scales complete this magnificent and neurasthenic vision.

Not only is the vision in *Star Maker* wider than in *Last and First Men;* it has become less coarse. Not only does a continuity operate among its parts which is much more various than the somewhat crude cause-and-effect which serves to perform changes of scene in the earlier book, but a concomitant flexibility works through the prose itself. The personal viewpoint, however attenuated it becomes, is a help in this respect, adding a cohesion which *Last and First Men* lacks.

Last and First Men is just slightly an atheist's tract, based largely on nineteenth-century thought. In *Star Maker,* the atheism has become a faith in itself, so that it inevitably approaches higher religion, which is bodied forth on a genuinely new twentieth-century perception of cosmology; thus it marks a great step forward in Stapledon's art, the thought unfolding with little sense of strain through chapter after chapter. It is magnificent. It is almost unbearable.

Stapledon also published several slightly more orthodox novels, of which mention need only be made of *Odd John* (1935) and *Sirius* (1944). *Odd John* is a pleasant superman tale, relating how John grows up, experimenting with his special powers until he discovers others of his kind and founds a community on a small island in the Pacific. Although this small and somewhat crazy utopia is eventually wiped out, the mood of the book is light and cheerful. The histories of all the supermen are different, and Stapledon clearly enjoys himself inventing past histories for them. Since this is the nearest the author ever came to "a good read," it is a suitable Stapledon for beginners, a vernal hill before tackling the dizzy and formidable heights that loom beyond.

Sirius is the most human of all Stapledon's novels, perhaps because its central figure is a dog. Sirius is a sheep dog that has the brain and consequently the perceptions of a man, although in other respects it remains dog. The product of a scientific experiment, the dog gradually wins its independence. Its life is made tolerable by a reciprocated love for the girl Plaxy. Love is a rare thing in Stapledon's work; here, reaching across species, it finds its warmest and most touching expression, to live on even when the mutated dog is killed.

These two novels are fine of their kind; the name of Olaf Stapledon would be remembered by them alone in the science fiction field, where memories are long. But *Last and First Men* and *The Star Maker* soar far beyond the accepted limits of science fiction. Or rather, one might say, Stapledon is the great classical example, the cold pitch of perfection as he turns scientific concepts into vast ontological epic prose poems, the ultimate sf writer. In particular, *Star Maker* stands on that very remote shelf of books which contains huge foolhardy endeavours, carried out according to their author's ambitions: Hardy's *Dynasts* stands there, the writings of Sir Thomas Browne, C. M. Doughty's epic poems, and maybe Milton's *Paradise Lost*.

How it is that the funeral masons and morticians who work their preserving processes on Eng. Lit. have rejected Stapledon entirely from their critical incantations is a matter before which speculation falls fainting away. His prose is as lucid as his imagination is huge and frightening. *Star Maker* is really the one great grey holy book of science fiction—perhaps after all there is something appropriate in its wonderful obscurity and neglect!

This chapter on thirties' writing could be extended greatly. But time and space preclude more than an affectionate mention of J. B. Priestley's time plays, such as *Time and the Conways* (1937) and *I Have Been Here Before* (1938)‡; the novels of S. Fowler Wright, such as *The World Below* (1929); Philip Wylie's *When Worlds Collide* (1932), with Edwin Balmer and later filmed, and his *The Disappearance;* James Hilton's best-selling novel, also filmed, *Lost Horizon*—another of the exotic sons of Haggard; the novels of John Taine (the mathematician Eric Temple Bell), such as *Before the Dawn* (1934); and whatever one's personal preferences may be. Instead, we must look at the sf magazines.

The writers gathered together in this chapter created their work in response to forces working in society and the ideas of their times. Their books are specific responses to specific conditions. Kafka, Huxley, Čapek, Stapledon, are full of *Weltanschauung;* and

‡ Priestley has more than once spoken up for the pleasures of science fiction, and was one of the first to praise *Last and First Men*.

at their best they rise through it to a sort of universality which permits their books to endure beyond their immediate age. In capturing the *Zeitgeist*, they defy it.

Most of the writings in the sf magazines have been unable to endure. They reflect little of the world and a lot more of the tricks of their trade. They created sf as a medium, but in so doing inevitably lowered its "once-for-once-only" aspect.

It is easy to argue that Hugo Gernsback (1884–1967) was one of the worst disasters ever to hit the science fiction field. Not only did the segregation of science fiction into magazines designed especially for it, ghetto-fashion, guarantee that various orthodoxies would be established inimical to a thriving literature, but Gernsback himself was utterly without any literary understanding. He created dangerous precedents which many later editors in the field followed.

Gernsback was born in Luxembourg, received a technical education, and emigrated to the United States in 1904, determined to make good as an inventor. In no time, he was marketing home radio sets and publishing the world's first radio magazine, *Modern Electrics*. In that journal, in 1911, he serialised his novel *Ralph 124C 41+: A Romance of the Year 2660*—a novel which gives us a pretty broad hint as to his lack of interest in anything but technical marvels and gimmicks.

A sample of this unique document is in order. This is the opening of Chapter 3, "Dead or Alive?"

> An apologetic cough came through the entrance of the laboratory. It was nearing one o'clock of the following day.
>
> Several minutes later it was repeated, to the intense annoyance of the scientist, who had left orders that he was not to be interrupted in his work under any circumstances.
>
> At the third "Ahem!" he raised his head and stared fixedly at the empty space between the doorjambs. The most determined optimist could not have spelled welcome in that look.
>
> Peter, advancing his neck around the corner until one eye met that of his master, withdrew it hastily.
>
> "Well, what is it?" came from the laboratory, in an irritated harsh voice.

This tawdry illiterate tale, which drifts into space and back, is packed with all sorts of technical predictions, each one of which has apparently been invented just before the story opens in 2660. But society is unchanged: boy meets girl in the same prissy 1911 way, and Ralph has a manservant; sleep, in this hideous world, is regarded as wasted time, so that during the night children are fed lessons, and adults—of all miserable things—the contents of newspapers. This is simple-minded Victorian utilitarianism. Gernsback's philosophy, far more than Stapledon's, is what C. S. Lewis would have loathed, had he known it; but Stapledon would have loathed it, too, had *he* known it.[20] The worst Gernsbackian sf neither thinks nor dreams.

Gernsback's sorry concoction met with great success. Its flow of inventions went down well, the dearth of Inwardness and Imagination notwithstanding. Gernsback began to publish more science fiction—mercifully by other hands—in his magazine. In April 1926, he launched *Amazing Stories,* with a first issue featuring stories by Verne, Poe, and Wells. Full of confidence, he launched *Amazing Stories Annual* in 1927, replacing it with *Amazing Stories Quarterly* in 1928—and running *Ralph 124C 41+* through in the latter during 1929.

He lost control of *Amazing Stories* early in 1929, but began publication of *Science Wonder Stories* in the summer of 1929, with a speed which says much for his initiative. Gernsback was an energetic and courageous publisher, always ready to follow up success. He also coined the term "science fiction," after juggling with the unpronounceable Gernsbackian uglyism "scientifiction." For all that, it is very difficult to understand why he should ever have been spoken of as "The Father of Science Fiction"[21]; but we have met enough of these claimants before to realise that Gernsback was just a midwife disguised as a Young Pretender.

The very existence of Gernsback's magazines attracted writers. Names such as Murray Leinster, David H. Keller, Stanton A. Coblentz, Jack Williamson, Bob Olsen, Harl Vincent, and Philip Francis Nowlan, who wrote of the Buck Rogers later to be immortalised in comic strip, were associated with his imprint. He also imported German writers in translation, so that such exotic names as Otfrid von Hanstein and Bruno H. Burgel appeared in his pages.

Gernsback laid great emphasis on the need for scientific accuracy in stories, and later competitors felt bound to copy him. Although this dictate was more honoured in the breach than the observance, it did have the effect of introducing a deadening literalism into the fiction. As long as the stories were built like diagrams, and made clear like diagrams, and stripped of atmosphere and sensibility, then it did not seem to matter how silly the "science" or the psychology was.

A typical story might relate how a scientist experimenting in his private laboratory found a new way to break up atoms so as to release their explosive power; in so doing, he sets up a self-perpetuating vortex of energy which kills either the scientist or his assistant, or else threatens the career of his beautiful daughter, before it rolls out of the window and creates great havoc against which the local fire brigade is powerless. The vortex grows bigger and more erratic all the while. Soon it is destroying New York (or Berlin or London or Moscow) and causing great panic. Tens of thousands of lunatics roam the open countryside, destroying everything in their path. The CID (or the militia or the Grenadier Guards or the Red Army) is helpless.

Fortunately, the scientist's favourite assistant, or the reporter on the local paper, or the boy friend of the beautiful daughter, has a great idea, which is immediately taken up by the President (or the Chancellor or the King or Stalin). Huge tractors with gigantic electromagnets are built in every country, and these move in on the vortex, which is now very large indeed, having just consumed San Francisco Bridge (or Krupp's works or Buckingham Palace or the Kremlin). Either everything goes well, with the hero and the beautiful daughter riding on the footplate of one of the giant machines as the energy vortex is repulsed into space—or else things go wrong at the last minute, until a volcanic eruption of unprecedented violence takes place, and shoots the energy vortex into space.

The hero and the beautiful daughter get engaged (or receive medals or bury Daddy or are purged) by the light of a beautiful new moon.[22]

The effect of this sort of story was to kill the vogue for the Burroughsian interplanetary romance. The bright colours of the latter were replaced by the grey contretemps and armistices of technocracy.

But talent will out, even in adverse circumstances. Gradually a synthesis between the Burroughsian and the Gernsbackian was reached.

The synthesis was reached by way of the "Gosh-wow!" type of

story, and not through Gernsback's magazines alone. (*Amazing*—
which amazingly still survives—has in fact contributed little to the
field.) Farnsworth Wright's grand old pulp, *Weird Tales*, published
a considerable amount of science fiction—without always calling it
that—ever since its first number in March 1923. And in January
1930, a new magazine joined the lists. It was named *Astounding
Stories of Super Science*. In it the synthesis would appear, making
a new kind of sense.

NOTES

1. And perhaps there is room in a note to be reminded of how
often opera uses a great fantasy theme. Wagner's *Twilight of the Gods*
immediately comes to mind, with its great climax of flood and fire.
Stravinsky's *Oedipus Rex* depicts the dangers inherent in seeking out the
truth. Bartók's one-act opera *Bluebeard's Castle* shows the disaster that
can attend a woman who seeks to know everything about her lover's
past. And so on. There is probably a case to be made for arguing that
opera, with all its colour, music, and ritual, is the most powerful way of
conveying fantasy.

2. Erich Heller, "The World of Franz Kafka," *The Disinherited
Mind*, Cambridge, 1952.

3. *Tagebucher 1910–1923*, translated into English as *The Diary of
Franz Kafka*, edited by Max Brod, 2 Vols., 1948–49. "Unnoticeable
life. Noticeable failure," reads one entry.

4. For the influence of psychoanalysis on Kafka, see Charles Neider's
The Frozen Sea, 1948. An extract from this book, under the title "The
Castle: A Psychoanalytical Interpretation," is included in a useful collection of critical essays, *Twentieth Century Interpretations of The Castle*,
edited by Peter F. Neumeyer, Englewood Cliffs, New Jersey, 1969.

5. Nesvadba's best collection is *In the Footsteps of the Abominable
Snowman*, 1971.

6. For my knowledge of this book and the next, I am indebted to
Mr. Peter Kuczka, the well-known Hungarian authority on science fiction.
The original title of *The Nightmare* is *A Gólya Kalifa*. An English
translation was published by Corvina Press, Budapest, in 1966.

7. Original Hungarian title: *Utazás Faremidoba Capillaria*. An
English translation by Paul Tabori was published by Corvina Press,
Budapest, in 1965.

8. In *Writer at Work: The Paris Review Interviews*, Aldous

Huxley claimed that *Brave New World* "started out as a parody of
H. G. Wells' *Men Like Gods,* but gradually it got out of hand . . ."

9. From Philip Toynbee's review of *Island. Observer,* Sunday,
Apr. 1, 1962.

10. There is an early critical book on Huxley: John Atkins, *Aldous
Huxley: A Literary Study,* revised edition, 1967. The latest study is
George Woodcock's *Dawn and the Darkest Hour,* 1972.

11. Isaiah Berlin's essay, with others, is contained in *Aldous Huxley,
1894–1963. A Memorial Volume,* edited by Julian Huxley, 1965.

12. Laura Archera Huxley, *This Timeless Moment: A Personal
View of Aldous Huxley,* 1969.

13. A passage that will remind admirers of A. W. Kinglake's
Eothen of the traveller's conversation with a pasha, from which it is
concluded that "the intervention of the dragoman is fatal to the spirit of
the conversation."

14. ALDISS: I would have thought that you constructed *Perelandra*
for the didactic purpose. LEWIS: Yes, everyone thinks that. They are
quite wrong . . . The story of this averted Fall came in very conveniently.
Of course it wouldn't have been that particular story if I wasn't interested in those particular ideas on other grounds. But that isn't what
I started from. (From C. S. Lewis' "Discussion of Science Fiction,"
recorded by Brian Aldiss. Published in *SF Horizons I,* 1964. Reprinted
in *Of Other Worlds.*

15. Perhaps the difficulty one has with *Perelandra* is suggested by
Lois and Stephen Rose, the authors of (what this critic regards as a fallible and partially informed study) *The Shattered Ring: Science Fiction
and the Quest for Meaning,* 1970, when they say "The evil antagonist,
Weston, is often compared to a nasty little boy. His 'naughtiness' is
epitomised by his cruel teasing and senseless torture of animals . . ."
Lewis gives us nastiness and a dose of horror. But he confronts us with no
real evil.

16. Those who find *A Voyage to Arcturus* readable but baffling
are advised to seek out the 1963 Gollancz edition, which includes a Note
examining the novel in the light of Milton's epic. This note is by E. H.
Visiak, who died in 1972, aged ninety-four. Like Lewis, Visiak was a
Milton scholar. His esoteric novel *Medusa* (1929) also bears Miltonic
traces.

17. Roger Lancelyn Green, *C. S. Lewis,* a Bodley Head Monograph,
1963, p. 26.

18. Very ambivalent. Lewis apologises to Wells in a special note in
Out of the Silent Planet; but Jules in *That Hideous Strength* is a
spiteful and personal caricature. It was hardly Wells' fault that he was a
Cockney, or that his legs were short.

19. For a full discussion of this theme, see Mark R. Hillegas, *The Future as Nightmare: H. G. Wells and the Anti-Utopians*, New York, 1967. Hillegas deals fully with Lewis, Forster, Zemyatin, and Orwell and looks rather tentatively at the world of standard science fiction. Hillegas' study was reviewed at some length by C. C. Shackleton in a two-part criticism in *New Worlds*, Nos. 182–83.

20. When an sf fan approached Stapledon in 1936, he was treated to his first glimpse of science fiction magazines. "My impression was that the stories varied greatly in quality," Stapledon politely said. The anecdote is told at greater length in Sam Moskowitz's *Explorers of the Infinite*, Chap. 16.

21. "The real 'Father of Science Fiction' is Hugo Gernsback and no one can take the title away from him." Sam Moskowitz, *Explorers of the Infinite*, Chap. 14.

22. A story suspiciously similar to this apocryphal one appears in the Apr. 1929 issue of *Amazing Stories*.

9

The Future on a Chipped Plate:

THE WORLD OF
JOHN W. CAMPBELL'S "ASTOUNDING"

> The boat-express is waiting your command!
> You will find the "Mauretania" at the quay,
> Till her captain turns the lever 'neath his hand,
> And the monstrous nine-decked city goes to sea.
> Kipling: *The Secret of the Machines*

> He opened his mind. All around him, stretching across
> the earth, the linked thoughts of the Baldies made a
> vast, intricate network, perhaps the last and mightiest
> structure man would ever build. They drew him into
> their midst and made him one with them. There were
> no barriers at all. They did not judge. They under-
> stood, all of them, and he was a part of them all. . . .
> Henry Kuttner (Lewis Padgett): *Humpty Dumpty*

It is fun to speculate on what might have happened if Hugo Gernsback's literary flair had been equal to his business sense, or if one
editor responsive to the main currents of the time had arisen in the
early thirties. Such an editor did not emerge until the end of the
decade.

Meanwhile, with the slumps and the strikes and the depres-
sions, it was a tough time both for literature and for people. The
reading public of America seemed to want only wonder and escapism. That was what they got, alike from Hollywood and the pulps.

For these reasons, the treasured sf magazines of the thirties now make painful reading. Yet, in a fashion they have survived; they have survived as artefacts of that now remote period. They are strange and beautiful to look at. Their covers are gaudy and gorgeous. The artwork, in fact, has survived well, for some of the artists such as Frank R. Paul—a Gernsback discovery—Wesso, Virgil Finlay, and Elliott Dold projected a genuine outré personality. They are now antiques, valued by connoisseurs, much as Meissen porcelain or English watercolours are valued.

These connoisseurs are, in the main, science fiction fans. Gernsback soon discovered and made use of an active fandom, lads who read every word of every magazine with pious fervour and believed every word of editorial guff. These fans formed themselves into leagues and groups, issued their own amateur magazines or "fanzines," and were generally a very vocal section of the readership. Many writers and editors later rose from their ranks.

This particular factor of a devoted and enthusiastic readership is peculiar to science fiction, then and now. The fans founded their own publishing houses, instituted their own international awards (called, of course, the "Hugos"), and organised their own conventions on local, state, national, and international scales. No writer can be other than grateful for this attention in an age when writers by and large complain of isolation from their audience. But there is an obverse side of every coin, and the truth is that several promising writers have been spoiled by seeking popularity exclusively from the fans who—like any other group of enthusiasts—want more of what they have already been enjoying. To attain true stature as a writer, one must look beyond the fervid confines of fandom— however cosy it may seem by the campfire, yarning of old times.

How far that campfire was from the civilised arts, back in the late twenties and thirties. Those gaudy covers, for instance, which in time became an art form of their own, were totally divorced from all the exciting new movements of the early twentieth century. Cubism, futurism, surrealism, exerted no influence. At the time when Burroughs began to write of Barsoom, the Italian painter Giorgio de Chirico was founding metaphysical painting; one of his inspirations was Jules Verne,[1] and surely those strange paintings of his would have touched the imagination even of Gernsback's stable. Yet it was not until the early sixties that modern science fiction met modern art, when the English Penguin Books launched their new science fiction series with surrealist and other covers, Bradbury and Blish with details of Max Ernst canvasses, Picasso with Roy Lewis' *The Evolution Man*, Hal Clement with Yves Tanguy, Frank Herbert with Paul Klee.[2]

By that time, science fiction and fantasy had produced many artists whose names and works were bywords within the field, even if they were unknown beyond it. Virgil Finlay, Paul, Wesso, and Dold have already been mentioned. Later came Orban, Charles Schneeman, Roy Krenkel, Hubert Rogers, Timmins, Edd Cartier, John Schoenherr, Kelly Freas, Jack Gaughan, and two exceptionally fine artists, Richard Powers, whose rise is roughly coincidental with the growth of sf in paperback, and the use of freer techniques, and "Emsh"—Ed Emshwiller, later to become famous as a film-maker (his *Relativity* was one of the early and lasting successes of the Underground cinema). Among their English counterparts are Brian Lewis, Eddie Jones, and Bruce Pennington.

The Japanese have also produced excellent sf artists, the wit and style of Hiroshi Manabe being especially impressive. The Italians have published some of the most striking art. The beautiful surrealist covers of Karel Thole, a Belgian artist, would stand out in any company. The French Phillipe Druillet's fantasy strips are magnificent creations.

The history of science fiction art deserves to be written. In some respects, it has been less provincial than the science fiction of the magazines—to which we now turn.

What we see in the thirties, after the rise of *Amazing*, is very minor competence. No writer or editor seems to have a clear idea of what he is doing, beyond producing safe variations on what has gone before. Basically, two disciplines predominate, the fantasy mode of Burroughs and Merritt, and the *Popular Mechanics* mode of Gernsback and his merry men.

The authors who most interest us today are those who somehow managed to embrace the two modes and add some quality of their own. Three names stand out above the morass of the thirties. Two of them, within the limits of the field, are innovators: Edward E. Smith, Ph.D., and John W. Campbell. Jack Williamson, a disciple of Merritt's, survives because he operates powerfully at the dreaming pole.

Within sf fandom—that is, the coterie of readers to whom science fiction virtually means the magazines—E. E. Smith, Ph.D.

(known as "Doc" Smith), is one of the greatest names, if not the greatest of all.

Well, we have met many superlatives by now, and E. E. Smith (1890–1965) certainly introduces us to many more. His is the logical development of Gernsbackian thought, the infinite extension of technology for its own sake, the glamorous disease of giantism. It was E. E. Smith who started science fiction off on the billion year spree which is now an integral part of its image.

Beneath Smith's advance, the light-years went down like ninepins and the sober facts of science were appropriated for a binge of impossible adventure. Smith set the Injuns among the stars.

Smith was a doughnut-mix specialist when he had his first story, *Skylark of Space* accepted by *Amazing* in 1928. It was full of super-science. Interstellar travel was taken for granted, and the heroes were super-heroes. At the onset of his career, Smith found a formula which he never abandoned. The Skylark series was followed by the Lensman series, Smith's magnum opus, which eventually spanned six volumes, running from *Triplanetary* (serialised in *Amazing* in 1934) to *Children of the Lens,* serialised in *Astounding* in 1947.[3]

This series postulated two extremely ancient cultures, mutually incompatible, the Arisians and the Eddorians, the former being good, the latter horrendously evil. They lived in separate galaxies, unknown to one another until the galaxies happened to drift into each other. The Arisians are gentle and For Civilisation, the Eddorians are utterly sexless and For Power. Lovely Dreamers versus Horrid Intellectuals.

The tale of their struggle, with certain Earthmen and other alien life aiding Arisia, fills the six books. *Triplanetary* begins: "Two thousand million or so years ago two galaxies were colliding; or rather, were passing through each other . . ." and goes on from there. Such events as the sinking of Atlantis, the decline and fall of the Roman Empire, and the world wars, have been but incidents in the long struggle against the Eddorians.

Doc Smith, in short, wrote the biggest game of Cops and Robbers in existence. His saga is loaded to its armpits in unstoppable forces and immoveable objects, in hyper-spatial tubes and super-weapons and planets full of stupefying life armed with terrible mental capabilities.

And then the doors and windows crashed in, admitting those whom no other bifurcate race has ever willingly faced in hand-to-hand combat—full armed Valerians, swinging their space-axes!

The gangsters broke, then, and fled in panic disorder; but escape from Narcotics' fine-meshed net was impossible. They were cut down to a man.

"QX, Kinnison?" came two hard, sharp thoughts. The Lensman did not see the Tellurian, but Lieutenant Peter van Buskirk did. That is, he saw him, but did not look at him.

"Hi, Kim, you little Tellurian wart!" That worthy's thought was a yell. "Ain't we got fun?"

"QX, fellows—thanks," to Gerrond and to Winstead, and "Ho, Bus! Thanks, you big, Valerian ape!" to the gigantic Dutch-Valerian with whom he had shared so many experiences in the past. "A good clean-up, fellows?"

"One hundred percent, thanks to you. We'll put you . . ."

"Don't, please. You'll clog my jets if you do. I don't appear in this anywhere—it's just one of your good routine jobs of mopping up. Clear ether, fellows, I've got to do a flit."

"Where?" all three wanted to ask, but they didn't—the Gray Lensman was gone.

The whole gigantic road show works by magic. The Lenses of the Lensmen, which resemble fantastic jewels, are semi-sentient life forms bestowed by Arisia, which provide their wearers with amazing paranormal powers. Spaceships travel across hundreds of light-years at faster than light speed by "inertialess drive." They become non-detectable when required, can evade thought-screens, can be converted to perform amazing feats hitherto unheard of in the realm of physics. The Lensmen wear non-detectable armour, can enter the minds of sinister aliens or harmless insects. They are unkillable, and encounter the most formidable situations with schoolboy glee.

Smith took great pains with his epic, rewriting its earlier parts to hang together in one entire enormous concept. And the concept is impressive. Unfortunately, everything moves at such breath-taking speed—or else stops entirely while everyone talks and the plot catches up—that what is good in theory is by-passed in practice. The author conveys no visual experience and does not make his immense distances real; his banal hearty style is obvious from the extract quoted.

Nevertheless, for youngsters, the entire astounding edifice holds a lot of joy and excitement, mainly because, whatever else Doc Smith could or could not do, he clearly *enjoyed* spinning out this doughtnut mix of galactic action.[4]

He died in 1965, loaded with honours by the science fiction field, unknown beyond it.[5]

It must have been a painful experience to write for the pulps in the thirties. One had to conform to formula or get out. There was no sort of cultural tradition or precedent to appeal to. Low rates of pay engendered much hack-work.

Perhaps things would never have changed, had not editors often been short of material and published stories which, to their amazement, readers liked. . . . However that may be, a few writers did spring up among such super-hacks as John Russell Fearn, who pillaged ideas from all quarters, including the cinema, and wrote under many names.[6] Many of them, such as Edmond Hamilton, chronicler of "Captain Future," are worth a chapter in their own right, but we must take as our representative the stalwart Jack Williamson.

Williamson began writing in Gernsback's *Amazing* and never looked back. He was much influenced by Abe Merritt, and managed to assimilate Merritt's sense of colour and movement without taking over the fairies as well. His output was fairly prolific, as outputs needed to be if one was to live by writing sf in a field where *Amazing* and *Wonder* were paying half a cent a word on publication. His greatest early success was with a serial in a 1934 *Astounding, The Legion of Space,* a Gosh-wow! epic which thundered along on the cloven heels of Doc Smith. But there are three later novels of Williamson's which have more to offer, and which—unlike some of the so-called "classics" of the field—have not been reprinted as often as they might be.

The Legion of Time was a serial in a 1938 *Astounding.* Its plot, while being philosophically meaningless, is a delight. Lanning, a Harvard man who becomes a reporter, is thinking of time. Because of this, he is visited by the fair Lethonee. Lethonee comes from far in the future; she carries an immense jewel, which allows her to travel back to Lanning. Later, Lanning is visited by the sexy Sorayina, also from the future. Lethonee's and Sorayina's futures are mutually exclusive. One will materialise at the expense of the other. Either Jonbar, Lethonee's capital, or Gyronchi, the tawdry capital of Sorayina, inhabited mainly by anthropoid ants, will come into being, depending on how their potentialities for realisation are strengthened in Lanning's own time.

After many desperate struggles, which Lanning's Legion of Time generally wins, it is discovered that the crucial moment at which the time-lines divide is a day in 1921. The Legion's timeship heads for 1921, closely pursued by Sorayina's dreaded black Gyronchi ship.

In 1921, they find a boy in a meadow. This is John Barr, who will either pick up a magnet in the grass and thus be moved to become a scientist (making great discoveries from which will develop Jonbar), or will fail to pick it up, will pick up a pebble instead and become a migratory worker. In the latter case, his great discovery will be made by "an exiled engineer from Soviet Eurasia and a renegade Buddhist priest," who will turn the discovery (something about mentally released atomic power) to evil ends, thus developing Gyronchi.[7]

Lanning battles through despite all the enemy can do, pitches the magnet at Barr's feet, and sees the "very light of science" dawn in the boy's eyes. So Gyronchi is defeated. Lanning sails the timestreams to Jonbar to get the girl, and is agreeably surprised (though not *very* surprised) to find that Lethonee and Sorayina have become merged into one. He's got them both!

Fairy tales have a way of revealing hard truths about everyday life. Science fiction so often turns out to be a fairy tale—never more so than in this instance! The significance of some of the inconsistencies in this tale have been discussed elsewhere[8]; but its charm obstinately remains. Like Doc Smith's saga, this one also works on magic. Most traditional sf does so. The magical spells are given such names as "mentally released atomic power"; the hyper-drives light the way to Babylon.

Not surprisingly, Williamson's best novel deals directly with magic. *Darker Than You Think* was published in *Unknown* in 1940. Barbee, like Lanning, is a reporter. He goes to cover the return of a scientific expedition from the interior of Asia, the members of which he knows. They return with an ironbound box which contains some terrible secret they guard with their lives.

Barbee gets mixed up with a beautiful girl called April Bell, who sends odd little shivers down his spine. She presents a Lethonee-Sorayina duality: by day, a beautiful girl; in his dreams, a superb wolf bitch. And Barbee finds he has the power to change to wolf in his dreams and pursue her into the wilds. In that dream state, she leads him to enter houses and kill. Barbee soon has proof that his dream state is no dream.

In the chest that Dr. Mondrick and his colleagues are guarding so anxiously is evidence that Homo lycanthropus once existed—a witch people, whose genes merged with mankind and may now, by skilful interbreeding, become dominant again. One by one, Mondrick, his expedition members, his wife, are killed. Barbee is there, responsible, although he tries to help them. Only his closest old friend, Sam Quain, survives, lugging the chest with its deadly secret. Barbee tried to help him, but Quain will not trust him. Despite the mounting crisis, Barbee tried to remain human. The taunting wolf with its green eyes and red tongue calls to him. Soon the Child of Night, the great new witch, will emerge and start a new reign of his kind.

Barbee is the Child. He turns into a pterosaur, kills Quain, and destroys the evidence that might make mankind rise against his kind. Then he follows the white wolf into the forest.

Preposterous though this sounds in outline, it is extremely well worked out, full of genuine suspense and excitement, and with a good hefty sense of evil working for it. The characters, though obvious, are clearly drawn; but the major advantage of the novel is that it is full of the pleasure of wild life, of running free in the dark, of the forests, the mountainside, and of the scents on the breeze. The novel works like a *novel*, not a diagram, showing us without lecturing how splendid it would be to chase a white she-wolf through the night. Here is a happier escape from the human than poor Jekyll achieved.

And suddenly he was free.

Those painful bonds, that he had worn a whole lifetime, were abruptly snapped. He sprang lightly off the bed, and stood a moment sniffing the odours that clotted the air in the little apartment—the burning reek of whisky from that empty glass on the chiffonier, the soapy dampness of the bathroom and the stale sweaty pungence of his soiled laundry in the hamper. The place was too close; he wanted fresh air.

He trotted quickly to the open window, and scratched impatiently at the catch on the screen. It yielded, after a moment, and he dropped to the damp, hard earth of Mrs. Sadrowski's abandoned flower bed. He shook himself, gratefully sniffed the clean air of that tiny bit of soil, and crossed the sidewalk into the heavy reek of burned oil and hot rubber that rose up from the pavement. He listened again for the white she-wolf's call, and ran fleetly down the street.

Free—

No longer was he imprisoned, as he had always been, in that slow, clumsy, insensitive bipedal body. His old human form seemed utterly foreign to him now, and somehow monstrous. Surely four nimble feet were better than two, and a smothering cloak had been lifted from his senses.

Free, and swift, and strong!

"Here I am, Barbee!" the white bitch was calling across the sleeping town.

The plot hinge of *Darker Than You Think* is characteristic of the period: humanity, or reality, is revealed by some accident of scientific research or discovery to be other than we have assumed. The revelation is always unpleasant. The great exemplar is Charles Forte's dictum, "We're property!" which was embodied in a novel by Eric Frank Russell, *Sinister Barrier* (published in *Unknown*, as was *Darker Than You Think*). Slightly later, Van Vogt's *Asylum* depicts Earth as a dumping ground for the scum of the universe, just as Thulcandra is the dumping ground for the Bent One. As the psychiatrist Glenn says in Williamson's novel, "The unconscious mind does sometimes seem a dark cave of horrors, and the same unpleasant facts are often expressed in the symbolism of legend and myth." Faced by the horrors of a global war, the sf writers were fashioning their own kinds of myth. Despite a slight clumsiness, *Darker Than You Think* still works in this manner.

Williamson's *The Humanoids* is less successful. As a novel-length sequel to a short story called "With Folded Hands," it appeared in *Astounding* in 1948 under the title . . . *And Searching Mind.* Williamson presents a well-constructed plot, buttressed with learned bits of pseudo-science, which centres around the coming of robots to a planet geared for war with its neighbour. The first robot that the hero, Forester, sees, strikes him as attractive when it drops its human mask.

> There was nothing really horrible about what emerged from that discarded mask.
> Rather, it was beautiful. The shape of it was nearly human, but very slim and graceful, with no mechanical awkwardness or angularity whatever. Half a head shorter than Forester, it was nude now, and sexless. The sleek skin of it was a shining black, sheened with changing lights of bronze and blue. (Chapter 9)

The humanoids arrive by the thousand and take over in the midst of the crisis. They are units of a cybernetic brain many light-years away, and their prime directive is "To Serve and Obey, and Guard Men from Harm." In effect, they bring peace by rendering men powerless—in the most benevolent possible way. Unlike Čapek's humanoids, Williamson's are utterly subservient, and he wisely leaves the ending open, as the humanoids lay their benevolent plans for Andromeda—is their peace-keeping a triumph or tragedy? As Damon Knight says in Chapter 4 of *In Search of Wonder*, the book is important because its theme is important.

Unfortunately, the impact is greatly muffled by having it set far away across the galaxy. To have set it on Earth would have been dramatically better. And, of course, the philosophical implications take second place to a tale of adventure. All the same, *The Humanoids* has plenty of readability, because Williamson's strong visual sense is at work, here as in *Darker Than You Think* (we are constantly reminded of the *presence* of the androgenous metal creatures), and his characters are not thick-ear supermen like Doc Smith's but pretty ordinary fallible people, in need of some sort of prop just like the rest of us.

Under his own name and pen names, Williamson wrote many other novels and stories. In the fifties, he wrote undersea novels of sf adventure with Frederik Pohl, since when he has produced comparatively little fiction, his latest novel being *Moonchild* (1972). He is currently teaching science fiction in university.

The third author who rose to eminence in the thirties' magazines is a controversial figure who has had a greater effect on magazine science fiction than any other man.

John W. Campbell (1910–71) was one of the field's intellectuals. He had strong ideas, some of them erroneous, but his positive side triumphed over many of his mistakes.

Campbell's first story was published in the January 1930 *Amazing*—"When the Atoms Failed." He rapidly made his name in the field of megalomaniac galaxy-busting being pioneered by "Doc" Smith, with stories whose very titles can still light the dim eyes of senior fans: "Piracy Preferred," "The Black Star Passes," "The Islands of Space," "The Mightiest Machine," "Invaders from the Infinite," and so on. Most of these stories show deep interest in complex machines and are studded with explanations of their workings.

In 1934, Campbell changed his approach. Taking on the pseudonym of Don A. Stuart (derived from his first wife's name), Campbell produced a series of short stories in a much more meditative mood. The first was "Twilight"; it imitates the dying fall of Wells' *Time Machine*, and features a man who goes into the far distant future when man is extinct because his curiosity is dead. A civilised regret is the mood aimed at. Campbell adopts a kind of singsong intonation and a faux-naïve style.

> Can you appreciate the crushing hopelessness it brought to me? I, who love science, who see in it, or have seen in it, the salvation, the raising of mankind—to see those wondrous machines, of man's triumphant maturity, forgotten and misunderstood. The wondrous, perfect machines that tended, protected, and cared for those gentle, kindly people who had—forgotten.

When "Twilight" was gathered into a collection by Shasta Publishers, Campbell claimed that it was "entirely different from any other science fiction that had appeared before," which is totally incorrect. It did, however, bring into magazine science fiction another alternative to Gernsback's utilitarianism, talking animals and Gosh-wow; its "all passion spent" mood was quickly taken up by other writers, most notably Lester del Rey and, later, Arthur C. Clarke.

Even in his lachrymose vein, Campbell continued to write

about huge engines and the vanishing tricks of supernormal power, interspersing them with rather plodding technical detail. Belief in incredible forces of ESP was to dog him all his life.[9] Here are four paragraphs from *The Cloak of Aesir,* first published in 1939, which demonstrate several of his literary characteristics. The Sarn-Mother, one of the rulers of a defeated Earth, is talking:

> "Aesir spoke by telepathy. Mind to mind. We know the humans had been near to that before the Conquest, and that our minds are not so adapted to that as are the humans'. Aesir used that method.

> "He stood before me, and made this statement that was clear to the minds of all humans and Sarn in the Hall of Judgment. His hand of blackness reached out and touched Darnell, and the man fell to the floor and broke apart like a fragile vase. The corpse was frozen glass-hard in an instant of time.

> "Therefore, I released Grayth and Bartell. But I turned on Aesir's blackness the forces of certain protective devices I have built. There is an atomic blast of one-sixteenth aperture. It is, at maximum, capable of disintegrating half a cubic mile of matter per minute. There was also a focused atomic flame of two-inch aperture, sufficient to fuse about twenty-two tons of steel per second.

> "These were my first tests. At maximum aperture the blackness absorbed both without sound or static discharge, or any lightening of that three-dimensional shadow."

By the time *Aesir* was published, Campbell was editor of *Astounding.* He took over in 1938, at the age of twenty-eight, to begin what proved to be a thirty-three-year reign.[10] As Donald Wollheim points out, Campbell could begin to draw on the first generation of young writers, raised on magazine sf; "science fiction builds on science fiction."[11]

The new editor was confronted by new competition. A promising and colourful *Marvel Science Stories* appeared on the stands in 1938, to be followed by *Startling Stories, Dynamic,* and *Science Fiction.* Thick and fast they came at last, and more and more and more. *Fantastic Adventures* arrived as a stable mate to *Amazing*—at that time owned by the Ziff-Davis chain—then *Planet Stories,* pursued by two magazines edited by a teen-age Frederik Pohl, *Astounding Stories* and *Super Science Stories. Future Fiction, Comet*

Stories, Cosmic Stories, and *Stirring Science Stories* pop up shortly thereafter. Most of these magazines were in the Burroughsian mode, *Planet Stories* especially.

Astounding itself acquired a sister magazine in the Street and Smith group. This was *Unknown,* which appeared on the newsstands in the spring of 1939 and ran for less than forty issues. Campbell edited both magazines in tandem. *Unknown* specialised in bizarre fantasy, which frequently operated close to reality but stood it upside down—*Darker Than You Think* is a good example. When *Unknown* died, so, it seems, did Campbell's love of that particular genre, and a wartime mood of "realism" spread over stories that were often far from realistic in essence.

Campbell soon proved himself a good and ambitious editor. He forced his writers to think much harder about what they were trying to say, and clamped down on Gosh-wowery, although, when a genuinely inspired madman like A. E. van Vogt came along, Campbell was wise enough to let him have his head. Also, he had the fortune to take over at a good time, when the monstrous footprints of Burroughs and Gernsback had, to some extent at least, obliterated one another. The stiffening breeze from Europe also introduced a more serious note.

He worked, too, on logic—a quality his competitors had always been short of. It was Campbell's own peculiar sideways logic (which accounted for his fondness for Lewis Carroll), but it led him to reject the Bug-Eyed Monsters—known in the trade as BEM's —and many of the trashy plots that went with them. As he remarked at a later date, while thinking genially about the unthinkable:

> Two motives standard in BEM-style science fiction can be dismissed quickly. Aliens aren't going to invade Earth, and breed human beings for meat animals. It makes a nice background for horror-fantasy, but it's lousy economics. It takes approximately ten years to raise one hundred pounds of human meat, and at that it takes high-cost feed to do it. Beef cattle make better sense—even though that louses up the horror motif.
>
> And that is, of course, assuming the improbable proposition that the aliens' metabolism can tolerate terrestrial proteins at all.
>
> If they can, of course, it's much easier to get local natives,

ideally adapted to the planet's conditions, to raise the cattle. Inherently much cheaper than trying to do it yourself. Besides, the local yokels can be paid off in useless trinkets like industrial diamonds, or tawdry little force-field gadgets, children's toys that won't cut anything with any accuracy better than a microinch.

Then there's the old one about raiding Earth and carrying "Earth's fairest daughters" away as love-toys on some alien planet. Possible motive . . . if you'd define "fairest" adequately. If the aliens happen to come from a bit heavier planet, the proposed raids on "Earth's fairest daughters" might turn out to be very distressing to the gorilla population. In those "Earth's fairest daughter" bits, I've noticed, nothing whatever is said about the intellectual capabilities of the "fairest"; a charming young gorilla maiden would pass the only test proposed . . . if your eye for looks were slightly different. And obviously these interstellar harem-agents aren't interested in offspring anyway; there couldn't possibly be any.[12]

A team of new writers, or old writers operating under pseudonyms—often a surprisingly effective way of altering writing habits—began to gather round Campbell. Unlike many editors before and after, Campbell knew when a story made sense and when it didn't. He argued strongly with his contributors—and his arguments were often well informed and fair. Thus he laid the foundations for what the gentle hearts of fandom call "The Golden Age."

One authority on the subject, Alva Rogers, is definite about the date. When he reaches 1939 in his chronicle, he says, "The July issue was unquestionably the first real harbinger of *Astounding's* Golden Age."[13] This issue carried a story by A. E. van Vogt, *Black Destroyer*, which later became part of his book *The Voyage of the Space Beagle*. Other new writers appeared that year, soon to become famous, among them Robert A. Heinlein, Isaac Asimov, and Theodore Sturgeon.

Heinlein's first short novel, *If This Goes On . . .* was published early in 1940—a brisk tale of total dictatorship in the United States operating under the cloak of religion, and this was followed by a serial from L. Ron Hubbard, *Final Blackout*, which supposed that the war in Europe dragged on until civilisation broke down. Hubbard had previously been known as a fantasy writer. His story and Heinlein's seemed at the time much more plausible than the lead stories *Astounding* had hitherto been publishing.

In 1941, Heinlein revealed the plans of his scheme for a Future History series, while Asimov began his long series of stories about robots with positronic brains whose behaviour is guided by three laws of robotics which prevent them from harming men.

In this respect, Heinlein and Asimov brought literary law and order into magazine science fiction. Asimov's robot stories are amusing little puzzles, without the philosophical implications of Williamson's *The Humanoids*, Čapek's robots, or Frankenstein's monster, from which they ultimately derive. But Asimov's achievement—which should not be forgotten—is that he banished those slavering metallic hordes, or those single mechanical men forever reaching for the nearest axe, which had been a boringly predominant feature of the magazines until Campbell's day.

Both Asimov and Heinlein brought intelligence and wide knowledge to their storytelling. Heinlein's preoccupation with power was sometimes to express itself disastrously, as in his novel *Starship Troopers*. But that was later; in the early forties, he could do no wrong. In 1941 alone, *Astounding* published three of his novellas which can still be read with pleasure, *Logic of Empire*, set on Venus, *Universe*, set on a gigantic interstellar ship, and *By His Bootstraps*, a time-paradox story which still delights by its ingenuity, as well as several excellent short stories.

It seemed that the cosmos was his oyster, so diverse was his talent. But no author has more than one secret central theme, or needs it; *Logic* is about resistance to authority; *Universe* is about what happens when authority breaks down; and *Bootstraps* is a good-humoured demonstration of the trouble that can come when the father-figure is removed.

The Golden Age was in full swing.

The change may be read in the magazine covers as vividly as anywhere. The symbolic always precedes the actual—a concept must be visualised before it can be realised. So the art side often flies ahead of the contents. The 1938 covers of *Astounding* span a wide range of subjects, are interesting, but have no unity. From 1939, a kind of coherence appears. The Campbell orchestra tunes up. The January covers for 1939 and 1940 both romanticise industrial processes (i.e., organisational action as opposed to individual action)[14] and might be used with perfect propriety as factual illustrations today. The age of the solitary Gernsbackian inventor is nearly over. The all-action scientist-adventurer is also on his way out. Campbell was bringing the mythology of the age up to date, in a magazine which, less than a decade earlier, had been planned as *Son of Amazing*.

What Campbell produced was a synthesis of the previous modes of magazine sf, plus the new contributions. The result was something that for the first time could stand comparison with the science fiction we have looked at in earlier chapters, the ex-ghetto science fiction. The flavour of the two kinds was very different, but the merits of the junior were apparent for the first time.

While magazine science fiction could produce no Swifts, no Mary Shelleys, no Wellses, it nourished a stream of accomplished entertainers who, at their best, were also thought-provoking and imagination-stirring.

Whereas Kafka, Huxley, Stapledon, and authors of that ilk were critics who arose to deal with a specific socio-technological situation, the very nature of the magazine sf field—its month-by-month continuity—nurtured something of another order: a dialogue between writers. The conditions had been there in embryo in the thirties; in the forties, under Campbell, they bore fruit. The constant cribbing of ideas became instead something of a genuine and rapturous exchange.

If some of the excitement generated then is hard to detect several decades later, it is because one of the electrifying factors was precisely that creative exchange, going on from issue to issue, year by year, conducted by Campbell and other editors such as Pohl—and nobody knew quite what was coming next. Every month brought the promise of something wilder and stranger— and the promise was always kept!

Something of that same fecundating situation occurred in the mid-sixties, when Michael Moorcock took over *New Worlds*. As Moorcock did later, Campbell seized on his editorial column to expound his theories, hoping that writers would pick up the trail. It is typical of the whole success story of *Astounding* that it is not only the fiction which has been anthologised again and again; a selection of Campbell's editorials has also been published.[15]

The magazine sf writers differed from the Huxleyan kind of writer in one other important way. That way is implicit in what has already been said. They did not question the basic value of technology. They saw that technology would bring big troubles (wasn't that what sf was all about?), but they were secure in the belief that more massive, more organised, doses of technology would take care of the problem. Such formalised beliefs helped make Campbell's magazine—their bastion until his death in 1971—much more of a force to be reckoned with than its predecessors.

The spaceships that Heinlein and Van Vogt dreamed up would have drained the energy systems of Earth many times over had they been built, as well as swallowing all its metallic ores. But what *symbols* those spaceships were!

For many years, science fiction fans were fond of saying jocularly, "A spaceship is just a phallic symbol." So it often may have been in terms of cover art—Emsh for one often used spaceships deliberately as phallic symbols.[16] But they symbolised a great deal more. In the thirties, as we have seen, they stood in for tramp steamers or ocean liners (such as the *Mauretania* mentioned in Kipling's verse at the head of this chapter). In the writings of Campbell's new wave, they might symbolise variously a spirit of dedication, manly togetherness, or a romanticised industrial process of gigantic proportions.[17]

While symbolising such matters, the spaceships, of course, served also as a convenient way of hefting their heroes across the paper light-years. But one need not be an avid searcher for symbols to see that, whatever else they stood for, spaceships meant the conquest of nature. Or vice versa.

Long rows of shops and warehouses stood deserted. Doors yawned open. Neglected roofs were sagging. Ruined walls, here and there, were black from old fire. Every building was hedged with weed and brush.

Far across the shattered pavements stood the saddest sight of all. A score of tall ships stood scattered across the blast aprons, where they had landed. Though small by comparison with such enormous interstellar cruisers as the "Great Director," some of them towered many hundred feet above the broken concrete and the weeds. They stood like strange cenotaphs to the dead Directorate.

Once they had been proud vessels. They had carried the men and the metal to build Fort America. They had transported labor battalions to Mars, dived under the clouds of

Venus, explored the cold moons of Jupiter and Saturn. They had been the long arm and the mighty fist of Tyler's Directorate, and the iron heel upon the prostrate race of man.

Now they stood in clumps of weeds, pointing out at the empty sky they once had ruled. Red wounds marred their sleek skins, where here and there some small meteoritic particle must have scratched the mirror-bright polish, letting steel go to rust. And the rust, in the rains of many years, had washed in long, ugly, crimson steaks down their shining sides.

An excerpt from Jack Williamson's *The Equaliser*, in a 1947 *Astounding*. This story is about a power beyond the atomic which makes every man his own master, so that the social contract is dissolved. Williamson appears to be in some confusion here—the rockets were used for oppression, yet their abandonment is "the saddest sight of all"—but the connection between spaceships and mastery of the environment is abundantly clear.

Astounding developed into a hymn to this connection. The hymn may not be fashionable nowadays; but fashions come and go.

So the magazine sf writers became able to do many things that the writers outside the field could not do. Above all, they could depict a technological culture as a continuing process—often continuing over thousands of millions of years. Although the writers (optimistically or blindly) neglected the vital factor of depletion of Earth's mineral and other resources, they perceived that Western civilisation rests increasingly on a non-random process of innovation, on R and D rather than Ralph 124 c4I+. The solitary inventor has gone down before the continuities of research laboratories.

This continuity of culture has its analogue in the continuity of *Astounding* over its vital years. As Don Wollheim puts it, "Science fiction builds on science fiction." It is no longer fruitful to speak of influences and derivations; future research has begun. *Astounding* in its best years was a collaborative work, the first think-tank. And was followed in that work by such later magazines as *Galaxy* and *Fantasy* and *Science Fiction*.

The stellar empires postulated by Asimov in his Foundation series or Van Vogt in his Child of the Gods series—though both may have been based on older models (such as Gibbon or Robert Graves' Claudius books)—owe a superior vitality over previous empires to their basic premise that technology demands continuity and expansion. The Manhattan Project, involving many specialists from many countries, drove the lesson home—but the lesson is fore- ✓ shadowed in science fiction before it emerges fully in society. That the way to the Moon lay through a door marked R & D is a perception one first encounters in Campbell's *Astounding*.[18]

Campbell's special field was atomic physics. This proved a rapid growth area of science in the period after he took over in *Astounding*'s editorial office. It was no accident that Military Intelligence agents visited that office in 1944, to investigate the background to Cleve Cartmill's story, "Deadline," which Campbell had just published.

"Deadline" deals with the development of an atomic bomb; Cartmill assembled facts that were known at the time. What he did not know of was the existence of the Manhattan Project, dedicated to identical lines of research. The story of this invasion of Campbell's office was immensely popular in sf circles; it was cherished as proof that sf was not just fairy tales, but seriously predicted coming nuclear weaponry. More significant is the fact that the Manhattan Project itself, that grandiose and secret conspiracy of talent, had also been foreshadowed in *Astounding*. The industrialisation of science, the rise of the industrial spy, the anxious guarding of new processes, the paranoia of high-funded laboratories —these themes emerge in preimago state in story after story.

As a corollary of this preoccupation, the typical *ASF* story was rather cold and impersonal in tone, and sometimes degenerated into a sort of illustrated lecture. Before many years were over, the gimmick or gadget story had fallen from popularity. At least one reader gave up reading (for a couple of months) after a confrontation with the glib superficiality of Harry Stine's "Galactic Gadgeteers" in 1951. In its heyday, the gadget story was best devised by writers such as Hal Clement, a MIT man whose novel *Mission of Gravity* (an *ASF* serial in 1953) is still a great favourite.

Clement's short story "Fireproof," in 1949, presupposes launcher satellites girdling the Earth in a continued East-West confrontation, with an Eastern spy aboard a Western satellite. The spy is going to blow up the launcher, but fails to do so because fire will not burn where there is no convection of air, as in the gravity-free conditions of the satellite (a fact on which the spy has not been briefed, happily for the West!). The story hardly exists as a story; nor does Campbell regard it as a story, but as part of the continuing *Astounding* debate. The evidence for this lies in the wording of Campbell's blurb for the story, a minor art of which Campbell was master:

> This yarn, gentlemen, introduces a brand new idea in the field of spaceship operation. There's twenty years of discussion gone by—and this beautiful, simple and exceedingly neat point has been totally missed! Before you reach the end, see if you can figure the answer!

There were times when *Astounding* smelt so much of the research lab that it should have been printed on filter paper.

Nevertheless, the research lab approach generated ideas. No popular magazine has ever been such an intellectual delight. Many later problems were foreshadowed in general terms and chewed over excitingly. Such superman stories as Mark Clifton's "What Have I Done?" discussed the relative meaning of equality in human society. Simak's "City" series investigated new relationships among living things. Eric Frank Russell imagined strange new symbiotic forms of life in stories such as "Symbiotica." Old hand Murray Leinster visualised a time when people might lose interest in maintaining the strenuous arts of civilisation. It's true that in this particular story, "Trog," interest is artificially occulted by a fiendish enemy brain wave, but the general thrust of the story points to a stage of culture which sometimes seems now to be approaching us.

Many writers argued about the role of the computer long before the computer cut its first transistor, wondering how it would fit into man's world. One of the most brilliant and pithy answers was contained in the one-page story by Frederic Brown, "Answer." (Though it did not appear in *Astounding*, its punch line, "*Now* there is a God!" has become a password in some circles.)

As for aliens, they were everywhere. In *Astounding* at least, the Burroughs emphasis sank below the surface, as the writers realised increasingly that man's behaviour, alone among species, was not species-specific, and that that plasticity could best be expressed by using aliens as if they were merely behaviourly

THE WORLD OF JOHN W. CAMPBELL'S "ASTOUNDING"

235

different kinds of men (though disguised maybe by fangs or scales). Simak's aliens are generally just men without sin. Later, in the fifties, this balanced attitude fell away, perhaps under pressure of Campbell's xenophobia—as Wollheim says, "No internationalist he"—and the aliens became warped symbols of fear. But, in the forties, all seemed well.

A. E. van Vogt was talking confidently of interstellar winds back in 1943, and dropping in casual word of large dollops of space—as when a survey ship reports that a small system of stars "comprises two hundred sixty billion cubic light-years, and contains fifty million suns."

Van Vogt was the ideal practitioner of "Doc" Smith's billion year spree. He was not hard and cold and unemotional, in the manner of Clement, Asimov, and Heinlein. He could balance his cubic light-years and the paraphernalia of super-science with moments of tenderness and pure loony joy. Intimations of humanity surfaced now and again among all his frenetic mental powers and titanic alien effects.

Van Vogt is not seen at his best in longer work (he becomes as hopelessly snarled up as his readers in *World of Null-A*). Among his short stories, one of the best—because it exhibits all his talents in dynamic balance—is "The Storm" (1943), which contains some moments of love between Maltby and the Lady Laurr (Van Vogt was a sucker for a title). Indeed, there's a hint that the story's title is intended to refer also to an internal storm of emotion. Very sophisticated! But, of course, it was the intergalactic storm which interested readers, and that was what they got.

> In those minutes before disaster struck, the battleship *Star Cluster* glowed like an immense and brilliant jewel. The warning glare from the Nova set off an incredible roar of emergency clamor through all of her hundred and twenty decks.
>
> From end to end her lights flicked on. They burned row by row straight across her four thousand feet of length with the hard tinkle of cut gems. In the reflection of that light, the black mountain that was her hull looked like the fabulous planet of Cassidor, her destination, a sun at night from a far darkness, sown with diamond shining cities.
>
> Silent as a ghost, grand and wonderful beyond all

imagination, glorious in her power, the great ship slid through the blackness along the special river of time and space which was her plotted course.

Even as she rode into the storm there was nothing visible. The space ahead looked as clear as any vacuum. So tenuous were the gases that made up the storm that the ship would not even have been aware of them if it had been travelling at atomic speeds.

Violent the disintegration of matter in that storm might be, and the sole source of cosmic rays, the hardest energy in the known universe. But the immense, the cataclysmic danger to the *Star Cluster* was a direct result of her own terrible velocity.

If she had had time to slow, the storm would have meant nothing.

Striking that mass of gas at half a light year a minute was like running into an unending solid wall. The great ship shuddered in every plate as the deceleration tore at her gigantic strength.

In seconds she had run the gamut of all the recoil system her designers had planned for her as a unit.

She began to break up.

The writing has clarity and brevity, ably conveying Van Vogt's excitement at his immense drama. Later, and beyond the pages of Campbell's magazine, Van Vogt was never to recapture his first fine careless rapture. Nor that mixture of kookie science—half a light-year per minute, indeed!—with lyric excitement.

Kuttner also was lyrical and gave the impression of seeing the whole picture.

Henry Kuttner's was a sensuous world, non-diagrammatic, blurred at the edges. Whereas Asimov concerned himself with robots and androids which men could not tell from fellow men, Kuttner's universe rejected such non-resonant themes. He posited a human society in which there was a sub-species of telepaths, all linked to each other by thought and sensation. They could be distinguished from ordinary men by their bald heads (hence the series was known as "The Baldies"*). In Kuttner's world, people marry and have babies and cry and upset milk. They enjoy the Earth and the Sun. Donne-like, they understand that no man

* Gathered into book form under the title *Mutant* (Gnome Press, 1953).

is an island, not even a mechanical island. "Each time a telepath
dies, all the rest within minds' reach feel the blackness close upon
an exhausted mind, and feel their own minds extinguish a little
in response."

Even at a time of tension, Kuttner's telepathic minds are open
to random impressions. In "Humpty Dumpty," in a 1953 *Astounding*, we read:

> By now Cody was at the little park before the long
> Byzantine building. Trees were wilting above brownish lawns.
> A shallow rectangular pool held goldfish, who gulped hopefully as they swam to the surface and flipped down again.
> The little minds of the fish lay open to Cody, minds thoughtless as so many bright, tiny, steady flames on little birthday
> candles, as he walked past the pool.

An image like that can burn in a reader's mind for decades
after he has read it. Henry Kuttner married another sensitive
writer from the pulps, Catherine Moore, and their collaboration
was fruitful. Kuttner died in 1958, at the ripe young age of forty-
three. Our own minds were extinguished a little in response.

Kuttner was given recognition by pre-war fans, who could
not accept his attempts to coax a little sex and sensuality into the
genre, mainly in *Marvel Science Stories*.[19] Of the two trusty
critics within the sf field, only James Blish puts in a really strong
word for Kuttner.[20] It is undeniable that, faced with the terrors
of earning a living in a field where the editor was all-powerful
(and hard-up to boot), Kuttner did turn in a lot of hack-work; yet
he was voted favourite living sf author at a 1947 sf Convention.

Kuttner was exceptional. Campbell liked to give the impression
that all stories were machine-turned off a lathe of truth. (*Astounding* stories were tested for popularity monthly and ranked in
order by readers, in a department labelled "The An Lab.")

Nevertheless, *Astounding* wisely never confined itself to what
was likely.[21] The technicalities of George O. Smith and Hal
Clement were always counterbalanced by one more chunk of the
Lensman saga, the wildness of A. E. van Vogt, or the doomed
psychiatric fun of Theodore Sturgeon. Campbell enjoyed a joke.
Eric Frank Russell was for years his licensed jester; there were
also "spoof" articles by Isaac Asimov, and John Brunner's *Report*

on the Nature of the Lunar Surface, which proved that the Moon really was made of green cheese.

The impossible was not ruled out, if only because nobody knows what is possible and what is not. Also, there is some evidence that sf writers are particularly prone to confuse science with magic.

Even the hardheaded Campbell, who saw in science and applied science "the salvation, the raising of mankind," even Campbell believed that the impossibility of getting something for nothing might be transcended by a formula or incantation—hence his extraordinary notion that seventy-five per cent of the brain (and the most powerful part) lay unused, his belief in psionics, and his pursuit of cults such as Dianetics (later Scientology, founder L. Ron Hubbard) and the Dean Drive, a neat little device which was supposed to generate thrust without producing an equal and opposite reaction. The Dean Drive sounded suspiciously like the device Jack Williamson had written about a few years earlier in *The Equaliser,* a solenoid wound in a special way which generated almost unlimited electrical power, thus enabling every man to be independent and ending dictatorship forever. Campbell, convinced of the profound worth of science fiction, tried to live some of it.[22]

"Cultural background" is a term much loved by literary critics. The reality behind the term is something that should never be forgotten when we look back at Campbell's achievements with *Astounding/Analog.* His magazine began as one of many hundreds of pulp magazines, most of them short-lived, short-sentenced, and short-changed. They were considered beyond the pale of literacy. Moreover, when Campbell arrived, the great era of the pulps was already over—some say it closed with the paper shortages induced by World War I.[23] These pulps are slowly gaining recognition as a new common culture, growing up in place of one that had shattered. Certainly they were churned out for a lower middle or working class —in many cases immigrant—entirely without privilege (another contrast with the prosperous audiences of a stable society addressed by the Huxley-type science fiction writer). The pulps gave a whole stratum of the American public, hit by the Depression and other economic evils, a sort of unified viewpoint.

Tony Goodstone points out that the "latent psycho-sexual

drama of the Depression" depended in part on the era's "unusually emasculating effect on the breadwinner."[24] More straightforwardly, we can agree that the effect on a man of being unemployed or underpaid is to induce a feeling of powerlessness.

All the successful pulps used strong, tough, all-action heroes with which the underprivileged could identify. All the air aces, cowboys, detectives, Tarzans, Conans, and mighty avengers such as Doc Savage and the Shadow (let's not mention Superman, Batman, and the extraordinary mob of comic-book heroes who followed) are in this succession. Science fiction offered an unusual and almost limitless extension of the hero role and of power. Campbell must have seized instinctively on this function. His response to his times was intuitive.

Nick Carter might set the New York underworld to rights. All the brave adventurers and aviators might vanquish their enemies. Doc Savage might own an inexhaustible gold mine under a mountain in South America. But only Campbell's heroes had the real equaliser: the infinite policing powers of the mind, the inexhaustible forces beyond the atom!

So sf transcended the pulps, by taking their simple strong-arm formulas and inventing new protagonists big enough to take on the universe. At the same time, very subtly, the problems those protagonists faced could be shown to have close bearing on day-to-day problems in a technological society, problems on both a "realistic" and a "mythological" level. Where other magazines messed about with the present, Campbell gave you the future on your chipped plate.

Even more, you could grow up still believing in the Campbellian magic. You couldn't grow up believing in Doc Savage's ludicrous gold mine, but it needs a very sophisticated mind to sort out prediction from fantasy. *Astounding* was a mag for all seasons.[25]

NOTES

1. Writing in an Italian magazine in 1919, De Chirico makes these remarks on Verne. "Joyful but involuntary movements of the metaphysical can be observed both in painters and writers, and speaking of writers I would like to remember here an old French provincial who we will

call, for clarity's sake, the armchair explorer. I refer to Jules Verne, who wrote travel and adventure novels, and who is considered to be a writer for children.

"But who was more gifted than he in capturing the metaphysical element of a city like London, with its houses, streets, clubs, squares and open spaces; the ghostliness of a Sunday afternoon in London, the melancholy of a man, a real walking phantom, as Phineas Fogg appears in *Around the World in Eighty Days?*

"The work of Jules Verne is full of these joyous and most consoling moments; I still remember the description of the departure of a steamship from Liverpool in his novel *The Floating City.*"

The essay "On Metaphysical Art," from which this extract is taken, is included in Massimo Carra's *Metaphysical Art*, 1971.

2. The art editor of the series was the Italian Germano Facetti. The covers mentioned were, in chronological order: *Penguin Science Fiction*, edited by Brian Aldiss—Oscar Dominguez, *Memory of the Future* (1961); *The Day It Rained Forever*, by Ray Bradbury—Ernst's *Jardin Gobe-Avions* (1963); *A Case of Conscience*, by James Blish—Ernst's *The Eye of Silence* (1963); *The Evolution Man*, by Roy Lewis—Picasso's first cover for *Minotaure* (1963); *Mission of Gravity*, by Hal Clement—Yves Tanguy's *The Doubter* (1963); *The Dragon in the Sea*, by Frank Herbert—Paul Klee's *Underwater Garden* (1963); *More Penguin Science Fiction*, edited by Brian Aldiss—Kandinsky's *Small Worlds* (1963); and *Deathworld*, by Harry Harrison—Pavel Tchelitchev's *Citron* (1963).

3. In sequence the series runs, *Triplanetary, First Lensman, Galactic Patrol, Gray Lensman, Second Stage Lensman, Children of the Lens.*

4. There is even a concordance to the works of "Doc" Smith, an honour he shares with Shakespeare, Charles Dickens, and other greats. It is Ron Ellik and Bill Evans' *The Universe of E. E. Smith*, Chicago, 1966—another publication from the dedicated House of Advent.

5. In 1971, the English firm of W. H. Allen began an expensive series of hard-cover reprints of the Lensman Saga. They are selling well and captivating a new generation of fans. But D. B. Wyndham Lewis pointed out long ago the folly of expecting progress in the arts.

6. Fearn's devoted biographer, Philip Harbottle, claims that the Liverpool-born Fearn used more pseudonyms than any other fantasy writer, and tells me of thirty-three; there were perhaps more. There were certainly other pseudonyms used for other fields. All the details are given in *The Multi-Man: A Biographic and Bibliographic Study of John Russell Fearn*, by Philip Harbottle. Privately printed by the author, 1968.

7. This is a magnificent example of what Franz Rottensteiner has called "the role of individual people being ridiculously exaggerated" (in *The Other Side of Realism*).

8. See the long article "Judgement at Jonbar," by the present writer in *SF Horizons I*.

9. Campbell's unremitting attempts to build telepathy, ESP, and other odd psychic phenomena into a science called psionics were based on unscientific premises. Those premises are revealed in something Campbell says in an article "The Story Behind the Story" about his novelette *The Double Minds,* published in the August 1937 issue of *Thrilling Wonder Stories*. What Campbell mildly calls a "pet idea" was in fact to become an obsession.

"In most instances, I think, authors have some 'pet' ideas, that gradually work themselves into the shape of a story, given time. The present yarn, *The Double Minds*, is based on the interesting fact that no man ever used, or began to use so much as a quarter of the capacity of his brain. The total capacity of the mind, even at present, is to all intents and purposes, infinite. Could the full equipment be hooked into a functioning unit, the resulting intelligence should be able to conquer a world without much difficulty." Leaving aside the question of whether greater intelligence might not reject the idea of conquest, this view of the brain is entirely erroneous. The superb functionalism of nature does not allow any organ to operate at twenty-five per cent capacity for many generations; that we still do not understand all the workings of the brain is entirely another matter. Campbell may have caught his "pet idea" from John Russell Fearn, whose very first story, *The Intelligence Gigantic* (*Amazing*, 1933), uses the same theme. "We only think and receive impressions in snatches, imperfectly understood, but—and this is the vital point—with a nerve connection to make the entire brain of use, we can operate our brain power to the full! It means a power of thought five times greater than we now have." What a gift to power-fantasy the idea was!

10. An analysis of Campbell is to be found in Chap. 17 of Donald Wollheim's delightful and dogmatic *The Universe Makers,* New York, 1971. He points out the frustrations of Campbell's long editorial job on *ASF* (a job so devotedly done, so wretchedly paid), and the way in which his policies later isolated him from the sympathies of fandom.

11. Ibid.

12. The quote is taken from a 1960 editorial, "Unimaginable Reasons," and incidentally gives a demonstration of the way in which Campbell loved to lecture his authors. As Harry Harrison has said, "When John Campbell was talking, a lot of solemn nodding went on all round!"

13. Alva Rogers, *A Requiem for "Astounding,"* Chap. 5, "The Dawn of the Golden Age, 1939–1940."

14. I owe this observation to Dr. Leon Stover of I.I.T., Chicago.

15. John W. Campbell, *Collected Editorials from Analog,* selected by Harry Harrison, New York, 1966. In his Introduction to the volume, Harrison points out the impact of Campbell on his writers and adds, "None of these writers has been so small as to deny the influence of John Campbell, and the number of books that have been dedicated to him gives evidence of this. At a guess I would say there are at least thirty, a record that I am sure is unique in literature."

16. For use of the submarine as phallic symbol, see Arnold Kohn's cover painting on *Fantastic Adventures* for Mar. 1949; mention of this cover is also made in Note 21 below. Submarines were customarily believed to be siblings of spaceships. Kohn applies the idea pictorially.

17. Examples: Van Vogt's "Far Centaurus," *Astounding Science Fiction,* Jan. 1944, uses the spaceship as symbolising the spirit of dedication—in this case ironically defeated. L. Ron Hubbard's "To the Stars," *ASF,* Feb.–Mar. 1950, uses it as a symbol of manly togetherness—most noticeable when the crew of the *Hound of Heaven,* travelling at near light speed, bursts out into its favourite chorus, "Viva la *Hound,* viva la *Hound,* viva la company." As for romanticised industrial processes, this is so all-pervasive it is hard to exemplify; but one might stipulate most of the Venus Equilateral stories by George O. Smith, or the same author's "The Impossible Pirate," *ASF,* Dec. 1946. For the spaceship as a symbol of the imprisonment of life that technological advancement can bring about, one must turn to a later generation of writers—for example, the present writer's *Non-Stop,* 1958, published as *Starship* in the United States.

18. Observations similar to these first saw the light of day in Dr. Leon Stover's acute study of the processes behind literature, *American Science Fiction: An Anthropological Exegesis,* Chap. 5. This thesis has been (to date) published only in France, as *La Science Fiction Américaine,* Paris, 1972.

19. For instance in "The Time Trap," in *Marvel Science Stories,* Vol. 1, No. 2, Nov. 1938. There are at least three naked ladies in this fantasia of Kuttner's. The voluntary stripper is Nirvor, priestess with silver hair, eternally accompanied by leopards. She declares her love for the hero and peels. He rejects her on the grounds that she was once a leopardess; vivisection has done a decent conversion job. How Dr. Moreau would have laughed!

20. For instance in *The Issue At Hand,* pp. 78–79, where I note with pleasure that Blish also seizes on that same passage about the candle-flame thoughts of goldfish. Blish has vigorously refuted Moskowitz'

view of Kuttner as a derivative back, in "Moskowitz on Kutter," an article in *Riverside Quarterly*, Vol. 5, No. 2; he concludes by saying that Moskowitz' "sole critical principle is one of infinite regress"—a remark not made any kinder by its high accuracy quota.

21. A comment that applies even more to the other magazines in the field. If the present author compiles a companion volume to this one, he will concentrate on the contemporary scene and on magazines other than *Astounding*, here perhaps given undue attention. Meanwhile, to take a lucky dip and pick up one issue of one magazine: *Fantastic* for Mar. 1949. Here are some of the story blurbs: "Beneath the ocean floor lay a great secret—guarded by the giant mer-race . . ."; "The people of Loran looked into the sky and saw the great spaceship approach. Was it possible that a God had returned?"; "Is existence as we know it but a series of locked doors in time? And is the mind the key that will open them?"; "Dave had to win the chess game—for if he lost, the Earth would be destroyed . . ." They give an idea, which pictures and stories powerfully reinforce, of the way the genre dealt with matters and images which have legendary power over us. The none-too-concealed erotic meaning of that particular issue's cover, with the immense mermaid clutching a submarine in one hand, reinforces the feeling that mere likelihood was not and should not have been given first consideration.

22. As a result, sf fans stayed away in droves from *Astounding* when it became the serious and stodgy *Analog*. Their judgement should be remembered by those who regard fandom as some sort of headless beast! Under a new editor, Ben Bova, *Analog* is becoming more lively once again.

23. See for instance, *The Pulps: Fifty Years of American Pop Culture*, edited by Tony Goodstone, New York, N.D.

24. Ibid., Chap. 7.

25. For further comments on *Astounding*'s effect on readers—and for a full selection of the best-remembered stories mainly from its Golden Years, see *The Astounding-Analog Reader*, edited by Harry Harrison and Brian Aldiss, New York, 2 Vols., 1972–73.

10

After the Impossible Happened:

THE FIFTIES AND ONWARDS, AND UPWARDS

> The claws got faster and they got bigger. New
> types appeared, some with feelers, some that
> flew. There were a few jumping kinds. The
> best technicians on the moon were working on
> designs, making them more and more intricate,
> more flexible. They became uncanny; the
> Ivans were having a lot of trouble with them.
> Some of the little claws were learning to
> hide themselves, burrowing down into the ash,
> lying in wait.
>
> Philip K. Dick: *Second Variety*

Since World War II ended, and the dropping of the atomic bomb
on Japan became the first move in the Cold War, science fiction has
diversified in a number of ways. That diversification leads us directly to the present.

Once magazine science fiction began to spread to traditional
publishing, and to appear in hard-cover, it reached the general public and the libraries. Success attended such pioneering anthologies
as Raymond J. Healy and J. Francis McComas' *Adventures in Time
and Space* and Groff Conklin's *The Best of Science Fiction* (both
1946). The way was open for sf to take itself more seriously. That
growing seriousness has been its most significant characteristic of
recent years, for better or worse.

Outcrops of sf include think-tanks, such as Herman Kahn's Hudson Institute, which have to some extent taken over sf's predictive role, much as ICBM's have taken over from the old-fashioned bombers of SAC.* To some of us steeped in the sf of the time, space flight itself—and the launching of the first sputniks and satellites—seemed like an extension of sf, just as the Wellsian atomic bomb had done.

For several years before the first space rockets lumbered up to lodge a human being in orbit, the sf magazines issued propaganda on the subject; when success came, one might almost have been forgiven for believing that "thinking made it so." Space flight had been the great dream, the great article of faith; suddenly it became hardware, and was involved in the politics of ordinary life.

The first sputnik went into orbit in October 1957, and the Space Age had begun. It is hard for people now to realise how stubbornly the idea of any form of space travel was opposed before that date, and not only by the supposedly ignorant. There was the British Astronomer Royal, who declared in 1956, "The future of interplanetary travel is utter bilge!" (He later compounded his error by saying that what he *really* said was that stories about interplanetary travel are utter bilge.)

Space travel was a dream, the precious dream of sf fans. It was part of the power fantasy of the sf magazines. When space travel became reality, the dream was taken away from them. No wonder that the sales of magazines dropped dramatically after that! Commentators have always had difficulty explaining that fact, but the reason is simple—withdrawal symptoms were going on.

If the transformation of dream to hardware brought disillusion to many sf fans, it also meant that sf and the general idiom of a life style that courted the unlikely became much more of a commonplace. The impossible had happened. People began to expect the unexpected.

As a result, the sf ghetto walls crumbled from outside; there was no longer reason to feel persecuted inside. The decor of new cities, the design of world's fairs and expos, the feel of offices and community centres, the gaga sophistication of TV ads, the sheen on

---

* Frederik Pohl, however, has a good argument to show that sf's role can still be fruitfully predictive, since it injects into the picture the emotional tone that the statistics leave out, thereby allowing us all to see whether we want to accept the futures the planners posit for us.

hundreds of motion pictures from the James Bonds onwards—all merged with the slick worlds of science fiction. The term "science fiction" increasingly became used as a sort of okay jargon term, meaning something futuristic, unlikely, and high-powered.

Moreover, evidence began to emerge during the late fifties that the USSR—that dark Communist alter ego of the capitalist Western world—harboured its own science fiction writers. Later, Russian sf found its way to the West in translation, while Western sf found its way to the socialist camp. Some of us found friends on the other side of what was once called "the Iron Curtain" whose greatest need—as desperate as ours several years earlier—was for science fiction magazines. Later still, an International Sf Symposium was held at which Russian and Western sf writers met, exchanged views, and became close friends.[1]

To say this is to anticipate to some extent the contents of this and the following chapter. To make sense of the present, we should look at developments after World War II, when science fiction was still a minority cult, little known to any but its devotees.

Astounding after the war was a very black magazine. Its writers and readers—to say nothing of its editor!—were digesting the implications behind the nuclear bomb, its unlimited powers for greatness or destruction. It was a painful process: the old power fantasies were rising to the surface of reality. Many stories were of Earth destroyed, culture doomed, humanity dying, and of the horrific effects of radiation, which brought mutation or insidious death. Nor were things depicted as much cheerier beyond the solar system.

Titles of late forties and early fifties' stories in *Astounding* reinforce the point: "Tomorrow and Tomorrow" (Kuttner), "The End Is Not Yet" (Hubbard), "There Is No Defence" (Sturgeon), "Dawn of Nothing" (Chandler), "Space Fear" (Schmitz), "And Then There Were None" (Russell). In Simak's "City" series, humans had passed from the Earth, leaving it to a rabble of dogs and miniature robots. Nor was the news much cheerier from Trantor, where the Mule was threatening Asimov's galaxy with thousands of years of slavery and barbarism. But the absolute supremacy of *Astounding* was almost at an end; new magazines, new writers, were assembling in the wings.

Terms such as "pessimism" and "optimism" are loosely used in the science fiction debate. There was plenty of pessimism in *As-*

tounding; that is a simple emotion. What it lacked was a natural and decent despair which has always characterised much of ordinary literature. But, even in 1972, editors in the sf field reject stories because they are "too down-beat"—a curious rejection, since sf has always been, on the whole, a gloomy literature.

We find that natural and decent despair in the writings of such authors as Bester, Sheckley, Harrison, and—later—Spinrad, Ballard, and Disch, a despair which lends zest to the rest of life. These authors relish humour, and have a reverence for other people and a regard for sex, vital elements often found with despair. Of these writers, only Harry Harrison found his métier in *Astounding.* His first two novels were published in the early sixties, just as the magazine's name was changing to *Analog.* They were *Deathworld* and *A Sense of Obligation* (in book form as *Deathworld II*), and marked Harrison out as one of the few authors capable of carrying the old vigour of earlier days forward into a new epoch.

As for Bester and Sheckley, they found their niches in *Galaxy,* edited by Horace Gold, which, with the *Magazine of Fantasy and Science Fiction,*† sprang up lustily in the early 1950s. (Gold had written for *Astounding* as early as 1934; with L. Sprague de Camp, he contributed the haunting "None But Lucifer" to Campbell's *Unknown.*) Alfred Bester produced two novels, both containing gaudy and exciting glimpses of future societies, *The Demolished Man* (serialised 1952) and *The Stars My Destination* (serialised 1956–57, and known also as *Tiger! Tiger!*).

The latter novel in particular is a definitive statement in Wide Screen Baroque—a kind of free-wheeling interplanetary adventure, full of brilliant scenery, dramatic scenes, and a joyous taking for granted of the unlikely. Bester writes with natty panache, a style more encouraged by Gold's type of madness than Campbell's.

> He jaunted.
> He was aboard the *Nomad,* drifting in the empty frost of space.
> He stood in the door to nowhere.
> The cold was the taste of lemons and the vacuum was a rake of talons on his skin. The sun and the stars were a shaking ague that racked his bones. (*Tiger! Tiger!,* Chapter 15)

† Known in common parlance as *F&SF.*

248 AFTER THE IMPOSSIBLE HAPPENED:

There are passages in Durrell's later *Alexandria Quartet* which are not dissimilar, and tied also to exotic backgrounds ("Long sequences of tempera. Light filtered through the essence of lemons. An air full of brick-dust—sweet-smelling brick-dust and the odour of hot pavements slaked with water").

After his two wild novels, Bester fell silent (though there is also *Rat Race,* an acid novel about TV biz). He evidently recognised that his statement was definitive, leaving it to others with a tenth of his perception and wit still to churn out pale imitations.

His few short stories are also cherished. Most of them concern long odds of one sort and another, a good example being "Time is the Traitor," in which one John Strapp travels round the galaxy in quest of a duplicate of the girl he loved ten years ago. He finds her at last, but he has changed. "The mind goes back, but time goes on, and farewells should be forever." So run the story's closing words. Unfortunately, they appear to represent Bester's personal philosophy.

Sheckley at his best is Voltaire-and-soda. His fizzing nihilism expresses itself most pungently at short-story length. His stories poured into *Galaxy* in the fifties, when he wrote too much. He has a wry inventiveness which skates him over profound depths.

In Sheckley's "Dimensions of Miracles," Carmody, a man who has won a galactic prize, meets a chap called Maudsley, who, as it turns out, built the planet Earth. Not too well, either.

Earth was my first test case [Maudsley says], and that is why I will always remember it.

A tall, bearded man old with piercing eyes had come to me and ordered a planet. (That was how your planet began, Carmody.) Well, I did the job quickly, in six days I believe, and thought that would be the end of it. It was another of those budget planets, and I had to cut a few corners here and there. But to hear the owner complain, you'd have thought I'd stolen the eyes out of his head.

"Why are there so many tornadoes?" he asked. "It's part of the atmosphere circulation system," I told him. (Actually, I had been a little rushed at that time; I had forgotten to put in an air-circulation over-load valve.)

"Three-quarters of the place is water!" he told me. "And I clearly specified a four-to-one land-to-water ratio!"

"Well, we couldn't do it that way!" I told him. (I had lost his ridiculous specifications; I can never keep track of these absurd little one-planet projects. (Chapter 12)

Sheckley appears to have no moral, religious, or political convictions clamouring for expression; no teacher lives to play enemy to the artist—one of the permanent dilemmas facing many an sf writer. Amis called him "science fiction's gadfly," and so he remains, the idle stinger of an idle song—and the more welcome for that.

Galaxy, under the editorship of H. L. Gold, and *F&SF*, under the editorship of Anthony Boucher, provided several other writers with a congenial platform. The original version of that slender modern classic, Ray Bradbury's *Fahrenheit 451*, appeared in *Galaxy's* second issue. Theodore Sturgeon's extraordinary "Baby Is Three" appeared in *Galaxy* in 1952, and later was built into the novel, *More Than Human*. The story is about six outcasts of society who together make a viable Gestalt entity; it transcends its own terms and becomes Sturgeon's greatest statement of one of his obsessive themes, loneliness and how to cure it.[2]

In general, 1952 was a good year at *Galaxy*. It also saw the serialisation of Frederik Pohl and Cyril Kornbluth's *Gravy Planet*, known in book form as *The Space Merchants*, and the start of the serialisation of Clifford Simak's best book, *Ring Around the Sun*. *Astounding* had nothing equivalent to offer; Asimov's serial, *The Currents of Space* based itself on the plot, old-fashioned even then, that the fate of Earth depended on one man, and he had lost his memory! Asimov's *The Martian Way*, appearing in *Galaxy* at the same time, was much more forward-looking.

Pohl and Kornbluth made one of the greatest combinations in the science fiction field, and the death of Kornbluth in his thirties was a minor disaster—perhaps not least to Pohl. Together, they produced some excellent novels. *Space Merchants* apart, *Gladiator-at-Law*, set in and out of the slummy Belly Rave, *Wolfbane*, and *Search the Sky* all have their supporters. All these novels appeared in *Galaxy*.

The strangest of them is *Wolfbane* (1957), in which Earth is moved out of its orbit by a runaway planet whose inhabitants are Pyramids. One Pyramid slices off the top of Everest and settles there. The central character, Tropile, is captured by the Pyramids and used as one component in their gigantic and grotesque computer. He wakes to find himself in a gigantic tank, floating spread-eagled and doing *something* automatically. Looking about, he finds he can see all round without moving his head. He has been given total vision. Then he looks at his hands.

> He could see them, too, in the round, he noted; he could see every wrinkle and pore in all sixteen of them. . . .
>
> *Sixteen hands!*
>
> That was the other moment when sanity might have gone.
>
> He closed his eyes. (Sixteen eyes! No wonder the total perception!) and after a while he opened them again.
>
> The hands were there. All sixteen of them.
>
> Cautiously, Tropile selected a finger that seemed familiar in his memory and, after a moment's thought, flexed it. It bent. He selected another. Another—on a different hand, this time.
>
> He could use any or all of the sixteen hands. They were all his, all sixteen of them.
>
> I appear, thought Tropile crazily, to be a sort of eight-branched snowflake. Each of my branches is a human body.
>
> He stirred, and added another datum. I appear also to be in a tank of fluid, and yet I do not drown.
>
> There were certain deductions to be made from that. Either someone—the Pyramids?—had done something to his lungs, or else the fluid was as good an oxygenating medium as air. Or both.
>
> Suddenly a burst of data-lights twinkled on the board below him. Instantly and involuntarily, his sixteen hands began working the switches, transmitting complex directions in a lightning-like stream of on-off clicks.

In *New Maps of Hell*, Amis refers to Pohl as "the most consistently able writer science fiction, in the modern sense, has yet produced." He perhaps gets nearer the truth when he calls Pohl "some sort of novelist of economic man." The best of Pohl—a distinctively surrealist best—comes in his collections of short stories with the attractive titles, *Turn Left at Thursday*, *The Man Who Ate the World*, *The Case Against Tomorrow*, and *Day Million*. Although, by the highest tests, he has never entirely managed a personal statement (and would probably laugh to hear that one was required), Pohl's contribution to the field has been enormous—and not least for his editorial skills. He edited *Star, If, Galaxy,* and other magazines, taking over the last named from Horace Gold, when his sanity proved just as effective as Gold's messianic drives.

Another maturing talent in the fifties was that of James Blish, who had hitherto been known mainly for his galaxy-spanning series of stories about the Okies in their flying cities (gathered together eventually in four volumes under the generic title of *Cities in Flight*).

The Okie series may have appeared at first blush to be staple *Astounding* diet, and in a way it was. The basic motivation behind the stories depends on two technological developments, the spindizzy, which powers the flying cities and—since they travel at sublight speeds—anti-agathic drugs, which render the crews virtually immortal. Blish explores only the implications of the spindizzy; the effects of immortality on the crews are never investigated, and so remain little more than a plot device.

But, while Van Vogtian conquest was going on in other stories all about them, Blish's cities sought work rather than thrones among the stars. This was a significant step away from Campbell's power fantasy, and a herald of the remarkably different writings Blish was to come up with later.

In the early mid-fifties, away from *Astounding,* Blish was publishing such remarkable and excellent stories as *Common Time, Beep,* and *A Case of Conscience,* the latter now accepted as one of the seminal novels of modern science fiction, a fine piece of work which stands squarely on its own accomplishment inside or outside the science fiction field. Blish is a cautious man who has taken heart from his own success—success at which, in direct contrast to many lesser writers, he always seems faintly surprised.

Of all contemporary writers, he is most notable for the persistence with which he has moved into new areas for exploration. Too many writers pretend to invent futures when they are busily rewriting past sf, with its tattered backdrop of telepathy, FTL drives, galactic conquest, and other shoddy goods; Blish stubbornly chooses difficult themes and pursues his own course. He had also proved himself a rancorous but acute critic of the sf field.[3]

In the early fifties, the sf field—as far as it was known at all—was generally misunderstood and condemned. Pornography got a better press. Yet the truth was, it was reforming itself from within, shuffling off the last of the Gernsback tradition.

Behind the violence of Harrison's writing, the power drives of Bester's, the comic reversals of Sheckley's, the eschatologies of Blish's, the social criticism of Pohl's, one senses the formation of liberal or liberal-inclined societies. Harrison's *Make Room, Make Room* (1966),‡ for instance, is a highly credible portrait of an over-crowded New York, the society of which hangs together, not only through dogged police and governmental coercion, but through an unstated acceptance of the social contract by millions of hard-pressed inhabitants; so that, at the end of the book, the *status quo* still holds, the entity survives. (A masterly stroke, and not only because it defies a long-established sf convention that Everything Falls Apart in the Final Chapter.)

Such liberal inclinations represent a rejection, however unconscious, of the old pulps-through-*Astounding* tradition of indulgence in power fantasy.

"Make trade not war," say Blish's Okies, thereby taking a step toward less authoritarian attitudes.

So with *Tiger! Tiger!* (the better title, with its Blakeian reference): "There's got to be more to life than just living," says Bester's Gully Foyle, looking ahead to Moorcock's Jerry Cornelius. "Who are we, any of us, to make a decision for the world?"

This evolution in thinking was more than simply literary. In a world confronted by Hitler and Stalin—and the millions who made their rise to power possible—the old pulp ethos began to seem positively indecent. But something larger may have been involved. Our understanding of human behaviour continues to broaden and deepen, as it has done ever since Darwin's time. Western society is still liberalising itself, tortuous though the process is (and threatened all the while). We used to hang people for stealing bread; now we pay unemployment benefits. We used to allow children to be used as slave labour; now we are extending the school-leaving age. We used to treat as criminal people who were merely sick. We have many hang-ups, but socially we are more enlightened than we were at the beginning of the century.

We have painfully begun to understand that the way to reintegrate the rejects of society—whether rejected on grounds of race,

‡ Since filmed by M-G-M as *Soylent Green*.

poverty, low IQ, or whatever—is to express our concern, not our hatred; to bring them nearer rather than shutting them farther away.[4] As Mary Shelley pointed out a while ago, for it is one of the lessons of *Frankenstein*.

This moral progress comes as a result of scientific developments—a positive thing science does, often forgotten in a time when science's failures claim our attention. The biological and biochemical springs of human action are still being examined; we can only say that they seem to undermine an authoritarian view of government, and equally to make moral judgments of the old kind irrelevant. The double helix of heredity may prove to be the next politico-religious symbol after the swastika.

Because this more understanding or science-based attitude has to fight its way to general acceptance—and has a painfully long way to go!—we can expect to find it worked out in novel form, filtered through various aspects by various minds.

So it is. As well as the novels mentioned, which have to be taken as representative of many more, we can see a whole post-war range of fiction in which man's performance in an authoritarian society is examined. The range includes George Orwell's *Animal Farm* (1945), B. F. Skinner's *Walden Two* (1948), Orwell's *1984* (1949), George Stewart's *Earth Abides* (1949), Kurt Vonnegut's *Player Piano* (1952), David Karp's *One* (1953), Evelyn Waugh's *Love Among the Ruins* (1953), Pohl and Kornbluth's *The Space Merchants* (1953), Ray Bradbury's *Fahrenheit 451* (1954), and so on, through Anthony Burgess' two sixties novels, *A Clockwork Orange* (1962) and *The Wanting Seed* (1962), and such a novel as James Blish and Norman Knight's *A Torrent of Faces* (1967).

All these novels, whatever else they are, treat the predicament of the individual in societies that represent varying degrees of repression. They may be classed as utopias (or anti-utopias), which they undoubtedly are, but behind that classification stands a greater one. From the slogan "All animals are equal" down to F. Alexander's remark to Your Humble Narrator, in *Clockwork Orange*, "A man who cannot choose ceases to be a man," the authors are searching for a definition of man that will stand in the terrifying light of twentieth-century knowledge.

In this uncertain currency of the intellect, the sf writers are the unacknowledged bankers of the Western world. And it may be that their persistence in drawing almost characterless central figures is no weakness of technique but rather, as it were, a blank cheque, written against each reader's account of himself.

To this debate, George Orwell (1903–50) brought little that strikes us as startlingly new. His *1984*, published in the year before his death, was an immediate success; its fame is now on the wane, but this may only be temporary, in that the novel embodies all too effectively the immense depression prevalent in England and Europe at that time, as an aftermath of war. Indeed, to reread *1984* now is to be struck with the truth of its psychic trace of civilian life in World War II, with the shifting populations, miserable housing, loosely packed cigarettes, rationing, and the endless security restrictions—including those alarming posters which said HITLER IS LISTENING.

Orwell's *1984* has also been under suspicion as a pastiche of the formidable Russian anti-utopia, Yevgeny (or Eugene) Zamyatin's *We*. Although *We* was not published in Britain until 1970, it was written in 1920, published in English translation in the United States in 1924, and done in various European languages before Zamyatin died in exile in Paris in 1937. It seems very likely that Orwell—and indeed Huxley before him—may have picked up a copy of *We* in France.

Be that as it may, the whole Orwellian paraphernalia of one man against a super-state was not new. In particular, it was not new within the pages of sf magazines.

It is entirely on the cards that Orwell, with his love of the outlawed in literature, read a lot of science fiction.[5] His *1984* reads rather like a lobotomised Van Vogt, with its Newspeak standing in for Van Vogt's General Semantics. The thought police and the whole psychotic plot of the solitary good guy against the universe is pure Van Vogt, the twist in the tail being that in Orwell's case the universe, represented by Big Brother, wins. Perhaps Winston Smith's attempts to unravel the past reflect some past Orwellian attempt to unravel *The World of Nul-A*.

To say this is partly to poke fun at the legions of learned commentators who find *1984* a nest of stolen ideas. For the novel possesses two cardinal virtues, one intellectual and one emotional, which, taken together, make an original contribution to the debate.

Firstly, Orwell states clearly that the object of a party in power is to hold power. His Party holds power and glories in it; hence that memorable line, "If you want a picture of the future, think of a boot stamping on the human face forever." Unlike his predecessors—unlike even Wells, forever on his way up—Orwell identified strongly with the lower classes, even when he found them repulsive[6]; and from this viewpoint, he saw lucidly that those who are down are kept down. It is this perception which makes *Brave New World* seem namby-pamby; for Huxley, secure in the upper classes, never thinks to give us a sight of the whip.

The emotional virtue of *1984* is that Orwell's utopian desires are so much more human than those of his greater predecessors, of Plato, More, and the others. His recipe for a good life is tender and fallen: something to eat, no nosey neighbours, a bit of comfort, and a girl to take to bed.[7]

Orwell succeeded in uniting intellectual and emotional. He shows what happens when power is all-powerful and what is human in man is eradicated in consequence:

> "What have you done with Julia?", said Winston. . . . "You tortured her?"
>
> O'Brien left this unanswered. "Next question," he said. "Does Big Brother exist?"
>
> "Of course he exists. The Party exists. Big Brother is the embodiment of the Party."
>
> "Does he exist in the same way as I exist?"
>
> "You do not exist," said O'Brien. (Part 3, Chapter 2)

Power obliterates character.[8]

An ability to unite intellectual and emotional is by no means simple. I would not want to suggest *1984* is a simple book. To whom is its warning directed? To the voters? If so, then it is an anti-prophetic book, in that the less this fictional world becomes reality by the test date, the better Orwell will have succeeded in his purpose. And so his intentions may have been, in part; but there are wider aspects of the novel, which are beautifully brought out by Richard Rees in his book on Orwell, when he says:

> The core of Orwell's message in *1984*, stripped of Winston's tragedy and all the sadism, is simply that our industrial machine civilization is tending to deracinate and debilitate us, and will finally destroy us; and the concensus of opinion on this point among thinkers as diverse as Orwell, Huxley,

Gandhi, Simone Weil, and D. H. Lawrence, to say nothing of
the many others, such as Eliot and Koestler, who would go at
least part way with them, is striking and depressing. All the
more so because no one seriously believes that the rhythm of
industrialisation and mechanisation could be relaxed or indeed
that it can possibly fail to go on accelerating (unless inter-
rupted by war) until the whole population of the world has
been incorporated into the mass-civilization.[9]

Many of the more thinking science fiction writers found themselves in this problem many years ago.[10]

Orwell's *Animal Farm* was published in 1945. It is a beautiful
and brief book—of all the books mentioned in this volume, possibly
the one most likely to get first to Pluto, tucked in microfiche edition in some visiting astronaut's pocket: a book with survival value.

Perhaps its meaning is little different from *1984*'s, but its impact is considerably different, and the story of the animals manag-
ing their own farm seems likely to live on to entertain future
innocents, just as we enjoy Gulliver's troubles in Lilliput without
bothering about the references to Queen Anne's court. Orwell's
1984 is much more time-bound.[11]

Clearly, *Animal Farm* is not science fiction in any accepted
sense. Equally clearly, it is one of those charming cases, such as
Alice, that has intense appeal for anyone with that sort of mind. All
animals are equal, but Orwell's animals are more equal than others.

Before World War II, such popular novels as were some kind of
kissing kin with sf were mainly fantasy. The prime example is
James Hilton's *Lost Horizon* (the last of the small-time Rider Hag-
gards?), which made a smashing film with Ronald Coleman in.

In the long period after the war, we can point to a wide range
of novels which have been just as popular and more serious in character, and nearer to many of the interests of sf.

One plunges into the list almost at random, but an interesting
tally it makes, including Nigel Balchin's *Small Back Room;* Nevil
Shute's *No Highway, On the Beach,* and *In the Wet;* C. P. Snow's
The New Men; John Bowen's *After the Rain;* Constantine FitzGib-
bon's *When the Kissing Had to Stop;* L. P. Hartley's *Facial Justice;*
Kingsley Amis' *The Anti-Death League* and his impressive later
novel *The Green Man* (which contains a marvellous encounter

with God); Michael Frayn's *The New Men;* all the near-future political thrillers of the *Fail-Safe* category; Angus Wilson's *The Old Men at the Zoo;* the two Anthony Burgess novels already mentioned; some of J. B. Priestley's novels; William Burroughs' extraordinary fractured novels, such as *The Ticket That Exploded;* Lawrence Durrell's *Alexandria Quartet,* and his *Tunc* and *Nunquam;* Nabokov's dazzling *Ada;* the stories of Donald Barthelme; John Barth's *Giles Goat Boy;* the puzzles of Jorge Luis Borges; the extraordinary creations of Samuel Beckett; and—most particularly—William Golding's novels, *Lord of the Flies* and *The Inheritors,* with its evocation of lost things. . . . There one must halt, since one must halt somewhere. But what an impressive array of novels! All of them look towards a definition of man and his status. All of them approach the science fiction condition; just as, on its own side of the fence, science fiction approaches the modern novel.

Such a rapproachement is probably due as much as anything to a change in emotional climate. On the one side, the evolution of McLuhan's global village has involved increasing numbers of people in a forward-directed world outlook which features sf. On the other side, the same cultural effect has meant that sf writers and readers have become more involved with the world, less content with the old artificial patterns of sf adventure.

Of course, sf adventure, redskins among the stars, will always survive. No medium is better equipped to deliver heart-wrenching surprises, desperate odds, and formidable mysteries—the whole Gothic package—than science fantasy. And, in the fifties, numerous practitioners rose to fame who specialised in such adventure, among them such prolific writers as Poul Anderson, Robert Silverberg, and John Brunner, all of whom sprouted pseudonyms. But there were signs elsewhere of diversification.

Ray Bradbury was the first to take all the props of sf and employ them as highly individual tools of expression for his own somewhat Teddy-bearish view of the universe. The trouble with genre material is that it becomes overused. On the whole, the props are few: rocket ships, telepathy, robots, time-travel, other dimensions, huge machines, aliens, future wars. Like coins, they become defaced by overcirculation (though it is true that some of them, adroitly used, acquire *baraka* by long association). In the fifties, with many new outlets for sf, writers combined and recombined these standard elements with a truly Byzantine ingenuity—indeed, to *aficionados,* this permutational aspect becomes one of sf's chief attractions—but there were signs even then that limits were being reached. By the sixties, the signs could not be ignored.

Those who became successful in the fifties refurbished the worn props. Either, like Bradbury and Clarke, by using them with fresh insight; or, like Heinlein and Frank Herbert, by expanding the field of vision and using the props together with exotic elements. Philip K. Dick and Kurt Vonnegut, who belong to the next chapter, make the props subservient to their own brands of existential wit.

It was the first writer to recombine the old props in his own way who won the greatest fame. Ray Bradbury's flamboyant rocket ships took him into a high literary orbit. It couldn't, as they say, have happened to a nicer guy.

> One minute it was Ohio winter, with doors closed, windows locked, the panes blinded with frost, icicles fringing every roof, children skiing on slopes, housewives lumbering like great black bears in their furs along the icy street.
>
> And then a long wave of warmth crossed the small town. A flooding sea of hot air; it seemed as if someone had left a bakery door open. The heat pulsed among the cottages and bushes and children. The icicles dropped, shattering, to melt. The doors flew open. The windows flew up. The children worked off their wool clothes. The housewives shed their bear disguises. The snow dissolved and showed last summer's ancient green lawns.
>
> *Rocket summer.* The words passed among the people in the open, airing houses. Rocket summer . . .

The first words, of course, of Bradbury's *Martian Chronicles* (also published as *The Silver Locusts*). That was way back in the earliest of the fifties. How delicate and nice it is, and what an extraordinary poetical idea, that rocket exhausts could change climates! Well, they changed political climates and helped to defreeze the Cold War, so perhaps a prophetic symbolism may be detected.

What one did not realise at the time was that Bradbury always dealt with a prepubertal world, and that his stories read like translations of Ukranian folk tales. He seemed like a magician.

The Illustrated Man! The Golden Apples of the Sun! Fahren-

heit 451! The October Country! How enchanting those early books were at the time, how we needed them.

They are perfect in their way, and their way is the way of *Wind in the Willows.* They belong to an imaginary American past where every town had wooden sidewalks, every house a verandah with a rocking chair, and every attic a dear old Grandma fading out under the rose-blossom wallpaper. In this milieu, rockets are just quaint novelties, like early Fords, Hudsons, and Packards. There are also sharp social comments, such as *The Pedestrian,* about a man arrested for that un-American activity, walking.

Bradbury is of the house of Poe. The sickness of which he writes takes the form of glowing rosy-cheeked health. It is when he makes functional use of this, contrasting sickness and health in one story, that he is at his most persuasive. For instance, in *The Third Expedition,* in *The Martian Chronicles.*

Here, an earth rocket lands on Mars and finds that it is like Earth long ago when the rocket crew were children. There are cute old Victorian houses with stained-glass windows, and white wooden houses, and houses of red brick, and church steeples with golden bells. And plenty of trees and green grass. The inhabitants of the town prove to be all the characters you knew and (since this is Bradbury's reality) loved as a kid, particularly Grandma and Grandpa, and Mom, pink, plump, and bright, and Dad, all set in a context of victrolas playing and turkey dinners being eaten.

Then Captain Black has to go upstairs to sleep in the old brass bed with his brother, who has golden shoulders, and the mood changes. Black grows very frightened when the lights go out, and suddenly realises that the whole setup is a terrible and evil alien trick.

> And suppose those two people in the next room, asleep, are not my mother and father at all. But two Martians, incredibly brilliant, with the ability to keep me under this dreaming hypnosis all of the time.

He never makes it to the bedroom door. His brother gets him.

Christopher Isherwood came along and announced that Bradbury was a poet. His name became famous overnight, and he has remained one of our eminent dreamers ever since, the Hans Christian Andersen of the jet age.

Arthur C. Clarke is another dreamer to make good into the

starry empyrean beyond the sf field. His escape velocity has been fueled by reserves of technical knowledge, and his career resembles in many ways the schoolboy dream of success. It has been said, unfairly, that Bradbury's science fiction is for those who do not like sf; but no such monstrous charge can be levelled at Clarke's writing. More than any other sf author, Clarke has been faithful to a boyhood vision of science as saviour of mankind, and of mankind as a race of potential gods destined for the stars. If Stapledon has successors, Clarke is the foremost. Egotistical in many ways, he has throughout his career remained humblingly true to that early faith, and to science fiction as the literature of the gods.

His literary abilities are traditional, and his prose workaday. But he rises to a certain strength when he manages to unite the thinking and dreaming poles of his nature (to amalgamate the Wellsian and the Burroughsian, as it were). This he achieves in several masterly short stories—especially in "The Nine Billion Names of God," justifiably famous—and in two novels, *The City and the Stars* (1956) and *Childhood's End* (1953). In the latter especially, a rather banal philosophical idea (that mankind may evolve into a greater being, an Overmind) is expressed in simple but aspiring language that vaguely recalls the Psalms, even down to the liberal use of colons; when this is combined with a dramatised sense of loss, Clarke's predominant emotion, the result has undeniable effect.

This passage is from the end of *Childhood's End,* when Karellen, a member of a menial alien race, has seen man vanish from Earth, and prepares to return to his own distant planet:

> For all their achievements, thought Karellen, for all their mastery of the physical universe, his people were no better than a tribe that had passed its whole existence upon some flat and dusty plain. Far off were the mountains, where power and beauty dwelt, where the thunder sported above the glaciers and the air was clear and keen. There the sun still walked, transfiguring the peaks with glory, when all the land below was wrapped in darkness. And they could only watch and wonder: they could never scale those heights.
>
> Yet, Karellen knew, they would hold fast until the end: they would await without despair whatever destiny was theirs.

They would serve the Overmind because they had no choice, but even in that service they would not lose their souls.

The great control screen flared for a moment with sombre, ruby light: without conscious effort, Karellen read the message of its changing patterns. The ship was leaving the frontiers of the Solar System: the energies that powered the Stardrive were ebbing fast, but they had done their work.

Arthur Clarke's success story lies in the main beyond the scope of a mere literary critic. His early work on earth satellites and his informed commentaries on the Apollo space launchings during the sixties and early seventies have made him almost as much a part of the space race as Cape Kennedy itself. He is also celebrated as co-author of the Stanley Kubrick film *2001*, one of the great cult successes of its day.**

There are many other successes of this period, and many we are going to omit, for reasons of both concision and folly. This is the way of histories; that as they come closer to the present and future, the errors of proportion become greater; so does the writer's subjectivity. The reader must be warned that I now write of a period on which I myself had some effect—and so venture here to use a personal "I."

Before we proceed to discuss the milestones cast by Tolkien, Peake, Heinlein, Herbert, Brunner, and Miller, at least a mention must be given to the swarming talents of the fifties, all of whom have their followers, and whose stories still give pleasure.

Among them most assuredly are some of the senior writers of the field, active earlier and still active. Such as L. Sprague de Camp, a scholar whose main work is in fantasy. Many recall with pleasure his Viagens Interplanetarias series, in which Brazil is top dog in twenty-second century—not an unlikely conjecture. Lester del Rey, an able and intelligent writer, also edited one of the better magazines, *Space Science Fiction*. Poul Anderson, a sword-among-the-stars man, has an immense following all round the world; his first novel, *Brain Wave*, remains his most memorable. Charles Beaumont, great fun writer, died in the old age of his youth. Algis

** Before *2001*, Kubrick made *Dr. Strangelove* from Peter George's *Red Alert* and, after *2001*, *A Clockwork Orange* from Anthony Burgess' novel of the same name. The latter may well come to be regarded as one of the masterpieces of the cinema. On the strength of this, Kubrick should perhaps be acknowledged the great sf writer of the age.

Budrys, once a power in the land, author of two fine novels, *Rogue Moon* and *Who*, among other good things, turned critic—always a fatal step. Kenneth Bulmer, great stalwart of the Carnell magazines, has recently taken over editorship of *New Writings in SF*. Colonel Theodore Cogswell's *Wall Around the World* is still being reprinted. The pseudonymous Robert Crane's *Hero's Walk* enjoyed a vogue. Gordon Dickson, ambitious and productive writer, is best known for his Dorsai series. David Duncan's novels had much to recommend them—*Another Tree in Eden; Dark Dominion*, with its strange new metal; *Occam's Razor*, with the great line, "Gentlemen, we are about to short-circuit the universe!" Philip José Farmer was breaking tabus before the sf field knew it had them. Jack Finney conveys a gentle and fantastic nostalgia. Daniel Galouye, a follower of Heinlein's, found his most individual voice in a striking novel, *Counterfeit World*. James Gunn is one of the almost-greats, whose *The Immortals* and *The Joymakers* deserve further attention. Daniel Keyes' *Flowers for Algernon* was immediately hailed (and later filmed as *Charly*). Damon Knight, now too well known as critic and anthologist, was once a spirited and elegant short-story writer. Fritz Leiber, most celebrated for his fantasies set in imaginary worlds, was also capable of producing short sf as stunning as "A Pail of Air." J. T. McIntosh began with great promise in such novels as *One in Three Hundred*. Charles Eric Maine was for a long time a regular producer of sensational and effective sf novels, of which the best was perhaps *The Darkest of Nights*. Richard Matheson roared away like an engine in the fifties before hitting Hollywood, where he scripted his own *Incredible Shrinking Man*. Ward Moore's *Bring the Jubilee* in *F&SF* has deservedly become a classic. Dan Morgan's telepathic series, *The Minds*, is still appearing in England. Kris Neville is a satirical man who writes too little. Alan Nourse brings a doctor's understanding to his fiction; that fiction includes a bundle of striking stories as well as several novels for boys. Edgar Pangborn, another respected name, is the author of such novels as *Mirror for Observers* and *Davy*. Fletcher Pratt, historian of the American Revolution, preferred writing fantasy. Frank Robinson's exciting novel *The Power* was filmed. James H. Schmitz wrote one of the best exo-ecology stories, *Grandpa*. E. C. "Ted" Tubb was for some years king of British sf, editor of *Authentic*, an imaginative writer. Wilson Tucker was a great fan, the author of several excellent novels, among them *The Long Loud Silence*

and the one with the beautiful title, *The Year of the Quiet Sun.*
Jack Vance swashbuckled on a million imaginary worlds. James
White's "Sector General" stories about sick extraterrestrials span a
couple of decades. Bernard Wolfe authored the massive amputee
utopia *Limbo 90.* Will Worthington is a great surrealist who writes
too little. Many other names—and I have left the ladies till last.

A few women, such as C. L. Moore, Katherine Maclean, and
Leigh Brackett, were working in the field earlier. On the whole,
they were romantics, though Katherine Maclean could do the hard
stuff magnificently (as in *Incommunicado*), or be extremely funny
(as in *The Snowball Effect*, in which, I swear, the Watashaw Sew-
ing Circle takes over America). Leigh Brackett had many successes before becoming a highly paid script writer in Hollywood,
among them *The Sword of Rhiannon* (1953), which I persist in
regarding as the most magical sub-Burroughs of them all, the best
evocation of that fantasy Mars we would all give our sword arm
to visit:

> Jekkara was not sleeping despite the lateness of the hour.
> The Low Canal towns never sleep, for they lie outside the
> law and time means nothing to them. In Jekkara and Barrakesh
> night is only a darker day.
> Carse walked beside the still black waters in their ancient
> channel, cut in the dead sea-bottom. He watched the dry wind
> shake the torches that never went out and listened to the
> broken music of the harps that were never stilled. Lean lithe
> men and women passed him in the shadowy streets, silent as
> cats except for the chime and whisper of the tiny bells the
> women wear, a sound as delicate as rain, distillate of all the
> sweet wickedness of the world. (Chapter 1)

With the arrival of *Galaxy* and *F&SF*, more women writers appeared, attracted by less dour technology and wider audiences.
Among the famous names are Zenna Henderson, whose stories
about "The People" were very popular, Marion Zimmer Bradley,
Rosel George Brown, Margaret St. Clair (author of many novels
and one short comic gem, "Prott"), and the senior lady of them all,
Miriam Allen de Ford, an accomplished writer of sexual fantasy, as
her collection *Xenogenesis* (1969) proves. Also the best-selling
André Norton, whose science fantasies are designed for teen-agers
and read by adults.

Dropping so many names all at once is perhaps one way of conveying the wealth of talent that filled the magazines in the fifties and later. The list is by no means complete—and will be continued in the next chapter.

In such an impersonal list, one passes too fast over many personal favourites. I'll indulge myself by naming two.

Any survey of contemporary sf, which this book does not claim to be, would have to examine the various works of De Camp. Like so many sf writers of the period—David Duncan's name springs to mind—De Camp never produces masterpieces, but is rarely dull. His books all give the impression of having been thrown off for fun while he equips himself for a second expedition to the delta of the Orinoco or wherever.

Many of De Camp's best books are collaborations, as are the two fantasies *The Incomplete Enchanter* (*Unknown* again) with Fletcher Pratt, and its follow-up, *The Castle of Iron*. Or there's a *Planet of the Apes* type novel, *Genus Homo,* with P. Schulyer Miller. But the saltiest De Camp is a solo effort, *Lest Darkness Fall,* in which the ingenious Martin Padway falls back in time to sixth-century Rome and proceeds to wreck history with his premature inventions.

De Camp also writes non-fiction. He is author of *The Science Fiction Handbook,* as well as several works of historical and mythological travel—among them *Lands Beyond,* another collaboration, this time with Willy Ley. The first sentence of the Introduction to *Lands Beyond* reads, "Three colossal figures stride across the landscape of the mind of early man: the warrior, the wizard, and the wanderer." It is a sentence, I believe, which also tells us much about the mind of early L. Sprague de Camp.

And secondly, Charles Harness, a small producer whose novel *The Rose* frequently appears with recommendations from such connoisseurs as Michael Moorcock, Judith Merril, and Damon Knight. The importance of *The Rose* lies in the question it asks: "Can science and art be made compatible and complimentary?"[12]

My own preference is for Harness' *The Paradox Men.* This novel may be regarded as the climax to the billion year spree. It plays high, wide, and handsome with space and time, buzzes round the solar system like a demented hornet, is witty, profound, and trivial all in one breath, and has proved far too ingenious for the hordes of would-be imitators to imitate. In my introduction to the

British edition of this novel, I call it Wide Screen Baroque[13]; other novels in the same category are Doc Smith's and A. E. van Vogt's, possibly Alfred Bester's: but Harness' novel has a zing of its own, like whisky and champagne, the drink of the Nepalese sultans.

The fifties were a crucial period. Sf came out of its shell, began to talk about the fullness of love as well as the emptiness of space, although interplanetary adventure still dominated all other themes. Magazines proliferated—later to dwindle again, but propagation had taken place. And what had been confined to magazine publishing became part of the ordinary publishing scene (including the burgeoning paperback market), so that sf would never again endure (or enjoy—it depends on your viewpoint) at least two decades out in a wilderness of its own.

Naturally, this major reorientation of audience had its effect. The whole operation became less ingrown. Another effect, to which we now turn in some awe, was that authors were able to write large books which existed as books rather than serials. They could be visualised as a whole; the results were sometimes enormous. Some of these giants had an immediate and powerful influence on our culture.

Beyond, or above, or outside science fiction—but watching over it as the Castle watched all that went on in the village in Kafka's novel—stands J. R. R. Tolkien's trilogy *The Lord of the Rings*.

This enormous structure was built, in the main, in the mid-fifties, although the Hobbit cult only started when Ace and Ballantine published their paperback editions in the States in 1965. Until then, the books had sold well, but Tolkien—a familiar Oxford figure, Merton Professor of English Language and Literature—was mainly known as editor of the best-selling Oxford University Press title *Sir Gawaine and the Green Knight*. The cult then spread back to England (the English write well but borrow enthusiasm from others).

Presumably this large-scale work has been the main influence for the tremendous growth of fantasy and private-world fiction since then—the other influence being the dreadful state of the real world.

One speaks of the cult. To speak of the work itself is more difficult. As Dr. Johnson is reported apocryphally to have said of *The*

Oxford English Dictionary, "It is an achievement which it would be irrelevant to admire, presumptuous to commend, and reckless to consult."

The saga takes the form of a quest, staged in Middle Earth. The Professor's learned apparatus helps to actualise his parallel world, establishing its language and cartography, as well as the full majestic regalia of fairy tales: Hobbits living in cosy dens, eating as voraciously as schoolboys; elves; dwarfs; trolls; thinking trees; dragons; black and white magicians; and so on. The kindly Gandalf presides over the sylvan scene but, in the East, lies Mordor, ruled over by the dreaded Sauron and his army of the living dead. Frodo the Hobbit finally wins a tremendous victory, and the magic ring, which confers absolute power on its wearer, is destroyed, together with the powers of Sauron and all that is his.

Such a large-scale work is open to many interpretations. There is no reason why it should be accepted at face value. One theory, now largely discredited, was that the work was an allegory on World War II. I like Lundwall's description of it as "a conservative man's Utopia,"[14] for the rigid class structure of Middle Earth, and the sense that the black industrial forces of Sauron may overcome the fair lands carries a strong reminder of the England of Tolkien's youth. And, indeed, where else can all the best fantasies start but in one's youth?

The writer most like Tolkien lies far outside the sf field. I refer to P. G. Wodehouse, Tolkien's senior by a decade. For Wodehouse, too, time stopped some while before World War I broke out, and the Hobbit dens may be likened to the Drones Club and other snug retreats, where chaps can gather for drinks and smokes and somewhat schoolboyish chat, secluded from the depraving company of women. The counterfeit gold of an Edwardian sunset lights the *oeuvre* of both men.

Where *Lord of the Rings* is like sf is in the way the heroes are all good, and evil is externalised and defeated—something which we know does not happen in real life, for evil is within us. But perhaps that is another reason for its popularity. One can have too much real life; Tolkien will blot it out for months at a stretch.

The success of Tolkien and the failure of reality have brought popularity to other great fantasists, such as James Branch Cabell, or the revered Mervyn Peake—not as much popularity, in Peake's case, because Peake's great Gothic trilogy, *Titus Groan, Gormen-*

ghast, and *Titus Alone* (1946–59) needs much more concentrated reading than Tolkien.

Compare the two texts.

Frodo is journeying to Orodruin with the ring. His faithful servant Sam is with him, and they are surrounded by threatening things, thirsty and alone. Night falls.

> They could not follow this road any longer; for it went on eastward into the great Shadow, but the Mountain now loomed upon their right, almost due south, and they must turn towards it. Yet still before it there stretched a wide region of fuming, barren, ash-ridden land.
>
> "Water, water!" muttered Sam. He had stinted himself, and in his parched mouth his tongue seemed thick and swollen; but for all his care they now had very little left, perhaps half his bottle, and maybe there were still days to go. All would long ago have been spent, if they had not dared to follow the orc-road. For at long intervals on that highway cisterns had been built for the use of troops sent in haste through the waterless regions. In one Sam had found some water left, stale, muddied by the orcs, but still sufficient for their desperate case. Yet that was now a day ago. There was no hope of any more.
>
> At last wearied with his cares Sam drowsed, leaving the morrow till it came; he could do no more. Dream and waking mingled uneasily. He saw lights like gloating eyes, and dark creeping shapes, and he heard noises as of wild beasts or the dreadful cries of tortured things; and he would start up to find the world all dark and only empty blackness all about him. Once only, as he stood and stared wildly round, did it seem that, though now awake, he could still see pale lights like eyes; but soon they flickered and vanished.
>
> The hateful night passed slowly and reluctantly. (Book 6, Chapter 3)

Now we visit Gormenghast Castle, and again it is night. The infatuated Irma has an assignation with Mr. Bellgrove in the garden:

> Involuntarily they moved together into the arbor and sat down on a bench which they found in the darkness. The night poured in on them from every side—a million cubic miles of it.

Oh, the glory of standing with one's love, naked, as it were, on a spinning marble, while the sphere ran flaming through the universe! This darkness was intensely rich and velvety. It was as though they were in a cavern, save that the depths were dramatized by a number of small and brilliant pools of moonlight. Pranked for the most part to the rear of the arbor these livid pools were at first a little disturbing, for portions of themselves were lit up with blatant emphasis . . .

From Irma's point of view the dappled condition of the cavernous arbor was both calming and irritating at the same time.

Calming, in that to enter a cave of clotted midnight, with not so much as a flicker of light to gauge her distance from her partner, would have been terrifying even with her knowledge of, and confidence in, so reliable and courteous a gentleman as her escort. This dappled arbor was not so fell a place. The pranked lights, more livid, it is true, than gay, removed, nevertheless, that sense of terror only known to fugitives or those benighted in a shire of ghouls.

Strong as was her feeling of gratification that the dark was broken, yet a sense of irritation as strong as her relief fought in her flat bosom for sovereignty. This irritation, hardly understandable to anyone who has neither Irma's figure, nor a vivid picture of the arbor in mind, was caused by the maddening *way* in which the lozenges of radiance fell upon her body.

She had taken out a small mirror in the darkness, more from nervousness than anything else, and in holding it up, saw nothing in the dark air before her but a long sharp segment of light. The mirror itself was quite invisible as was the hand and arm that held it, but the detached and luminous reflection of her nose hovered before her in the darkness. At first she did not know what it was. She moved her head a little and saw in front of her one of her small weak eyes glittering like quicksilver, a startling thing to observe under any conditions, but infinitely more so when the organ is one's own. (*Gormenghast,* Chapter 36)

Tolkien's prose, the very shaping vehicle of his story, is bland and universalised. It has no particular characteristic, apart from the joining of long sentences by "and," which can become wearying. Peake's prose is sharp and particularised. It cannot be mistaken for anyone else's writing or vision; wit moves through it, so that it is anti-sentimental—considerably less lulling than Tolkien's. On the other hand, it is decidedly quirky, too *dense*. A little at a time is all you need. Tolkien's prose is designed for the long, long, empathic read. Nevertheless, Peake conjures the special flavour of a special night, and gets much nearer to the things that haunt shadows. Well, perhaps it's all a matter of taste.

So to other milestones and large books that take us into the sixties.

We have already met Isaac Asimov and Robert Heinlein, labouring lustily in the pages of *Astounding*. Like Bester, Asimov seemed to know when enough was enough, and stopped writing sf novels somewhere after his best novel, *The Naked Sun* (1957). He has recently resumed: *The Gods Themselves* (1972).

Asimov employed the wide-angle lens for his view of life and it is a pity that his largest milestone, the *Foundation* trilogy, was written before sf authors were able to think of their books as books, rather than as short stories or serials in ephemeral magazines (or magazines that would have been ephemeral but for the dedication of fans). Conceived as one organic whole, the *Foundation* series would have undoubtedly risen to greater majesty.[15]

Instead of becoming a novelist, Asimov has developed into one of the polymaths of our day, producing a stream of popularisations of various scientific disciplines. The popularity of his novels continues. Like many another writer, Asimov began in subversive vein, prophesying change and barbarism; but, a generation later, such ideas lose their sting and become safe for a general public. Increasingly, one sees the solid conservative faith in technology in Asimov's novels. His short stories often err on the side of facetiousness.

Heinlein's transition from magazine writer to novelist is dramatic. His great and rare virtue is that he has never been content to repeat a winner or rely on a formula; and this, as we know from our study of Edgar Rice Burroughs, is a way of defying popularity. Nevertheless, wide popularity has been his.

He is very much a pulp writer made good, sometimes with his strong power drives half-rationalised into a right-wing political

philosophy, as in *Starship Troopers* (1959), a sentimental view of
what it is like to train and fight as an infantryman in a future war.
Anyone who has trained and fought in a past war will recognise the
way Heinlein prettifies his picture. But realism is not Heinlein's
vein, although he has an adroit way of dropping in a telling detail
when needed, sometimes giving the illusion of realism. This technique is notably effective in his boys' novels, such as *Starman Jones*
(1953), where close analysis of character and motive is not de-
manded.

For my taste, Heinlein's most enjoyable novel is *Double Star*,
which first ran as a serial in *Astounding* in 1956. *Double Star* is a
hymn to behaviourism. For once Heinlein begins with a "little" man,
almost a Wellsian Cockney, a pathetic failed actor, Lawrence Smith,
who liked to style himself Lorenzo the Great.

Because of his chance resemblance to Bonforte, one of the leading politicians of the solar system, Lorenzo is forced to impersonate
the politician and take on his powers, until he eventually becomes
the man himself, clad in his personality and office. People in other
Heinlein novels often have to fit into unaccustomed roles, become
revolutionaries, become space troopers, wear slugs on their backs,
or—like Smith in *I Will Fear No Evil*—live in a woman's body.

Heinlein's grasp of politics has always been remarkably frail,
and the political issues concerning liberty which lie close to the
heart of *Double Star* are absurdly falsified by the coarsely impractical methods the politicians employ. Thus, Lorenzo is shanghaied
into playing his role, while Bonforte is kidnapped by the opposing
party, the Humanists. This Chicago gangsterism is rendered the
more silly because an effort is made to model political procedures
on British parliamentary method: Bonforte is a Right Honourable,
and "leader of the loyal opposition."[16]

Despite this monstrous drawback, *Double Star* survives somehow because at its centre is the process whereby Lorenzo becomes
Bonforte, and Heinlein handles this with a clarity he is rarely able
to sustain in his other adult novels. The scene on Mars where
Lorenzo as Bonforte goes to be adopted into a Martian Nest (rare
honour for Earthmen) is effective. There are parallels between this
novel and Hope's *Prisoner of Zenda*.

In a juvenile novel, *Red Planet* (1949), Heinlein presents another effective picture of Mars. Heinlein is obscurely moved by

Mars. As a thinker, he is primitive; perhaps this is the source of his appeal. The critic Panshin says that "Heinlein's idea of liberty is wolfish and thoroughgoing."[17] Although it is true that several of his novels are about revolution and wars, this does not make of Heinlein a Zapata. The dark and blood-red planet shines only in the complex universe of his own mind; his ideas of liberty boil down to what a man can grasp for himself.

More nonsense has been written about Heinlein than about any other sf writer. He is not a particularly good storyteller, his characters are often indistinguishable, his style is banal, and to compare him with Kipling is absurd. A better comparison is with Nevil Shute, who also loved machines and added mysticism to his formulae; but Shute is more readable.

Shute, however, is not as interesting as a character. The interest in Heinlein's writing lies in the complexity of Heinlein's character as revealed through the long autobiography of his novels. He is a particular case of that magic-inducing not-growing-up which marks so many sf writers.

And this is best exemplified in his best novel, *Stranger in a Strange Land* (1961). Though it is a faulty book, Heinlein's energy and audacity are turned to full volume. It also is an ambitious book and that, too, one respects.

Mars hangs just below the horizon again.

The central figure of *Stranger in a Strange Land* is Valentine Michael Smith, twenty-five years old and a distant relation of Tarzan; he was born on Mars and brought up by Martians. Back on Earth, his strange Martian ways threaten political stability. He is even better equipped than Tarzan, materially and mentally—materially because oddities of his birth have left him heir to several considerable fortunes and have possibly made him owner of Mars as well; mentally, because he has picked up all sorts of psi powers, learnt from his Martian parents.

Although the novel is by no means "a searing indictment of Western Civilization," as the blurb on one edition†† would have it, it does pitch in heartily against many of our idiocies, just as the early Tarzan books did.

But the odd attraction of *Stranger* is that it mixes the Burroughs tradition with the Peacock-Aldous Huxley tradition. It is full

†† New English Library edition, 1965.

of discussions of religion and morals and free love. For Smith comes
under the protection of Jubal Harshaw, a rich old eccentric know-
all, who holds forth about everything under the Sun. He is a distant
and tiresome relation of Propter in *After Many a Summer* (and is
later to spawn the even more distant and tiresome Chad Mulligan
in *Stand on Zanzibar*).

Smith's ideas of sharing come from his Martian Nest, which
sounds much like the Martian Nest in *Double Star*.

All the characters talk a great deal, their verbosity only ex-
ceeded by the characters in *I Will Fear No Evil*. Here's a sample,
where Jubal and Ben discuss Smith's rejection of conventional
moral codes, and Jubal calls Smith a "poor boy."

> "Jubal, he is *not* a boy, he's a man."
>
> "Is he a 'man'? This poor ersatz Martian is saying that sex
> is a way to be happy. Sex *should* be a means of happiness. Ben,
> the worst thing about sex is that we use it to hurt each other.
> It ought *never* to hurt; it should bring happiness, or at least,
> pleasure.
>
> "The code says, 'Thou shalt not covet thy neighbor's wife.'
> The result? Reluctant chastity, adultery, jealousy, bitterness,
> blows and sometimes murder, broken homes and twisted
> children—and furtive little passes degrading to woman and
> man. Is this Commandment ever obeyed? If a man swore on
> his own Bible that he refrained from coveting his neighbor's
> wife *because* the code forbade it, I would suspect either self-
> deception or subnormal sexuality. Any male virile enough to
> sire a child has coveted many women, whether he acts or not.
>
> "Now comes Mike and says: 'There is no need to covet my
> wife . . . *love* her! There's no limit to her love, we have every-
> thing to gain—and nothing to lose but fear and guilt and hatred
> and jealousy.' The proposition is incredible. So far as I recall
> only pre-civilization Eskimos were this naive—and they were
> so isolated that they were almost 'Men from Mars' themselves.
> But we gave them our 'virtues' and now they have chastity and
> adultery just like the rest of us. Ben, what did they gain?"
>
> "I wouldn't care to be an Eskimo."
>
> "Nor I. Spoiled fish makes me bilious."
>
> "I had in mind soap and water. I guess I'm effete." (Chap-
> ter 33)

Smith also has a number of psi powers at his command, from the ability to slow his heartbeats, to psychokinesis, to making objects vanish—and those objects include clothes, guns, and human beings.[18] He is also represented as being of high intellect *and* is a great success with the girls. In fact, as James Blish knowingly puts it, Smith "can work every major miracle, and most of the minor ones, which are currently orthodox in Campbellian science fiction."[19]

So Smith is ideally equipped by his author to found a new religion—and he does. After "discorporating" quite a few troublesome people, Smith allows himself to be killed by the mob, and discorporates on to the astral level himself.[20]

Stranger in a Strange Land has an odd fascination, despite its faults; it reminds one of Huxley's *Island* in its attempt to offer a schema for better living, but one imagines that Huxley would have been horrified by its barely concealed power fantasy. One might go even further than Blish (who was writing at time of publication) and say that *Stranger* in fact represents the apotheosis of Campbellian science fiction, and so of the long pulp tradition.

Stranger has a strange case history. When first published, it did not sell very well, although, within the sf field, it collected a Hugo. It slowly got up a head of steam and became one of the campus best sellers, along with *Lord of the Flies* and *Lord of the Rings*, spreading then to Underground success.

Panshin, writing possibly in 1965, has a startlingly prophetic thing to say. Speaking of the fact that the religious premises of Heinlein's novel are untrue, and super-powers do not exist, he adds, ". . . without these anyone who attempts to practise the book's religion (which includes mass sex relations) is headed for trouble. In other words, the religion has no point for anybody."[21]

The sixties, so good for so many people in the West, began with the success of *Lolita* and the trial of *Lady Chatterley* and ended with the trial of the hippie murderer Charles Manson, whose family messily took care of Sharon Tate and other victims, and whose career magnificently encapsulates all the slummier manifestations of the decade. Manson's grotesque "religion" was compounded of many straws drifting in the atmosphere, among them Bible texts and Beatle music and drugs. He also picked up some Scientology from a defrocked renegade from that movement—and we recall with pride that Scientology, too, was the brain child of an sf writer, L. Ron Hubbard, alias René LaFayette. *And,* in the words of Manson's biographer,

> . . . another book that helped provide a theoretical basis for Manson's family was *Stranger in a Strange Land* by Robert Heinlein. . . . Initially, Manson borrowed a lot of terminology and ideas from this book—not, hopefully, including the ritual cannibalism described therein. Manson, however, was to identify with the hero of the book, one Valentine Michael Smith [Manson's first follower's child was named Valentine Michael Manson]—a person who, in the course of building a religious movement, took to killing or "discorporating" his enemies. . . . To this day Manson's followers hold water-sharing ceremonies . . .[22]

Of course, only a moralist would be silly enough to imagine, during the Vietnam War, that the Sharon Tate murders and all the rest of Manson's odious mumbo-jumbo might be any sort of logical end result of the well-established and respectable pulp tradition of the all-powerful male, so largely epitomised in Campbell's swaggering intergalactic heroes.

Before leaving Heinlein, one more thing remains to be said. Old-time fans still think of him as a hardware specialist. In fact, he moved over very early to writing a different kind of sf, and one, I believe, much more in tune with the sixties and seventies—a variant which we may call Life-Style Sf[23]; that is to say, a fiction which places the emphasis on experimental modes of living more in accord with, or forced on us by, pressures of modern living.

Another vogue which we may regard as having been hastened on by Robert Heinlein is the vogue for very long novels. If you can't be great, be big! Frank Herbert's *Dune* (1965) is certainly big, and many people have found it great.

Dune is enjoying something like the same success as *Stranger in a Strange Land,* and probably for the same reason, because its readers can indulge in a fantasy life of power and savour a strange religion. But there is more than that to *Dune* and its successor, *Dune Messiah* (1969).[24] Although Campbellian science fiction is still present, so, too, is an attention to sensuous detail which is the antithesis of Campbell; the bleak, dry world of Arrakis is as intensely realised as any in science fiction. The obvious shortage of water,‡‡ for instance, is presented not just diagrammatically, but as living fact which permeates all facets of existence.

In the dining hall of the Arrakeen great house, suspensor lamps had been lighted against the early dark. They cast their yellow glows upward onto the black bull's head with its bloody horns, and onto the darkly glistening oil painting of the Old Duke.

Beneath these talismans, white linen shone around the burnished reflections of the Atreides silver, which had been placed in precise arrangements along the great table—little archipelagos of service waiting beside crystal glasses, each setting squared off before a heavy wooden chair. The classic central chandelier remained unlighted, and its chain twisted upward into shadows where the mechanism of the poison-snooper had been concealed.

Pausing in the doorway to inspect the arrangements, the Duke thought about the poison-snooper and what it signified in his society.

All of a pattern, he thought. *You can plumb us by our language—the precise and delicate delineations for ways to administer treacherous death. Will someone try chaumurky tonight—poison in the drink? Or will it be chaumas—poison in the food?*

He shook his head.

Beside each plate on the long table stood a flagon of water. There was enough water along the table, the Duke estimated, to keep a poor Arrakeen family for more than a year.

Flanking the doorway in which he stood were broad laving basins of ornate yellow and green tile. Each basin had its rack of towels. It was the custom, the housekeeper had explained, for guests as they entered to dip their hands ceremoniously into a basin, slop several cups of water onto the floor, dry their hands on a towel and fling the towel into the growing puddle at the door. After the dinner, beggars gathered outside to get the water squeezings from the towels.

How typical of a Harkonnen fief, the Duke thought. *Every*

‡‡ It was the shortage of water on Mars which led to the "water-brotherhood" that Smith establishes in *Stranger in a Strange Land.*

degradation of the spirit that can be conceived. He took a
deep breath, feeling rage tighten his stomach.

"The custom stops here!" he muttered.

He saw a serving woman—one of the old and gnarled ones
the housekeeper had recommended—hovering at the doorway
from the kitchen across from him. The Duke signalled with
upraised hand. She moved out of the shadows, scurried around
the table toward him, and he noted the leathery face, the blue-
within-blue eyes.

"My Lord wishes?" She kept her head bowed, eyes
shielded.

He gestured. "Have these basins and towels removed."

"But . . . Noble Born . . ." She looked up, mouth gaping.

"I know the custom!" he barked. "Take these basins to the
front door. While we're eating and until we've finished, each
beggar who calls may have a full cup of water. Understood?"

And these were from *Analog* in its maligned days![25] The two
Herbert serials about Arrakis ran in 1963, 1964, and 1965. They are
dense and complex books, repaying careful reading.[26] While they
contain many ideas, the main informing idea is an ecological one;
which makes them—together with all the other things they are!
—very trendy books.

Herbert has long been known as an impressive writer. His
great 1955 serial in *Astounding, Under Pressure*—reprinted variously
in book form under much less apposite titles, *Dragon in the Sea,* and
21st Century Sub—also has strong religious elements, and is well
worth seeking out for its study of obsessed men engaged in undersea warfare some time in the future. Herbert's *The Santaroga
Barrier* portrays a small utopian community that isolates itself from
the rest of the United States.

Our next giant is John Brunner's *Stand on Zanzibar* (1968).
Zanzibar does not enter the matter; it is simply the area of land you
would need on which to stand all the inhabitants of Brunner's 2010
world elbow to elbow. For this is a slick overpopulation novel,
the crowded scene built up by slabs of close-ups, newspaper cut-
tings, conversation, jokes, and what the author calls "Contexts"—
bulletins of one sort and another. All these buttress the narrative,
and greatly increase its sense of density and complexity.

This is an extract from a party conversation, which shows some of the period slang at work:

"One thing about this crazy party, I do depose—I never expected to see so many shiggies at Guinevere's place looking like shiggies instead of like sterile-wrapped machines. Do you suppose she's testing the temperature to see if she should move the Beautiques over to the natural trend?"

"Happened all in a moment. One second, just a bunch of people walking down a street, not going any place in particular, and the next, these brown-noses clanging on big empty cans with sticks like drummers leading an army and all sorts of dreck flying through the air and windows being smashed if they weren't out already and screaming and hysteria and the stink of panic. Did you know you can actually smell terror when people start rioting?"

"Louisiana isn't going to last much longer, you know. There's a bill up for next session in the state legislature which will ban child-bearing by anyone who can't prove three generations of residence. And what's worse they're only offering five to two against it being passed. The governor has his two prodgies now, you see."

"I was in Detroit last week and that's the most eerie place I ever did set foot. Like a ghost town. All those abandoned factories for cars. And crawling with squatters, of course. Matter of fact I went to a block party in one of them. You should hear a zock group playing full blast under a steel roof five hundred feet long! Didn't need lifting—just stand and let the noise wipe you out."

"It's more than a hobby, it's a basic necessity for modern man. It fulfils a fundamental psychological urge. Unless you know that if you have to you can kill someone who gets in your way, preferably with your bare hands, the pressure from all these people is going to cave you in."

Among all its diversions, *Zanzibar* produces three well-integrated stories centred round three characters. House is the black director of General Technics, a gigantic company planning to invest massively in Benina, an African country ripe for development. House's roommate, a white called Hogan, is taken and turned into an assassin, to be dropped in a Far Eastern country called Yatakang, where they are breeding improved men. And both House and Hogan form part of the scene at home, which is dominated by a big bad hippie philosopher called Chad Mulligan.

General Technics owns a computer called Shalmaneser, which is both vulnerable and unprotected, although tourists are allowed to view it. A girl tries to clobber it with an axe, and House—one of the directors of the company—has to come and sort out the trouble (he uses a liquid helium hose which snaps the girl's hand off at her arm). This sort of unlikely and unpleasant melodrama militates against the lively intellectual dance going on elsewhere, and eventually overwhelms it. Before that, Brunner conducts a gleeful teach-in on present discontents, aided by Chad Mulligan. As with all Propter-figures, as with Jubal Harshaw, Mulligan wearies, being an author mouthpiece. He puts us all to rights and even out-talks Shalmaneser. The book becomes too long.

Towards the end, faced with winding up a complex affair, Brunner takes refuge in a welter of action in which coincidences pile up, jaws drop, testicles hammer pavements, brains chill, and key scientists are smuggled out of police states at dead of night. The power of the statement is dissipated.

But it is an interesting experiment, not least to a critic because it marks a stage along the road, midway between pulp and social commentary. Commendably ambitious, Brunner had not prepared himself sufficiently in his previous writing, mainly countless Ace sf thrillers, for the creation of a major book. A man of intelligence and wit, he seems—perhaps like Pohl—unwilling to make a personal statement. In *Zanzibar*, he takes courage from the new developments in sf in the sixties, and may yet give us something bigger and better— or preferably smaller and better.

With many popular novels behind him, Brunner resembles Robert Silverberg, another energetic producer. Silverberg decided, very bravely, to throw up productivity in favour of creativity and begin a new career for himself. Such determination deserves nothing but applause, and will win Silverberg large new audiences in the seventies.

We turn now to the last book in our parade of giants. Like all the others except *Zanzibar*, it shows some concern for religion. Here, the concern is central.

In World War II, Walter Miller, Jr., like his fellow American, Kurt Vonnegut, Jr., became involved with the hostilities in Europe.

Vonnegut experienced the fire-bombing of Dresden and eventually produced *Slaughterhouse Five*. Miller experienced the assault on the Benedictine Monastery at Monte Cassino and wrote *A Canticle for Leibowitz*. So we digest our own experiences and offer them as nourishment for others.

Canticle has the dryness, toughness, and nutritional value of *cordon bleu* pemmican. All sf writers are astonishing but some sf writers are more astonishing than others. *Canticle* appears to be the rocky summit of Miller's brief writing career.

He came on strong with stories in—to mention it yet again—Campbell's *Astounding—Izzard and the Membrane, Blood Bank, The Big Hunger*, using interstellar space as some sort of obscure private metaphor, in 1951 and 1952. But the stories that got turned into *Canticle* appeared in *F&SF*.

An aside about that magazine, since more has been said of *ASF* and *Galaxy*. It would be a shabby history of sf which held no warm word for the shade of Anthony Boucher, *F&SF*'s tremendous editor. Boucher's real name was William Anthony Parker White. He entered the sf field through Campbell's *Unknown*—as did his rival editor, Horace Gold.

As Gold, through *Galaxy*, brought in the divine razzmatazz of Bester, Pohl, Sheckley, and the incredible William Tenn, so Boucher, through *F&SF*, brought in literary standards and a much wider appreciation of what was implied by "science." As Judith Merril has said, "Until Boucher and McComas started *Fantasy and Science Fiction*, in 1949, the Campbell-dominated specialty field had no place in it for the kind of stories Beaumont, Budrys, Clingerman, Cogswell, Dick, Henderson, Matheson, Miller, MacDonald, Moore, Nourse, Pangborn, Tenn, Vance, Vonnegut, and a score of others, began to produce—as did Asimov, Bester, Leiber, Wyndham, and others, many of whom had virtually stopped writing until the necessary new magazine came along."[27]

Since Boucher's day, *F&SF* has been maintained successfully through several editorships, among the most distinguished being those of Robert Mills, Avram Davidson, and Ed Ferman, present incumbent of the diocese.

Canticle was published in book form in 1960, and was immediately greeted with the warmest praise by reviewers—i.e. they said it was so good it couldn't possibly be sf.[28] It has its longueurs, but emerges as the best of the after-the-bomb novels.[29]

A Dark Age follows the nuclear holocaust, and such shreds of learning as can be picked from the ruins are preserved by the Catholic Church, and in particular by the holy men of the Order of Saint Leibowitz. This is far from being one more tedious exercise in revamped feudal history. Miller's sense of irony and of place ensure that. He takes us towards another Renaissance, when once more technology builds up to its previous level. Give or take a few mutants, everything is as before. Then the bombs begin to fall again.

In synopsis, this suggests an exercise in heavy message-dropping. *Canticle* is nothing of the sort.

> The two-headed woman and her six-legged dog waited with an empty vegetable basket by the new gate; the woman crooned softly to the dog. Four of the dog's legs were healthy legs, but an extra pair dangled uselessly at its sides. As for the woman, one head was as useless as the extra legs of the dog. It was a small head, a cherubic head, but it never opened its eyes. It gave no evidence of sharing in her breathing or her understanding. It lolled uselessly on one shoulder, blind, deaf, mute, and only vegetatively alive. Perhaps it lacked a brain, for it showed no sign of independent consciousness or personality. Her other face had aged, grown wrinkled, but the superfluous head retained the features of infancy, although it had been toughened by the gritty wind and darkened by the desert sun.
> The old woman curtsied at their approach, and her dog drew back with a snarl. "Evenin', Father Zerchi," she drawled.

This pathetic old creature wants the abbot to baptise Rachel. Which raises a nice theological point, for Rachel is her sleeping and mutated extra head. How many souls has an old two-headed woman? Many years before this, Old Father Heinlein wrote a story called *Common Sense*, in which there is a tough two-headed mutant, Joe-Jim. Joe-Jim is the leader of a gang of mutants. Both heads, Joe and Jim, can talk and behave as brothers; in the end, one of them gets stabbed through the eye. Old Mrs. Grales in *Canticle* represents an inspired improvement on the early model; Miller invests the sleeping head with mysterious significance.

The bombs drop. The monastery falls on Father Zerchi. Pinned down, he sees Mrs. Grales approach. But no, the face of Mrs. Grales is pale and withered; her eyes have closed; she appears to be dying.

Rachel has woken to transient life. Unlike that dull yellow eye of Frankenstein's creature, the eyes the bomb has opened are cool green eyes, alert with curiosity. Rachel is young and beautiful, only just born, full of wonder at the wounded world. The dying priest sees in her eyes a primal innocence and hope of resurrection as she kneels before him. More bombs fall.

Science fiction is like an ocean. The images come and go, mysteriously linked through transformation after transformation. Many rivers pour into the ocean, all the tributaries of our life, both waking and dreaming. These days, we all have two heads. Frankenstein's monster plunges along beside us, keeping just below the Plimsoll line of consciousness, buoyant with a life of its own.

NOTES

1. Characteristically, on neutral ground! This was the First International SF Symposium, held in Tokyo in 1970, to coincide with Expo '70; organised by Sakyo Komatsu, Chairman, and first suggested by the present writer. Those present included Frederik Pohl, Judith Merril, Vasily Zakharchenko, E. I. Parnov, Julius Kagarlitski, Arthur C. Clarke, and Brian Aldiss.

2. Damon Knight refers to *More Than Human* and *The Demolished Man* as "the two most famous sf books of the fifties," in his Introduction to *A Science Fiction Argosy*, edited by Damon Knight, New York, 1972.

3. Under the name of William Atheling, Blish has written two books of sf criticism, both published by Advent House: *The Issue at Hand*, 1964, and *More Issues at Hand*, 1970. His critical work in the field of James Joyce studies is also well known.

4. The point has been made many times. One statement of it, from the viewpoint of a "human biologist," may be found in Alex Comfort's *Nature and Human Nature*, 1966.

5. While examining boys' magazines in his famous article "Boys' Weeklies," written in 1939, Orwell comments, "The one theme that is really new is the scientific one. Death rays, Martians, invisible men, robots, helicopters, and interplanetary rockets figure largely; here and there there are even far-off rumours of psychotherapy and ductless

glands." He had *Modern Boy* and *Champion* mainly in mind. The same article also mentions "threepenny Yank Mags"—the Woolworths' counter which was the traditional spot at which future British addicts were infected with the sf virus.

6. Orwell was one of the Angry Young Men of his day, in a line stretching back through Shelley and Wells and forward to Amis and Osborne—men whose sympathies, at least during the flush of youth, lay with the submerged classes. Like calls to like over the years; as Desmond King-Hele notes in *Shelley: His Thought and Work,* Chap. 8, the song "Beasts of England" in *Animal Farm* is a parody of Shelley's challenge to the ruling classes, "Song of the Men of England":

> Men of England, wherefore plough
> For the lords who lay ye low?
> Wherefore weave with toil and care
> The rich robes your tyrants wear?

Again like Shelley, Orwell wrote a parody of the national anthem. It appears in *Animal Farm,* as "Comrade Napoleon." This was the book banned, not in England, but in the USSR.

7. The point is made with different emphasis by Chad Walsh in his *From Utopia to Nightmare,* 1962. See Chap. 8.

8. Something of the same viewpoint appears more diffusely in H. F. Heard's *Doppelgängers,* New York, 1947. Heard postulates two worlds, an upper and a lower, both ruled by tyrants, one rather like *Brave New World* and one similar to *1984.* The central character has his personality wiped out as Winston Smith does, but by means of very elaborate and futuristic behaviourist devices.

9. Sir Richard Rees, *George Orwell: Fugitive from the Camp of Victory,* 1961. The passage quoted comes in Chap. 8.

10. Another way in which to portray the corrosive effects of technological civilisation upon us is to depict man as dehumanised, as a robot or android—the message of *R.U.R.* and most significant robot stories since. Stories of robots becoming "humanised" have always struck me as perverse, a confusion of symbols.

11. In this respect, it is interesting to compare the translation of the two books into other media. Orwell's *1984* was one of the early successes of post-war British television—the serial everyone watched—its gritty subject matter well matched by the gritty techniques of the flickering small screen. Later, it was made into a less successful film, with Michael Redgrave as O'Brien and Patrick O'Brien as Smith. *Animal Farm* became an animated cartoon.

12. The question, presumably, which interested Michael Moorcock. See his introduction to the Roberts and Vinter edition of *The Rose,*

1966. This short novel had previously been published in the British *Authentic* sf magazine, edited by H. J. Campbell.

13. British edition published by Faber & Faber in 1964. Introduction by Brian Aldiss. Paperback edition, 1967. Referring to this and the previous note, one sees that a British rescue operation was carried out on the reputation of Charles Harness. Edmund Crispin has performed a similar operation for Cyril Kornbluth. We have already noted transatlantic rescues carried out in the opposite direction, with Lin Carter's revival of Arnold's Mars novel. Indeed, many other cultural debts are owed to Lin Carter. David Hartwell at Signet has recently been instrumental in reprinting several Aldiss titles. Such two-way traffic is one of the pleasures of sf; next chapter instances many more.

14. Sam Lundwall, *Science Fiction: What It's All About*, 1971, Chap. 5.

15. "The loss is everybody's that the youthful Asimov's literary technique was not a match for his theme—indeed Tolstoi himself might have blenched and turned away." Brian Aldiss, *The Shape of Further Things*, 1970. In this volume, which was by way of being a dry run for the present book, I have a good deal to say about my personal involvement with science fiction.

16. Despite which, one critic claims this novel is "not melodramatic, but sure and real." The remark occurs in Chap. 3 of Alexei Panshin's *Heinlein in Dimension: A Critical Analysis*, Chicago, 1968. This is a long, honourable, and painstaking study of Heinlein's work, recommended simply as a popular guide. But Panshin has no grasp of critical method, or of what makes literature. His own prose style is blind to grace and meaning; "By 2075 one assumes that everybody will talk enough differently from the present to need translation into our terms."

17. Panshin, op. cit., Chap. 7.

18. A lively discussion of the wish-fulfilment aspects of the novel is contained in Dr. Robert Plank's article, "Omnipotent Cannibals: Thoughts on Reading Robert Heinlein's *Stranger in a Strange Land*," *Riverside Quarterly*, Vol. 5, No. 1.

19. James Blish, "Cathedrals in Space," in *The Issue at Hand*.

20. It is interesting to compare Heinlein's novel, written before the hippie thing, with my own *Barefoot in the Head* (1969). In the latter, the entire culture is freaked out after the Acid Head War, and the central character, Charteris, is elevated to the role of Messiah. But such power as he has comes from abnegation and, when he finds himself on the brink of believing in his ability to work miracles, he deliberately throws away the Christ role.

21. Panshin, op. cit., Chap. 4, portions of which appeared in

Riverside Quarterly in 1965. Which demonstrates that Panshin has some of the qualities needed to criticise sf, *pace* Note 16!

22. From Chap. 1, Sec. 1 of Ed Sanders' *The Family: The Story of Charles Manson's Dune Buggy Attack Battalion*, New York, 1971. Manson was also turned on by Dr. Eric Berne's *Transactional Analysis* and the Beatle's totally innocuous "I Wanna Hold Your Hand."

23. As far as I know, this coinage is first used in my Afterword, "A Day in the Life-Style of . . ." in *Best SF: 1971*, edited by Harry Harrison and Brian Aldiss, where it is applied to such novels as Luke Rhinehart's *The Dice Man*.

24. How the two novels are intricately connected (rather than the second book's being a mere sequel to the first) is examined in Robert C. Parkinson's interesting article "*Dune*—An Unfinished Tetralogy," *Extrapolation*, Vol. 13, No. 1. As the title implies, Mr. Parkinson sees room for yet more Dune.

25. *Dune World* and *The Prophet of Dune* were serialised in *Analog*. *Dune Messiah* appeared in *Galaxy*.

26. Your critic regrets that he is such a recent convert to them that he is unable to offer proper elucidation; that must wait for strength and a second volume.

27. Judith Merril, "What Do You Mean—Science Fiction?" Pt. 2., *Extrapolation*, Vol. 8, No. 1. One of Miss Merril's great gifts as anthologist and catalyst—not to mention female incendiary—has been her enthusiasm. Here it runs away with her slightly, but in the main what she says is incontrovertible. She goes on to add of Boucher that "he would not buy a story just for the idea; he had to like the writing. And unlike most earlier editors, he was not style-deaf."

28. Strictly as codified in the immortal couplet written by Kingsley Amis and/or Robert Conquest:

> "Sf's no good," they bellow till we're deaf.
> "But this looks good."—"Well, then, it's not sf."

29. Although I have a weakness for Pat Frank's novel *Alas, Babylon* (1959), in which World War III breaks out and the States is bombed back to the Stone Age. A little community survives, cut off in Florida. At last, a helicopter arrives, and the community can get some news of the outside world. One of the survivors asks, "Who won the war?" The helicopter pilot is amazed: "You mean you really don't know? . . . We won it. We really clobbered 'em!"

11

The Stars My Detestation:

YESTERDAY AND TOMORROW

> That picture of the Earth with the Moon in the fore-
> ground should be in every classroom and home in the
> world. Plenty of clouds and water are visible, but
> very little land. No national boundaries are visible at
> all.
>> Isn't that message clear enough?
>> Harry Harrison: *Men on the Moon*

The grand official opening of the Space Age took place in October
1957, when the first Earth satellite was lobbed into orbit. From
then on, we could escape from our planet.* A little later, with those
striking satellite photographs, came another realisation which may
stand us in even better stead: that our planetary air, soil, water, are
limited and must be treated with proper respect if we are to survive.

In 1969, Donald Wollheim, then guiding light of Ace Books,
published an anthology called *Men on the Moon*. He persuaded
twenty-seven writers to give their views on the first lunar landing,
which took place in July of that year. Isaac Asimov, John Brunner,
E. C. Tubb, Alan Nourse, and others had their say. Only Philip K.
Dick, Ray Bradbury, and Poul Anderson were full of unqualified
praise and excitement. Most of the authors took a very sceptical

---

* I admit to a highly specialised use of the pronoun.

view of the proceedings. The phrase on the plaque, "We Came in Peace for All Mankind," stuck in their gullets; they started remembering the Indians.

Michael Moorcock quoted J. G. Ballard's wry remark: "If I were a Martian I'd start running now!" Isaac Asimov hoped we might find a nobility in space of which many dream and some practise. Bob Shaw thought that the plaque should have borne not words but a symbol whose significance would have been universally understood—"something like a grabbing hand, with its fingers clawed into the Moon's soil." Harlan Ellison talked about little old ladies getting mugged. Harry Harrison was the one person who mentioned Vietnam, pointing out that it was war, not the Apollo missions, which wasted everyone's substance. Other writers felt that the lunar walk could have brought small cheer to the oppressed and impoverished on Earth.

The general consensus was cautionary. Ever since the beginning of the Space Age, sf writers have been less romantic about space flight, although there are exceptions such as Poul Anderson. The C. S. Lewis view is winning through, that we are liable to spread destruction wherever we go. There may be something to Kenneth Bulmer's remark in *Men on the Moon:* "We're in the creative instant of the paleolithic man who's just hand-paddled a log across the estuary—now all the oceans lie beyond"; but the old joy in bigger and better logs is somehow less spontaneous than before. Now that the Moon had become real estate, can it so easily be dreamed about and handled as a symbol? Has the grandiose vision of interstellar flight lost its potency as it approaches reality? Do we now regard the stars in detestation rather than hope? Is the billion year spree over?

My answer to these questions is perhaps a personal one. I do not set great store by the prophetic side of sf. To prophesy a war in 1999 means nothing in 1973; and it can make no difference in 1999. The gesture is even less meaningful if it happens to be the only correct one among ninety-nine failed prophecies. To prophesy as warning (as I believe Orwell did in *1984*) is entirely a different matter.

But if sf as prophecy is out, sf as prodromic utterance is definitely in. We have seen how Mary Shelley has a prodromic gift. My belief is that sf as a whole has something of the same ability.

To lay out the evidence for this fully would need a long monograph. But the point may be explained briefly.

Every few years, a great submerged theme moves through science fiction like a ground swell. There are always crosscurrents but,
with insight or hindsight, we may catch the main drift. In the sixties,
this ground swell moved towards environmental topics. To elaborate, the most important work done tended to direct itself towards
new socio-scientific attitudes, towards the complex factors involved
in the technological culture's slow debasement of man and his natural world. This has found expression in many of the writings we
are about to examine, which characteristically deal with affairs on
this overpopulated world rather than any other, or with the role of
malfunctioning or discontented individuals—what we have termed
Life-Style Sf.

Moreover, I believe that this sixties ground swell, which points
the way to a general public concern in the seventies with these
same issues, had its inevitable precedents in the sf of the fifties, in
its most characteristic ground swell. The fifties' ground swell might
be called Fear of Dehumanisation in the Face of the Stars.

Depersonalisation was not a new fear. What was new was the
characteristic science fictional form of expression it now achieved.
And since it never achieved perfection of expression (or not on
more than miniature scale), it came and passed, and has hitherto
been unremarked.

Because the theme never clarified into perfection, it remains
somewhat surrounded by similar material. Nevertheless, its crest
emerges clearly in 1953.

Robots can embody depersonalisation fears. This is perhaps
their most obvious psychological function. They then stand for man's
anxieties about surviving the pressures of modern society, as in
R.U.R. Since then, sf has taken the matter further and used symbolism less accessible than the robot to express anxieties about the
blow to the psyche experienced by achieving space travel and con-
fronting other worlds; or, to phrase it another way, the cultural
shock of the alien.

There were several sf precedents before 1953: John W. Campbell's *Who Goes There*, as far back as 1938, Eric Frank Russell's
Metamorphosite in 1946 (a curious story with a frighteningly beautiful symbol of flowering nuclear power), and Van Vogt's *The
Sound* in 1950, are three examples.

Then in 1952 came Alan Nourse's *Counterfeit,* and there the theme was, almost full-grown.

Counterfeit appeared in *Thrilling Wonder,* and was necessarily melodramatic, but it made its point. A spaceship is returning to Earth from Venus. Aboard are men and an alien posing as a man, almost indetectable, right down to cellular level. (Nourse is a doctor, and made the details convincing.) The alien can imitate a human being to perfection. Dr. Crawford detects one of them and kills the "man," whereupon it dwindles down into a little red blob.

But there is more than one alien aboard. The ship returns to Earth, the crew depart, and Crawford goes back on his own. He hears something in the ship. Another alien is there. He comes face to face with it. He is glaring at himself! The alien kills him, and heads into the city.

A perfect fable of dehumanisation in the face of the stars.

In 1953, one finds several versions of the same fable, among them another tale by Nourse, *Nightmare Brother.*

This time, a man is being trained on Earth to confront the horrors on alien planets. These horrors are never described. All we know is that, as in the previous Nourse story, nothing is what it seems. The horrors can twist men's minds, inflicting illusions on them that may prove fatal.

Even the training is almost too much for Cox, Nourse's hero. His girl pleads for him.

"It may kill him! You're asking too much, he's not a superman, he's just an ordinary, helpless human being like anyone else. He doesn't have any magical powers."

And this was in *Astounding,* where magical powers had been the order of the day. Before the test case of actual space flight, the mask of pulp fantasy was slipping.

Cox learns to master the alien threat, but not all the characters facing similar peril in 1953 were as fortunate. For instance, the heroes of two Philip K. Dick variants, *Imposter* and *Colony*—in the first of which a man discovers he is an android manufactured on an alien world—a robot, moreover, with a bomb in his chest! In the second, the engulfing alien takes on the form of a spaceship, into which the humans meekly troop, thinking to return to Earth.

James Gunn's *Breaking Point* appeared in Lester del Rey's short-lived but excellent *Space Science Fiction.* Here, the spaceship crew are subjected to intolerable mental forces, again expressed as hallucinations, by the aliens outside. Fear was the key-note. Curiosity rather than fear informs Damon Knight's *Four in One,* in which Nourse's horrendous blob, now lying inert on Knight's planet, is big enough to absorb several rash Earthlings. The idea was used humorously twice by Sheckley, also in 1953, in *Diplomatic Immunity* and *Keep Your Shape.* Always the alien took over, always he had an unfair advantage. The great powers enjoyed by Earthmen in the previous decade's fiction were now possessed solely by his enemies.

In the next year, the theme of dehumanisation is already on the wane. But two good examples appear in *Galaxy.* Fred Pohl's *The Tunnel Under the World,* where the man up against the inexplicable happenings discovers he is just a table-top robot, is the only one of this group of stories in which a menace from space is not involved. This is a Pohl story—the menace is Advertising. William Tenn's *Down Among the Dead Men* is the most gruesome of all. In Earth's battle against insect invaders from space, we are running short of men. But bits of bodies can be patched together and revived by new techniques. The trouble is, the zombies smell a bit, which is unpleasant for the live men who lead them into battle. . . . Dehumanisation in the face of the stars can't go much further than this.†

Which is presumably why this theme now peters out in this particular form. Note that it is essentially an American form, possibly one culmination of the Injuns-among-the-Stars obsession.[1]

In the nature of things, no theme becomes extinct in sf.[2] The aliens-turning-into-anything straggle on, for instance in Fredric Brown's *The Mind Thing* (1961) and John Brunner's *Double Double* (1967), but by then the heat was off. However, back comes the theme in full creative force—i.e., transformed—in Stanislaus Lem's *Solaris* (English translation, 1970, but first published in Polish in 1961), where his world-ocean can create human-analogues which invade the satellite station. The Russian film *Solaris* (1972) very successfully re-creates the novel.

To my mind, this Dehumanisation in the Face of the Stars theme was one of the psychic birth pangs of the Space Age, a prodromus of the new stresses with which Russian and American space

† But how often sf reads like religion-for-unbelievers. Dehumanisation is an atheist's version of demonic possession. The two disciplines are fused in the Bent One's seizure of Weston in *Perelandra.*

missions have faced society. The theme also functions within science fiction to prepare us for a movement away from the stars and towards Earth, which is the dominant theme of the most vital sf of the sixties.

The fears expressed in the fifties have led, also, to a much less glib readiness to poise and solve a major problem, which was once a characteristic of magazine sf. Or maybe life's just become trickier; as the problem of ending the Vietnam War demonstrates.

Certainly the significant recent changes in science fiction have been towards a more land-locked and cerebral model, with problems poised rather than solved.

Let us trace the train of events which leads us to the present through the career of one writer, a career which accurately graphs the state of sf (and the world) in its succeeding phrases.

The writer is John Wyndham. He changed his name and tune more than once. He went through several larval stages before emerging as a resplendent butterfly.

Wyndham had several given names, all of which were utilised at one stage or another of his development. His full name was John Wyndham Parkes Lucas Beynon Harris, and he was born in 1903 in the Warwickshire countryside. His most famous novels would carry memories of the country, either wrecked or triumphing.

He started selling science fiction to the American sf magazines in the thirties under the name of John Beynon Harris, and became very popular. His manner was light and amused; he wrote about space flight but, one feels, without any burning faith in the possibility of its becoming reality. In *Exiles on Asperus,* Earthmen are enslaved by the batlike inhabitants of an asteroid and grow to love their chains.

In 1935, a popular British family magazine called *The Passing Show* ran a serial in the summer months to catch the seaside trade. It was illustrated by a remarkable artist, Fortunino Matania, who had already done a sexy job on two of Edgar Rice Burroughs' *Venus* novels for the same magazine. *The Secret People* was by one John Beynon. Harris had dropped his "Harris."

The French, with Italian cooperation, have flooded part of the Sahara to create a huge new sea in an attempt to bring fertility to the barren land about its shores. Hero and heroine in plane

crash into sea and are drawn by a swift-flowing current into vast
subterranean caves. There they fall into the hands of a race of
subterranean pigmies (the last of the British submerged nations?).
They escape at the end of the story, bearing with them the pigmy
secret of "cold light." The pigmies are all drowned when sea floods
their caves. *The Secret People* was evidently popular with its
audience; it had few unfamiliar elements in it to disturb them. It
was published as a hard-cover book in the same year.

The Passing Show later serialised *Stowaway to Mars,* which
also appeared in hard-cover. Both books were published in paperback later, and reprinted in 1972. Wyndham was established as a
success, although his literary talents had not revealed themselves
as other than modest.

Other men who wrote science fiction in the mid- and late
thirties have since been almost forgotten. But they did not seek
magazine publication, and their novels had more literary style.
We should pause to recall two of the most striking before following
the next phase of the Wyndham life cycle.

A year before *The Secret People* was serialised—in 1934—Alun
Llewellyn's *The Strange Invaders* was published. It is beautiful,
cold, and remote, and created so far from the preconceptions of its
day that it carries conviction still. The Ice Age is returning. The
scene is somewhere in the south of Russia, where cold winds speak
of coming winter; Moscow is already under the ice. Interest centres
on a mediaeval community whose religion has likewise undergone
a long freeze. Marx, Lenin, and Stalin are worshipped super-
stitiously as gods. All details are intense and chilly, like a novel by
Ursula Le Guin. And then the big reptiles return.

> They turned. At first they could see nothing.
>
> The walls stood bare of guards, for those set there had
> come down to ward off the attack of Tartars upon the gate,
> and men had been too much preoccupied to station sentinels
> there again. The crenellations jutted raggedly against the sky
> of thick and rolling cloud. But there was something un-
> familiar about their pattern, in one place.
>
> A dark shape thrust above the walls, a shape they could
> not make out; a shape that seemed of stone, so motionless
> it was. The day broadened.
>
> A head, long and narrow and flat. Shoulders that humped

as if about to thrust the arms for a mighty leap. A head covered with horny scales that glittered and winked with a sheen of smooth polished colour. Hands that gripped the top of the battlements with clawed fingers, glowed with the same shining scales. From the base of the head, over the shoulders, it appeared as if some supple mail were stretched, wrinkled and gleaming. Stiff, unbreathing it stood; it seemed immaculate, bright, shaped of some strange metal by an inhuman, precise craftsman. Its scales were laid with a cunning geometry of design. The nostrils were bored in its snout in horny circles; its ears, or what seemed its ears, were also incised hollows. The grim line of its mouth slit its head and curled up with the hint of an emotionless grin far back from the nostrils. It did not appear to look at them, and yet it watched. Sidelong it gazed with an eye close to the top of its brainless head, an eye that had a glassy shimmer over a hint of twinkling green. An eye that witnessed without consideration, like a mechanism that would catch apprehension of what was about it and instruct some mighty, cold and purposeful force to action. It watched.

Its long shadow spread hugely over the city. One hand in its jewelled mail curved down into the fortress; the other rested on the wall and they saw the fourth finger, three feet long, longer than its fellows, curl slenderly into the air.

Their breath was stopped in their nostrils.

The creature moved. Its jaws opened silently and shut; a black tongue flickered, forked, out and in.

The people shuddered and they sighed like a moaning wind. The Chief of Fathers neither stirred nor breathed.

Karasoin swayed upon his steed; then sprang from the saddle.

An alien scene, alien creatures, an alien faith—all were staple diet of magazine fiction. Never were they so hauntingly combined as here.[3]

Much more a period piece is R. C. Sherriff's *The Hopkins Manuscript* (1939). Sherriff is the author of *Journey's End. The Hopkins Manuscript* is a cosy catastrophe, much in the style that Wyndham was to adopt two decades later. It reads now as a gorgeous parody of all things British and thirties-ish.

The hero, Hopkins, is in his fifties, has a Cambridge education, and comes of an old and honourable family. He breeds poultry. In true Edwardian style, he lives alone with his housekeeper in a large and comfortable house. When the Moon comes crashing down to Earth, says Hopkins, ". . . after careful reflection I decided to meet the crisis in the dining-room." He takes down the china ornaments and stacks them in cupboards.

The Moon splashes down in the Atlantic, raising the sea level, and bringing certain unpleasant problems with it.

> And how were we to live if, as I imagined, the whole fabric of civilization had collapsed? No butter, no milk, no bread, no meat? . . . The grim, unanswerable problems paraded before me in the dawn like spectres: no electric light —no sanitary services—no pure water . . .
> I missed the morning paper, too; I missed the dawn song of birds in the spring. And even the cheerful whistling of the milkman . . . (Chapter 22)

Rich mineral deposits are found on the Moon. War breaks out among the European powers. Hopkins, in desperation, goes to live in Notting Hill. His manuscript is presented as being found a thousand years later, by members of the Eastern races who invaded and conquered a divided Europe.

The divided Europe idea very soon became reality. War broke out, and eventually John Wyndham—like more than one British science fiction writer—found himself in the Royal Corps of Signals. He took part in the Normandy landings. After the war, when the fruits of victory were rapidly turning into the ashes of peace, he was without career or direction.

It was then that he embarked on the course that was to make him master of the cosy catastrophe. *The Day of the Triffids,* by John Wyndham, was serialised in *Colliers,* and appeared in hardcover in England in 1951. Its success was immediate and prolonged, to nobody's surprise more than the modest Wyndham, who was having a sherry in a pub one day when he overheard two gardeners discussing their weeds over a pint of beer; one said, "There's one by my tool shed—a great monster. I reckon it's a triffid!" The word had entered the language, as unobtrusively as Heinlein's waldoes.

The triffids are huge perambulating vegetables with poisonous flails who arrive on the scene just as everyone but the hero has been blinded by unusual meteors. Rarely has there been a less promising start to a story. Yet there is magic in *Day of the Triffids*, and in the excitement of the hero and his girl moving through a collapsing London. It may be reminiscent of Conan Doyle's *Poison Belt*, but here everything goes gleefully to pot with no possibility of a subsequent cleaning up. The map has been irrevocably changed.

It changed again in 1953, when the krakens succeeded the triffids. *The Kraken Wakes* (plonkingly called *Out of the Deeps* in the United States) has the world invaded by things which settle in the ocean and melt the icecaps to give themselves more *liebensraum*. Motorboats in Oxford Street. Like the earlier novel, *Kraken* was an immense success, and adapted for radio—although it never made a (disastrous) motion picture like *Triffids*. Both novels were totally devoid of ideas but read smoothly, and thus reached a maximum audience, who enjoyed cosy disasters. Either it was something to do with the collapse of the British Empire, or the back-to-nature movement, or a general feeling that industrialisation had gone too far, or all three.

Wyndham's popularity continued. Short stories poured out, all urbane and pleasing. More novels appeared, one of which, *The Midwich Cuckoos* (1957), was later made into a very effective movie, *The Village of the Damned*. His best novel is *The Chrysalids* (1955, retitled *Rebirth* in the United States). *The Chrysalids* is set in a New England environment after nuclear war, when the fathers of the community sternly wipe out any mutated children. Not an original theme, but the characters and settings are beautifully realised. Much less successful was *The Outward Urge*, by John Wyndham and Lucas Parkes—Lucas Parkes being more components of Wyndham's name. Wyndham died in 1969.

Many heroes besides Sherriff's decided to meet the crisis in the dining room, so to speak. The essence of cosy catastrophe is that the hero should have a pretty good time (a girl, free suites at the Savoy, automobiles for the taking) while everyone else is dying off. The best and most memorable example of this sub-genre is American: George Stewart's *Earth Abides*, but it was the British writers—less preoccupied with aliens than their American counterparts—who specialised in Wyndham-esque comeuppances.

Among the afflictions visited on Earth by British writers are snow (John Boland's *White August*); gales (J. G. Ballard's *The*

Wind from Nowhere); insanity (Dighton Morel's *Moonlight Red*); plague (John Blackburn's *The Scent of New-Mown Hay*); disappearing oceans (Charles Eric Maine's *The Tides Went Out*); and super-beasts (J. T. McIntosh's *The Fittest*).

Such novels are anxiety fantasies. They shade off towards the greater immediacy of World War III novels, a specialist branch of catastrophe more usually practised by American writers. Perhaps the extreme example here is Poul Anderson's *After Doomsday*, which opens with the Earth already destroyed.

Recent versions of the catastrophe, which eschew natural cataclysm and predict merely a deterioration of the present world situation, strike an immediately convincing note. Christopher Priest's *Fugue for a Darkening Island* (1972) shows England disrupted by civil war, following the incursion of millions of African refugees. It marks a development from Robert Bateman's *When the Whites Went* (1963), in which, as the title implies, the blacks take over.

Striking though such novels are—Priest is particularly effective in his use of a foiled sexuality to counterpoint the ravished body of England—they are understandably less strong meat than their American counterparts. For instance, Wilson Tucker's *The Year of the Quiet Sun* (1970), or a less miniaturist version of what might be the same colour wars as Tucker's, in Alan Seymour's *The Coming Self-Destruction of the USA* (1969). Here the British catastrophe theme coalesces with the American colour obsession. Cosiness has fled.

Master of the semi-cosy was John Christopher, whose name is often linked with Wyndham's.

With Christopher, the catastrophe loses its cosiness and takes on an edge of terror. Though the terror is slightly muted in his best novel, *Death of Grass* (1956), in which a mutated virus attacks all grains and grasses, there is sound writing strategy in the way that the central character, John, operates less than well in the crisis which overtakes the world, and falls under the shadow of his brother, David, while both become almost subsidiary to Pirrie, a memorably formidable character the brothers meet in a gunshop. The novel shows a remarkable grasp of political as well as psychological possibilities.

Christopher had already shown his mettle with a frolicsome intellectual novel, *The Year of the Comet* (1955). Under his own name, Sam Youd, and many pen names, he poured forth a stream of lucid and successful novels. After his great popular success, *Death of Grass*, his catastrophes grow increasingly dark and uncosy. Perhaps the best of these is *The World in Winter* (1962). *Pendulum* (1968), with the brutish young taking over, is merely painful. There is also the anti-cosy aliens-will-get-you shocker, *The Possessors* (1965), set in a decidedly chilly Switzerland.

Christopher is now making a new reputation with his children's books. An intelligent and witty man, marvellously equipped as a writer, John Christopher seemed poised at one time to become the country's leading sf writer. But the race is not always to the swift, etc., etc.

Perhaps time was running against Christopher and Wyndham; for the catastrophe novel presupposes that one starts from some kind of established order, and the feeling grew that even established orders were of the past.

Christopher and Wyndham made elegant appearances in E. J. "Ted" Carnell's magazines, *New Worlds* and *Science Fantasy*, which—with the love and dedication characterising sf buffs—had been founded by fans when nobody else wanted to know. The two magazines bumbled along on a minimum of talent and an occasional infusion of good red American blood, kept going mainly by the persistence of Carnell.‡

All British writers went through Ted Carnell's hands. Almost despite himself, he built a literary agency to look after their interests, and gradually established a pocket empire to which such outside authors as Harry Harrison and Frederik Pohl were attracted. Carnell was good for British sf, not least because he was utterly dogged, completely dependable, and entirely honest. He knew nothing about literature; but he did know what he liked.

The props of his magazines were such stalwarts as E. C. "Ted" Tubb, for many years the *doyen* of British sf, Kenneth Bulmer, John Rackham, John Brunner (who was selling sf to *Astounding* at the age of seventeen), and Michael Moorcock, whose talents for swirling fantasy began to crystallise round the enigmatic figure of Elric of Melniboné, the crimson-eyed albino, with his broadsword Stormbringer.

Carnell being Carnell, the magazines appeared with scrupulous

‡ Meanwhile, rival British magazines like *Nebula* and *Authentic* faded out in the fifties. The pioneering *Tales of Wonder* was killed by the paper shortage during World War II.

regularity until the last issue of his *New Worlds* in April 1964. The final words of his last editorial were, "Let us not look upon this as the end of the line, but merely as a natural stage of metamorphosis in the development of science fiction." Sage advice! He then went on to edit *New Writings in SF*, a successful series of paperbacks which he continued until his death in 1972, when Ken Bulmer became editor.

His magazines were taken over by new publishers. *Science Fantasy* was edited by Kyril Bonfiglioli, a Balliol man. *New Worlds* was edited by Michael Moorcock, who proceeded to take Carnell's words literally; metamorphosis was his thing. England was *swinging* by then, with Beatlemania gripping the country, hair growing, and mini-skirts flying. A new mood of hedonism was in the air. The British Empire had dissolved; the Romans were becoming Italians.

Moorcock's particular Stormbringer was J. G. Ballard, a young writer who had already shown his abilities as a surrealist in the Carnell days, with such stories as *Billenium,* one of the best over-population stories, and *The Terminal Beach,* which is essentially a Ballard story and hard to define in other terms. With great courage and foresight, Moorcock seized on this unsettling Ballardian quality and cried its virtues. The old gang was kicked out. A new gang entered.

The very first Moorcock *New Worlds,* in the summer of 1964, contained the beginning of a two-part Ballard serial and an article by Ballard on William Burroughs. "In *The Naked Lunch,* Burroughs compares organised society with that of its most extreme opposite, the invisible society of drug addicts. His implicit conclusion is that the two are not very different, certainly at the points where they make the closest contact—in prisons and psychiatric institutions . . ." It was to these extreme points that Ballard instinctively journeyed, the poles of mental inaccessibility, where normal and abnormal met on apotropaic neutral ground.

Moorcock's energy and Ballard's imagery attracted a new audience to science fiction. It was, in fact, an audience already around, grokking the more way-out strata of the life of their time, but not at all tuned to the old pulp idiom, of which the Carnell magazines were tired inheritors.

The new *New Worlds* seized on an essential truth: that the speculative body of work contained in the sf of the past had been directed towards just such a future as the mid-sixties: the Sunday colour mags, proliferating LP's, drugs, promiscuity, cheap jet flights, colour TV, pop music that suddenly spoke with a living mouth—and the constant threat that the Middle East or Vietnam or South Africa or Somewhere would suddenly blow up and end the whole fantastic charade forever and ever amen—this actually *was* the Brave New World, nor were we out of it!

Around *New Worlds* and the flamboyant figure of Moorcock gathered a staff who often doubled as writers, among them the redoubtable Charles Platt, Langdon Jones, Hilary Bailey, Mal Dean, M. John Harrison, Diane Lambert, and the anthologist Douglas Hill. The word got about, and soon young American writers began to arrive, many of them to settle in London. Of their number, the names of Thomas Disch, John Sladek, and Pamela Zoline must be mentioned, three writers full of talent and energy. Tom Disch's fine dark novel, *Camp Concentration*, was serialised in *New Worlds* in 1967.

By that time, matters were getting slightly out of hand. *New Worlds* had been in financial trouble again, but was baled out by a magnificent Arts Council Grant, an appeal for which had been supported by such worthy figures as Edmund Crispin, Anthony Burgess, Roy Fuller, Kenneth Allsop, Angus Wilson (for many years a staunch friend of science fiction), J. B. Priestley, and Marghanita Laski.[4]

Later Americans to arrive on the scene included James Sallis and Norman Spinrad, whose thumping novel about life in deep-freeze and the power of TV, *Bug Jack Barron*, was serialised throughout most of 1968. Its four-letter words (and perhaps its marked disrespect for politicians) led to Spinrad's being referred to as a "degenerate" in the House of Commons—a notable if not singular honour—and the magazine's being banned by W. H. Smith, the biggest retail outlet in Britain. More trouble. Paradoxically, at the same time the Arts Council Grant was extended for a further period.

Meanwhile, Ballard—perhaps made slightly frenzied by having been so firmly nailed to the masthead of Moorcock's pirate ship—rejected linear fiction and was writing "condensed novels," impacted visions of a timeless, dimensionless world, lacerated by anguish, desiccated by knowledge, and illustrative of William Burroughs' dictum, "A psychotic is a guy who's just discovered what's going on."

New Worlds had gone not only dirty but glossy. Art was represented by such respected names as Christopher Finch, Eduardo Paolozzi, M. C. Esher, Jim Cawthorne, Richard Hamilton, and, inevitably, Mervyn Peake, another Moorcockian obsession. Typical issues from those early glossies contain the names of Giles Gordon, C. C. Shackleton, John Brunner (with an extract from *Stand on Zanzibar*), Disch, Platt, Dr. Christopher Evans, Roger Zelazny, Gene Wolfe, James Sallis, Peter Tate, Michael Butterworth, Zoline, with her superlative *Heat Death of the Universe*,[5] David I. Masson, George MacBeth, Sladek, and Aldiss doing his Acid Head War series. And the great Ballard.

Pentax Zoom. In these equations, the gestures and postures of the young woman, Trabert explored the faulty dimensions of the space capsule, the lost geometry and volumetric time of the dead astronauts.

1) Lateral section through the left axillary fossa of Karen Novotny, the elbow raised in a gesture of pique: the transliterated pudenda of Ralph Nader.

2) A series of paintings of imaginary sexual organs. As he walked around the exhibition, conscious of Karen's hand gripping his wrist, Trabert searched for some valid point of junction. These obscene images, the headless creatures of a nightmare, grimaced at him like the exposed corpses in the Apollo capsule, the victims of a thousand autocrashes.

3) *The Stolen Mirror* (Max Ernst). In the eroded causeways and porous rocktowers of this spinal landscape Trabert saw the blistered epithelium of the astronauts, the time-invaded skin of Karen Novotny.

One "chapter" from *The Death Module,* powerfully conveying some of the dislocations and unexpressed connections of its time.

As a novelist, Ballard was less successful. *The Wind from Nowhere* has already been mentioned as a cosy catastrophe. The purest draught is contained in *The Drowned World* (1963), a picture of a landscape glowing in flood and heat, in which man is an amphibious thing beyond disaster but lured towards some ultimate and wished-for nemesis.

Drowned World sets the pattern for the other Ballard novels, all of which are novels of catastrophe, and in form—if form only—owe a good deal to John Wyndham; which may be why Ballard has had cutting things to say about Wyndham. *The Crystal World* (1966) shows Ballard's style glittering darkly and reduplicating itself like the jewels encasing his saturnine forests. But the central problem of writing a novel without having the characters pursue any purposeful course of action—even more acute in *The Drought* (1965) —is not resolved. Ballard has never resolved it.

His short stories are far more successful: they hinge upon in-action, their world is the world of loss and surrender, their drama the drama of a limbo beyond despair where action is irrelevant. The novels invent colourful doom-worlds; the best short stories stick to a region on the outskirts of London or Los Angeles only too horrifyingly familiar. Ballard's singular gift has been to give this landscape its voice.

Some of Ballard's condensed novels were published together as *The Atrocity Exhibition* in England in 1970. American publishers were more squeamish. Read together, the condensed novels become repetitive, and Ballard's habit of pushing jargon as others push dope is too apparent. Taken singly, they are more impressive; but it is perhaps the stories of Ballard's *Terminal Beach* period which will last the longest. His ferocious intelligence, his wit, his cantankerous-ness, and, in particular, his extraordinary rendering of the perverse pleasures of today's paranoia, make him one of the grand magicians of modern fiction. His is an uncertain spell, but it spreads—as Moor-cock was the first to perceive—far beyond the stockades of ordinary science fiction.

Here is a passage from *The Terminal Beach* which incorporates some of the symbols later to return in more compacted form to Ballard's fiction.

The Naval Party

When the search party came for him Traven hid in the only logical place. Fortunately the search was perfunctory, and was called off after a few hours. The sailors had brought a supply of beer with them and the search soon turned into a drunken ramble.

On the walls of the recording towers Traven later found balloons of obscene dialogue chalked into the mouths of the shadowy figures, giving their postures the priapic gaiety of the dancers in cave drawings.

The climax of the party was the ignition of a store of

gasoline in an underground tank near the air-strip. As he listened, first to the megaphones shouting his name, the echoes receding among the dunes like the forlorn calls of dying birds, then to the boom of the explosion and the laughter as the landing craft left, Traven felt a premonition that these were the last sounds he would hear.

He had hidden in one of the target basins, lying among the broken bodies of the plastic models. In the hot sunlight their deformed faces gaped at him sightlessly from the tangle of limbs, their blurred smiles like those of the soundlessly laughing dead.

Their faces filled his mind as he climbed over the bodies and returned to his bunker. As he walked towards the blocks he saw the figures of his wife and son standing in his path. They were less than ten yards from him, their white faces watching him with a look of almost overwhelming expectancy. Never had Traven seen them so close to the blocks. His wife's pale features seemed illuminated from within, her lips parted as if in greeting, one hand raised to take his own. His son's face, with its curiously fixed expression, regarded him with the same enigmatic smile of the child in the photograph.

"Judith! David!" Startled, Traven ran forwards to them. Then, in a sudden movement of light, their clothes turned into shrouds, and he saw the wounds that disfigured their necks and chests. Appalled, he cried out. As they vanished, he ran off into the safety of the blocks.

Moorcock's campaign converted a lot of fans. They began to grok. The pulp formula had withered in the wind. In *Science Fantasy*, too, new names came up, such as Keith Roberts, excellent illustrator as well as writer (his "Pavanne" series appeared here). There were also writers of promise such as Jael Cracken, John Runciman, Daphne Castell, and Chris Priest, as well as Johnny Byrne and Thom Keyes, who later materialised in the pop world (Byrne wrote *Groupie* and Keyes *All Night Stand*, both novels packed with zip and grot).

Strange people; but none so flamboyant as *Science Fantasy*'s editor, with his Rolls-Royces decaying before his twenty-seven-room house in North Oxford—which was once tenanted by a bishop, the bishop's brother, and a shared mistress, a North German princess. Oxford fantasy had struck again.

Eventually, Bonfiglioli bought for a peppercorn fee a Tintoretto valued at 40,000 pounds and handed over his magazine, now called variously *Impulse* and *Sf Impulse,* to Keith Roberts, then J. G. Ballard (for six days), then the amazing Harry Harrison, who happened to be on one of his periodical migrations through England at the time.

Another startling immigrant was Judith Merril, already well known as a writer and anthologist, producing a *Year's Best Sf,* which grew more autobiographical—and more confusing—as the years passed. Her madness and excitement, and her travels round England, drew other writers and poets into the movement; she was priestess to the prophet. Mainly through Judy's proselytising, the Moorcock-Ballard-*New Worlds* thing became known as "The New Wave."

The Wave spread to the United States. Any writer with a freaky style became an honourable member of New Wave. The mistake was in assuming that style was all and meaning nowhere. At the heart of *New Worlds* New Wave—never mind the froth at the edges—was a hard and unpalatable core of message, an attitude to life, a scepticism about the benefits of society or any future society.

Tired of the new hoo-ha (and it was pretty tiring unless you were young, high, and living in Ladbroke Grove), Isaac Asimov said, "I hope that when the New Wave has deposited its froth and receded, the vast and solid shore of *science fiction* will appear once more."

What the New Wave deposited was much needed alluvial soil on that overtilled strip of shore. For the New Wave is but one of many tides and comes much nearer to the source and impetus of creative writing than did the pulp formulae. Its heroes did not swagger around in magnetised boots. They were generally antiheroes, their destination more often bed than Mars.

To argue for either side in such a controversy is a mistake; phonies are thick on either hand, good writers few. The new movement certainly widened both the scope of sf and its audience. Moreover, as the whole course of this volume demonstrates, the new movement was only revolutionary in magazine sf terms. In the main, by rejecting genre pulps, it was more in the grand tradition than the magazines—which may, in course of time, be seen as no more than a vitalising tributary to the great stream of sf. One may, nevertheless, recall the point that George Melly made about the Beatles in *Revolt into Style*, that they "destroyed Pop with their intelligence." The New Wave did the same to sf; intelligence and irreverence did it. Ballard's is not the only view of the world, Moorcock's not the only approach.

By the time Judy Merril's great anthology appeared, horrendously entitled *England Swings SF*, published in New York in 1968, the swinging had swung, Miss Merril's giant enthusiasm had been diverted to other things, and it was left to others to sweep up after the party.

In the States, meanwhile, great young names such as Roger Zelazny, Samuel "Chip" Delany, and Harlan Ellison (destined to be called by the *New Yorker* "the chief prophet of the New Wave," to his endless embarrassment) were springing up. The itinerant Disch was making a solid reputation (though sometimes with such be-all and end-all titles as *White Fang Goes Dingo*), followed later by a renegade Robert Silverberg and writers as diverse as Harvey Jacobs, Barry Malzberg, and many others.

Several less iconoclastic writers were adding to their already considerable reputations in recent years and extending the margins of sixties' sf, even if not as showily as the demolition crew over at Moorcock's place.

Such names as Mack Reynolds, who brought passionate left-wing debate to *Analog;* and Phil José Farmer, whose *Strange Relations* (1960) was among his earlier explorations into unorthodox sexuality; Poul Anderson, prolific vacuum-buster with a large fan following; Robert Bloch, whose *Psycho* was turned into one of the hit movies of the sixties; Ben Bova, who took over *Analog* after Campbell's death; John Brunner, producing such novels as *Squares of the City* (1965) and *Quicksand* (1967); Terry Carr, writer and editor; Lin Carter, emerging as an editor of lost fantasy; D. G. Compton, dramatist with a considerable sf following; Edmund Cooper, urbane novelist and enthusiastic book reviewer; Lee Harding, one of the best known of the new Australian writers; Fred Hoyle, famous and controversial astronomer, now a knight, whose *Black Cloud* (1957) was only the first of several sf novels and TV serials; Damon Knight, branching out into one of the

unshakeable authorities of the field, and founding the SFWA
(Science Fiction Writers of America); Cyril Kornbluth, whose
posthumous reputation has been growing, not least because of the
dedication of Edmund Crispin, who brought together *The Best
Science Fiction Stories of C. M. Kornbluth* (1968) and saw that
The Syndic was published in a proper hard-cover edition; Keith
Laumer, one of the great new popular and prolific sf entertainers
to emerge in the sixties; Sam Lundwall, with novels to follow his
genial and perceptive survey of sf; Larry Niven, still cleaving the
paper light-years with mighty machines and alien races; Christopher Priest, with two elegant novels behind him; Bob Shaw,
whose short and lucid novels display quiet understanding of human
nature; Cordwainer Smith, surrealist, poet, man of amazing inventiveness, whose very titles, such as *Game of Rat and Dragon,
Think Blue, Count Two,* and *The Lady Who Sailed the Soul,* were
full of evocation; Theodore Sturgeon, returning in force to the field
in the late sixties; Van Vogt, back with such novels as *Rogue Ship*
(1968), in which one Lesbee utters a cry many sf writers must
have woken crying, "Hey, I've figured out the true nature of the
universe!"; Ted White, sparkily if unavailingly trying to edit *Amazing* into a force to be reckoned with.

And writers whose reputation is still newer, such as Mark
Adlard; T. J. Bass; Richard Cowper; G. C. Edmondson; David
Gerrold; Mark S. Geston; Jon Hartridge; Vincent King; R. A.
Lafferty; Bruce McAllister; Andrew Offut; Emil Petaja; Jannick
Storm; Leon Stover; James Tiptree; George Zebrowski, and many
other names, some of whom were given a chance to shine in
Harlan Ellison's mammoth anthology *Again, Dangerous Visions*
(1972), triumphal successor to his first mammoth, *Dangerous
Visions* (1967). There is now a new generation of sf writers in the
States—young and eager—the men of the eighties—who are more
concerned with life styles than technologies. For them, the New
Wave is as much an accepted part of the scene as Edgar Rice
Burroughs.

Some writers will feel slighted to appear in these lists; others,
not to appear. To be conscious of injustice is not the same as
remedying it. All the same, I am aware that the writings of such
men as "Chip" Delany and Roger Zelazny need more careful
examination than this chapter can afford them. Both have great
strengths—Zelazny's despite what seem perverse attempts to trans-

late whole mythologies into sf mythology, Delany's despite defiance of C. S. Lewis' dictum that to tell how odd things struck odd people is to have an oddity too much—which need the perspectives of time for full appreciation, so elaborate are the garments they weave. Both are true practitioners of Burke's sublime.

Nor have I mentioned the women writers of this period. Even a brief list must contain the names of Angela Carter (the prankish *Infernal Desire Machines of Doctor Hoffmann*); Jane Gaskell; Hilary Bailey; Sonya Dorman; Carol Emshwiller; Ursula le Guin; Anne McCaffrey; Naomi Mitchison; Kit Reed; Joanna Russ; Josephine Saxton; Kate Wilhelm; and Pamela Zoline. Of these ladies, Kit Reed and Kate Wilhelm have already built solid reputations as short-story tellers and novelists; and Ursula Le Guin is becoming one of the powerful novelists of the seventies.

She began well with *The Left Hand of Darkness* (1969), and has developed from there with such novels as *The Lathe of Heaven* (1971). A review appears in today's *Guardian* of her *The Tombs of Atuan* (1972), the successor to *A Wizard of Earthsea*. The review is by John Rowe Townsend; he begins by speaking of fantasy in general and mentioning Tolkien, after which he adds that he is not sure whether it is a compliment to compare Miss Le Guin with Tolkien. Of the new book and its Earthsea predecessor, he says, they "seem to me to be as good as anything that's been done in this field."

One must add that Le Guin is a rarity in that she writes beautifully. Not prettily. Beautifully. Her prose is a pleasure to read.

Estraven did not answer for a while. He sat gazing at the fire, whose flames winked, reflected, from his tankard and from the broad bright silver chain of office over his shoulders. The old house was silent around us. There had been a servant to attend our meal, but Karhiders, having no institutions of slavery or personal bondage, hire services not people, and the servants had all gone off to their own homes by now. Such a man as Estraven must have guards about him somewhere, for assassination is a lively institution in Karhide, but I had seen no guard, heard none. We were alone.

I was alone, with a stranger, inside the walls of a dark

palace, in a strange snow-changed city, in the heart of the Ice Age of an alien world.

Everything I had said, tonight and ever since I came to Winter, suddenly appeared to me as both stupid and incredible. How could I expect this man or any other to believe my tales about other worlds, other races, a vague benevolent government somewhere off in outer space? It was all nonsense. I had appeared in Karhide in a queer kind of ship, and I differed physically from Gethenians in some respects; that wanted explaining. But my own explanations were preposterous. I did not, in that moment, believe them myself.

"I believe you," said the stranger, the alien alone with me, and so strong had my access of self-alienation been that I looked up at him bewildered. "I'm afraid that Argaven also believes you. But he does not trust you. In part because he no longer trusts me."

This is from the first chapter of *The Left Hand of Darkness*. The setting is another planet, and a magnificently visualised planet it is; but the writer's attention never wavers from the strange interplay of character between human and alien.

I concur with Harlan Ellison; much of the best writing in science fiction today is being done by women (and he didn't even mention Christine Brooke-Rose, author of *Such*, 1966, and a fine modern novelist).

What has made the difference is the disappearance of the Philistine-male-chauvinist-pig attitude, pretty well dissipated by the revolutions of the mid-sixties; and the slow fade of the Gernsbackian notion that sf is all hardware. Science fiction, in other words, has come back to a much more central position in the world of art. The all-male escapist power fantasy had at one time devoured all but what we have called the Huxleyan branch, those writings which occurred only irregularly as specific social criticism. Science fiction has returned from the Ghetto of Retarded Boyhood; and, truth to tell, it seems not to have suffered from its imprisonment.

Various segregated areas are still around. Indeed, there is probably more power fantasy than ever before; but this now mainly concentrates itself in the Sword-and-Sorcery end of the market. I believe that the chief diet of sf is much more reality-oriented than before. And I believe this has certain artistic advantages. It means more careful writing (reader more alert, less drugged), better characterisation (characters less subordinated to exigencies of certain-victory plot), and greater diversity of subject matter (stars aren't the only destination).

To say this is to generalise to an appalling degree. And it is, as ever, a mistake to speak of science fiction per se. Science fiction per se does not exist. There is only the will—or the lack of will—of individual writers.

Certainly there are more writers writing some form of speculative fiction than ever before. There is also more reprinting than ever before. If the gap between the sf novel and the traditional one is narrowing, so is the gap between looking forward and nostalgia. The new frontiers are in the mind; and yesterday's novels may hold as much strange territory as tomorrow's.

The conformist society, of which we heard so much in the fifties, did not materialise. Instead, society diversified; even in suburbia, there are more people "doing their own thing" than ever before. Sf has diversified in the same way. Diversification is one of the individual's instinctive defences against the machine principle which—in the present day at least—imposes an artificial uniformity of societal goals.

For the sake of brevity, I have abridged the diversity of today's sf; for instance, I have not mentioned the great European writers of the period. Vercors, one of the heroes of the French resistance in World War II, wrote one of the seminal books towards a definition of man in *Borderline*, also translated as *Ye Shall Know Them* and, I'm sorry to say, *The Murder of the Missing Link*. From Czechoslovakia we have had the marvellous stories of Josef Nesvadba. From Poland, the ingenious fantasies of Slavomir Mrozek, author of *The Ugupu Bird*, as well as that weighty and wise novel of Stanislav Lem's *Solaris*—now filmed—which contains an ocean with as much spiritual substance as the one in *Perelandra*, and shares *Perelandra*'s sub-theme of demonic possession. From the Soviet Union, Yefremov's *Andromeda* and many other stories. From India, Lee Tung's extraordinary surrealist fantasia on overpopulation, *The Wind Obeys Lama Toru*. From Norway, Axel Jensen's touching *Epp*, a study of the old and failed. From Sweden, Harry Martinson's dramatic poem *Aniara*, made into a fantastic opera. And so on, from the tremendous activity in Japan to the unknown goings-on in China.

Nearer home, the last few years have witnessed a phenomenon which is even more pleasing than the rise of new young authors: an accession of new powers in older and more established authors.

Moorcock, for example, has been so far from exhausted by his labours on *New Worlds* that he has poured forth a stream of novels. Some of the fantasies have gone to subsidise the magazine, and are potboilers. Yet there has also been the creation of Jerry Cornelius, whose adventures have featured in such novels as *The Final Programme, A Cure for Cancer* and *The English Assassin.*[6] In Cornelius, the worlds of Ronald Firbank and Ian Fleming meet; Cornelius embodies many aspects of the present day projected into an art deco international future, with Ladbroke Grove as important a destination as ever Alpha Centaurus was. Moorcock's *Behold the Man* is in more serious vein, with time-travel back to the life of Christ.

Harrison has produced a string of entertainments, among them most notably *Bill the Galactic Hero*, which, in its lighthearted way, has more than a lick of New Tide in it, good-naturedly parodying as it does the worlds of Heinlein's Starship Troopers and Asimov's Trantor. *The Technicolor Time Machine* followed on the good work, to be capped by *A Transatlantic Tunnel, Hurrah!* (retitled *Tunnel Through the Deeps* in the United States), a parallel world novel in which the United States never broke away from Britain. These three novels almost constitute a category of their own, buoyed as they are by Harrison's individual grasp of life. (Harrison is, incidentally, one of the rare writers, like Mack Reynolds, who has travelled extensively on the globe he writes about.)

Many of his lesser novels appear hastily written. Hardly surprisingly, for he is also one of the field's major editors, most notable among his productions being a *Year's Best SF* (edited with the aid of a junior assistant).

His novel *Make Room, Make Room*—one of the definitive overpopulation novels—has already been mentioned.

While they are popular, Harrison's Stainless Steel Rat books, featuring the exploits of one Slippery Jim DiGriz, hardly add to his reputation. All the same, they burst out now and again with peculiarly Harrisonian virtues—for instance his love of horrible

Paleo-Industrial artifacts. Here is the scene where DiGriz (incognito) is in the smoke-filled castle of Count Rdenrundt on some remote and ill-visaged planet.

Something came in through the door and I recoiled, thinking the war was on. It was only a robot, but it made such a hideous amount of hissing and clanking that I wondered what was wrong with it. The Count ordered the ghastly thing to wheel over the bar; as it turned away I saw what could only have been a *chimney* projecting behind one shoulder. There was the distinct odor of coal smoke in the air.

"Does that robot burn *coal*–?" I gurgled.

"It does," the Count said, pouring us out a pair of drinks. "It is a perfect example of what is wrong with the Freiburian economy under the gracious rule of Villelm the Incompetent. You don't see any robots like this in the capital!"

"I should hope not," I gasped, staring bug-eyed at the trickle of steam escaping from the thing, and the stains of rust and coal dust on its plates. "Of course I've been away a long time . . . things change. . . ."

"They don't change fast enough! And don't get galactic-wise with me, Diebstall. I've been to Misteldross and seen how the rubes live. You have no robots at all—much less a contraption like this." He kicked at the thing in sullen anger and it staggered back a bit, valves clicking open as steam pumped into the leg pistons to straighten it up. "Two hundred years come next Grundlovsday we will have been in the League, milked dry and pacified by them—and for what? To provide luxuries for the King in Freiburbad. While out here we get a miserable consignment of a few robot brains and some control circuitry. We have to build the rest of the inefficient monsters ourselves."

He drained his glass and I made no attempt to explain to him the economics of galactic commerce, planetary prestige, or the multifold levels of intercommunication. He was still glaring at the robot when he leaned forward and suddenly tapped a dial on the thing's side.

"Look at that!" he shouted. "Down to eighty pounds pressure! Next thing you know the thing will be falling on its face and burning the place down. Stoke, you idiot—*stoke!*"

A couple of relays closed inside the contraption and the robot clanked and put the tray of glasses down. I took a very long drag on my drink and enjoyed the scene. Trundling over to the fireplace—at a slower pace now I'll admit—it opened a door in its stomach and flame belched out. Using the coal scoop in the pail it shovelled in a good portion of anthracite and banged the firedoor shut again. Rich black smoke boiled from its chimney. At least it was housebroken and didn't shale out its grate here.

"Outside, dammit, outside!" the Count shouted, coughing at the same time. The smoke was a little thick. I poured another drink and decided right then that I was going to like Rdenrundt. (*The Stainless Steel Rat*, Chapter 16)

The humour and imagination are characteristically Harrison.

James Blish's latest work demonstrates new powers. In particular, the twin novels *Black Easter* and *The Day After Judgement* carry sf into another dimension. The fantastic latter novel, set on an Earth where God is dead and the infernal city of Dis rises red-hot in Death Valley, is *sui generis*. Although it belongs somewhere in the eschatological school where lives the spirit of C. S. Lewis, its peculiar wit in mingling the idioms of technological overkill with ecclesiastical parlance removes it to a niche of its own. While its remorseless argument makes it one of science fiction's most powerful intellectual novels.

Philip K. Dick is another intellectual, although of a different school—the school of Pirandello. In his novels, things are never what they seem. Between life and death lie the many shadow lands of Dick, places of hallucination, illusion, artificial reality, dim half life, paranoid states. All his novels are one novel, elegant, surprising—like Blish's world, like Ballard's world, witty—full of disconcerting artifacts, scarecrow people, exiles, robots with ill consciences. It is invidious to pick out titles, in a way, except that some of the novels are hastily written (an inept start to *Ubik* all but ruins an excellent novel); but *Martian Time-Slip, The Penultimate Truth, The Three Stigmata of Palmer Eldrich,* and the unforgettable *Man in the High Castle,* all continue the Dickian meditation on a high level.

Because he is so much an anti-materialist, because he so mistrusts appearances, Dick's name is less widely known than that of more accessible writers such as Heinlein or Vonnegut. Yet Dick in the United States, like Ballard in England, has created a live and original body of work that challenges close attention.

The Man in the High Castle (1962) represents his talents best. It depicts a future world in which World War II was won by the Axis Powers. North America has been divided into three north-south strips. The large Eastern strip is occupied by the Nazis; the narrow Western seaboard is occupied by the Japanese. There is a middle section, the Rocky Mountain States, a neutral and powerless buffer state. Dick populates this world with a number and variety of characters, some of whom can act with more effect than others, but all of whom are subservient to the currents of history.

In the Rocky Mountain States, however, lives a man whose vision runs counter to history. He is a novelist (rather a Heinlein figure in some ways) who has written a novel called *The Grasshopper Lies Heavy*. *The Grasshopper Lies Heavy* postulates a world in which both Germany and Japan were defeated in the war; it is therefore subversive, and suppressed; but its message begins to revitalise a few defeated Americans.

One of many attractive features about the novel is the way in which conqueror and conquered alike gain our sympathy. A central character is Mr. Takomi of the Japanese Trade Mission, a good man who consults his I Ching at every turn. Like many good Dick characters, he is vouchsafed an actual glimpse of evil, which materialises like God in Amis' novel *The Green Man*.

Evil manifests itself to Takomi when he is listening to a debate on who will become German Führer following the death of Martin Bormann. Dick expresses the terrible dislocations that follow in a telling dislocated prose:

> The Foreign Office spokesman ceased his dry, slow recitation.
>
> Mr. Takomi thought, I think I am going mad.
>
> I have to get out of here; I am having an attack. My body is throwing up things or spurting them out—I am dying. He scrambled to his feet, pushed down the aisle past other chairs and people. He could hardly see. Get to lavatory. He ran up the aisle.

Several heads turned. Saw him. Humiliation. Sick at important meeting. Lost place. He ran on, through the open door held by embassy employee.

At once the panic ceased. His gaze ceased to swim; he saw objects once more. Stable floor, walls.

Attack of vertigo. Middle-ear malfunction, no doubt.

He thought, Diencephalon, ancient brainstem, acting up.

Some organic momentary breakdown.

Think along reassuring lines. Recall order of world. What to draw on? Religion? He thought, *Now a gavotte perform sedately. Capital both, capital both, you've caught it nicely. This is the style of thing precisely.* Small form of recognizable world, *Gondoliers.* G. & S. He shut his eyes, imagined the D'Oyly Carte Company as he had seen them on their tour after the war. The finite, finite world . . .

An embassy employee, at his elbow, saying, "Sir, can I give you assistance?"

Mr. Takomi bowed. "I am recovered."

The other's face, calm, considerate. No derision. They are all laughing at me, possibly? Mr. Takomi thought. Down underneath?

There is evil! It's actual, like cement.

I can't believe it. I can't stand it. Evil is not a view. He wandered about the lobby, hearing the traffic on Sutter Street, the Foreign Office spokesman addressing the meeting. All our religion is wrong. What'll I do? he asked himself.

Despite a high production rate, Dick's novels are enviably capable even when not more than that. True, there is much that is shoddy in them—his writing is maddeningly inconsistent—but his world *is* shoddy, in both appearance and speech, for it is but an outcrop of a universe in which good and evil battle, with evil always about to win. It may be that Dick will emerge as one of the significant writers of our day, more inventive than C. S. Lewis (who depicts another area of the same cosmic battle), and as fundamental as Mary Shelley.

It can be observed, too, that throughout Dick's books and titles blows the horn of freedom. We catch its note in *The Crack in Space, Galactic Pot-Healer,* and the novels already mentioned. Most Dickian protagonists are captives, oppressed rather than oppressors, victims of a society too large and complex for them. His elaborate plots, deriving from Van Vogt, are necessary to depict that engulfing size and complexity. This is Dick's way of defining the bars and spaces beyond. Even to be prisoner of an illusion is to possess that illusion. Even death leads to another form of existence, as in *Counter-Clock World* and *Ubik.*

That tallyho for freedom—for solitude or for rebellion or for a change in the restrictions of society—blows steadily through sf, however dark its forests, from Mary Shelley, Verne, Wells, London, Stapledon, Orwell, to the present day. In Dick it sounds faint and ghostly, as befits our darker world picture; but its note is thrillingly distinct. It goes deeper than a gesture; it is a habit of mind.

One catches the sound also in Vonnegut's work, although there it becomes mannerist.

He is one of the masters of present-day discontents, in the grand tradition of despairers which runs through Swift and Huxley. No simple solutions for Dick, no easy identifications with all-powerful heroes. His figures stand knee-deep in technological kipple, gazing at visions beyond their comprehension. The mood is often one of grey metaphysical comedy—Rick Decard, for instance, in *Do Androids Dream of Electric Sheep?* (1968), is brought to final disillusion by discovering that a toad he picked up in the desert is just another artifact, with a control panel set in its belly. The toad brings us as much disgust and laughter as Harrison's coal-driven robot; perhaps we unconsciously set a toad and robot against a vision of Man, Son of God, seeing them as symbols at once of our achievement and failure.

Here is one paragraph from *Do Androids Dream.* Technological man—represented by Rick Decard—stands in an empty San Francisco apartment building.

Silence. It flashed from the woodwork and the walls; it smote him with an awful, total power, as if generated by a vast mill. It rose from the floor, up out of the tattered gray wall-to-wall carpeting. It unleashed itself from the broken and semi-broken appliances in the kitchen, the dead machines which hadn't worked in all the time Isidore had lived here. From the useless pole lamp in the living room it oozed out, meshing with the empty and wordless descent of itself from the fly-specked ceiling. It managed in fact to emerge from every object within his range of vision, as if it—the silence—meant to supplant all things tangible. Hence it assailed not only his ears but his eyes; as he stood by the inert TV set he experienced the silence as visible and, in its own way, alive. Alive! He had often felt its austere approach before; when it came it burst in without subtlety, evidently unable to wait. The silence of the world could not rein back its greed. Not any longer. Not when it had virtually won.

Dick never faileth. But Kurt Vonnegut has not improved since he has been voted one of America's heap big gurus.

The purest Vonnegutian delights are to be found in his early novels, *Sirens of Titan* (1959) and *Cat's Cradle* (1963), with its elegant new religion, Bokononism. *Sirens of Titan,* in particular, is a cascade of absurd invention, its hither-thither technique a sophisticated pinch from the Wide Screen Baroque school. The elaborations of plot make it read like an exceptionally sunny Dick novel (which is to acknowledge, too, Dick's father-figure, Van Vogt); the spoof "explanations" of the origins of Stonehenge and the Great Wall of China are in that tradition. But the narrative is extremely well integrated—a perfect little cartwheel of a performance.

The same complex plotting and infolding of event went into what is Vonnegut's best novel, the remarkable *Mother Night* (1961). It represents a triumph of ambiguity which even Dick has never excelled. Is the central character a traitor or one of his country's great heroes? Even *he* does not know. Although this novel is not science fiction, its central character is called Howard W. Campbell, Jr. Whether by this Vonnegut intended merely a jest at John W. Campbell, Jr.'s expense, or whether he implied a profound commentary on Campbell as the greatest purveyor of pulp power fantasy, I must leave wiser critics to decide. It is a fact that

Vonnegut harps on sf, its themes and characters, while denying that he writes anything of the kind.

An instance of this occurs in *God Bless You, Mr. Rosewater* (1965). By now messages are replacing ambiguities. The message of *Mr. Rosewater* is that non-conformists are more fun than conformists—hardly galvanising news! Here the obsession with science fiction is embodied in the figure of Kilgore Trout, writer of interplanetary romances, author of eighty-seven paperbacks, unknown outside the science fiction field.

Eliot Rosewater, the central character, visits the Milford Conference, an actual science fiction event organised by Damon Knight. Rosewater tells them

> "I love you sons of bitches. You're all I read any more. You're the only ones who'll talk about the really *terrific* changes going on, the only ones crazy enough to know that life is a space voyage, and not a short one, either, but one that'll last for billions of years. You're the only ones with guts enough to *really* care about the future, who *really* notice what machines do to us, what wars do to us, what cities do to us . . . You're the only ones zany enough to agonize over time and distances without limit, over mysteries that will never die, over the fact that we are right now determining whether the space voyage for the next billion years or so is going to be Heaven or Hell."

Vonnegut's tribute to the billion year spree—too long and lingering to be wholly satire.

Slaughterhouse Five (1969, since filmed) is a restless book; whether its hither-thither methods sufficiently emphasise the horrors of the bombing of Dresden, whether social conscience is not paraded a little too conspicuously, is a moot point. The time-travel and other sf apparatus seem intrusive, fascinating though they are. Vonnegut's hither-thither technique worked much better on the more frivolous subject matter of *Sirens of Titan*, where tremendous enterprises (such as a message brought right across the galaxy just saying "Greetings!") are only pseudo-tremendous and carry none of the Death of Dresden with them.

The spiritual desiccations of Dresden were apparent before Vonnegut wrote. But Dick, I believe, give us new insight into the desiccations of everyday. Despite these reservations, there is much

in Vonnegut to admire—not least an exuberance of invention
which he shares with most of the better sf writers.

Vonnegut sped right out of the sf field as soon as he had cash
for the gasoline. For that he should not be blamed, though he
cannot have failed to notice that he still writes sf. The traffic is
not one way. Other writers from other disciplines come in and
make their contribution. To think of sf as some sort of closed shop
is ridiculous, and the quickest way of getting the shop closed for
good.

We end as we began, with a woman. This one, like Mary Shelley,
wrote science fiction without knowing it. In so doing, she created
one of the great science fiction novels.

I should have to start searching for her all over again.
The repetition was like a curse. I thought of placid blue seas,
tranquil islands, far away from war. I thought of the Indris,
those happy creatures, symbols of life in peace, on a higher
plane. I should clear out, go to them. No, that was impossible.
I was tied to her. I thought of the ice moving across the world,
casting its shadow of creeping death. Ice cliffs boomed in my
dreams, indescribable explosions thundered and boomed, icebergs crashed, hurled huge boulders into the sky like rockets.
Dazzling ice stars bombarded the world with rays, which
splintered and penetrated the earth, filling earth's core with
their deadly coldness, reinforcing the cold of the advancing
ice. And always, on the surface, the indestructible ice-mass
was moving forward, implacably destroying all life. I felt a
fearful sense of pressure and urgency, there was no time to
lose, I was wasting time; it was a race between me and the
ice. Her albino hair illuminated my dreams, shining brighter
than moonlight. I saw the dead moon dance over the icebergs, as it would at the end of our world, while she watched
from the tent of her glittering hair.

I dreamed of her whether I was asleep or awake. I
heard her cry: "One day I'll go . . . you won't see me again
. . ." She had gone from me already. She had escaped. She
hurried along a street in an unknown town. She looked
different, less anxious, more confident. She knew exactly
where she was going, she did not hesitate once. In a huge

official building she made straight for a room so crowded she could hardly open the door. Only her extreme slimness enabled her to slip between the many tall silent figures, unnaturally silent, fantastically tall, whose faces were all averted from her.

In its terror and beauty, its mercurial shifts of mood, its cunning sliding panels which bring us abruptly from one level of reality to another, this is unmistakeably a passage from Anna Kavan's *Ice* (1967).

I have told Anna's story already[7]—how she had the heroin habit for several decades and came to terms with it, how she travelled from country to country, and how she committed suicide one week before the news arrived of *Ice*'s acceptance by Doubleday. The story of *Ice* in many respects bodies forth her inner life. It is the ultimate in catastrophe—the advance of the ice is real enough, but also always the ice of the soul, the heroin encroaching, the habit of death you can't kick. For me, it embodies one of the high points of science fiction, and so becomes unclassifiable.

> And through the drifts the snowy clifts
> Did send a dismal sheen:
> Nor shapes of men nor beasts we ken—
> The ice was all between. . . .

Some of *Ice*'s illustrious relations are clear. Kafka for a start. Anna Kavan's assumed name began with a K in his honour. There is also the surrealist vein, as exhibited in some of Cocteau's work and in the painter De Chirico's only novel, *Hebdomeros*. Again, this is a catastrophe novel that goes far beyond Ballard as Ballard is beyond Wyndham, sailing into the chilly air of metaphysics. It looks sideways at its great contemporary among pornographic novels, Pauline Réage's *Story of O*. Even more, it is its own self, mysterious, in some ways unsatisfactory, an enigma—like all the greatest science fiction, approaching despair; but, in its acceptance of the insoluble, also full of a blind force much like hope.

As in our inner beings, there are only three persons in *Ice*. The pursued and the pursuer often change roles, become indistinguishable. In that respect, they remind us of Frankenstein and his monster, and remind us how Frankenstein and monster, and their many later progeny, come to us from the inner being, where life, art, and science all begin.

ENVOI

In the best traditions of the genre, I shall predict.

The last few years bear testimony to the enormous diversity of science fiction—so great that one wing does not recognise the other as the same creature.

My belief is that this diversification will increase, thus merging on the one side with comic books, the flickerings of television, and Dayglo Middle Earth posters; and on the other side with the sort of literature-of-extremity practised by such very individual men as Samuel Beckett, William Burroughs, Lawrence Durrell, Anthony Burgess, et al. There will be plenty of middle ground; some areas will be commercially viable, some creatively viable.

From this, one can postulate that the sf field will undergo—is already undergoing—the same stratification already undergone in the general category, with high-brow novels and low-brow novels and several brows in between. And, as ever, whatever is genuinely new will be suspect until it has won its way. The intensification of sf-as-study-course will increase this tendency towards stratification. (University courses in sf, originated by Mark Hillegas and Leon Stover in the States and Philip Strick and Peter Nicholls in the United Kingdom are now a commonplace.)

The days when one person desired to—or could—read all that was published have probably vanished already. In the reading field, more than enough is better than less than enough. There are advantages as well as disadvantages in increasing stratification.

At present, the major awards in the field, such as the Hugo and the Nebula (awarded by the SFWA) and the newly instigated Europa, are awards for popularity or repetitive novelties. Sooner or later, the Prix Goncourts of the field will arrive, to be bestowed for works of genuine creation. We hope that the new John W. Campbell Memorial Award will be a step towards this end. Academia and the middle class are moving in on sf[8] and will create order out of chaos.

Although helping to create that order is one of the objectives of this book, its author bows with deepest affection towards the chaos of the past.

NOTES

1. Three slightly later British versions may be noted, Brian Aldiss' *Outside,* 1955, which appears to be an examination, rather than a variant; Eric Frank Russell's *Three to Conquer,* 1955, and Kingsley Amis' *Something Strange,* 1960.

2. More accurately, a theme will not die while there is a socio-economic reason for its survival. The British theme of "submerged nations"—derived from Disraeli's two nations—finally petered out at the end of World War II, interred between Party and prole in *1984,* when there was no longer justification for it in reality. From which we may deduce that aliens-among-us will continue for some while to be a feature of American sf.

3. Personal footnote. I bought this remarkable novel in Barnstaple market place for one shilling, in the early months of war, 1940. Although I had read much sf before, it had been in magazines. This was the first time I discovered that it existed in novel form; and the formal beauty of its writing overwhelmed me. It still embodies some of the most compelling elements of storytelling: vivid characters, the elements active, a sense of terror, strong pictorial sense, striking situations, and destinies as remote and illuminating as the Moon!

4. This list gives some idea of the way in which popular science fiction always had good intellectual and cultural support in Britain, possibly because the pulps were not a native phenomenon. In the States, support in the main came from scientists rather than literary people —from John R. Pierce rather than J. B. Priestley. America's answer to C. S. Lewis and Marghanita Laski was Clifton Fadiman and Spring Byington. When popular science fiction began to be published in hardcover during the early fifties, critics such as Amis and Conquest and Philip Toynbee did a great deal to see that it received a favourable reception. Edmund Crispin's *Best Sf* anthologies from Faber & Faber, starting publication in 1955, were crucial in establishing valid critical standards.

5. My critical essay on Pamela Zoline's story "The Heat Death of the Universe," appears in *The Mirror of Infinity: A Critic's Anthology of Science Fiction*, edited by Robert Silverberg, New York, 1970. Also included are useful essays by Amis, Conquest, Knight, Blish, Willis McNelly, Harrison, and others, on a number of authors, including Asimov, Ballard, Clarke, Campbell, and Heinlein.

6. Jerry and his friend, Miss Brunner, became Underground favourites when Mal Dean's Cornelius strip appeared in *International Times*. His adventures were chronicled by several other writers, among them Langdon Jones, James Sallis, Maxim Jakubowski, Norman Spinrad, and Brian Aldiss. These adventures were collected in *The Nature of the Catastrophe*, edited by Michael Moorcock and Langdon Jones, 1971.

7. In my Introduction to the American edition and British paperback edition of *Ice*. "Her catastrophe victims do not leap up and embrace their catastrophe; nor do they flee from it; they accept it as part of life."

8. See, for a recent instance, *Above the Human Landscape: A Social Science Fiction Anthology*, edited by Willis E. McNelly and Leon E. Stover, Pacific Palisades, California, 1972. An excellent anthology, full of famous names, illustrated, and with appendices by the two learned professors: "Apeman, Superman—or, *2001*'s Answer to the World Riddle," by Leon E. Stover, and "Vonnegut's *Slaughterhouse Five*: Science Fiction as Objective Correlative," by Willis E. McNelly. For all its fun, sf has long been a cerebral field, and rewards such analysis.

CRITICAL BIBLIOGRAPHY

The following books and monographs have
been most frequently consulted. The list includes only writings which refer to authors
within the sf field; for further items, see
chapter notes.

Allen, Dick (Editor). *Science Fiction: The Future*, New York, 1971.
Amis, Kingsley. *New Maps of Hell*, 1961.
Armytage, W. H. G. *Yesterday's Tomorrows: A Historical Survey of
Future Societies*, 1968.
Atheling, William, Jr. *The Issue at Hand: Studies in Contemporary
Magazine Science Fiction*, Chicago, 1964.
———. *More Issues at Hand: Critical Studies in Contemporary Science
Fiction*, Chicago, 1970.
Atkins, John. *Tomorrow Revealed*, 1955.
Bailey, J. O. *Pilgrims Through Space and Time: Trends and Patterns
in Scientific and Utopian Fiction*, New York, 1947.
Bergonzi, Bernard. *The Early H. G. Wells: A Study of the Scientific
Romances*, Manchester, 1961.
Bloch, Robert. *The Eighth Stage of Fandom: Selections from 25 Years
of Fan Writing*, Chicago, 1962.
Bretnor, Reginald (Editor). *Modern Science Fiction: Its Meaning and
Its Future*, New York, 1953.
Chesneaux, Jean. *The Political and Social Ideas of Jules Verne*, 1972.
Churchill, R. C. *A Short History of the Future*, 1955.
Clareson, Thomas D. (Editor), *SF: The Other Side of Realism:
Essays on Modern Fantasy and Science Fiction*, Ohio, 1971.
Clarke, I. F. (Collected and compiled by). *The Tale of the Future:
From the Beginning to the Present Day: A Check-list*, 1961.
———. *Voices Prophesying War, 1763–1984*, 1966.
Cohen, John. *Human Robots in Myth and Science*, 1966.

Davenport, Basil; Heinlein, Robert A; Kornbluth, C. M.; Bester, Alfred; Bloch, Robert. *The Science Fiction Novel: Imagination and Social Criticism*, Chicago, 1964.

Derleth, August. *Thirty Years of Arkham House 1939–1969: A History and Bibliography*, Sauk City, Wisconsin, 1970.

Ellik, Ron, and Evans, Bill. *The Universes of E. E. Smith*, Chicago, 1966.

Eshback, Lloyd Arthur (Editor). *Of Worlds Beyond: The Science of Science Fiction Writing*, 1965.

Evans, I. O. *Jules Verne: Master of Science Fiction*, 1956.

Franklin, H. Bruce. *Future Perfect: American Science Fiction of the Nineteenth Century*, New York, 1966.

Green, Roger Lancelyn. *Into Other Worlds: Space-Flight in Fiction, from Lucian to Lewis*, 1957.

Harbottle, Philip (Compiler). *The Multi-Man: A Biographic and Bibliographic Study of John Russell Fearn*. Privately printed, 1968.

Harrison, Harry (Editor). *The Light Fantastic: Science Fiction Classics from the Mainstream*, New York, 1971.

Hillegas, Mark R. *The Future as Nightmare: H. G. Wells and the Anti-utopians*, New York, 1967.

Knight, Damon. *In Search of Wonder: Essays on Modern Science Fiction*, Chicago, 1956. Revised edition, 1967.

Leighton, Peter. *Moon Travellers: A Dream That Is Becoming a Reality*, 1960.

Lewinsohn, Richard. *Prophets and Predictions: The History of Prophecy from Babylon to Wall Street*, 1961.

Lewis, C. S. *Of Other Worlds: Essays and Stories*, 1966.

Lundwall, Sam J. *Science Fiction: What It's All About*, New York, 1971.

Lupoff, Richard A. *Edgar Rice Burroughs: Master of Adventure*, New York, 1965.

Meadows, A. J. *The High Firmament: A Survey of Astronomy in English Literature*, Leicester, 1969.

Moore, Patrick. *Science and Fiction*, 1957.

Moskowitz, Sam. *Explorers of the Infinite: Shapers of Science Fiction*, Cleveland and New York, N.D.

——. *Seekers of Tomorrow: Masters of Modern Science Fiction*, New York, 1967.

——. (Editor). *Under the Moons of Mars: A History and Anthology of "The Scientific Romance" in the Munsey Magazines, 1912–1920*, New York, 1970.

Nicolson, Marjorie Hope. *Voyages to the Moon*, New York, 1949. Paper, 1960.

Panshin, Alexei. *Heinlein in Dimension: A Critical Analysis*, Chicago, 1968.

Philmus, Robert M. *Into the Unknown: The Evolution of Science Fiction from Francis Godwin to H. G. Wells,* Berkeley and Los Angeles, 1970.

Praz, Mario. *The Romantic Agony,* Second Edition, 1970.

Rogers, Alva. *A Requiem for Astounding,* Chicago, 1964.

Rose, Lois and Stephen. *The Shattered Ring: Science Fiction and the Quest for Meaning,* 1970.

Silverberg, Robert (Editor). *The Mirror of Infinity: A Critic's Anthology of Science Fiction,* New York, 1970.

Stella Nova, The Contemporary Science Fiction Authors, Los Angeles, Limited Edition, 1970.

Summers, Montague. *The Gothic Quest: A History of the Gothic Novel,* 1968.

Trout, Kilgore (Compiler). *SF-1: A Selective Bibliography,* New York, 1971.

Walsh, Chad. *From Utopia to Nightmare,* 1962.

Wollheim, Donald A. *The Universe Makers: Science Fiction Today,* 1972.

The invaluable indexes:

Index to the Science-Fiction Magazines, 1926–1950, compiled and arranged by Donald B. Day, Portland, Oregon, 1952.

Index to the S-F Magazines, 1951–1965, compiled by Erwin S. Strauss, MIT Science Fiction Society, Cambridge, Massachusetts, 1966.

Index to the Science-Fiction Magazines, 1966–1970, New England Science Fiction Association, West Hanover, Massachusetts, 1971.

The Complete Checklist of Science-Fiction Magazines, edited by Bradford M. Day, New York, 1961.

And the equally invaluable amateur magazines, or fanzines. In particular, I have relied on long runs of:

Extrapolation, edited by Thomas Clareson.
Riverside Quarterly, edited by Leland Sapiro.
SF Commentary, edited by Bruce Gillespie.
Speculation, edited by Peter Weston.

INDEX

INDEX

Camp Concentration. See Disch, T.
Candide. See Voltaire
Canticle for Leibowitz. See Miller, W.
Čapek, K., 26, 182, 184–85, 229
    Makropoulos Case, 183
    R.U.R., 183–84, 282n, 287
Carnell, E. J., 296–97
Carr, T., 303
Carroll, L., 104–5, 116
Carter, A., 305
Carter, L., 283n
Cartier, E., 217
Cartmill, C., Deadline, 233
Castell, D., 301
Castle, The. See Kafka, F.
Castle of Otranto, The. See Walpole, H.
Chesney, G. T., Battle of Dorking, 100–2, 104, 118
Chesterton, G. K., 147
Childers, E., Riddle of the Sands, 145–46, 155
Childhood's End. See Clarke, A. C.
Chirico, G. de, 216, 239, 317
Christianopolis. See Andreas, J.
Christopher, J., 295–96
    Death of Grass, 295
Chrysalids, The. See Wyndham, J.
Cities in Flight. See Blish, J.
City of the Sun. See Campanella, T.
City series. See Simak, C.
Clarke A. C., 225, 259–61, 281n
    Childhood's End, 260
    2001, 261
Clarke, I. F., Voices Prophesying War, 99, 100, 111n
Clement, H., 217, 233–34, 237
    Mission of Gravity, 233

Clifton, M., 234
Cloak of Aesir. See Campbell, J. W.
Clockwork Orange, A. See Burgess, A.
Cogswell, T., 262, 279
Collins, W., 18, 91, 103
Compton, D. G., 303
Conklin, G., 244
Conquest, R., 284n, 320n
Contes Cruels. See De l'Isle Adam, V.
Cooper, E., 303
Counterfeit. See Nourse, A.
Cowper, R., 304
Crispin, E., 248n, 298, 304, 320n
Cummings, R., 170

Darker Than You Think. See Williamson, J.
Darwin, C., 13, 30, 89, 110n
Darwin, E.
    evolutionary theories, 13ff.
    ideas, 13, 25, 36n, 108n
    influence, 15, 24, 26, 38n, 91n
    poetry, 14, 15, 17, 30
Davidson, A., 279
Day After Judgement. See Blish, J.
Day of the Triffids. See Wyndham, J.
Deadline. See Cartmill, C.
Dean, M., 298, 321
Death of Grass. See Christopher, J.
De Bergerac, C., 10, 61, 63–65, 79, 80n
De Camp, L. S., 247, 261, 264
Découverte Australe, La. See De la Bretonne, R.
Defoe, D., 9, 33, 70
    Robinson Crusoe, 70–71, 78, 79